Digital Piracy

Non-commercial digital piracy has seen an unprecedented rise in the wake of the digital revolution, with wide-scale downloading and sharing of copyrighted media online, often committed by otherwise law-abiding citizens. Bringing together perspectives from criminology, psychology, law and business, and adopting a morally neutral stance, this book offers a holistic overview of this growing phenomenon. It considers its cultural, commercial, and legal aspects, and brings together international research on a range of topics, such as copyright infringement, intellectual property, music publishing, movie piracy, and changes in consumer behaviour. This book offers a new perspective to the growing literature on cybercrime and digital security.

This multi-disciplinary book is the first to bring together international research on digital piracy and will be key reading for researchers in the fields of criminology, psychology, law and business.

Steven Caldwell Brown is an early career researcher based at The University of Strathclyde. Receiving his PhD in 2015 from Glasgow Caledonian University, his doctoral research was the first major psychological approach to understanding music piracy. A Chartered Psychologist, Steven is an expert in both the cultural and commercial impact of the digital revolution on contemporary music listening practices.

Thomas J. Holt is a Professor in the School of Criminal Justice at Michigan State University. He received his PhD in criminology and Criminal Justice from the University of Missouri-Saint Louis in 2005. His research focuses on cybercrime, cyberterror, and policy responses to these global problems.

Routledge Studies in Crime and Society

Digital Piracy
A Global, Multidisciplinary Account

Edited by
Steven Caldwell Brown and Thomas J. Holt

Routledge
Taylor & Francis Group

LONDON AND NEW YORK

First published 2018 by Routledge

2 Park Square, Milton Park, Abingdon, Oxon OX14 4RN
605 Third Avenue, New York, NY 10017

Routledge is an imprint of the Taylor & Francis Group, an informa business

First issued in paperback 2021

British Library Cataloguing in Publication Data
A catalogue record for this book is available from the British Library

Library of Congress Cataloging in Publication Data
Names: Brown, Steven Caldwell, editor. | Holt, Thomas J., 1978- editor.
Title: Digital piracy : a global, multidisciplinary account / edited by
    Steven Caldwell Brown and Thomas J. Holt.
Description: Abingdon, Oxon [UK] ; New York : Routledge, 2018. |
    Includes bibliographical references and index.
Identifiers: LCCN 2017049530| ISBN 9781138067400 (hardback) | ISBN
    9781315158679 (ebook)
Subjects: LCSH: Piracy (Copyright) | Copyright infringement. | Copyright–
    Music. | Sound recordings–Pirated editions. | Cultural property–
    Protection. | Copyright and electronic data processing.
Classification: LCC K1485 .D54 2018 | DDC 345/.02662–dc23
LC record available at https://lccn.loc.gov/2017049530

ISBN: 978-1-138-06740-0 (hbk)
ISBN: 978-0-367-48238-1 (pbk)

Typeset in Times New Roman
by Taylor & Francis Books

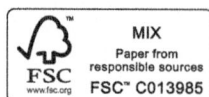

MIX
Paper from
responsible sources
FSC
www.fsc.org   FSC™ C013985

Printed in the United Kingdom
by Henry Ling Limited

The editors wish to dedicate this work to the scholars whose research and ideas are driving the field of inquiry into the phenomenon of media piracy around the world.

Contents

List of illustrations

Acknowledgements

Steven would like to thank Tom for taking on this project, as well as all of the contributors and to all at Routledge for bringing it to life. Thanks also to Paula Sonja Karlsson for her support throughout the process.

Tom wishes to thank Steven for all of his efforts with this book, as well as the editorial staff at Routledge, including Hannah Catterall for her support throughout the process.

Contributors

Adam Bossler is a Professor in the Department of Criminal Justice and Criminology at Georgia Southern University. His research focuses on the applicability of traditional criminological theories to cybercrime offending and victimization, the law enforcement response to cybercrime, and innovative policing and correctional strategies. His work has been published in three co-authored books and outlets including *Journal of Criminal Justice, Crime & Delinquency, Deviant Behavior,* and *Policing.*

Steven Caldwell Brown is an early career researcher based at The University of Strathclyde. Receiving his PhD in 2015 from Glasgow Caledonian University, his Doctoral research was the first major psychological approach to understanding music piracy. A Chartered Psychologist, Steven is an expert in both the cultural and commercial impact of the digital revolution on contemporary music listening practices.

George Burruss is Associate Professor of Criminology at the University of South Florida and affiliated with the Florida Center for Cybersecurity (FC2). He received his PhD in criminology and criminal justice from the University of Missouri St Louis in 2001. His research areas include criminal justice organizations and cybercrime.

Manuel Cuadrado-García is an Associate Professor of Marketing at the University of Valencia, Spain. His main research interest is arts marketing (performing arts, music, cinema and museums) both from a consumer and a managerial perspective. He is engaged in master's and PhD programs in cultural management and marketing in different universities and collaborates with several arts organizations.

Cassandra Dodge is a doctoral student at the University of South Florida. Her areas of research interest include technology and crime, and police technologies.

Tyler Edwards is a graduate student at Georgia Southern University with an interest in law enforcement and cybercrime.

Kenneth Forbes (PhD) is a Lecturer in Commercial Music at the University of the West of Scotland. His research interests lie broadly in the field of live music, applying a particular focus on liveness and live music memories, with a number of publications emerging as result. He received his doctorate from the University of Glasgow in 2015, with a thesis investigating the 'legendary' reputation of the Glasgow Apollo theatre (1973–85).

Thomas J. Holt is a Professor in the School of Criminal Justice at Michigan State University. He received his PhD in criminology and Criminal Justice from the University of Missouri-Saint Louis in 2005. His research focuses on cybercrime, cyberterror, and policy responses to these global problems.

Mateja Kos Koklic is an Associate Professor of Marketing at the Faculty of Economics, University of Ljubljana in Slovenia. Her research focuses on consumer behaviour, particularly in the digital piracy and sustainable consumption context. Her work has been published in the *Journal of Business Research, Journal of Business Ethics, Computers in Human Behavior, Behavior & Information Technology*, and other outlets.

Amanda Elizabeth Krause is a Research Fellow at The University of Melbourne. She is interested in the social and applied psychology of music with a focus on everyday music interactions. In particular, Krause's research interests concern listening technologies as well as the relationship between everyday music behaviours and well-being.

Monika Kukar-Kinney is a Professor of Marketing and the F. Carlyle Tiller Chair in Business in the Robins School of Business, University of Richmond, Richmond, VA. Her research focuses on compulsive buying, behavioural pricing, retailing and electronic commerce. Her work has appeared in journals such as the *Journal of the Academy of Marketing Science, Journal of Consumer Research, Journal of Retailing*, and *Journal of Business Research*, among others.

Juan D. Montoro-Pons is Associate Professor of Applied Economics at the University of Valencia, Spain. His main research interests are the economics and management of cultural consumption and the cultural industries, with an emphasis on live and recorded music. He also serves as vice-president of the International Music Business Research Association (http://www.im bra.eu).

Alexandra Pimentel is a doctoral student in the Department of Sociology, Anthropology and Social Work at Kansas State University.

Miguel Puchades-Navarro is Professor of Applied Economics at the University of Valencia. His main research areas are Public Choice, Constitutional Economics and Law and Economics. He has published and edited several books in this fields and papers in prestigious international journals, such as Public Choice and International Review of Law and Economics.

Valentina Re is Associate Professor of Film and Media Studies at Link Campus University of Rome. In 2005 she obtained a PhD in Film and

Theatre Studies at the University of Bologna, where she was subsequently post-doc researcher. From 2009 to 2014, she was Assistant Professor at Ca' Foscari University of Venice. She is senior editor of the international journal *Cinéma & Cie* and co-editor of the book series 'Narrazioni seriali' and 'Crossroads – Film, literature and other languages'. Her research focuses on film analysis methodologies, the relationships between film and media theories, literary theory and aesthetics, media distribution and circulation in the digital environment.

Gary Sinclair is a Lecturer in Marketing in Dublin City University. He specializes in consumer behaviour and has published a number of articles and book chapters on research regarding music and sport.

Kevin F. Steinmetz is an Assistant Professor in the Department of Sociology, Anthropology and Social Work at Kansas State University.

Hyojung Sun obtained her PhD in the Digital Disruption in the Recording Industry from the Science, Technology and Innovation Studies, University of Edinburgh. Her thesis will be published as a book titled *Digital Revolution Tamed: The Case of the Recording Industry* with Palgrave MacMillan. She is currently a visiting fellow at The Institute for the Study of Science, Technology and Innovation, University of Edinburgh.

Holly Tessler is Senior Lecturer in Commercial Music and MA Music Programme Leader at the University of the West of Scotland. Holly completed both her MBA (Music Industries) and PhD at the Institute of Popular Music, University of Liverpool. Her research interests include the Beatles, music industries as creative industries, music and cultural branding, music and media and Garage Rock.

Irena Vida is a Professor of Marketing at Faculty of Economics at University of Ljubljana. Her research focus is on application of consumer behaviour theories and models in cross-cultural settings and on strategic issues in international marketing. She published articles in various journals such as *Journal of Business Research*, *European Journal of Marketing*, *Journal of International Marketing*, and *International Marketing Review*, among others.

Part I

Introduction

1 Contextualising digital piracy

Thomas J. Holt and Steven Caldwell Brown

Digital piracy, sometimes called illegal downloading (or any number of other terms), refers to the act of acquiring intellectual property without remuneration to the artist, creator, or producer of the content. Piracy is a controversial area of academic research and is of interest not only to industry bodies and governments, but to legal scholars and law enforcement. Much research to date comes from economists (see Kariithi, 2011), which is representative of the natural tendency for research to focus on the economic impact of digital piracy. A similarly substantive area of research considers if digital piracy is 'bad', and if so, in what ways and for whom based on criteria such as lost revenue, lost taxes, dilution of property (e.g. Gopal et al., 2004). Other research from the social sciences has explored other areas such as who engages in digital piracy, and what factors are associated with pirating behaviours (e.g. Higgins & Marcum, 2011). This ever-growing body of research that encompasses a variety of scholars from a broad range of disciplines, is sufficient enough to now present convincing answers to these important questions.

The term piracy has been called ambiguous (David, 2010) and elusive (Higgins & Marcum, 2011), reflecting the difficulty in providing a good summary of the scope of digital piracy. Some researchers have defined piracy as a white-collar crime (see Nelken, 2012), only affecting the individual copyright holders whose intellectual property is infringed upon. There is some legitimacy in this point of view, though it is unclear how much commercial piracy, or profiteering from selling copyrighted products on the black market takes place and who is involved in this activity. Instead, the majority of research tends to focus on what can be considered user-end piracy performed by otherwise law-abiding citizens principally using the Internet to obtain copyrighted media for free, violating copyright laws in various nations around the world. This behaviour may again appear to only affect the copyright holders, though research demonstrates that individuals who pirate materials are likely to experience malicious software infections and data loss in the event they download incorrect files (Holt & Copes, 2010; Wolfe, Higgins & Marcum, 2008).

The problem of end-user piracy is also complicated by the fact that there are various platforms that can be used to acquire materials, including the use of direct downloads of files hosted on websites and servers, to more surreptitious methods of distributed peer-to-peer file sharing. In this case, users access and download portions of media or content from multiple user systems, making it more efficient, and difficult to determine the source of materials. In fact, file-sharing software has facilitated digital piracy on a mass scale, by becoming simpler and safer. The methods routinely change, where it has even been argued that file-sharing may soon become a relic of the past, due to emerging technologies (Mendis, 2013), and shifting piracy practices often occur in the face of legal action which seeks to inhibit access to copyrighted materials online via illegal sources. The reasons for seeking out content appear to remain consistent, and copyright remains misunderstood (Towse, 2013).

The development of Internet-based piracy stems from the digitization of media and content. Prior to the creation of the Internet, individuals could find ways to obtain bootleg or pirated versions of music and other media through the use of magnetic audio and video tape cassettes and recorders. Individuals could tape record songs off of the radio, or directly record a duplicate copy of media. The same was true for television and films. The digital revolution spurred by the development of Compact Discs and MP3 compression software, however, inspired widespread copyright infringement of protected works on an unprecedented scale. Scharf (2013) referred to these factors (the Internet, MP3, and peer-to-peer file sharing) as a *holy trinity* that created the phenomenon of digital piracy as we now know it and indeed it is the music industry that has been hit harder than any other creative sector due to such digital technologies (Watson, 2016). Since the spread of file-sharing technologies, recorded music revenues have dropped all across the world (Aguiar & Waldfogel, 2015), though it is overly simplistic to attribute this directly to digital piracy (Nowak, 2015). Music remains the most pirated type of media, lending due to its popularity (particularly amongst young people) and the fact that digital music files are small and easy to transfer online. The majority of research into digital piracy focuses on music.

The media used to exchange copyrighted digital files such as MP3 music files change on a regular basis; *Bit-Torrent* (a protocol supporting the transmission of large volumes of data over the Internet) dominated throughout the 00s, outliving previous trends (Sockanathan, 2011). In recent years however, new technologies have risen to prominence with the International Federation of the Phonographic Industry (IFPI), a not-for-profit organisation who represent the interests of the recorded music industry globally, now focusing on *stream-ripping* applications, which record content being streamed on the likes of YouTube. As with wider music trends, it could be said that music piracy changes with the times – the key constant however, is that many consumers to refuse pay for music legally when illegal options are also available. The individuals running piracy websites and services that enable illegal downloading profit from doing so, and as such, are what can be better thought of as commercial pirates. On the surface, user-end piracy is straightforwardly free (as are most activities online) but ultimately, engagement in digital piracy unfairly grants commercial pirates profits they are not entitled to. It is likely that most people do not realise this. YouTube is a major focus for the music industry, with IFPI (2016) discussing the 'value gap' wherein such services bypass normal licensing rules, leading to unfair remuneration. The organisation believes that stream-ripping via the likes of YouTube is now the dominant mode of music piracy (see Garrahan, 2016).

Since the Internet and computer technology are nearly ubiquitous in modern society, it is thought that millions of people engage in digital piracy every day. The true scope of piracy is, however, difficult to document as clear statistics are difficult to obtain. Rates of arrest for digital piracy are not published in traditional crime statistics and are largely unavailable, save for reports from industry advocacy groups. Conservative estimates of Internet users actively downloading copyrighted media illegally tend to cluster around one third of the global population: this perhaps amounts to the single most prevalent crime in history.

Calculating a worst-case scenario estimation on the impact of digital piracy, Ian Hargreaves (2011), who was tasked to investigate the need for copyright reform in the UK by then Prime Minister David Cameron, argues that even when working from industry estimates the cost of piracy is *underwhelming* in economic terms. Elsewhere, Pakinkis (2014), reflecting on a report from the then UK Prime Minister's IP Adviser Mike Weatherly, claims that piracy costs the UKs creative industries approximately £400 million per year – this cannot be said to be negligible. However, some estimates from the United States project truly astronomical costs due to piracy, as legislators argued that the US economy lost between $200 and $250 billion per year as a justification for the failed Stop Online Piracy Act (SOPA) in 2012 (Sanchez, 2012). In July 2015, Google received 54,810,885 notifications to remove or delete items from search indexes infringing copyright (Jun Lee & Watters, 2016). A costly process, IFPI (2016) research finds that 94% of all takedown requests sent by IFPI during 2015 related to recordings that were routinely uploaded to sites *already notified* that the content was breaching copyright.

The conflicts noted above are common throughout research into digital piracy from all across the globe. There is very little information currently available that is viewed with trust and grounded in reproducible evidence. As a result the three principal stakeholders in the debate on digital piracy, industry, government, and consumers (and/or so-called 'pirates'), are frequently at odds with one another. There is a perception amongst the latter party that digital piracy is a victimless crime. Yet, with so many new bills introduced in the past decade designed specifically to minimise digital piracy (particularly in North America and Europe), one can readily assume that there must be a negative impact on the creative and cultural industries in order to justify such costly and often aggressive, costly, and unpopular measures (e.g. Brenner, 2011). Anti-piracy measures have largely failed, with pirates easily adapting their methods to circumvent any technical and legislative changes. Higgins and Marcum (2011) explain that knowledgeable Internet users always seem to outsmart new technologies faster than they can be produced. In fact, many anti-piracy strategies also appear to inadvertently *encourage* digital piracy. Wikström (2011) suggests that: 'Perhaps the single most enduring effect of these [music piracy] initiatives has been a negative impact on the reputation of the music industry' (p. 155).

In recent years, the most effective anti-piracy measure appears to be the rise of attractive legal alternatives to digital piracy. For instance, there are now over 500 legal digital music services globally, and the International Federation of the Phonographic Industry (2015) report that subscription services are now an integral part of the music business. Subscription and ad-supported streaming services have grown from 9% to 27% of digital revenues in the last five years. The preference for all things digital has been clearly acted upon by industry, striving to meet consumer demands. The likes of Spotify, market-leader in music subscription services, can be said to accommodate the same driving forces behind accessing music legally – convenient, free access to large databases of music, at low cost. The impact of digital media on traditional bricks-and-mortar music retailers, or on cinemas over the long term remains to be seen. Furthermore, where Spotify rests in the bigger digital picture is at present unclear. It has been shown that individuals engaging in music streaming are also more likely to engage in music piracy (Borja, Dieringer & Daw, 2015). At the same time, multiple studies demonstrate that individuals engaging in digital piracy also spend more money on legal media (Huygen et al., 2009; Karaganis & Renkema, 2013; Thun, 2009; Watson et al., 2015; and Zentner, 2006).

These mixed findings reinforce the need for nuanced research considering the impact of piracy from multiple perspectives. Thus, this book attempts to address these issues through different contributors that collectively help provide a far richer understanding of digital piracy. For instance, it has been suggested that piracy offers a 'try before you buy' means to make more informed pur-chasing decisions (Peitz & Waelbroeck, 2006). Research frequently finds that individuals engaging in digital piracy assert this reason to justify their beha-viour (e.g. Holt & Copes, 2010; Ingram & Hinduja, 2008). Certainly, a recent trend in research shows how many people who access media illegally also purchase it illegally, increasingly making use of different platforms to satisfy different needs (Sinclair & Green, 2016).

This book addresses the need to critically evaluate the current research to date into digital piracy in order to better present a clear and concise account of 'the good', 'the bad', and 'the unclear'. This book does so by bringing together the collective expertise of a wide range of scholars from across the globe, sharing their expertise from a range of academic disciplines. The often competing interests of an array of stakeholders are considered, including not only government, industry, and consumers, but Internet service providers, and other parties who are affected or influenced by digital piracy.

This book draws on the expertise of academics from a wide range of dis-ciplines from all over the globe. Their collective contributions offer rich insight into the many interrelated facets of digital piracy in the real world, and invite readers to challenge their beliefs and consider the broader context in which digital piracy is rooted. In defence of academics' favourable advantages in researching the music industry, Williamson et al. (2011) explain that:

> As academics we have not only methodological expertise but also, on the whole, more knowledge of our specialist field than its practitioners – we understand its broader context, we can draw on comparative international and institutional material, we have a longer historical perspective, we have the advantages of disinterest, we are not constrained by encrusted conceptual frameworks
>
> (p. 471)

The academic has, amongst other things, a better understanding of the wider context in which digital piracy takes place in order to make more informed decisions, rather than resting on notions of it being 'good' or 'bad', or even 'right' or 'wrong' (as we will see, rudimentary notions of duality are problematic). The academic can review research on the topic in a balanced way (as is their obligation) and point towards the generally weak research methods used or the fact that researchers from different disciplines bring with them particular biases (to name but a few limitations in the research which follows). Put simply, the contributions from the scholars in this book are authoritative.

In their critical and timely addition to the literature in 2015, Watson and associates review the findings from hundreds of research articles on the topic, working from an initial database of over 54,000 sources. The authors conclude that the present knowledge on digital piracy is skewed by methodology, and that most research does not draw from actual data. The academic can conclude that in a lot of specific areas, *we just don't know what is going on*; we must interpret findings with caution due to *x*, *y*, and *z*.

Yet, people are reluctant to trust information that does not conform with their viewpoints. In order to fully understand digital piracy and the interrelated politics of the digital economy, it is essential to either a) spend more time reviewing information on the topic or b) start trusting those who have spent more time reviewing information on the topic. The former is unlikely, with people sorting through new information in ways that reinforce what they already believe (Watts, 2012), actively searching for information that exaggerates existing beliefs (Fisher, Goddu & Frank, 2015). To complicate matters, search results are increasingly refined to support your world view, helping you find more the same information. And, for every piece of information online, another exists that challenges it (Kelly, 2011). Correct opinions are no more likely to be found than incorrect ones (Levitin, 2014).

Though this book aims not to be *the* authoritative source on digital piracy (but rather a central hub of knowledge for interested parties to make up their own minds), it very much aims to position itself in a world where option b is more feasible: regrettably, much academic knowledge is out of the reach of the general public due to issues concerning copyright. Even if laypersons wanted to discover more about digital piracy, they would not be able to. Furthermore, this book takes research methodology into account when interpreting findings, providing the reader with an overview of how conclusions are drawn from empirical research.

In this book, the origins and evolution of digital piracy over time will be presented, along with the consequences the ensuing shifts on consumer preferences have had on the creative and cultural industries. In doing so, a review of anti-piracy strategies and legal responses will be presented, evaluating the effectiveness of these retaliations against digital piracy. Pondering the recent rise of legitimate alternatives to digital piracy (with a particular emphasis on music piracy), this book looks ahead to the future of what is an ever-increasing digital world and what this means for future generations of digital consumers. Broader questions concerning the ethical implications of living in a digital world will also be considered, with digital piracy underscoring the shifting moral landscape of a world in which the consequences of actions carried out online are invisible.

Importantly, scholars from different academic backgrounds from all over the world come together in this book, and it is in this new territory where the real contributions from this book emerge. The book is, however, designed to allow for particular chapters of interest to be read independently.

More than anything, this book aims to open up long-term dialogue between different parties and hopes that readers will respond engage in much needed debate on this topic. Having read this book, readers will be in a better position to do so. Furthermore, readers will also be well equipped to challenge and confront 'research' on other topics in the future and be more sceptical and critical of *who* says *what* (and *why*). Just because something does not appear to *look* or *sound* right does not mean that it is not, in fact, right (and by this we of course mean *correct*) and it is for this reason that a broader understanding of the context in which digital piracy takes place is necessary in order to fully understand the legal, commercial, and cultural ramifications of this contentious activity which has risen to prominence since the turn of the millennium.

Research into digital piracy emerged as a major topic of interest for scholars of different disciplines in the early 00s and shows no signs of stopping, so long as widespread copyright infringement remains a burden on the creative and cultural industries. To once more focus on music, though legal services such as Spotify continue to prosper, music piracy is very much still alive and well (Snickars, 2016), and, as noted earlier, evolving constantly. This book aims to get to the heart of the constants which motivate copyright infringement, aiding policy development in the process.

In the first section of the book, three chapters demonstrate widely different approaches to mapping how digital piracy has impacted upon the creative and cultural industries. Sun, assuming an *Informatics* position, charts the disruption which occurred in the recorded music industry, providing a detailed overview of music streaming. In doing so, she demonstrates that dated notions of how music generates revenue must be updated to accommodate new modes of music listening. *Popular Music* scholars Tessler and Forbes demonstrate how emerging musical trends demand new ways of thinking about copyright, specifically illustrating the shift from 'consumer' to 'prosumer' and how digital technologies afford great opportunities to manipulate music creatively. Copyright is at the heart of Re's chapter on the film industry. A *Film Studies* scholar, Re adopts a case study approach of the Italian market, reviewing recent anti-piracy initiatives and the rise of video on demand. Though the section is eclectic, a core theme of the book is gently introduced here in that *change* dominates all three chapters – this is discussed in the conclusion chapter.

In the second section of the book, four chapters demonstrate unique approaches to understanding digital piracy engagement, coming as they do from different disciplines. Krause and Brown draw from a psychological perspective, proposing a new model for understanding why individuals prefer one music format over another, illustrating the decision-making process involved when selecting music. Sinclair also focuses on music, from a marketing perspective. He demonstrates the imperfect understanding of how musicians are paid and how music pirates rationalise their engagement in piracy, further demonstrating compelling aspects of decision-making. Adopting an *Economical* stance, Montoro-Pons, Cuadrado-Garcia and Puchases-Navarro explain that while streaming may dissuade some from engagement in digital piracy, it may also lead to those paying for content legally to switch to streaming, thereby 'downgrading' their contribution to the creative and cultural industries. This chapter incorporates discussion not only of music, but of film and books. Kukar-Kinney, Vida and Kos Koklic, also coming from an economics perspective, highlight the impact of culture on piracy, zooming out of the general focus of earlier chapters in the section on individual factors.

In the third section of the book, three chapters hone in on the consequences of digital piracy. All three are criminological in nature. Burruss and Dodge argue that online deviance in the form of digital piracy is related to offline deviance too, with the implication that digital piracy may be a gateway to more serious offending. In Bossler and Edwards' wide-ranging review of criminology, a comprehensive summary of the theoretical contributions from criminology is mapped out. Steinmetz and Pimental, criticising the typical focus of much research on individual factors, such as those featured in Bossler and Edwards' review, take into account the wider political, economic and social circumstances. Overall, the section demonstrates the core contributions made by criminologists in understanding digital piracy.

A concluding chapter is presented that aims to pull together key findings from the chapters as well as provide useful commentary on the field more broadly. There is much overlap between the chapters – nowhere more so than in the final section – but the conclusions drawn are not always uniform. This is representative of the wider state of the field, a likely consequence of differing approaches to conducting research into digital piracy. As discussed in the conclusion, recent meta-analyses provide robust evidence for what is in fact known about digital piracy, rather than what is thought to be known. The findings of such work supports the conclusions drawn from the authors in the book.

References

Aguiar, L. and Waldfogel, J. (2015). Streaming reaches flood stage: Does Spotify stimulate or depress music sales? (Working paper 21653). Retrieved from The National Bureau of Economic Research website: www.nber.org/papers/w21653.

Borja, K., Dieringer, S. and Daw, J. (2015). The effect of music streaming on music piracy among college students. *Computers in Human Behavior*, 45, 69–76.

Brenner, S.W. (2011). Defining cybercrime: A review of federal and state law. In R. D. Clifford (Ed.), *Cybercrime: The Investigation, Prosecution, and Defense of a Computer-Related Crime*, 3rd edition. (pp. 15–104). Raleigh, NC: Carolina Academic Press.

David, M. (2010). *Peer to Peer and the Music Industry.* London: Sage.

Fisher, M., Goddu, M.K. and Frank, C. (2015). Searching for explanations: How the Internet inflates estimates of internal knowledge. *Journal of Experimental Psychology*, 144(3): 674–687.

Garrahan, M. (2016)*Music industry faces 'stream ripping' piracy threat*, September. Retrieved from www.ft.com/content/d31ff954-793a-11e6-a0c6-39e2633162d5.

Gopal, R.D., Sanders, G.L., Bhattacharjee, S., Agrawal, M., and Wagner, S.C. (2004). A behavioral model of digital music piracy. *Journal of Organizational Computing and Electronic Commerce*, 14(2): 89–105.

Hargreaves, I. (2011). *Digital Opportunity: A Review of Intellectual Property and Growth.* London: HM Treasury.

Higgins, G.E. and Marcum, C.D. (2011). *Digital Piracy: An Integrated Theoretical Approach.* Durham, NC: Carolina Academic Press.

Holt, T.J. and Copes, H. (2010). Transferring subcultural knowledge on-line: Practices and beliefs of persistent digital pirates. *Deviant Behavior*, 31(7): 625–654.

Huygen, A., Helberger, N., Poort, J., Rutten, P. and van Eijk, N.A.N.M. (2009). *Ups and Downs: Economic and cultural effects of file sharing on music, film and games* (Working Paper No. 1350451). Retrieved from Social Science Research Network website: http://papers.ssrn.comlsol3/papers.cfm?abstractJd=1350451.

Ingram, J.R. and Hinduja, S. (2008). Neutralizing music piracy: An empirical examination. *Deviant Behavior*, 29(4) 334–366.

International Federation of the Phonographic Industry (2015). *IFPI Digital Music Report 2015: Charting the Path to Sustainable Growth.* Retrieved from www.ifp Lorg/downloads/Digital-Music-Report-2015.pdf.

International Federation of the Phonographic Industry (2016). *Global Music Report: Music Consumption Exploding Worldwide.* Retrieved from: www.ifpi.org/downloads/ GMR2016.pdf.

Jun Lee, S. and Watters, P.A. (2016). Gathering intelligence on high-risk advertising and film piracy: A study of the digital underground. In R. Layton and P. A. Watters (Eds), *Automating Open Source Intelligence* (pp. 89–102). New York: Elsevier.

Karaganis, J. and Renkema, L. (2013). *Copy Culture in the US and Germany*. New York: The American Assembly.

Kariithi, N.K. (2011). Is the devil in the data? A literature review of piracy around the world. *The Journal of World Intellectual Property*, 14(2): 133–154.

Kelly, K. (2011). The waking dream. In J. Brockman (Ed.), *How is the Internet Changing the Way You Think?* (pp. 18–23). New York: HarperCollins.

Levitin, D.J. (2014). *The Organized Mind*. New York: Dutton.

Mendis, D. (2013). Digital Economy Act 2010: fighting a losing battle? Why the 'three strikes' law is not the answer to copyright law's latest challenge. *International Review of Law, Computers and Technology*, 2(1–2): 60–84.

Nelken, D. (2012). White-collar and corporate crime. In M. Maguire, R. Morgan and R. Reiner (Eds.), *The Oxford Handbook of Criminology* (pp. 733–770). Oxford: Oxford University Press.

Nowak, R. (2015). *Consuming Music in the Digital Age: Technologies, Roles and Everyday Life*. Basingstoke: Palgrave Macmillan.

Pakinkis, T. (2014, March). *Back With a Vengeance*. Retrieved from www.musicweek.com.

Peitz, M. and Waelbroeck, P. (2006). Why the music industry may gain from free downloading – The role of sampling. *International Journal of Industrial Organisation*, 24(5): 907–913.

Sanchez, J. (2012). SOPA, Internet regulation and the economics of piracy, January. Retrieved from www.wired.com/2012/01/sopa-piracy-costs.

Scharf, N.F. (2013). *Digital Copyright Law: Exploring the Changing Interface Between Copyright and Regulation in the Digital Environment* (Doctoral dissertation).

Sinclair, G. and Green, T. (2016). Download or stream? Steal or buy? Developing a typology of today's music consumer. *Journal of Consumer Behaviour*, 15(1): 3–14.

Snickars, P. (2016). More music is better music. In P. Wikström, and B. DeFillipi (Eds), *Business Innovation and Disruption in the Music Industry* (pp. 191–210). Cheltenham: Edward Elgar Publishing.

Sockanathan, A. (2011). *Digital Desire and Recorded Music: OiNK, Mnemotechnics and the Private BitTorrent Architecture* (Doctoral dissertation).

Thun, C. (2009). *Introducing Hollywood's Best Customers Vuze User vs. General Internet: Comparative Data* (Research Repoli). Retrieved from Frank N. Magid Associates website: www.magid.comlsites/defaultlfiles/pdf/vuze.pdf.

Towse, R. (2013). The quest for evidence on the economic effects of copyright law. *Cambridge Journal of Economics*, 37(5), 1187–1202.

Watson, A. (2016). Digital disruption and recording studio diversification: Changing business models for the digital age. In P. Wikström, and B. DeFillipi (Eds), *Business Innovation and Disruption in the Music Industry* (pp. 95–113). Cheltenham: Edward Elgar Publishing.

Watson, S.J., Zizzo, D. J. and Fleming, P. (2015). Determinants of unlawful file sharing: A scoping review. *PLoS ONE*, 10(6): e0127921.

Watts, D.J. (2012). *Everything is Obvious: How Common Sense Fails Us*. London: Atlantic Books.

Wikström, P. (2011). *The Music Industry: Music in the Cloud*. Cambridge: Polity Press.

Williamson, J., Cloonan, M. and Frith, S. (2011). Having an impact? Academics, the industries and the problem of knowledge. *International Journal of Cultural Policy*, 17(5): 459–474.

Wolfe, S., Higgins, G.E. and Marcum, C.D. (2008). Deterrence and digital piracy: A preliminary examination of the role of viruses. *Social Science Computer Review,* 26(3): 317–333.

Zentner, A. (2006). Measuring the effect of file sharing on music purchases. *Journal of Law and Economics,* 49(1): 63–90.

Section I
Evolving media consumption practices

2 The times they are a-changin'

Digital music value in transition from piracy to streaming

Hyojung Sun

Introduction

Napster, a pioneering P2P file-sharing network, set music free. It suggested a potential to disrupt the fundamental logic of music economics built around physical artefacts, and the fad of free music ensued and prevailed. The claim that inadequate remuneration for musicians would endanger our culture was used to support the music industry's battle against free music, often equated with digital piracy. iTunes and a myriad of other digital music services arose to valorise music on digital music networks, but a large proportion of digital music users remained unwilling to pay for music. In the midst of a diverse degree of failures, a viable method of digital music valorisation finally emerged in 2008 with the rise of subscription-based streaming music services spurred by Spotify. The growing digital music revenue not only saved the economic downturn for the industry, but also enabled pay-per-stream as a currency for digital music valuation (Wilson, 2017). However, debates still remain over the value of music on the new valorisation platform.

The issue here, however, is much more complicated than its broad portrayal in the media. In this chapter, I attempt to project the issue from a longitudinal perspective and discuss the fluidity of the way we value music. I demonstrate this by illustrating how the way we value music has evolved in the context of social, economic, industrial and legal settings. What this attests to is that the valuation of music has been subject to change in diverse variables and that the modern system of music valuation emerged as an interplay of power struggles, negotiations and conflicts. At the centre of this system lay the music industry's commercial interest, through which the copyright licensing scheme purported the commodification of music. Against this backdrop, this chapter recasts the current debate on digital music value as a continuation of the previous means of generating revenue and the belief in the copyright licensing scheme. The chapter, however, is not intended to offer a solution for a proper valuation of digital music, but instead to provoke interest in exploring the multifaceted and shifting value of music.

A brief history of music valuation

The common belief of music valuation holds that every use of music has to be compensated and the law subsists to serve the irrefutable logic of economics built around physical artefacts. This section challenges this widely perceived notion by illustrating the way we value music has been shaped by a myriad of factors that have evolved over time.

Experience

We now live in an era of what Kassabian (2001, 2013) has termed "ubiquitous listening", in which instant access to any music is available at any time on any device. The sheer abundance of choice and the readiness of music availability in the networked environment have certainly brought about an unprecedented convenience in music listening. The disposability of music, however, has diluted the very experience of appreciation of the music listening experience that had long been "a temporal, fleeting experience – and a rare treat" (Coleman, 2004: 1) available only in a church or near marching bands on a street. Listening to music in a private parlour was exclusive to aristocrats, not available to anyone else. As Frith has said, "In the eighteenth century even the most committed listener would not have expected to hear any particular piece more than once" (Frith, 2007: 285). The value of music hence lay in its ephemerality; it perished after the performance, resulting in a uniqueness that could not be repeated and an act of listening that existed only in that time and space (Katz, 2010). The characteristic of live performance is that "the work of the performer is an end in itself, not the means for the production of some other good" (Baumol & Owen, 1966: 164)

Sheet music

Technological developments, in conjunction with societal change, changed the value of music. The first change came with the printing press, invented by a German goldsmith, Johannes Gutenberg, in the mid-fifteenth century. This led to the invention of sheet music printing in 1501, which ultimately became a small business of producing music copies for a few aristocratic music admirers (Tschmuck, 2012: 9). With the societal and technological changes that followed subsequently, this copper engraving technology sowed the seed of a deep change in music value. The eighteenth century witnessed the emergence of the middle class, who had enough purchasing power for culture (Plumb; 1973). Concerts and theatre life began to grow markedly (Peacock & Weir, 1975: 37). As the piano became an essential item in the respectable home, home performance increased dramatically (Ehrlich, 1985). All of this contributed to the distribution of sheet music for public performances in concerts or operas, which became an important business for music publishers. This interplay between the burgeoning music publishing business and the growth of concert culture established an industrial basis for the music industry (Tschmuck, 2012: 9). In this market structure, sheet music was the driving force for the mass production of music as a commercial form (Garofalo, 1999). By the nineteenth century, music publishers stood at the centre of the business, with their market power dependent on the technological base of music concerts and the subsequent distribution of music through mass-produced sheet music (Tschmuck, 2012: 10).

Copyright

Legal protection for music took shape over a long period of time as a result of the interplay between technological advances, power struggles and social needs. The first modern copyright law, the Statute of Anne, was enacted in 1710 to grant protection of the right to copy for three subject matters: books, plays and maps, meaning that music was left out of protection coverage (Rosen, 2008). The first copyright protection conferred upon music was made by Johann Christian Bach (Johann Sebastian Bach's younger son) in England in 1777; it was under the category of books and other writings, citing the right to be read, rather than to be played (Kretschmer et al., 1999). This decision did not have much impact in terms of making legal protection for music more widely practised. In fact, copyright protection had long been little related to artists' earnings or stimulation of creative works. Copyright initially bestowed upon creators does not stay in their hands for long: for their work to be marketed, copyright is consigned to publishers (Kretschmer et al., 1999: 163). Also, music publishers by and large did not lobby for statutory protection during this period; instead, they endeavoured to strike market deals that, through strategies such as limit pricing (setting prices below the threshold of profit maximisation), prevented new entrants from establishing themselves. According to Hunter, this was because "for music publishers, the maintenance of copyright protection over 14 or 28 years was unnecessary, as most musical works would not remain in fashion that long" (Hunter, 1986: 276).

Phonograph

Another notable change in music value came with Thomas Edison's phonograph, invented in 1877. Prior to phonography, music remained live music, limited to a single performance. Phonography fixed sounds, which were then multiplied and distributed to the public. Sound recording was only the fourth out of the ten initial visions of this technology, stenography being the first. It was becoming apparent that sound recording constituted the largest commercial value of this technology when the Columbia Phonograph Corporation licensed and developed it as a "nickel-in-the-slot" machine. Allowing people to listen to a recording for a nickel marked the beginning of pay-per-play music. The commercial value of music evolved to a royalty system with Emile Berliner, who envisioned the future of this technology as "a machine for home entertainment and mass production of music discs" through which artists could earn royalties (Frith, 2007: 96). The creation of a master recording opened up an easy and less expensive way of duplicating and distributing sound recordings (Negus, 1992). By the 1910s, it was clear that records would become a powerful cultural force (Garofalo, 1999).

Collecting society

Phonography turned music into a "thing" and enabled "an unprecedented freedom to travel" (Katz, 2010: 14). When it came to monetisation, this was a challenge. Before the invention of phonography, monetising music was straightforward: the major avenue was music performances at theatres and concert halls, which involved intensive promotion.[1] When the phonograph enabled multiplied use of sounds, it was difficult, or nearly impossible, for individual composers to monitor each and every use of their music. Publishers, composers and songwriters felt an impending need for a more effective way to secure a performance royalty system. The legal protection granted by Statute of Anne was to be practised; an incident in Paris in 1847 ignited this change. Composers Ernest Bourget and Victor Parizot visited the Paris concert café *Ambassadeur*, where they heard, much to their surprise, a piece of Bourget's being played by an orchestra to whom he had never proffered performance permission. They refused to pay the bill for their drinks, arguing, "You consume my music, I consume your beverages, property against property" (Kretschmer, 2000: 211). The first collecting society for music, *Societé des Auteurs, Compositeurs et Deiteurs de Musique* (SACEM), was established in Paris. Albeit rudimentary, this society opened the door for monitoring sound usage and distributing royalties (Kretschmer, 2000). Its legal foundation to utilise performing rights for works played on sound recordings became the model for collecting societies in other countries, including the Performing Rights Society (PRS) in the UK and the American Society of Composers, Authors and Publishers (ASCAP) in the US.

Royalties

Royalties from the sales of recorded music were, for a long time, not considered significant to writers or publishers (Kretschmer, 2000). For publishers, sheet music was the main revenue-generating outlet. The way composers earned money varied greatly, from working for churches to conducting, teaching and even marrying a rich widow in the case of Debussy (Peacock & Weir, 1975). Working for noble courts or subsidies from noble patrons were, once acquired, considered an honourable and significant source of income.

Following the proliferation of new technologies, royalties from sound recordings became deeply associated with the music business and artists' earnings. It was sparked by the popularity of radio, whose airplay played a central role in disseminating new records and therefore record sales (Hirsch,

1969; Peterson, 1990). When radio had yet to be conceived as a popular medium for music listening, however, record companies feared that its free airplay would lessen people's desire to purchase records. Some famous artists also resisted the idea of their songs being played on the radio, with Bing Crosby famously putting the stamp "Not licensed for radio airplay" on his records. However, as radio became an increasingly important gatekeeper that dictated which songs would grab consumers' attention, record companies were naturally keen to get their artists on the airwaves in order to sell more units (Burnett, 1996). Record companies and radio stations soon developed a "symbiotic relationship" in which radio airplay became the "lifeline" of a record company (Hirsch, 1969). It was not long before radio became the main music consumption medium, and the royalties resulting from this phenomenon became a significant source of profit for the industry (Frith, 1987). By the end of the nineteenth century, royalties from sound recordings well superseded revenue from sheet music sales (Kretschmer, 2000).

Piracy

Music, by nature, easily crosses linguistic or cultural barriers; therefore, piracy has long been an issue (Laing, 2004). A series of technological developments and societal change made the issue particularly acute. The widespread use of magnetic tape and television in the 1940s, the unprecedented popularity of American rock and roll in the 1950s and the "British Invasion" of the 1960s all contributed to the predominance of Western culture on a global scale. Through a series of mergers and acquisitions, the global music industry was established. The music industry faced two major obstacles – *bootlegging* and *home-taping* – which the industry argued were responsible for the overall sales decline during the recession. With subsequent advances in technology allowing even more refined bootlegging and home-taping potential, the line between commercial use of unauthorised copying and private sharing became less clear, and the industry quickly lobbied to ensure that any unauthorised use of their copyrighted works was condemned as "piracy" (Marshall, 2004).

The decentralised control over the production and consumption of music enabled by the arrival of the cassette tape and Sony Walkman brought home-taping and bootlegging into the popular consciousness. The industry's response to this new technology was to fit new modes to the edifice of the existing model set up for the global entertainment business (Frith, 1988). Frith's remark below succinctly captures the nature of this trend.

> While the cause of the home-taping problem is new technology, the solution rests on an old-fashioned picture of creativity and commerce – we're asked to imagine ... This picture is being painted just as record companies' primary interest is no longer selling records to domestic consumers, but packaging multi-media entertainment, servicing programme-greedy satellite and cable companies, providing Hollywood soundtracks,

seeking sponsorship deals, coming to terms with advertising agencies. This is the context in which rights have become so important to the music business – publishing rights to be exploited in the increasing use of music on television, recording rights to be licensed to record packagers, whether TV merchandisers or genre specialists like Demon, video rights to the clips shown on the cable."

(Frith, 1988: 72)

CDs

CDs appeared in the market in the 1980s. Initially, this new medium did not receive much attention from consumers, who already owned their music in different formats such as cassette and LP. From consumers' perspective, CD meant buying a new music player and replacing all their music in a new format. From record companies' perspective, it meant higher margins, and a recovery from the economic downturn in the 1980s. Soon, consumers replaced the records they already owned on LP with CDs. This change was a result of a "conscious policy instituted by record companies", who promoted this new format vigorously (Mcleod, 2005: 526), only to realise later that it allowed users to "retrieve digital music information for new uses" and "undermine(d) the material distinction between production and reproduction on which copyright law rests" (Toynbee, 2004: 3).

In the 1980s, the recording industry shifted its attention from international conventions to lobbying trade regulations (Laing, 2004). Through subsequent international conventions, protection for neighbouring rights became consolidated. The recording industry's global strategy to exploit rights took on increased significance (Frith, 1988). As a consequence, copyright as an economic incentive became an integral part of the global recording business (Towse, 2001). Collecting societies were conceived as a convenient and efficient mechanism for collecting and distributing revenue to rights holders. The establishment of collecting societies resounds with the development of copyright – which was driven by publishers, not authors or artists – in that they, in an effort to boost their own bottom lines, "used the now familiar rhetoric of authors' rights to foster their own ends" (Kretschmer, 2000: 212). This led to the issues of a record-dependent music industry and the pay-per-use-driven business model, which later became problematic, especially in the digital era (Burkart & McCourt, 2006).

Copyright as an economic incentive

Michael Jackson's 1982 album "Thriller" became a sensation, not only culturally but also economically. The unprecedented sales of over 40 million copies indicated that the superstar economy could solve the industry's economic woes by reaping greater income from fewer artists (Garofalo, 1999). It also signalled a shift in the focus of recording companies' business from production to copyright exploitation (Garofalo, 1999). The ability to exploit copyright was firmly established as a central strategy for profit in the recording industry (Bettig, 1996; Frith, 1988; Negus, 1992). At the centre of the consolidation of the recording industry lay copyright, through which multinational firms' rights-based business was structured: endogenous sunk costs led to vertical integration, through which multinationals could build economies of scale to reap profits from their own labels (Bakker, 2012). The recording industry's global strategy of exploiting rights has taken on increased significance (Frith, 1988). As a consequence, copyright as an economic incentive has become an integral part of the global recording business (Towse, 2001).

The economic justification of copyright is to provide an incentive for artists to continue to create artistic works by guaranteeing commercial exploitation and, as a result, financial compensation. The substantial financial investment required to produce music, compounded by consumers' fickle and unpredictable musical tastes, makes the music business particularly high-risk, with a high ratio of failure. This market condition is associated with the market failure that creative works carry as public goods; that is, as a public good, music is non-excludable and non-rival. One person listening to music does not diminish its value or exclude its usage by another. When packaged in physical formats, music is turned into a rival good. This leads to the argument that the absence of protection could result in a "tragedy of the commons" – where no exclusive right to common goods would eventually lead to the destruction of the common resource (Hardin, 1968). To counteract these problems, the government can intervene and grant exclusive rights to the owner of the property as a remedy to the threat of over-consumption. Posner (1998) argued that the absence of legal protection for property rights would result in less or no incentive for investment. An efficient use of resources and continuous production is emphasised in order to ensure the recovery of the cost of development through exclusive rights. Another important economic aspect of copyright is that it is a trade of interests between costs and benefits (Towse, 2004). No benefit of copyright, in other words, will reduce the incentive to produce works, because the benefit will increase the price. Therefore, in determining copyright policy, it is of the utmost importance to strike a balance between the protection of artists and the costs of copyright in order to maximise creative output (Landes & Posner, 1989). However, the best way to overcome the dilemma of copyright as a mechanism for incentive to create access for users while avoiding concentration of copyright ownership in enterprises with excessive market power is still a matter of dispute (Towse, 2004). The role of copyright as an economic incentive has also been questioned. Towse (1999) and Kretschmer et al. (1999) have evidenced that asymmetry in information, risk-sharing and power structure favours record companies over artists; furthermore, the skewed distribution of royalties, where top-tier artists account for the majority of revenue, requires us to adopt a more sophisticated account of copyright as an economic incentive. Earning revenue from sound recordings has a very short history, and only a chosen few have received great rewards

(Caves, 2000; Towse, 2001). Marshall (2005) denounced this as romanticism inherited from the Romantic era, when "author" was elevated to a profession, and authors themselves were considered to be both artists and masters of their domain; this has mostly served the expansion of intellectual property.

The value of free music

The previous section described how the value of music has evolved from performance to sales of sheet music and to copyright-oriented business constructed around physical artefacts. In the context of sociotechnical, legal and institutional settings, the value of music built around copyright royalties fixed on physical artefacts, purported by the global music industry's interest, has been consolidated and validated over time in the music community.

The advent of P2P technology disrupted this model. With the potential to decentralise the commodification and commercial control of capital-intensive intellectual property, P2P technology was celebrated as a way of building a "communal innovation", in which an individual information-sharing and filtering mechanism would diversify user tastes through exposure to lesser-known artists (Pasquale III et al., 2002). This originates from the "hacker ethic" forged in the 1960s, which represented a counterculture, free distribution of information and an alternative to capitalism (Allen-Robertson, 2013). Hacker ethics were situated in a firm belief that computers were a vehicle for forming a powerful collective to challenge authority (Levy, 2001), and ultimately would emancipate the community from the constraints of capitalism (Himanen, 2001). These values became strongly tied to the subsequent development of P2P technology and the academic and policy discussion on digital culture (Benkler, 2006; Lessig, 2001; Vaidhyanathan; 2001).

The idea that information should be treated differently began with John Perry Barlow's famous article, "The economy of ideas", in which he argued that information is fundamentally different in that its value can be derived from "supporting and enhancing the soft property ... rather than selling it ... or embedding it" (Barlow, 1994). Furthermore, the idea of information as "free as the air to common use" was developed in order to suggest that information, unlike physical objects, should flow freely in the best interest of the public (Benkler, 2007). In a similar vein, criticism was raised of the copyright system, pointing out that it was an ancient system of privilege and hence did not fit into the information age (Deazley, 2006; Drahos, 1996). Extending this outmoded system to the protection of information, it was argued, would bring about a "second enclosure" that would reinforce the concentration of the commercial interests of the industry, compromise diversity and hence fail to serve the economic justification of the system (Boyle, 2008). All these ideas point to the fact that increasing protection of copyright for digitised cultural products could come at the risk of reinforcing concentrated, commercial production in the vertically integrated business structure (Benkler, 1999).

That semantic umbrella has infused these laws with the conceptual attitudes we have toward property in physical things. We expect things to be owned and exclusively controlled by someone. We think that protecting private property is good policy, good political theory, and just.

(Benkler, 1999: 355)

While celebrating the digital future as a means to connect authors to their fans, Goldstein (1994) held the view that the best way to achieve this would be to extend legal rights into every corner and therefore derive the value of every transaction of digital commodities.

The digital future is the next, perhaps ultimate phase in copyright's long trajectory, perfecting the law's early aim of connecting authors to their audiences, free from interference by political sovereigns or the will of patrons... [T]he best prescription for connecting authors to their audiences is to extend rights into every corner where consumers derive alive from literary and artistic works. If history is any measure, the results should be to promote political as well as cultural diversity, ensuring a plenitude of voices, all the chance to be heard.

(Goldstein, 2003: 236)

The music industry, which conceived free music as sales displacement, argued that free music constitutes a depreciated value of copyright and loss of royalties for artists, ultimately detrimental to innovation and creativity (IFPI, 2000). Different views also arose, proposing alternative ways to derive value from free music. In general, we can categorise these into three types: gift economy, network effect and indirect appropriation.

First is the *gift economy*, in which the sharing communities of P2P sharing networks would facilitate the giving and receiving of digital cultural products (Leyshon, 2003). By reversing the industrial control constructed around intellectual property, this "distributed knowledge system" was argued to provide an end to capitalism's expansion (Thrift, 2001). Second is the *network effect* (Shapiro & Varian, 1999), where the more users on the network, the better the experience. For example, there would be more files of better quality, access would therefore improve and efficient circulation of free music on digital networks could provide popularity and ultimately commercial success to musicians. Radiohead's "In Rainbows" album is the most widely mentioned case when referring to this effect. Lastly, the *indirect appropriation* of P2P filesharing could induce users to consume other relevant products. Free downloads of music could be used as a "free sample". The merit of "free samples" would invite users to listen to music in which they would otherwise would not be interested, which could lead to legitimate sales (Belleflamme & Peitz, 2014). Among legitimate sales, "revalorisation of performance" (Leyshon, 2003) has received the most attention, predicated on the idea that free music would bring back the very essence of the way music was valued: face-to-face intimacy and uniqueness that took place only at a certain time and in a certain space (Power & Hallencreutz, 2002; Vaidhyanathan, 2001).

Digital music valorisation process

The process of finding ways to derive value from digital music consuming networks, however, was by no means straightforward. A series of trial and error followed as various players sought to valorise music, culminating in the emergence of successful streaming services. This section discusses the uneven trajectory of business model developments in the digital music industry.

Non-free streaming model

Napster was a pioneering P2P technology-based music file-sharing service developed by a 19-year-old college student named Shawn Fanning. Its simple and easy means of exchanging files of copyrighted materials drew 70 million users at its peak. In the landmark case of A&M Records, Inc. v. Napster, the court sided with the entertainment industry, affirming that Napster was liable for contributory and vicarious copyright infringement.[2] Following the court decision, the original model of Napster was shut down. Nonetheless, P2P file-sharing persisted. Napster's progeny followed, developing ever-increasingly decentralised distribution networks.

The music industry's response to this challenge was contradictory. On the one hand, they resisted the change. They battled to stamp out the proliferation of unauthorised use of copyrighted digital content by lobbying for stronger and longer legal measures, employing digital rights management (DRM) systems, and litigating against companies and fans involved with P2P file-sharing. At the same time, they endeavoured to ensure they were not excluded from this new form of digital music distribution. Their solution was to devise their own digital music service in terms they envisioned themselves. Two large majors, Sony and Universal, began a joint-venture digital music service called Press-Play. Warner, EMI and Bertelsmann set up another service, MusicNet. Backed by major labels, these online subscription-based streaming music services were well equipped with top-selling catalogues. However, they fell far short of meeting digital music users' desires: the price was "set artificially high" and had "cumbersome digital rights management restrictions" (Sheffner, 2011). Rhapsody and EMusic were two more digital music services that emerged during this period, independent of the major record labels. They were more affordable and user-friendly, but were disadvantaged by their lack of popular catalogues, as the major labels had "collectively agreed not to do business with potential licenses" (Sheffner, 2011). Major labels might have successfully obstructed competitors' business, but they did not fulfil digital music users' demands either. Napster and its progeny empowered users to withhold their willingness to pay. The absolute lack of attention to digital music users' requirements led these services not only to fail but later to land at number nine on the "25 Worst Tech Products of All Time" list by PC World (Tynan, 2006).

Download model

None of the above approaches were enough to counteract the eroding business: CD sales continued to decline, label-led music services were apparently failing and P2P file-sharing appeared unstoppable. The key breakthrough was made by a technology firm, Apple. Its market share in the PC industry around 2001 was only 2%, and needed music content to promote their newly developed portable media player, iPod, and its management application, iTunes. From Sony's Walkman experience, major labels had learnt that the integration of music catalogues and music devices could have a great synergy effect.

iTunes debuted in April 2003, and sold one million tracks within a week. Its remarkable success can be attributed to various factors: legal *à-la-carte* choice from a breadth of music catalogues, at reasonable prices, as well as seamless integration with a chic gadget. The music industry, who had control over pricing and choice, had succeeded in bundling a subset of tracks as an album as a way to maximise profit (Zhu & Macquarrie 2003). Apple broke this down by introducing *à-la-carte* choice of music. By allowing digital music users to purchase licensed digital music at a relatively lower price compared to CDs, iTunes claimed to have brought digital music users to a legal platform, as well as contributing to the increase of digital music sales to a certain degree (Koh et al., 2014). This set the stage for the pay-per-download model.

However, it also laid the foundation for the tamed digital revolution (Sun, 2016). First, iTunes' desire to have legitimate digital music catalogues came at the price of consolidating the existing power relationship (Wikström, 2013). It eventually "len[t] itself to concentrating power in the major record labels. The walls that digital distribution broke down have been replaced by distribution barriers in the form of iTunes" (Arditi, 2014: 422). Although iTunes' *à-la-carte* choice of music purchase was revolutionary at that time, pay-per-download was still a continuation of pay-per-unit and was not enough to mitigate digital music users' unwillingness to pay. Its deliberate decision to constrain consumers' choices in part explains the unabated P2P file-sharing and the continued erosion of digital music sales revenue (Medford, 2008). Eventually, it provided leeway for other services to spring up.

Free streaming model

Although iTunes opened the gate for legitimate digital music consumption, it did not keep piracy at bay, and left room for other innovations. Free music seemed to be a *tour de force*. The next generation of digital music valorisation was modelled on the "free" streaming model. YouTube, Last.fm, Grooveshark and many other business services mushroomed during this period, offering free streaming music.

Last.fm began as a college project for Richard Jones, who studied computer science at the University of Southampton in the UK. He invented a music recommendation program called "Audioscrobbler", which collected and stored people's music listening history data. Its music recommendation system, along with a free and near-unlimited choice of music, brought great growth for the service. It became "one of the most well established, fastest growing online community networks", with around 20 million active users (Kiss, 2007). Last.fm's user base was growing very fast, and this large network of users made its recommendations more relevant to individuals (McCarthy, 2007). This success led to an acquisition by CBS, one of the largest acquisitions at that time. Since its acquisition by CBS, Last.fm has become much more compliant with copyright laws. Due to the hefty licensing fee, however, Last.fm closed down its free on-demand service, which was its most popular feature. This resulted in the waning popularity of the service.

Around the same time, in 2005, YouTube arose in the market as a free video-sharing website. The essence of the business lies in allowing users to upload and share videos through which advertisements are tied to generate revenue. While YouTube was not the first or only service of this kind, it gained exponential popularity due to its ease of use: instant, free and unlimited access to global catalogues, simple uploading of videos in any format and easy sharing (O'Brien & Fitzgerald, 2006). By allowing users to upload user-generated videos, it became a platform for "vernacular creativity". This lifted the barrier to entry and facilitated a "participatory culture" (Jenkins, 2006). In 2006, it became a Google company. Since then, YouTube has been embroiled in legal allegations by entertainment companies, including Viacom. Over the course of these legal actions, YouTube has put a few copyright-compliance policies in place and reached resolutions with entertainment firms.

YouTube is widely epitomised as the incarnation of Web 2.0, and is still the most popular music listening destination for free video streaming (Mulligan, 2017). However, its abundance of free content could not prevail over its limitations, such as the inconsistent quality of sound and the annoyance of advertisements (Jarrett, 2008).

These free-streaming based models accommodated the needs of digital music users, who wanted a vast number of catalogues by the cheapest means possible. Services, however, had to be compromised when they did not benefit the record labels. More importantly, contrary to the widely believed idea that digital music should be free – although free is important – the free streaming development process shows that free music was not all that mattered to digital music users. With hindsight, we can conjecture that there were four factors digital music users wanted from digital music services: a wide breadth of catalogues, convenience, legality, and price (as cheap as possible). None of the services ticked all the boxes. Besides, services had to find a balance between the conflicting interests of users and the labels who wanted to extend their power as far as possible.

Freemium streaming model

None of the previous models seemed to be able to stop piracy. Spotify, however, arose in 2006 in the midst of piracy's golden era. The business began with a vision to provide a solution better than P2P file-sharing. The key attraction of P2P file-sharing lay in its ease of use and free and unlimited access to music, with a major weakness of illegality. Spotify's solution was an easier-to-use service with a lowered fixed price, providing legal access to a worldwide catalogue. This strategy of "[f]ighting piracy with free" (Halmenschlager & Waelbroeck, 2014) through a freemium model suited a different segment of consumers, who were used to free music but had more willingness to pay, and proved to be sufficiently attractive to consumers to be commercially viable. For a new technology to survive in a harsh selection environment, a protected space, also known as a niche, can provide breathing room for a new sociotechnical configuration to arise (Kemp, 1994; Kemp et al., 1998; Geels, 2002).[3] For Spotify, this protected space was created in the least likely place, Sweden, the stronghold of piracy and the birthplace of two major pirate organisations, the Pirate Bay and the Pirate Party. The failed copyright policy in Sweden had created a legal vacuum, leaving nothing to lose in this experiment. The downturn of business forced Per Sundin, Chairman and CEO of Universal Music Sweden, to lay off 200 employees. The Swedish election debate in 2006 was heated on the subject of piracy, and Sundin's mother, who was watching this debate on TV, urged Sundin to find a new job (Lynskey, 2013). Sundin was in dire need of a saviour. Spotify's technical superiority and its willingness to license was impressive enough to convince his bosses to support the service.

However, it is also important to note that this was the result of an alignment between two major players with highly conflicting interests: digital music users and labels. Spotify's licensing deals were traded with the company's equity for a meagre amount from the labels (Jerräng, 2009). Labels' ownership of Spotify therefore raised a serious concern that this signified an usurpation of control by majors in the digital music business (Barr, 2013; Teague, 2012). The total lack of consideration for artists in this negotiation partly explains the debate over improper compensation for artists on this new music consuming platform.

Technological trajectory of P2P technology

With an increasing number of paying subscribers, streaming music services are well poised to be the de facto digital music consuming platform. The current digital music valorisation platform arose in the legitimate digital distribution networks, however, is distinct from the widely held vision that P2P networks could be at the centre of digital music distribution, promotion and discovery. P2P networks evolved as a response to the court decisions relating to their precedent P2P technologies. Since the decision by Ninth Circuit about

Napster, the trajectory of P2P technology has developed following the "road-map" of the court decisions of the precedent P2P technologies (Allen-Robertson, 2013; Giblin, 2011). The court rulings suggested that the more decentralised P2P networks are, the more legitimate they could be. This forced subsequent P2P networks to avoid having a central control (Nasir, 2005). However, not only the victory has been rather pyrrhic (Bridy, 2009), the entertainment industry faced the dilemma that the very legal measures they lobbied for became the bottleneck of controlling the problem they wanted to solve: legal precedents directed the P2P file-sharing networks to be decentralised to the extent that even their own legal measures are incapable of controlling them. That is, even if the client site is shut down, the legacy users still can swap files, new clients can easily be made, and the legal measures might have to go too far-fetched to control the globally distributed files (Edwards, 2011). As a result, the entertainment industry have turned to seek for different types of measures which involves "ISP-co-coperation" by introducing "graduated response" or "three strikes" laws for ISPs that control access to the Internet, or cutting off access to torrent sites or "cyber lockers".

Controversies over digital music value

There is an increasing amount of literature that provides evidence of the correlation between the increased number of Spotify users and the decrease in piracy (Aguiar & Waldfogel, 2015; IFPI, 2015; Page, 2013; Wlömert & Papies, 2016). It also signals a recovery of the music business. Amidst the growing optimism emerging in the industry, however, disputes remain over the value of music. The most widely known arguments are about the undervaluation of music generated from the streaming music platform. The argument that music is undervalued has been magnified in the wake of a few celebrities' vociferous critique. Thom Yorke, lead singer of Radiohead, denounced Spotify as "the last desperate fart of the dying corpse" (Dredge, 2013), while David Byrne, lead singer of Talking Heads, raised concerns that "the Internet will suck the creative content out of the whole world until nothing is left" (Byrne 2013). Later in 2014, Taylor Swift withheld her repertoire from Spotify, arguing that Spotify's meagre payout was not an appropriate price for her works of art (Swift, 2014). As of this writing, however, the high-profile artist has changed her mind, reportedly to "thank her fans" and is now back together with Spotify (Nicolaou 2017). According to Lalonde (2014), the current model of digital streaming services devalues music: free advertisement-based services give away music, and the subscription fee is considerably lower than other equivalent services such as pay-per-view ("PPV") or video-on-demand ("VOD").

While streaming services have largely been blamed for the paltry amount of royalties generated by pay-per-stream, some of the focus shifted to labels when the contract between Sony Music and Spotify was leaked in May 2015 (Singleton, 2015). This revealed that a considerable amount of money generated from streaming services, such as upfront payments, equity stakes and streaming rates, remains in the hands of labels and is not paid out to artists. Market power skewed toward the major labels appears to persist in the digital age, and this arguably leads to an "unfair" distribution (Erickson, 2015). This is manifested in the fact that 70% of streaming revenue goes to the labels, and no streaming services have proved to be profitable despite continuous growth (Tschmuck, 2015). This is linked to another major problem: lack of transparency (Hirschhorn, 2015). The opaqueness of the negotiation between services and labels and the contracts between artists and labels are said to constitute a primary impediment to remedying the problem (Rethink Music, 2015). This has led to a desire to build a "fair" compensation scheme and create a "virtuous" value chain in the music industry (ECSA, 2015; Lalonde, 2014; Music Managers Forum, 2016; Rethink Music, 2015), in a context where every "listen" can be tracked globally. One argument is that a centralised global digital music database could help ease the problems of fragmented use of digital music repertoires and revitalise the digital music market by providing better services to consumers, and ultimately compensate artists better (Ghafele, 2014).

Although this discussion is meaningful in its own right, its exclusive focus on the distribution of the revenue generated from streaming services falls short of understanding the full implication of the valuation of music in the digital era. A growing body of studies is therefore being developed to address derivative value generated from streaming music services. Recognising the inadequacy of the previous economics of music value, they stress that platform-based music consumption requires us to reconsider pay-per-unit music value and pay more attention to consuming patterns. Belleflamme (2016) has rightly pointed out the inadequacy of the previous means of valuing music on digital music networks. He questions the way we value music based on the pay-per-unit mechanism through three aspects: (1) the pay-per-unit model disregards new intermediaries such as services who play a crucial role in the digital music consuming platform; (2) the streaming model is at odds with the previous method of music valuation, which was modelled on a system where sales of a unit were equated with sales of one copyrighted piece of material; and (3) there is a variety of pricing in the streaming model. He therefore suggests a new model for a multi-sided platform that can account for the role of intermediaries and diverse external effects. Datta et al. (2017) draw upon the variety of choices enabled by the streaming platform. By illustrating that the abundance of choice enhances the diversity and better quality of digital music contents, they evince the need to attend to the changing behaviour on this new digital music platform. These views serve as a timely assurance of the impending need for a new dimension for digital music valuation.

The conventional music industry rested on the single-sided economics in which money is acquired through artificial scarcity and ownership. Its preoccupation with the pecuniary value and copyright royalties reflects a key belief that copyright protection properly compensates artists, and that economic valuation of music based on royalties is the best currency for measuring the value of music. Not only has the reality of copyright often been accused of remaining at odds with its primarily proclaimed economic justification (Caves, 2000; Kretschmer, 2000; Towse, 2001); the current discussion also takes the industry reports at face value, and rarely questions their validity, which Marshall (2013) has pointed out in the context of a more plural concept of the music industry. Its attempt to explain a new change in a pre-confined system can lose sight of the full implications of the digitally networked economy (Ng, 2014).

From a longitudinal perspective, the current music industry signals a shift of technological regime in which digital novelties embedded in the previous regime produce new kinds of development, and in tandem constrain others. The impact that digital technology has made far exceeds economic concerns, triggering contestations of what we value in a digitally networked society. The legacy of piracy fused with liberalism and the continued enforcement of existing industrial power structure is producing a new change in the digital music economics. Mangematin et al. (2014) call this "disassembly and reassembly", where old and new converge to produce a new trend. This new change takes place at all levels, from production to distribution and consumption; therefore, the authors emphasise, a fundamental reconfiguration of value chain is required. The complexity of the innovation process, which is subject to conflicts and struggles, begs us to understand the constellations of value creation in a networked context.

Conclusion

This chapter has discussed the malleable nature of music value and the way the modern system of music valuation has been established around copyright licensing, a scheme purported by the music industry. It has also investigated the digital music valorisation process and the diverse interests and power struggles involved in forming the digital music value that we have now come to agree upon. In the protracted process of technological innovation, it identified interplay amongst a wide array of actors with different interests, motivations and commitments (MacKenzie & Wajcman, 1985; Williams & Edge, 1996). In this case, it was two major players whose bargaining power exerted tremendous influence over the shaping of the business development: major labels, who wanted to extend the power gained from large and popular music catalogues, and users, who withheld their willingness to pay. Lastly, the chapter has demonstrated the inadequacy of the modern economics of music valuation and the need for a new dimension of music valuation in the digitally networked economy.

Despite the increasing revenue generated on the new digital music consuming platform, we're facing an irony that the primary concern of digital music value is centred on insignificant remuneration for artists, an issue that the music industry claimed would be solved if people paid for music. We observed the complexity of the issue involved in arriving at the value and the difficulty of finding a commercially viable valorisation business model. At the centre of this tribulation was the tension between the legacy of piracy and the extended power of existing major players. Large-scale access at low price came as the solution to this stalemate. The stark absence of concern for artists in this negotiation process reveals where the problem started. Alongside addressing revenue distribution issues, the chapter calls for the way forward by attending to the shifting value of music in which the value of piracy heritage and existing market value are converged.

Notes

1 Performance royalty systems were common practice in Paris throughout the era predating phonograph and gramophone technology (Kretschmer, 2000).
2 Vicarious liability rests on the ability to control and potentially receive financial benefit, and contributory liability is applied based upon the knowledge of infringing activity.
3 The discussion of protected space in radical innovation so far is limited to a space created artificially to nurture a promising technology. Spotify's case challenges this concept in broader contexts.

Bibliography

Aguiar, L. and Waldfogel, J., 2015. *Streaming reaches flood stage: Does Spotify stimulate or depress music sales?* National Bureau of Economic Research, Working Paper No. 21653.

Allen-Robertson, J., 2013. *Digital culture industry: A history of digital distribution.* Houndsmills, Basingstoke: Palgrave Macmillan.

Antal, A.B., Hutter, M., and Stark, D., 2015. *Moments of valuation exploring sites of dissonance.* Oxford: Oxford University Press.

Arditi, D., 2014. iTunes: Breaking barriers and building walls. *Popular Music and Society*, 37(4): 408–424.

Bakker, G., 2012. Adopting the rights-based model: Music multinationals and local music industries since 1945. *Popular Music History*, 6(3): 343.

Barlow, J.P., 1994. The economy of ideas [online]. *Wired*. Available from: www.wired.com/1994/03/economy-ideas/ [Accessed 31 May 2017].

Barr, K., 2013. Theorizing music streaming: Preliminary investigations. *Scottish Music Review*, 3(2): 1–20.

Baumol, W.J. and Owen, W.G.B., 1966. *Performing arts: The economic dilemma; a study of problems common to theater, opera, music and dance.* New York: Twentieth Century Fund.

Belleflamme, P., 2016. *The economics of digital goods: A progress report.* Rochester, NY: Social Science Research Network, SSRN Scholarly Paper No. ID 2903416.

Belleflamme, P. and Peitz, M., 2014. Digital piracy: An update. *IDEAS Working Paper Series from RePEc.*

Benkler, Y., 1999. Free as the air to common use: First Amendment constraints on enclosure of the public domain. *New York University Law Review*, 74(2): 354–446.

Benkler, Y., 2006. *The wealth of networks: How social production transforms markets and freedom.* New Haven, CT and London: Yale University Press.

Benkler, Y., 2007. Free as the air to common use: First Amendment constraints on enclosure of the public domain. In: *Economics of intellectual property law. Volume 2.* Elgar Reference Collection. Economic Approaches to Law, vol. 16. Cheltenham and Northampton, MA: Elgar, 3–13.

Bettig, R., 1996. *Copyrighting culture: The political economy of intellectual property.* Boulder, CO and Oxford: Westview Press.

Boyle, J., 2008. *The public domain: Enclosing the commons of the mind.* New Haven, CT: Yale University Press.

Bridy, A., 2009. Why pirates (still) won't behave: Regulating P2P in the decade after Napster. *Rutgers LJ.* 40, 565.

Burkart, P. and McCourt, T., 2006. *Digital music wars: Ownership and control of the celestial jukebox.* Lanham, MD and Oxford: Rowman & Littlefield Publishers.

Burnett, R., 1996. *The global jukebox: The international music industry.* London: Routledge.

Byrne, D., 2013. The internet will suck all creative content out of the world [online]. *The Guardian.* Available from: www.theguardian.com/music/2013/oct/11/david-byrne-internet-content-world [Accessed 31 May 2017].

Caves, R.E., 2000. *Creative industries: Contracts between art and commerce.* Cambridge, MA and London: Harvard University Press.

Coleman, M., 2004. *Playback: From the Victrola to MP3, 100 years of music, machines, and money.* New York: Da Capo Press.

Datta, H., Knox, G., and Bronnenberg, B.J., 2017. *Changing their tune: How consumers' adoption of online streaming affects music consumption and discovery.* Rochester, NY: Social Science Research Network, SSRN Scholarly Paper No. ID 2782911.

Deazley, R., 2006. *Rethinking copyright: history, theory, language.* Cheltenham: Edward Elgar.

Drahos, P., 1996. *A philosophy of intellectual property.* Aldershot: Dartmouth.

Dredge, S., 2013. Spotify launches artist Spotlight feature with Haim and Lorde. [online]. Musically. Available from: http://musically.com/2013/10/01/spotify-launches-artist-spotlight-feature-with-haim-and-lorde/ [Accessed 18 Feb 2016].

ECSA, 2015. ECSA position paper – What music creators want – ECSA–Composer Alliance [online]. *European Composer & Songwriter Alliance.* Available from: http://composeralliance.org/ecsa-position-paper-what-music-creators-want/ [Accessed 25 Aug 2015].

Edwards, L. 2011, *Role and responsibility of the internet intermediaries in the field of copyright and related rights.* Geneva: WIPO.

Ehrlich, C. 1985. *The music profession in Britain since the eighteenth century: A social history.* Oxford: Clarendon Press.

Erickson, K., 2015. Five things to understand about that Spotify contract leak [online]. *Future of Music Coalition.* Available from: www.futureofmusic.org/blog/2015/05/27/five-things-understand-about-spotify-contract-leak [Accessed 25 Aug 2015].

Frith, S., 1987. The industrialization of popular music. In: J. Lull, ed. *Popular music and communication.* Newbury Park, CA: Sage, 53geu.

Frith, S., 1988. Copyright and the music business. *Popular Music,* 7(01): 57–75.

Frith, S., 2007. Adam Smith and music. In: *Taking popular music seriously: Selected essays.* Aldershot and Burlington: Ashgate.

Garofalo, R., 1999. From Music publishing to MP3: Music and industry in the twentieth century. *American Music*, 17(3): 318–354.

Geels, F.W., 2002. Towards sociotechnical scenarios and reflexive anticipation: Using patterns and regularities in technology dynamics. In: K.H. Sørensen and R. Williams, eds. *Shaping technology, guiding policy: concepts, spaces, and tools.* Cheltenham and Northampton, MA: Elgar.

Ghafele, R., 2014. Europe's lost royalty opportunity: A comparison of potential and existing digital music royalty markets in ten different EU member states. *Review of Economic Research on Copyright Issues*, 11(2): 60–91.

Giblin, R., 2011. *Code wars 10 years of P2P software litigation.* Cheltenham: Edward Elgar.

Goldstein, P., 1994. *Copyright's highway: From Gutenberg to the celestial jukebox.* New York: Hill and Wang.

Goldstein, P., 2003. *Copyright's highway: From Gutenberg to the celestial jukebox.* Stanford, CA: Stanford University Press.

Halmenschlager, C. and Waelbroeck, P., 2014. Fighting free with free: Freemium vs. piracy. Available at SSRN:https://ssrn.com/abstract=2475641.

Hardin, G., 1968. The tragedy of the commons. *Science*, 162(3859): 1243–1248.

Himanen, P., 2001. *The hacker ethic: And the spirit of the information age.* London: Secker & Warburg.

Hirsch, P., 1969. *The structure of the popular music industry.* Survey Research Centre, Ann Arbor: University of Michigan.

Hirschhorn, J., 2015. Less money, mo' music & lots of problems: A look at the music biz [online]. Available from: www.linkedin.com/pulse/less-money-mo-music-lots-p roblems-look-biz-jason-hirschhorn [Accessed 22 Jun 2017].

Hunter, D., 1986. Music copyright in Britain to 1800. *Music & Letters*, 67(3): 269–282.

IFPI, 2000. *IFPI Music Piracy Report 2000.* IFPI (International Federation of the Phonographic Industry).

IFPI, 2015. *IFPI Digital Music Report 2015: Charting the Path to Sustainable Growth.* London: The International Federation of the Phonographic Industry.

Jarrett, K., 2008. Beyond Broadcast Yourself[TM]: The future of YouTube. *Media International Australia*, 126(1): 132–144.

Jenkins, H., 2006. *Convergence culture: Where old and new media collide.* New York: New York University Press.

Jerräng, M., 2009. Documents reveal major labels own part of Spotify [online]. *Computer Sweden*. Available from: http://computersweden.idg.se/2.2683/1.240046/docum ents-reveal-major-labels-own-part-of-spotify [Accessed 28 Feb 2016].

Kassabian, A., 2001. *Hearing film: Tracking identifications in contemporary Hollywood film music.* New York and London: Routledge.

Kassabian, A., 2013. *Ubiquitous listening: Affect, attention, and distributed subjectivity.* Berkeley, CA: University of California Press.

Katz, M., 2010. *Capturing sound how technology has changed music.* Revised edition. Berkeley, CA and London: University of California Press.

Kemp, R., 1994. Technology and the transition to environmental sustainability: The problem of technological regime shifts. *Futures*, 26(10): 1023–1046.

Kemp, R., Schot, J., and Hoogma, R., 1998. Regime shifts to sustainability through processes of niche formation: The approach of strategic niche management. *Technology Analysis & Strategic Management*, 10(2): 175–198.

Kiss, J., 2007. Last.fm fetches $280m. *The Guardian*, 30 May.

Koh, B., Murthi, B.P.S., and Raghunathan, S., 2014. Shifting demand: Online music piracy, physical music sales, and digital music sales. *Journal of Organizational Computing and Electronic Commerce*, 24(4): 366–387.

Kretschmer, M., 2000. Intellectual property in music: A historical analysis of rhetoric and institutional practices. *Studies in Cultures, Organizations & Societies*, 6(2): 197–223.

Kretschmer, M., Klimis, G.M., and Wallis, R., 1999. The changing location of intellectual property rights in music: A study of music publishers, collecting societies and media conglomerates. *Prometheus*, 17(2): 163.

Laing, D., 2004. Copyright, politics and the international music industry. In: S. Frith and L. Marshall, eds. *Music and Copyright*, Second edition. New York: Routledge.

Lalonde, P.-E., 2014. Study concerning fair compensation for music creators in the digital age [online]. *CIAM*. Available from: www.songwriters.ca/studyconcerningfaircompensation2014.aspx [Accessed 2 Aug 2015].

Landes, W.M. and Posner, R., 1989. An economic analysis of copyright law. *Economic Analysis of the Law*, 83–99.

Lessig, L., 2001. *The future of ideas: The fate of the commons in a connected world.* New York: Random House.

Levy, S., 2001. *Hackers: Heroes of the computer revolution.* New York and London: Penguin.

Leyshon, A., 2003. Scary monsters? Software formats, peer-to-peer networks, and the spectre of the gift. *Environment and Planning D*, 21(5): 533–558.

Lynskey, D., 2013. Is Daniel Ek, Spotify founder, going to save the music industry ... or destroy it? [online]. *The Observer*. Available from: www.theguardian.com/technology/2013/nov/10/daniel-ek-spotify-streaming-music [Accessed 27 Jan 2016].

Mangematin, V., Sapsed, J., and Schüßler, E., 2014. Disassembly and reassembly: An introduction to the special issue on digital technology and creative industries. *Technological Forecasting & Social Change*, 83: 1–9.

Marshall, L., 2005. *Bootlegging: Romanticism and copyright in the music industry.* London: Sage.

Marshall, L., 2004. Infringers. In: S. Frith and L. Marshall, eds. *Music and copyright.* Edinburgh: Edinburgh University Press.

Marshall, L., ed., 2013. *The international recording industries.* Abingdon and New York: Routledge.

McCarthy, C., 2007. What does CBS want with Last.fm? [online]. *CNET*. Available from: www.cnet.com/news/what-does-cbs-want-with-last-fm/ [Accessed 25 Feb 2016].

MacKenzie, D. and Wajcman, J., 1985. *The social shaping of technology.* Buckingham: Open University Press.

Mcleod, K., 2005. MP3s are killing home taping: The rise of internet distribution and its challenge to the major label music monopoly 1. *Popular Music and Society*, 28(4): 521–531.

Medford, C., 2008. *Report: Apple killed music industry.* Red Herring.

Mulligan, M., 2017. Who's leading the streaming music pack? *MIDiA Research*. Available from: www.midiaresearch.com/blog/whos-leading-the-streaming-music-pack/.

Music Managers Forum, 2016. Dissecting the digital dollar. *CMU Insights*. Available from: http://cmuinsights.com/digitaldollar/.

Nasir, C., 2005. Taming the beast of file-sharing – legal and technological solutions to the problem of copyright infringement over the internet. *Entertainment Law Review* 16(4): 82–88.

Negroponte, N., 1996. *Being digital*. First Vintage Books edition. New York: Vintage Books.

Negus, K., 1992. *Producing pop: Culture and conflict in the popular music industry*. London: Arnold.

Ng, I.C.L., 2014. *Creating new markets in the digital economy: Value and worth*. Cambridge: Cambridge University Press.

Nicolaou, A., 2017. Taylor Swift changes her tune and returns to Spotify. *Financial Times*, 9 Jun.

O'Brien, D.S. and Fitzgerald, B.F., 2006. Mashups, remixes and copyright law. *Internet Law Bulletin*, 9(2): 17–19.

Page, W., 2013. Adventures in the Netherlands: New Spotify study sees encouraging downwards trend in music piracy in the Netherlands. *Spotify Press*.

PasqualeIII, F.A., Weatherall, K.G., and Fagin, M.B., 2002. Beyond Napster: using antitrust law to advance and enhance online music distribution. *Boston University Journal of Science & Technology Law*, 8: 451.

Peacock, A. and Weir, R., 1975. *The composer in the market place*. London: Faber Music.

Peterson, R.A., 1990. Why 1955? Explaining the advent of rock music. *Popular Music*, 9(1): 97–116.

Plumb, J.H., 1973. *The commercialisation of leisure in eighteenth-century England*. Reading: University of Reading.

Posner, R.A., 1998. *Economic analysis of law*, fifth edition, New York: Aspen Law & Business.

Power, D. and Hallencreutz, D., 2002. Profiting from creativity? The music industry in Stockholm, Sweden and Kingston, Jamaica. *Environment and Planning A*, 34(10): 1833–1854.

Rethink Music, 2015. Fair music: Transparency and payment flows in the music industry [online]. *Rethink Music*. Available from: www.rethink-music.com/research/fair-music-transparency-and-payment-flows-in-the-music-industry [Accessed 15 Aug 2015].

Rosen, R.S., 2008. *Music and copyright*. New York: Oxford University Press.

Scherer, F.M., 2004. *Quarter notes and bank notes: the economics of music composition in the eighteenth and nineteenth centuries*. Princeton, NJ and Oxford: Princeton University Press.

Shapiro, C. & Varian, H.R., 1999. *Information rules: a strategic guide to the network economy*. Boston, MA: Harvard Business School Press.

Sheffner, B., 2011. The antitrust case against major record labels, in perspective [online]. *Billboard*. Available from: www.billboard.com/biz/articles/news/1179723/the-antitrust-case-against-major-record-labels-in-perspective [Accessed 10 Feb 2016].

Singleton, M., 2015. This was Sony Music's contract with Spotify [online]. *The Verge*. Available from: www.theverge.com/2015/5/19/8621581/sony-music-spotify-contract [Accessed 25 Aug 2015].

Sun, H., 2016. *Digital disruption in the recording industry*. PhD Dissertation. University of Edinburgh.

Swift, T., 2014. For Taylor Swift, the future of music is a love story – WSJ [online]. *The Wall Street Journal*. Available from: www.wsj.com/articles/for-taylor-swift-the-future-of-music-is-a-love-story-1404763219 [Accessed 31 May 2017].

Teague, J., 2012. Saving the Spotify revolution: Recalibrating the power imbalance in digital copyright. *Case W. Res. JL Tech. & Internet*, 4: 207.

Théberge, P., 2006. Everyday fandom: Fan clubs, blogging, and the quotidian rhythms of the internet. *Canadian Journal of Communication*, 30(4): 485–502.

Thrift, N., 2001. "It's the romance, not the finance, that makes the business worth pursuing": disclosing a new market culture. *Economy and Society*, 30(4): 412–432.

Towse, R., 1999. Copyright and economic incentives: An application to performers' rights in the music industry. *Kyklos*, 52(3): 369–390.

Towse, R., 2001. *Creativity, incentive, and reward: An economic analysis of copyright and culture in the information age*. Cheltenham: Edward Elgar.

Towse, R., 2004. Copyright and economics. In: S. Frith and L. Marshall, eds. *Music and copyright*. Edinburgh: Edinburgh University Press.

Toynbee, J., 2004. Musicians. In: S. Frith and L. Marshall, eds. *Music and copyright*. New York: Routledge.

Tschmuck, P., 2012. *Creativity and innovation in the music industry*. Second edition. Berlin and New York: Springer.

Tschmuck, P., 2015. Music streaming revisited – the problem of income distribution | music business research [online]. *Music Business Research*. Available from: https:// music businessresearch.wordpress.com/2015/07/18/music-streaming-revisited-the-proble m-of-income-distribution/ [Accessed 21 Jun 2017].

Tynan, D., 2006. The 25 worst tech products of all time [online]. *PCWorld*. Available from: www.pcworld.com/article/125772/worst_products_ever.html [Accessed 10 Feb 2016].

Vaidhyanathan, S., 2001. *Copyrights and copywrongs: The rise of intellectual property and how it threatens creativity*. New York: New York University Press.

Von Hippel, E., 2005. *Democratizing innovation*. London: MIT Press.

Wikström, P., 2013. *The music industry: Music in the cloud*. Second edition. Cambridge: Polity Press.

Williams, R. and Edge, D., 1996. The social shaping of technology. *Research Policy*, 25(6): 865–899.

Wilson, S., 2017. Streaming to overtake sales of physical music in the UK for the first time ever. *FACT Magazine: Music News, New Music*.

Wlömert, N. and Papies, D., 2016. On-demand streaming services and music industry revenues – Insights from Spotify's market entry. *International Journal of Research in Marketing*, 33(2): 314–327.

Zhu, K. and Macquarrie, B., 2003. The economics of digital bundling: the impact of digitization and bundling on the music industry. *Communications of the ACM*, 46(9): 264–270.

3 Digital piracy, new media and consumer choice

Kenneth Forbes and Holly Tessler

This chapter aims to critically assess the ontological, cultural and industrial implications of the notion of 'digital music piracy'. Starting from the position that there is a lack of precision surrounding each element of this concept, chiefly, 'digital', 'music' and 'piracy', we thus make a first assertion that 'digital music piracy' has become a kind of straw man for the various elements within the music, legal, and creative industries. Indeed, many of these sectors have attributed declines in revenue and changes in consumer behaviours to the digital music piracy bogeyman, rather than take more proactive and future-facing steps to understand and engage with the evolving practices, interests and activities of contemporary music fans and consumers. In many respects, we mirror the views of Jeremy Wade Morris (2015: 5), who shares our apprehension about:

> ... how heavily weighted public discussion around digital music has been toward piracy and economics. Driven largely by the major record labels and the major industry associations, the campaign against 'piracy' has created a heated rhetorical ground around digital music. ... (However,) piracy and the availability of 'free' digital music is only one factor driving the current shift in the music industries. There are bigger changes taking place with the form and function of cultural commodities in the current moment.

Such obvious disdain for the varying levels of user consumption, interaction and 'connectiveness' within the wider digital-media environment of everyday life can be regarded as a culture in which rights owners and their representatives refuse to engage with for fear of adding further to the widely held belief that contemporary copyright legislation is an anachronism that is more relevant to works of Dickens than it is to an artist like Drake.

To support this argument, in the second half of the chapter we draw on several illustrative examples intended to counter the predominant music industries' (Williamson & Cloonan, 2007) narrative warning of the ills of digital music piracy in an aim to demonstrate not only the limitations of the term 'digital music piracy' but also to highlight the fact that if major music industries stakeholders continue to cling onto outmoded business models reliant on centuries-old interpretations of copyright law, they will continue to miss out on both new opportunities for the production, distribution and consumption of music by their artists. Furthermore, and perhaps even more significantly, they will also continue to fundamentally misunderstand and ultimately alienate passionate music fans and consumers who increasingly see major record labels and publishers in an oppositional light. Ultimately, the discussion to follow will endeavour to endorse Sinnreich's view (2013: 17) that:

> Instead of supporting or embracing exciting new platforms that allow people to enjoy music to the fullest extent possible, the industry has attempted to squelch innovation at every turn, using copyright laws, security technologies, and propaganda as their weapons.

In attempting to pursue this claim, we recognise that there is insufficient space within the scope of this chapter to closely scrutinize the many intricacies of copyright legislation to the same extent as other key sources (such as Stokes, 2014). We therefore apply a caveat that our broad-brush analysis of copyright serves to focus instead on the way in which current content ownership laws function to demonize and inconvenience ordinary music fans by imposing needless restrictions on habitual forms of consumer usage, sharing and re-appropriation in an era of media convergence culture. As such, the discussion to follow will serve to underline that connectivity, sociality and participation all trump such misguided presumptions that originated in the eighteenth century about how music content should be consumed in the twenty-first century.

Problematizing 'digital'

Of obvious note, the notion of 'digital' and what it symbolizes within the current media environment lies at the heart of the conflict that we address. In this respect, 'digital' is problematized by its fragile links with 'copyright' in the twenty-first century. Within this realm, rights owners attempt to maintain their fragile grip on copyright and the key economic value that it represents, principally in order to bolster their long-term business agendas. Plácido Domingo, chairman of the global record industry body, the International Federation of Phonographic Industries (IFPI), proclaimed in a report (2014a: 4), that:

> Investment in music cannot be taken for granted. Like the creativity of the artist, it is something that needs to be supported and protected by a secure legal environment. That is why a safe, adequate copyright framework for artists and labels is so crucial. It is more crucial than ever before in today's digital world, where copyright is fighting for its place against those who would have music and culture disseminated for free or who

would erode copyright protections in the name of "copyright reform". It is copyright that makes investment in music possible. It is copyright that allows the industry that helps artists gain a return on its investment, and therefore plough back new funds and resources into the next generation of talent.

In addition to reiterating the historical and often sacrosanct trope about the record industry's control over all aspects of copyright (and rebuking those who would question their position), Domingo serves to confirm Tschmuck's (2017: 63) assertion that the record industry must rely on regularly extended copyright terms in order to minimize levels of uncertainty within their business models, with this functioning to provide a "kind of long-term insurance against poor business decisions". Notwithstanding the fact that very few, if any, industries rely on a 90% failure rate (Jones, 2012: 35) to facilitate a 10% megastar tier, the IFPI fail to acknowledge that the record industry's global dominance in the latter half of last century was ultimately a 'historical blip' (Williamson & Cloonan, 2013: 13), thus greatly marginalizing any claims about their ongoing control of copyright and our consumption habits. Indeed, the 'copyright' that Domingo refers to represents a bygone analogue age, where audiences merely read fixed, tangible goods, whereas now the reading-*writing* of cultural goods represents the normal everyday practice of consumer life, with the author–audience distinction becoming blurred (Sinnreich, 2013: 196). Such a trajectory leads Boon (2010: 6) to claim that the 'copyright', as applied in the twenty-first century "… itself sounds a little desperate, as though one had to actually suture the words 'copy' and 'right' together in order to associate consistency".

The main issue at stake here is the aforementioned intangibility and flexibility of creative texts that circulate within the digital environment. Of course, as Ginsburg (2001) and numerous others (Lessig, 2008; Knopper, 2009; Morris, 2015) have all clearly demonstrated, the record industry has, throughout its relatively long history, been reliant on locking down innovations within audio technology and the dissemination of music, restricting consumer choice within this process, in order to sustain their grip on copyright.

Certainly, from a historical perspective, the record industry's reluctance to embrace new technology in order to maintain their control over both copyright and how music should be consumed, can be garnered through a short analysis of an IFPI promotional video, which was commissioned in 2014 for their Music Remains initiative (Music Remains, n.d.). Entitled 'A history of recorded music in 90 seconds' (IFPI, 2014b), the video uses an array of recorded formats, which appear in chronological order from over the last one hundred-plus years. Starting with a gramophone and ending with an iPad, selected songs are used to soundtrack the specific format within the chain, with the 1970s being represented by ABBA's 'Dancing Queen' and vinyl albums (despite the song's key existence as top selling single) and Run-DMC and Aerosmith's 'Walk This Way' and the 1980s being symbolized by a Sony

Walkman. Lyrics performed by a 'rising artist' Pepstar (DJ/Producer Ian Opuko) relate to the artist's personal experiences with recorded music, ending with the lines (ibid.):

> Look at you, you're still beaming
> No CDs but you're still streaming
> Years have passed, and nothing's the same but
> You're the one thing that always remains ...

Music

Intended as an amusing reminder to viewers and consumers about the continuing significance of music despite 'frequent' format changes, the video serves to expose the fallacy of the record industry's approach to technology, with only three basic physical formats (variations of vinyl discs, tape and Compact Disc) being introduced over a period stretching past one hundred years. However, at the 1:01 mark in the video, at the point of transition between the CD and MP3 formats, we witness the moment where the record industry lost control of both technology and the physical manifestation of copyright. Whilst both Pepstar and Moore may suggest that music 'remains' the same despite such technological changes, this serves to ignore the fact that the production, storage and retrieval of music were profoundly changed by the conversion from a predominately analogue to predominately digital marketplace (Taylor, 2001: 3). Thus, by downplaying such implications, the Music Remains video leads the viewer–consumer to assume that the connection between recording format and intellectual property connotes a copyright continuum, remaining intact despite this clearly evident digital paradigm shift. Certainly, this resultant *dematerialization* of copyright (Barlow, 1994) and the 'temporary' nature of digital format technology requires further analysis.

Copyright dematerialization

Sterne (2012: 194) considers digital music a, 'container technology', representing a materiality that only exists within hard drives. Similarly, Kernfield (2011: 201) suggests that digital songs have become transparent, where, "Only the invisible part remains, the electronic representation of a string of numbers. Popular songs have been removed from their containers and packaging." In short, the music may remain, but its invisibility within the digital realm problematizes record industry notions of physical control of copyright. As Morris (2015: 2–3) reminds us, whilst the CD may have relied on the same industrial infrastructure as the music formats that emerged beforehand, the consumption of music thereafter relied upon a range of digital technologies. It therefore asks us to reconsider "… issues of ownership, cultural value and aesthetics, particularly as they relate to objects that are digital rather than tactile, abundant and infinitely reproducible rather than scarce and available in limited runs ..." (ibid.: 8). As such, as Morris (2015: 14) suggests, where music's value was previously inscribed within its physical manifestation, its immateriality in the digital environment removes many of its defining attributes, and its link with the past associations, its physical aura in general, more so its associations with format-related intrinsic copyright.

Problematizing 'music'

Of course, there is a converse side to music's invisibility in the digital environment. Its representation as a series of ones and zeros requiring electronic conversion (Katz, 2010: 157) continues to raise questions about its tangibility, leading Sterne (2012: 186) to ask, "Either music has dematerialized, or its materiality exists on a different scale. ... Is music a thing? If it was, is it still?" Indeed, music can be seen to be subsumed within digital media that "... combine and integrate data, text, sounds, and images of all kinds" (Flew, 2005: 2). The 'different scale' of materiality that Sterne refers to was initially, and most readily, realized through the example of music videos, where the physicality of music – for instance, the array of packaging, images and written notes contained within a typical album or CD – was materially and aesthetically apart from the sensorial and environmental experiences of *watching* music. In addition, the introduction of MTV in the early 1980s not only signified new working relationships between music and mass media (Goodwin, 1993: xvii), but further detached the record industry from the source of its global dominance and its traditional business model based on its longstanding oligopoly of production, distribution and promotion. These developments led Anderson (2015: 568) to conclude that popular music is now more effectively analysed through the modes of its production and consumption: "A new mode of popular music requires a multi-institutional reorientation around new sets of practices to replace what has been lost." Indeed, as Cupid and Files-Thompson (2016) clearly articulate in relation to Beyoncé's visual album of 2013, such music-media releases serve to establish and enhance new platforms and digital spaces for fandom, empowering the artist in the process. Thus, MTV and music video culture can be seen as early examples of an emerging convergence culture, defined by Pool (1983: 23) as an environment where different types of media interact on new platforms, eroding the individual's direct relationship with the previously isolated text.

Ultimately then, where the record industry previously relied on the imposition of unfair recording contracts (Greenfield & Osborn, 2007) and regularly expended terms of copyright to monetize the star economy (Toynbee, 2004: 133–134), the MTV era foreshadowed that of the digital music economy a generation later, where mixed and converged media outputs replaced recorded music as the central popular music product. As a result, record companies lost control over how its core business, sound recordings, were now being used and were compelled to regroup and restructure. As Tschmuck (2017: 63) notes, the vast range of mergers, acquisitions and takeovers that have materialized within the music and media industries since the 1990s demonstrates how record companies have frantically attempted to reconfigure and consolidate their media rights empires, ultimately leading to the current three remaining major music companies (Vivendi, Sony and Access Industries) to assume increasing levels of creative copyright within the wider digital economy, consequently enhancing the oligopolization of music as media content.

Problematizing 'piracy'

Continuing our discussion of terminological problems and limitations, we now turn our attention to the notion of 'piracy'. In short, our position remains that, as applied to the digital music environment of the twenty-first century, 'piracy' is not only an inappropriate term, but is one which is further encumbered by the rhetorical contexts in which it is normally articulated, which often serve to demonize the everyday practices, connectivity, interaction and diverse ways that ordinary consumers interact with media content. First applied in the late 1920s to designate the activities encapsulating the illegal reprints of song sheets 'against' the wishes of music publishers, the term piracy has endured, despite paradigm shifts in music dissemination technology, format and consumer practice, since its inception. However, as Marshall (2013: 196) highlights, piracy is not an absolute, neither is an economic concept; more so it remains an ideological issue, being 'socially mediated' between rights owners and the public.

Indeed, the term piracy is becoming increasingly vilified, applied to everyday music consumption activities like sharing music on social media or 'ripping' a CD, where these kinds of quotidian acts of music fandom and engagement have challenged outdated record industry notions of how media *should be* used, as Tehranian (2011: 1) notes:

> Copyright's growing ubiquity, when combined with the particular way in which our legal regulations have been written and interpreted, has put us in constant danger of running afoul of the law. In the twenty-first century, we have become, technically speaking, a nation of constant infringers.

Inevitably, the blurring and conflating of various and expanding definitions of piracy only generates further *anti*-piracy crusades by marginalizing – if not also alienating – the most ardent music consumers and fans:

> The content industry calls some things that are unquestionably legal 'piracy' … They've succeeded in persuading a lot of people that any behavior that has the same effect as piracy must be piracy, and therefore must reflect the same moral turpitude that we attach to piracy, even if it is the same behavior that we all called legitimate before.
>
> (Litman, 2000: 8)

Similarly, for Fairchild (2008: 77), these expansive definitions of piracy are both legal and ethical attempts to compel users to use content in the 'right way'. Certainly, whilst all-you-can-eat streaming services may be regarded by some providers as facilitating freedom of music choice and offering an almost infinite gateway to content, Morris and Powers (2015) provide strong evidence to show that such platforms are tightly controlled and curated towards prime brands, offer only limited listen-only forms of access within this process. Naturally, however, attempts such as these have proven deeply problematic as consumers have progressively grown more inventive in their everyday practices and more independent in their beliefs as the digital economy expands.

Most evidently, the pragmatic and cultural limitations of labelling unwanted consumer activity as acts of 'digital piracy' is most clearly evidenced by the fallout from 1999 RIAA v Napster lawsuit. The lobbying organization, and by extension, the artists and record labels it represented, hastened to make an implicit connection between loss of control over consumer behaviour and loss of sales revenue. As Fairchild (2008: 68–69) relates, a somewhat 'hysterical' report by the IFPI echoed the RIAA's claims, suggesting that P2P activity was said to disrupt if not also challenge the record industry's own manu-facturing competencies. Furthermore, the report also stated that such unsup-ported assertions failed to recognize that the consumption of an unauthorized musical text is not necessarily equivalent to a lost sale of one that is author-ized (Kernfield, 2011: 3). More directly, the RIAA failed to acknowledge that this unauthorized practice of 'try before you buy', might not have harmed sales at all, and indeed may actually have increased the likelihood of many P2P users to purchase the music they first heard and downloaded for free (Sinnreich, 2013: 77). Simply put, for where a number of allegedly negative outcomes of piracy are regularly articulated, there are also a number of analogue positive developments, which are less often discussed or acknowl-edged. It is an inconvenient truth that many inventive and 'disruptive' tech-nologies and practices first labelled as acts of piracy (with the recorded music industry itself once labelled as a pirate by music publishers), have long since been assimilated into the 'normal' music industries, with yesterday's 'pirates' becoming the establishment of today (Sinnreich, 2013: 35). Charges of 'piracy' therefore can be seen as having diminishing impact within a digital environment where antiquated laws mean little or nothing to a new generation whose practices and activities operate squarely beyond the bounds of traditional copyright law.

Collaborative digital culture: prosumers

Now that we have identified inherent problems with each constituent ele-ment, we can now present a more holistic analysis of why traditional copy-right law and its concomitant concept of 'digital music piracy' are chronically out of step with the way many of today's cultural consumers engage with music.

In their investigation into copyright and creation in the twenty-first century, Cammaerts, Mansell and Meng (2013) note that new and emerging digital media have meant there are more channels for the recorded music industry to realize profit than ever before: streaming, online and satellite radio, and gaming amongst them. Yet by remaining focussed on ultimately futile attempts to prevent music consumers from engaging with these new forms of media, the RIAA and major record labels missed their opportunity to innovate rather than litigate. More substantially, this enduring and belligerent truculence towards their most passionate and enthusiastic consumers underscored the fact that major record labels had fallen critically, if not fatally, out of touch with how music fans interact with music in the digital age. As noted above, one of the most self-evident changes between the analogue and digital eras has been the rise of 'prosumption', a practice that involves, "*both* production and consumption rather than focusing on either one (production) or the other (consumption)" (Ritzer & Jurgenson 2010: 14, emphasis original). Paralleling this blurring and merging of two formerly discrete activities has been the emergence of prosumer-oriented industrial practices like crowdfunding or music patronage, where in lieu of record company investment, a large number of private individuals provide collective support for independent musicians, music projects or events. Read together, what becomes clear is that traditional copyright law is both uneasy about and ill-suited to the grey areas created by these types of cultural and industrial digital prosumption. Rather than remain hampered by the limitations of copyright, prosumer-entrepreneurs have developed innovations and traditional copyright 'work-arounds' allowing them to collaborate and share creative work with like-minded individuals, thereby claiming back some of creative practices once labelled as digital music piracy.

One needs to look no further than YouTube for examples of just how fully participatory and shared online music activity has become enculturated into everyday life. Now five years after its original upload date, the music video 'Gangnam Style', by South Korean performer Psy, remains one of YouTube's most-viewed clip. Originally created and released without the aid or benefit of major-label support, at the time of writing, the video has had over 2.8 billion views (Billboard, 2017). Yet in addition to the original release itself, the track has also spawned over 2.5 million adaptations and remixes (YouTube.com, 2017), evidencing Cammaerts, Mansell and Meng's (2013: 10) assertion that:

> Insisting that people will only produce creative works when they can claim exclusive ownership rights ignores the spread of practices that depend on sharing and co-creation and easy access to creative works; this insistence privileges copyright owners over these creators.

This idea is further borne out through participatory and collaborative applications like SoundCloud and Indaba. Through the use of Creative Commons licences,[1] SoundCloud allows its users to upload and share their music, retaining any many (or as few) rights as they desire. As a result, other Sound-Cloud users may download, edit, remix and/or re-upload these new creations, thereby establishing a cyclical creative–collaborative online process that would be a practicable impossibility under traditional copyright law. Perhaps even more progressive than SoundCloud, Indaba defines itself as, 'a 21st century music community,' where, 'we provide people with the resources and opportunities they need to make the songs that people love' (Indabamusic, 2017). Indaba members begin by uploading (or downloading) 'stems', or individual tracks, or components, of songs to the site.[2] Other Indaba users will download the original stem and add their own enhancements and contributions before uploading the new version to the application, again, creating an endless loop of creative collaboration. Significantly, however, beyond just independent and/or unsigned musicians, Indaba is notable for the number of globally known acts who participate in remix events. At the time of writing, musicians including Enrique Iglesias, Aloe Blacc, Usher and Wyclef Jean have all posted stems for other users to remix. Under Creative Commons licences, these musicians (and their labels) cede any revenue generated from the resulting tracks, instead seeking other types of recognition for their work. For instance, speaking in 2014, Aloe Blacc observed, '"One of the things I thought when I was signing the contract to be on a major label was, 'There is no real reason for me to sell my music. If I'm an artist I can create art, and that's it ... But if I want to sell it ... there's got to be a bigger reason, and for me it's positive social change"' (Blacc, cited in Grammy.com, 2014). Thus, it might be concluded that there is emerging evidence that at least some performers within the recorded music industry are beginning to acknowledge that consumer activity that infringes traditional copyright law is not always, necessarily bad. Collaborative digital culture can not only generate new opportunities for unsigned and local musicians to have their music heard by anyone with a computer and Internet access, but also for major labels and their acts to begin to claw back some consumer good will through engagement with the kinds of participatory online music environments afforded by sites like YouTube, SoundCloud and Indaba, which in turn, engender brand loyalty and fan interest in copyrighted, for-profit new music releases.

Democratizing lip synching as performance

As the discussion above has shown, the levels and rates of enforcement shown by rights owners towards infringements of copyright within the digital music era have been unfailingly inconsistent. When there are multiple copyright stakeholders, for instance, those of an artist's record label and those of his music publisher, matters become even less straightforward. For example, 'professional-amateur' social network covers, such as those featured on television shows like Glee, have been called, 'a licence to print money' for publishers like BMG, due to the immense value of their synchronization rights (Cvetkovski, 2015: 120). However, record labels will derive little, if any, direct monetary income from these kinds of uses. At the same time, music publishers have been more vigorous in enforcing copyright protection over other, less financially and culturally valuable activity, such as amateur covers of songs uploaded to YouTube, where record labels and their artists may see both a material and indirect marketing benefit generated through such kind of fan-driven efforts. Furthermore, the risk posed by any non-sanctioned versions of songs and/or sound recordings can pose considerable threats to markets or product lines that have not yet been fully developed by the rights owners (Anderson, 2006: 59). Indeed, as Gaines observes, "Copyright protection is always and at the same time (about) circulation *and restriction*" (1991: 122, emphasis added).

Musical.ly and the grey areas of copyright

One current music media platform successfully navigating the grey areas of copyright is Musical.ly, a video–music messaging app, providing an online setting for its targeted tween–teenage audience to showcase their aptitude for lip-synching to current hit songs (Hahm, 2016). Uploaded tracks can be edited and filtered, but are limited to a maximum length of 15 seconds. Launched in 2014 by Chinese entrepreneurs Luyu Yang and Alex Zhu, it has attracted $116 million (USD) in venture capital and presently has over 200 million users, who create 13 million short videos daily (Robehmed, 2017). The app has helped to launch the career of several new artists including Baby Ariel, Jacob Sartorius and the Perkin Sisters, becoming the most popular platform for music discovery by teenagers in the USA. It also serves as a major media publicity platform for new releases by established artists, such as Ariana Grande and Selena Gomez (Rys, 2017). Perhaps the main attraction of Musical.ly is that, like Indaba, it enables amateur performers to interact with an original, professional track, but also affords them a chance to showcase their own creative flourishes, for instance, adding original dance or performance moves whist lip-synching to current hit songs, resulting in a kind of hybrid amateur–professional artefact.

Whilst the process of lip-synching may be anathema to traditional rock ideology (Frith, 2002: 284), such mimicry is ideal for pop music and its demographic. Representing a cultural change in music consumption that never could be envisaged by rights owners, "It is consumption in its own right, and like we've never really seen before. The 15 second hook is the song. The other 3 minutes are unnecessary baggage" (Mulligan, 2016). In this respect, Musical.ly represents a clear evolution from previous music industry-approved formats, one where consumer engagement, not copyright control, drives innovation.

Within this innovative context, music-related apps like Musical.ly serve a multitude of purposes within the digital realm, while rights owners attempt to play catch-up with regard to copyright control within this intertextual digital environment. In Musical.ly's case, despite its huge popularity, the developers took two years to acquire the appropriate licences on an ad-hoc, provider-by-provider basis (Rhys, 2017). Musical.ly's circumspect and protracted licensing process stands somewhat in opposition to the experiences of an earlier app, Flipagram. Launched in 2013, Flipagram used music to soundtrack user-generated photo-video uploads. Like Musical.ly, it too proved vastly popular, extending its market to 85 countries and frequently acquiring 'best app' accolades. However, as their CEO Farhad Mohit clearly admitted, the company was knowingly guilty of massive copyright infringement by failing to acquire any licences during the first few years of its very successful existence (Resnikoff, 2016). History would suggest that such frequent and substantial repeated copyright violations should have led to swift and emphatic legal action by rights owners. Yet Flipagram were allowed to continue to operate unimpeded for years, only acquiring full licences in March, 2016 (ibid.). Overall, such inconsistencies only serve to underline the fact that rights owners have yet to fully grasp how much music can be reimagined within the digital environment, where prosumer-generated content can both extend and reinvigorate copyrighted materials, simultaneously redrafting the boundaries between performers and audiences, between protectionism and innovation, between creativity and collaboration.

Conclusion

We began this chapter by problematizing both the constituent elements and collective implications of the concept digital music piracy. Doing so allowed us to demonstrate that the lack of clarity around each element inevitably leads to an ontologically, legally and culturally outmoded idea, often invoked by copyright stakeholders more concerned with attempts to prevent new forms of consumer engagement with their works than efforts to understand how music consumption has changed in the digital era. Specifically, we noted that one of the most evident developments of the twenty-first-century music industries has been the shift from consumer to prosumer. Inherent within this change is the assertion that consumption of music is no longer a 'one-way' process from rights owner to consumer. Instead, through discussion of websites and applications like YouTube, SoundCloud, Indaba and Musical.ly, we have made the case that music consumption in the digital age is often a shared and collaborative activity, which often involves some degree of copyright violation, intentional or not (Litman, 2000). From the 1999 RIAA v Napster lawsuit to the recently revised and enacted Digital Economy Act of 2017, it seems to be the case that many traditional copyright stakeholders seem intent on pursuing (seemingly futile) efforts to stem the tide of sharing music on social media and mobile applications rather than embrace the potential and substantial opportunities these collaborations may afford. Scholars and industry analysts both have presented compelling cases that not only are social and collaborative music practices here to stay, but that if incorporated into a strategically managed digital campaign, they can actually create substantial new income and brand-loyalty opportunities, which can offset any losses sustained through stricter copyright interpretation and enforcement (see Sinnreich, 2013 and Cammaerts, Mansell & Mang, 2013).

It is important to note that some musicians and labels are cognisant of the potential within collaborative digital music practices, grasping the notion of music as a kind of 'taster' or perhaps even a 'loss-leader,' encouraging music consumers (or prosumers) to invest both financially and emotionally in the bigger music/lifestyle 'brand' or 'experience.' Social media stalwarts like Katy Perry, Lady Gaga and Justin Bieber lend credence to the conclusion that a carefully managed digital music campaign, including tolerance of and inter-action with online and collaborative activity, can yield tremendous returns in terms of consumer loyalty and brand engagement. In addition to its brand-building value, more innovative musicians and software developers are con-stantly finding new ways of embracing the opportunities the collaborative online environment can provide, which in turn, are extending the scope and blurring the boundaries between previously discrete music industries sectors. For instance, in 2014, the Australian electronic music duo Knife Party used Twitter to invite fan submissions of original music compositions the act could use in a live performance the next night. The band received over 300 sub-missions in a 24-hour period, ultimately selecting 20 tracks which were mixed together as part of the act's 45-minute set (O'Connell, 2017). With seemingly little care or regard for traditional copyright ownership and protection, Knife Party as well as their fans instead privileged the *collaborative experience* of artist–fan interaction to create a unique musical event infused with more emotive power than a traditional album or single release or even live event could offer. For these reasons, it is our position that the ongoing digital music piracy crusade is in fact counterproductive to the creative, technical and industrial realities of the twenty-first-century music industries.

Notes

1 Creative Commons is a non-profit organization seeking to promote alternatives to traditional copyright law and regulation. Artists who release music under a Crea-tive Commons licence have a range of options allowing their work to be circulated more openly and with less restrictions than traditional copyright (Creative-Commons, 2017).
2 For a wider discussion of remix culture see: Brown, S.C. (2014) and Brown, S.C. (2011).

References

Anderson, T.J. (2006) *Making Easy Listening*. Minneapolis and London: University of Minnesota Press.
Anderson, T.J. (2015) 'Modes of production: The value of modal analysis for popular music studies.' In: Bennett, A. and Waksman, S. (eds) *The Sage Handbook of Popular Music*. London: Sage, 567–583.

Barlow, J.P. (1994) 'The economy of ideas.' *Wired* (Online) 1 March. Available at: www.wired.com/1994/03/economy-ideas/ [Accessed 1 May 2017].

Billboard. (2017). 'YouTube's 10 most-watched videos.' (Online) 2 March 2017. Available at: www.billboard.com/articles/news/magazine-feature/7709247/youtube-m ost-watched-videos [Accessed 7 June 2017].

Boon, M. (2010) *In Praise of Copying*. Cambridge, MA and London: Harvard University Press.

Brown, S.C. (2011). 'Artist autonomy in a digital era: The case of Nine Inch Nails.' *Empirical Musicology Review*, 6(4): 198–213.

Brown, S.C. (2014). 'With a little help from my friends: Peer production and the changing face of the live album.' *International Journal of Music Business Research*, 3(1): 52–66.

Cammaerts, B., Mansell, R. and Meng, B. (2013) *Copyright and Creation: A Case for Promoting Inclusive Online Sharing*. London: London School of Economics. Also available online at: www.lse.ac.uk/media@lse/documents/MPP/LSE-MPP-Policy-Brief-9-Copyright-and-Creation.pdf.

Creative Commons. (2017). 'Share your work.' (Online). Available at: https://creative commons.org/share-your-work/ [Accessed 10 August 2017].

Cupid, J.A. and Files-Thompson, N. (2016) 'The visual album: Beyoncé, feminism and digital spaces.' In: Trier-Bieniek, A. (ed.) *The Beyoncé Effect: Essays on Sexuality, Race and Feminism*. Jefferson, NC: McFarland & Company.

Cvetkovski, T. (2015) *The Pop Music Idol and the Spirit of Charisma: Reality Television Talent Shows in the Digital Economy of Hope*. Reston, VA: AIAA.

Fairchild, C. (2008) *Pop Idols and Pirates*. Aldershot: Ashgate.

Flew, T. (2005) *New Media*. Oxford: Oxford University Press.

Frith, S. (2002) 'Look! Hear! The uneasy relationship of music and television.' *Popular Music*, 21(3): 277–290.

Gaines, J.M. (1991) *Contested Culture: The Image, the Voice, and the Law*. Chapel Hill: University of North Carolina Press.

Ginsburg, J.C. (2001) 'Copyright and control over new technologies of new dissemination.' *Columbia Law Revenue* 101(7): 1613–1647.

Goodwin, A. (1993) *Dancing In The Distraction Factory*. London: Routledge.

Grammy.com. (2014) 'Aloe Blacc is the answer.' (Online). 3 September. Available at: www.grammy.com/grammys/news/aloe-blacc-answer [Accessed 10 August 2017].

Greenfield, S. and Osborn, G. (2007) 'Understanding commercial music contracts.' *Journal of Contract Law*, 23, 248–268.

Hahm, M. (2016) '60 million teens are crazy about this lip-sync app.' *Yahoo! Finance* (Online) 12 April. Available at: https://finance.yahoo.com/news/musical-ly-60-m illion-snapchat-instagram-facebook-twitter-periscope-200300415.html [Accessed 18 June 2017].

IFPI (2014a) 'Investing in music' Report (Online) Available at: www.ifpi.org/content/library/investing_in_music.pdf [Accessed 1 June 2017.

IFPI (2014b) 'A history of recorded music in 90 seconds.' YouTube (online video), published 12 February. Available at: www.youtube.com/watch?v=wcfLolnmLl4 [Accessed 11 June 2017].

Indabamusic (2017) 'Indaba music'. (Online). Available at: www.indabamusic.com/ [Accessed 7 June 2017].

Jones, M. L. (2012) *The Music Industries*. London: Palgrave MacMillan.

Katz, M. (2010) *Capturing Sound*. Berkeley: University of California Press.

Kernfield, B. (2011) *Pop Song Piracy*. Chicago, IL and London: The University of Chicago Press.

Knopper, S. (2009) *Appetite for Self Destruction*. New York: Simon and Schuster.

Lessig, L. (2008) *Remix*. New York: Penguin Press

Litman, J. (2000) 'The demonization of piracy.' CFP 2000: Challenging the Assumptions. Tenth Conference on Computers, Freedom and Piracy, Toronto, 6 April.

Marshall, L. (2013) 'Infringers' In: Frith, S. and Marshall, L. (eds) *Music and Copyright*. Edinburgh: Edinburgh University Press, 189–207.

Morris, J.W. (2015) *Selling Digital Music Formatting Culture*. Oakland: University of California Press.

Morris, J.W. and Powers, D. (2015) 'Control, curation and music experience on streaming music services.' *Creative Industries Journal*, 8(2): 106–122.

Mulligan, M. (2016) 'Welcome to the 15 second song.' *Music Industry Blog* (Online) 4 March. Available at: https://musicindustryblog.wordpress.com/2016/03/04/welcome-to-the-15-second-song/ [Accessed 18 June 2017].

Music Remains (n.d.) 'The one thing that always remains.' (Online) Available at: www.musicremains.org [Accessed 11 June 2017].

O'Connell, R. (2017) '11 Electronic musicians who collaborate with fans in unique ways.' Mental Floss (Online). Available at: http://mentalfloss.com/article/58154/11-electronic-musicians-who-are-collaborating-their-fans-unique-ways [Accessed 7 June 2017].

Pool, I. (1983) *Technologies of Freedom*. Harvard, MA: Harvard University Press.

Rys, D. (2017) 'Musical.ly, Apple Music ink new partnership, with more to come.' *Billboard* (Online) 28 April. Available at: www.billboard.com/articles/business/7776302/musically-apple-music-partnership [Accessed 18 June 2017].

Ritzer, G. and Jurgenson, N. (2010) Production, consumption prosumption: The nature of capitalism in the age of the digital 'prosumer.' *Journal of Consumer Culture*, 10(1): 13–36.

Resnikoff, P. (2016) 'Flipagram CEO admits to massive copyright infringement.' *Digital Music News* (Online) 14 March. Available at: www.digitalmusicnews.com/2016/03/14/flipagram-ceo-admits-to-massive-copyright-infringement/ [Accessed 18 June 2017].

Robehmed, N. (2017) 'From musers to money: Inside video app Musical.ly's coming of age.' *Forbes* (Online) 11 May. Available at: www.forbes.com/sites/natalierobehmed/2017/05/11/from-musers-to-money-inside-video-app-musical-lys-coming-of-age [Accessed 18 June 2017].

Sinnreich, A. (2013) *The Piracy Crusade. How the Music Industry's War on Sharing Destroys Markets and Erodes Civil Liberties*. Amherst and Boston, MA: University of Massachusetts Press.

Sterne, J. (2012) *MP3 The Meaning of a Format*. Durham, NC and London: Duke University Press.

Stokes, S. (2014) *Digital Copyright: Law and Practice*. London: Hart Publishing.

Taylor, T.D. (2001) *Strange Sounds*. London and New York: Routledge.

Tehranian, J. (2011) *Infringement Nation*. Oxford: Oxford University Press.

Toynbee, J. (2004) 'Musicians.' In Frith, S. and Marshall, L. (eds) *Music and Copyright*. Edinburgh: Edinburgh University Press, 123–138.

Tschmuck, P. (2017) *The Economics of Music*. Newcastle Upon Tyne: Agenda Publishing.

Williamson, J. and Cloonan, W. (2007) 'Rethinking the music industry.' *Popular Music*, 26(2): 305–322.

Williamson, J. and Cloonan, M. (2013) 'Contextualising the contemporary recording industry.' In: Marshall, L. (ed.) *The International Recording Industry*. London and New York: Routledge, 11–29.

YouTube.com (2017) 'Gangam Style remix' (Online). Available at: https://www.you tube.com/results?search_query=gangnam+style+remix [Accessed 07 June 2017].

4 Anti-piracy policies and online film circulation

The Italian context, between formality and informality

Valentina Re

Introductory remarks

This chapter aims to show how the concepts of formal and informal economies can provide innovative perspectives on digital piracy research and, more specifically, how the categories used to analyse the interactions between formal and informal areas (functions, effects and controls) can provide an effective theoretical model for the study of the relationships between anti-piracy communication and the online media ecology. The chapter is structured in four parts. In Section 1, I discuss how the 'economic issue' has affected the piracy debate in past years, focusing in particular on the polarization between commercial and non-commercial piracy (and its moral implications) and the controversial issue of financial harm. In Section 2, I illustrate how the study of formality and informality, as well as of their interactions, provides a multidimensional approach that enables us to go beyond problematic polarizations, and account for a complex, unstable scenario. Finally, having provided a brief overview of the main features of the online film circulation in Italy in Section 3, in the fourth and final part I analyse a series of recent, Italian anti-piracy initiatives. This aims to illustrate how formal actors express and disseminate their interpretations of the functions of informal practices in formal markets, and of the effects of informal activities on the formal audiovisual industry. The study of these interpretations contributes to an understanding of how online film circulation is socially perceived and how formal actors can shape the development of the digital distribution sector.

1 Piracies and profit: some premises

In recent years, the categories of formal and informal economies of cinema (Lobato, 2012a, 2012b; Lobato & Thomas, 2015) have provided an invaluable theoretical tool for scholars dealing with the definition of film piracy, and particularly its commercial (or non-commercial) dimensions and their implications. Before addressing the notions of formality and informality and their relevance for the study of piracy, it is useful to provide a brief overview of the multiple ways in which the 'economic question' has affected research and debates on digital piracy, particularly in the first decades of the 2000s. More specifically, I discuss, first, the polarization of commercial and non-commercial piracy, which has (more or less implicitly) forced the debate to adopt a moral, rather than legal, framework, and has partially hidden a greater diversification of pirate activities. Indeed, the rich variety of existing digital 'piracies'[1] is related to different aims, needs, players and interests, and all piracies are intertwined with larger economic, cultural, and social aspects. Second, I discuss[2] a further polarization: between the notion that piracy, considered as a separate, homogeneous entity, harms the creative and cultural industries (which are taken as a separate entity); and, contrarily, the idea that creative industries, and society as a whole, can actually benefit from piracy.

Dangerous liaisons: commercial and non-commercial piracy

In 2004, Lawrence Lessig clearly distinguished between two kinds of piracy that he called 'piracy I' and 'piracy II'. 'Piracy I' consists of businesses 'that do nothing but take others people's copyrighted content, copy it, and sell it – all without the permission of a copyright owner' (Lessig, 2004: 63). This is the case, for instance, of pirated DVDs or counterfeited items on sale. 'This is piracy plain and simple', comments Lessig and 'this piracy is *wrong*' (my emphasis). Conversely, 'piracy II' falls into the category of 'non-monetary markets', which, according to Chris Anderson, concern 'anything people choose to give away with no expectation of payment' (Anderson, 2009: 20). This kind of piracy, which is related to copyrighted content shared on P2P protocols (such as BitTorrent) and is generally labelled as 'file sharing', is very closely related to the 'sharing economy' (Lessig, 2008) and 'gift economy', where 'incentives to share can range from reputation and attention to less measurable factors such as expression, fun, satisfaction, and simply self-interest' (Anderson, 2009: 20). Sharing networks can be used as 'substitutes for purchasing content', to sample content before purchase, or to access content that is no longer sold (Lessig 2004: 68).

It is this second kind of 'piracy', that also plays a significant role in Henry Jenkins' research on fandom and participatory culture (Jenkins, 2006), where file sharing and the transformative reworking of content by fans express values such as passion, collaboration, engagement, and prove the increasing importance of fans and audiences in shaping how content circulates in the digital environment. In *Spreadable Media*, Jenkins, Ford and Green write: 'We are reserving the term "pirate" in this book for people who profit economically from the unauthorized sale of content produced by others. This is not a legal distinction but a moral one that matters for many of those whose activities we will discuss' (Jenkins, Ford & Green 2013: 16).[3]

Critics have consciously employed the term 'file sharing' – which emphasizes the role of individuals both as consumers and distributors, as well as the importance of communities in P2P collaborative networks – in place of the more industrial label 'piracy', in order to reject what appeared to be an all-encompassing metaphor with an implicit negative moral judgment.[4] However, as Jenkins, Ford and Green observe, the term file sharing has actually preserved that moral framework. In addition to stressing the role of audiences in media circulation, it effectively replaces a negative moral judgment with a positive one based on a non-commercial nature, therefore providing a 'moral' justification to copyright infringement.[5]

Moreover, the moral issue is often confirmed in the discourses produced on file sharing forums, and there are examples of P2P portals which expressly promote ethical conceptions of file sharing and demonstrate the 'social side' of piracy. An interesting example is the Italian P2P forum TNT Village, which proposes an idea of 'ethical sharing'[6] that seeks to promote culture and protect consumers' rights. As we can read in the forum's Statute (TNT Village 2005), its main premise is the 'essential and urgent need' for a 'substantial reformulation of copyright law', based on the belief that 'the long duration of rights' protection is a hindrance to culture and to the diffusion of knowledge'. In order to achieve its objectives, TNT proposes, on the one hand, to establish a system of Collective Licensing in order to legalize non-commercial file sharing and protect the rights of both owners and consumers. On the other hand, the forum presents a form of 'ethical sharing', i.e. file sharing with a few self-imposed restrictions, concerning for instance the need to preserve the 'commercial life' of copyrighted works by sharing them only after an established amount of time after their original release.

And yet: how should we respond to the fact that many P2P portals actually *do have* a commercial dimension? Can they be considered new examples of the 'moral economy of piracy' discussed by Johns, which has ethical justifications while pursuing economic aims? With regard to the audiovisual sector, a recent report commissioned by the MPA (Motion Picture Association) to Incopro (2015) reveals how the majority of cyberlockers and linking sites, as well as, especially, popular P2P portals (such as Torrent forums and search engines)[7] have important advertising revenues (which, in the case of cyberlockers, must be added to subscriptions). Another report (Digital Citizens Alliance, 2015) calculates an estimated $209 million in aggregate annual revenue from advertising for the 589 sites examined (which includes the well-known torrentz.eu and rapidgator.net). This implies that what at a first glance appeared to be connected to the idea of a 'gift economy' might ultimately be an 'unauthorized' version of the traditional media model of the 'three-party market', 'where a third party pays to participate in a market created by a free exchange between the first two parties' (Anderson, 2009: 19).

On the one hand, the data offered by Incopro and the Digital Citizens Alliance may challenge those more optimistic views that emphasize the ideas of community, participation, engagement, bottom-up practices, and disintermediation in relation to the heterogeneous practices grouped under the label 'file sharing'. On the other hand, such an emphasis on advertising revenues related to presumably 'non-commercial' piracy, especially on behalf of corporate associations like the MPA, is to be expected. As I will discuss more extensively later in the chapter, it can clearly be understood as both a reformulation of the controversial argument of 'financial harm' and losses due to piracy,[8] and a response to the 'rhetoric' of sharing economies, which serves to discredit 'good' piracy.

I would nevertheless suggest that moral evaluations like 'bad' or 'good' should be set aside, and that we should not allow the possible commercial aspects of file sharing to overshadow the problems it reveals. Irrespective of its commercial implications and of the various motivations of those involved in file sharing activities – both 'actively' (uploading and downloading) or 'passively' (only downloading) – what file sharing reveals is that piracy is ultimately a matter of cost/price adequacy, access to cultural production and business models.

Beyond the moral issue: accessibility and business models

Beyond the distinction between profit and not-for-profit piracy, pirate activities are in fact marked by a more complex mix of different issues such as the efficiency of existing business models and copyright laws, the accessibility of cultural products, the balance between costs and prices, the consumers' role in shaping how media circulate, and social engagement.

As Anderson states, piracy can be considered as 'a form of imposed Free. You may not have intended your product to be free, but the marketplace thrust Free upon you' (Anderson, 2009: 59). He adds:

> Piracy happens when the marketplace realizes that the marginal cost of reproduction and distribution of a product is significantly lower than the price asked. In other words, the only thing propping up the price is the law protecting intellectual property. If you break the law, the price can fall, sometimes all the way to zero.
>
> (Anderson, 2009: 189)

Most consumers do believe that the work of artists is worth adequate remuneration. However, they are somehow aware that, in most cases, production and distribution costs in the digital economy no longer justify the prices they find online. In this respect, the international success of Netflix can also be explained by the equilibrium of near-zero marginal costs (for the media company) and near-zero marginal prices (for the final user): as in any subscription model, the more I consume, the less I pay (Anderson 2009).[9]

Furthermore, piracy concerns access to culture and the cross-border availability of content, and nowadays it continues to represent the most efficient way to meet the needs of our new, pervasive 'on demand culture'. Chuck Tryon (2013) has effectively defined this in terms of the widespread promise and expectation of 'anytime, anywhere' access or, more precisely, of new forms of immediate, personalized, ubiquitous and expanded access to media content. More specifically, piracy undermines the very 'key mechanisms' that the audiovisual sector considers as the basis of the 'funding and financing cycle', namely 'exclusive territorial licensing' and 'inter-temporal pricing', or the traditional window release system. It is interesting to note that the reference to these operations as essential funding mechanisms does not come from an informative industry report on the impact of piracy in the audiovisual sector. The references are rather taken from an industry report denouncing the potential effects of cross-border access measures proposed by the European Commission: 'If the European Commission introduces cross-border access measures which erode the territoriality of audiovisual rights in Europe, less content will get made and consumers will be worse off overall' (Oxera & O&O, 2016, booklet).

The audiovisual sector's powerful opposition to the EU's proposed 'modern copyright rules fit for the digital age' (European Commission, 2016) illustrates clearly how, beyond piracy alone, it is content circulation in the wider digital ecosystem that encourages to consider renewing a long-lasting business model grounded in copyright laws: a business model that protects intermediaries, which media company seem determined to preserve as long as possible, despite its inefficiency (Currah, 2006; Karaganis, 2011). As John Howkins states: 'The question remains whether the conventional music and film industries will reinvent themselves and regain it. Whether they do, and how they do, will affect the future of all creative products, and all industries, that depend on digital copying' (Howkins, 2007).

For copyright-based industries, 'the most important element of copyright ownership in terms of distribution is that intellectual property is divisible; namely, any or all of the exclusive rights vested in the copyright owner may be transferred or licensed separately' (Ulin, 2009: 63–64). With respect to the audiovisual media, the window strategy optimizes the content's value and maximizes profits by creating multiple licences and discrete periods of exclusivity (worldwide or in specific territories), which also allow repeated consumption and differential pricing (Ulin, 2009: 5).

The window system is generally adaptable to new distribution platforms. For many years the window system has 'protected' the theatrical release from the home video market by providing theatres with exclusive access to motion pictures for several months. And yet, as soon as the DVD market became more remunerative, studios started to experiment with different ways of narrowing the theatrical window in order to maximize their revenue. Until the late 2000s, the entire system worked efficiently. However, by driving towards a 'simultaneous, non-exclusive, flat-priced access' (Ulin, 2009: 5), online circulation now represents an unprecedented challenge to that market, even in its authorized forms. As Ulin has observed:

> Because VoD [Video on Demand] can largely fulfil the consumer's appetite for access to all "when I want it, how I want, where I want it", there

was [an] attack on [...] the elements of exclusivity and timing upon which windows are constructed.

(Ulin, 2009: 299)

The myth of financial harm

Another way in which attention on the economic question has extensively oriented the 'piracy debate' concerns what has been labelled as 'the myth of financial harm' (Yar, 2008), or, as Crisp has put it, 'the central question of whether (and to what extent) the cultural industries are being negatively affected by copyright-infringing activities' (2015: 85).

In the concluding chapter of *Piracy*, Adrian Johns develops and discusses the very stimulating notion of the 'intellectual property defense industry'. This is 'an exemplary postindustrial enterprise' that took its current form in the 1970s, and sought both to directly prevent and fight piracy, and to promote wider changes in legislation. 'What we "know" about piracy – its rates, locations, costs, and profits', writes Johns, 'is usually what this industry sees and transmits to us' (Johns, 2009: 500).[10]

As Yar demonstrates, data about piracy provided by lobby groups or corporate associations, which is often the only data available, does not simply 'describe' facts, as corporate reports claim to do thanks to the use of various objectifying strategies. More correctly, 'one should view [data] as discursive strategies for attempting to construct a political and public consensus about the immorality of piracy' (Yar, 2008: 608).

One of the main strategies used to this end can be defined as the 'rhetoric of financial harm', which aims to demonstrate and emphasize the economic damage that piracy causes to content producers, creative professionals, artists, authors and, more or less directly, consumers. In many cases, statistics are employed to support anti-piracy campaigns. In recent years the website of FAPAV, the Italian Federation for the safeguarding of multimedia and audiovisual content, has presented various alarming claims, such as 'in Italy, in 2010, piracy caused 500 million euros worth of economic damage to the audiovisual sector'.[11] The figure of 500 million euros came from research that the FAPAV commissioned from IPSOS in 2011, which in fact offers a clear example of what is known as the 'level of substitution' problem. Indeed, the only question asked in the FAPAV/IPSOS survey, when assessing the impact of piracy, is: 'What would you have done if you couldn't obtain an illegal copy?' As a consequence, every download substitutes one cinema ticket or DVD sold, and the economic impact can be more easily determined.[12]

As mentioned above, the issue of financial harm is related to a harsh polarization in the piracy debate.[13] On the one hand, corporation associations, relying on their own statistics and the substitution argument, have supported for a long time the assumption that piracy reduces industry profits and that we must first fight and eliminate digital piracy in order to encourage the development of legal digital distribution.[14] On the other hand, independent research[15] has mainly emphasized the limited appeal of the content that's available online legally, the length of release windows and territorial exclusivity as the main reasons why consumers resort to piracy.[16] Moreover, academic studies have underlined the questionable methodological rigour of industry reports, and particularly of the substitution argument,[17] demonstrating instead how authorized and unauthorized channels are not mutually exclusive.

In a well-known paper discussing the cultural and social aspects of file sharing, van Eijk, Poort and Rutten discuss at length how 'not every file downloaded does result in one less CD, DVD or game sold. The degree of substitution is difficult to determine' (van Eijk, Poort & Rutten, 2010: 46). Rather, it is vital to note that piracy *can* also have positive influences, such as, in particular, the sampling effect and the network effect. According to the former, by participating in file sharing activities, consumers discover new films, TV shows and directors, which in turn can create new demand – for instance, I might discover a TV show on an unauthorized platform and then decide to buy the DVD box set. Following the network effect, on the other hand, file sharing enhances the wider popularity of products, thus creating new canons and 'must see' phenomena, therefore raising demand as well.[18]

Finally, and more generally, it has been noted that 'domestic piracy may well impose losses on specific industrial sectors, but these are not losses to the larger national economy' (Karaganis, 2011: 16). Certainly, we cannot over-look its positive effects, such as encouraging participation in cultural life and personal development, and stimulating creativity. Irrespective of the fact that increased accessibility to content creates an increased demand (where it does not yet exist) that media companies will be able to meet, sooner or later, it is necessary to consider its implications in terms of access to a global, diverse culture. The right 'to participate in the cultural life of the community, to enjoy the arts and to share in scientific advancement and its benefits' is internationally recognized exactly as a common right 'to the protection of the moral and material interests resulting from any scientific, literary or artistic production of which he is the author' (United Nations, 1948): there should be no hierarchy between these cultural rights, and balance and harmonization should be a paramount aim in policymaking (Crisp, 2013).

2 Piracy, between formality and informality

Let us try to summarize these points. The term 'piracy', as well as the term 'file sharing', are overloaded with multiple meanings, provided by multiple actors. The terms also imply a counterposition between commercial and non-commercial piracy, which ambiguously overlaps with ideas of immoral and moral piracy. What is more, whatever label we use, piratical activities appear as a homogenous 'body' that is able to damage or alternatively to foster the creative economy, though it remains, in either case, clearly separated from it.

The ideas of the formal and informal economies provide us with a fresh vocabulary that has many qualities. First, they allow us to go beyond problematic polarizations like moral and immoral,[19] or commercial and non-commercial; second, they imply intertwined rather than oppositional relationships between a plurality of different players; finally, by setting aside the counterposition of legal and illegal, they also enable us to recall that neither status is an intrinsic feature that emerges simply from 'the nature of things': rather, they are specific political, historical and geographical conditions (Lobato, 2010), based on a particular copyright law, that could be reformed in any case. As such, these terms remind us that the copyright-based window system is not 'intrinsically' legal, just as BitTorrent and cyberlockers are not 'inherently' illegal, insofar as they have the potential to be used for authorised forms of sharing.

Formal and informal economies: a definition

In Lobato's view, the concept of 'informal' is particularly important to the study of media distribution in a 'globalised convergent world', where ongoing processes call for a definition of 'distribution' that is open and general enough to account for the multiple and variable ways – including also piratical ways – in which 'movies travel through space and time' and 'film is being accessed' (Lobato, 2012a: 1). Rather than 'a defined field or category', the concept of the informal is a 'heuristic device' that can be defined only in relation to that of the formal. While the idea of 'formality' concerns all economic activities and revenue sources that appear consolidated, documented and measurable, and thus coincides with what is conventionally taken as *the* economy of a specific sector, the idea of 'informality' allows us to conceive and recognize the unconventional, what is uncertain and scarcely measurable, which does not correspond to pre-established categorizations and thus which corporate and academic studies struggle to grasp. Formal economic activities encompass traditional players and business models, systems of statistical enumeration, regulation systems and legal frameworks; conversely, informal activities highlight unexpected players and unusual economic deals, and include a wide array of unmeasured, unregulated, extra-legal and not documented practices.

The categories of formality and informality should not be intended as marked by an intrinsic, stable meaning. They are flexible tools that can describe and analyse a particular economic scenario in any given time and space, rather than fixed and pre-established components of that scenario. The idea of informal or 'shadow' economies emerged in the early 1970s to identify and quantify 'economic production and exchange occurring within capitalist economies but outside the purview of the state' (Lobato, 2012a: 39–40). Research in Latin America, Eastern Europe and African nations demonstrated that 'the assumption that formality is the rule is implicitly ethnocentric', and that 'in many settings informality is the norm, not an aberration' (Lobato, 2012a: 42 and 40). Comparisons with Western countries proved that 'formal economies can become informal and viceversa' and that 'governments and formal enterprises can actively *produce* informality' (Lobato, 2012a: 41–42). Finally, it has been noted that:

> while criminal activities are typically informal, [...] informality can be found on both sides of the law. Many informal activities are both legal and reputable. [...] Informal activities are neither inherently good nor bad. It is difficult to make any kind of moral claims about either formality or informality as an organisational principle.
>
> (Lobato, 2012a: 42)

In addition to its displacement of the 'moral issue', Lobato's argument is particularly helpful and productive given that the theoretical opposition between formal and informal, whose definitions are mutually interdependent, helps understand how formality and informality work together in practice, and to stress the idea there is not one single 'real' economy but an ecology of different economies. 'In film economics, the formal and the informal are closely linked' (Lobato, 2012a: 41): it is their combination that reveals that 'what we typically call the international film industry is one kind of distribution among many others' and underlines the urgent need to study 'the many ways in which [informal practices] interface with conventional film industries' (Lobato, 2012a: 3 and 1).

By stressing the conceptual interdependency between the two categories, we can also conceive of informality/formality as a 'continuous line' rather than a binary division, and thus start to see how not only entire economic sectors, but also specific actors and entities, present a mix of formal and informal elements. YouTube, for instance, 'functions as a professional vehicle for professional producers and a distribution system for unauthorized uploads and amateur content' (Lobato & Thomas, 2015); moreover, it has recently started to provide a TVOD (Transactional Video on Demand) service.[20] Thus, the theoretical framework provided by the formality/informality couple helps us to understand piracy 'as an inherent feature of audiovisual distribution rather than an aberration' (Lobato, 2012a: 70). It furthermore enables us to 'disaggregate' the notion:

> Instead of thinking piracy as a singular practice, it is necessary to think in terms of *piracies*. Depending on the context, piracy may be theft or a legitimate business practice, a free speech act or a form of political resistance. Sometimes it is all these things at once.
>
> (Lobato, 2012a: 70)

If the rhetoric of piracy as theft or financial loss can be easily explained from a formal perspective, it is only when adopting an informal point of view that piracy as a form of 'free enterprise' and the monetization opportunities presented by its consumption become equally relevant.

My reference to YouTube here also draws attention to the fact that – although they are not exclusive to the digital mediascape – the interdependency and instability of formal and informal areas have been exacerbated, especially in Western economies, by the introduction of digital technologies. It is habitual to refer to countries like Nigeria or India, or South-East Asia, when discussing the existence and features of grey economies, where 'the lines between formal and informal businesses are [...] blurred' and piracy fosters the development of an indigenous culture 'where accessing media legally is not an option' (Lobato 2012a: 75 and 82). However, as noted in the previous section, digital technologies have had a disruptive impact on the existing relationships between formal and informal activities in Western, capitalistic economies. As Lobato writes: 'The Internet is now generating an expanded range of viewing platforms that integrate legal and black markets. The lines between the formal and informal are very faint here' (Lobato, 2012a: 95).

The Internet has presented both opportunities (additional revenue streams such as digital downloads and rentals, for instance) and challenges (SVOD, new players and new intermediary services or gatekeepers) for the formal sector of film and media distribution, and especially the well-established and profitable windows system. At the same time, it has hugely impacted on the informal side, too, by expanding the scope of movie piracy and creating unprecedented conditions for the development of file sharing, thus fostering the myths of complete disintermediation and limitless access to film culture. Moreover, new intermediary services like linking sites and cyberlockers 'represent a new combination of the formal and informal, combining legal display ads and subscription payments with illicit access to unauthorised content' (Lobato, 2012a: 96). In this context, the unstable balance between formality and informality in the film industry (as well as in the larger area of the cultural and creative industries) has come under threat. The need for a multidimensional approach that accounts for the changes in the complex and multifaceted relationships between the two areas,[21] and therefore grasp fully the contemporary media ecology, is today a priority for scholars.

The interactions between formality and informality: functions, effects, and controls

In order to analyse the multiple relations between the formal and informal, I briefly present and apply the methodological framework recently provided by Lobato and Thomas in *The Informal Media Economy* (2015). Lobato and Thomas propose that interactions between formality and informality can be studied within three categories (Table 4.1): *functions* (how informal components can be used within formal economies), *effects* (what happens to media economies when formal systems incorporate informal aspects), and *controls* (how formal actors manage and understand informal activities).

Starting from *functions*, Lobato and Thomas point out six basic services that informality can provide within a formal market. *Gap-filling* is when informal tactics and solutions are employed to solve problems in the formal area, i.e. 'consumers sharing infrastructure, such as satellite dishes'.[22]

Table 4.1 Understanding the interactions between formality and informality (Lobato and Thomas 2015).

Functions	Effects	Controls
Gap-filling	Substitution	Restriction
Incubating	Dispersal	Codification
Outsourcing	Extension	Authorization
Taste-testing	Revaluation	Measurement
Priming	Redeployment	Promotion
Education	Reconfiguration	

Incubating occurs when skills, technological innovations or innovative business solutions are transferred from the informal economy, where they have been able to develop, to the formal economy, as in the case of 'start-up companies selling rights for new digital innovations [that] are bought up by major broadcasters or media conglomerates, as a cheap means of R&D'. *Outsourcing* concerns the direct acquisition, by a formal entity, of expertise, services and labour related to the informal sector, for reasons of efficiency. This is the case for 'freelance creatives in the media world work' as well as for many forms of crowdsourcing, 'as when users of social media platforms are called upon to contribute to branding and market research efforts for major corporations'. *Taste-testing* is when formal media companies use informal services and practices to test the audience's appetite for their products, such as when SVOD services such as Netflix monitor 'the most downloaded shows on Bit-Torrent networks as a way of estimating the market for future productions'. *Priming* occurs when no legal distribution channels exist or are accessible to consumers, and informal systems are exploited by formal actors to increase revenue streams. This was (infamously) the case for Susan Boyle's audition at *Britain's Got Talent*, which had no official distribution outside the UK. Illegally uploaded on YouTube, the video has generated further economic outcomes and a wider, stronger engagement over time. Finally, *educating* refers to the pivotal role played by informal services 'in building popular literacy within changing technological environments': 'informal services are sometimes the first places where businesses and consumers acquaint themselves with emerging technologies, services and products'.

The second category, *effects*, encompasses all of the 'changes to the original, formal market as a result of interaction with informal elements'. Lobato and Thomas identify six kinds of effects. *Substitution* describes:

the changes when one technology or medium emerges to provide a comparable service, overtaking the previous standard [...]. Additionally, it could describe the substitution of one group of workers for another [...]. Sometimes, substitution involves a shrinking or disappearing market, as when the *Encyclopedia Britannica* was killed by Wikipedia.

As noted in the previous section, the 'substitution argument' – that piracy cannibalizes paid forms of consumption and traditional revenue streams – has played a key role in anti-piracy communication and piracy debates. *Dispersal* occurs when 'market activities are replaced by activities in a different category, or transactions move into many diffuse areas of the economy simultaneously' – i.e. when informal music or video streaming creates value for advertisers, platforms or internet service providers but not for traditional actors like networks and copyright holders. Conversely, *extension* happens when new markets are created 'on top of existing ones' – as in the case of YouTube, which 'has created new advertising markets around uploaded content'. *Revaluation* is when the economic value or other kinds of intangible value decrease or increase due to informal activities. An instance of this occurs when informal circulation in online communities leads to success for independent bands or filmmakers. Finally, *redeployment* happens when 'particular elements originating in the informal economy are taken up in formal commerce' (as the peer-to-peer protocol used in formal applications like Skype), and *reconfiguration* occurs 'when formal players restructure their business models in response to informal competition' – i.e., the reduction of DVD prices or the implementation of VOD platforms to compete with pirates.

The final category that can be employed to examine the interactions between the formal and informal areas is that of *controls*. This includes all of the strategies used by formal actors 'to manage, contain, organise, systematise or curtail informal activity'. Lobato and Thomas identity five main strategies of control. *Restriction* includes 'disciplinary and enforcement mechanisms' meant to 'reduce or contain informal activity', such as the widespread example of anti-piracy enforcement. *Codification* is when new rules are elaborated to partially formalize informal activities, as in the case of digital rights management technologies, 'that enable limited but not extensive sharing within a household'. *Authorization* implies the extension of the legal framework to 'encompass new phenomena'. *Measurement* refers to information collection and knowledge generation 'about the size and nature of the informal sector, enabling regulation and other formalizing strategies'. Finally, *promotion* is when specific interventions are carried out by governments or other formal entities to 'encourage particular informal practices', and thus to take advantage of 'the innovative energies of informal economy'.

My main hypothesis is that, by considering the category that Lobato and Thomas define as *controls* (how formal actors try to manage informality), and especially the sub-categories of *restriction*, *measurement*, and *promotion*, we can also elucidate how formal actors express and disseminate their interpretations of the *functions* that informal practices perform in formal markets, and of the *effects* of informal activities on the formal market. Studying these interpretations has particular relevance for two reasons. First, it helps to understand how online film circulation is socially perceived in all its dimensions (economic, legal, cultural). Second, it illustrates how formal actors can shape the development of the digital distribution sector. Before discussing my hypothesis in relation to the Italian context, it is necessary to provide a brief overview of the main features of the contemporary, Italian online distribution ecology.

3 The online distribution ecology in Italy

AGCOM regulation on copyright protection: digital works are valuable

Within the category of *restriction* actions, in recent years the Italian legal framework has been characterized by the introduction, on 31 March 2014, of a new 'Regulation on copyright protection in electronic communication networks' (AGCOM, 2013b), ratified by AGCOM (the Italian Communications Regulatory Authority) on 12 December 2013 following a lengthy development process and heated debate in the press. AGCOM was created in 1997 (Law no. 249/1997) as an independent, administrative authority with the purpose of regulating and supervising the telecommunication, audiovisual media and publishing sectors, therefore protecting the rights of both players and consumers. Starting from 2000 (Law no. 248/2000) it was progressively provided with supervisory powers with regard to copyright enforcement (Legislative Decree no. 70/2003 and Legislative Decree no. 44/2010). In order to elaborate the final Regulation AGCOM launched three public consultations (AGCOM, 2010b; AGCOM, 2011b; AGCOM, 2013a) while pursuing independent research activities on copyright issues (AGCOM, 2010a and AGCOM, 2011a).

As Francesca Pellicanò explains, AGCOM's activity 'has been two-fold and takes into equal consideration both, firstly, the support of the legal offer of digital works and the promotion of education and information for the public, and secondly, enforcement proceedings in case copyright violations should occur' (Pellicanò, 2014). With regard to the former aim, the procedure starts only when a rights holder makes a complaint. At that time AGCOM informs the uploader, the website manager and the providers (ultimate users are not involved). If the infringement is attested and the challenged material is not immediately taken down, AGCOM addresses its requests only to providers. In other words, if the website is hosted in Italy, AGCOM requires the Internet hosting provider to perform a 'selective removal'. If the website is hosted abroad, or in case of massive infringement, AGCOM requires the Internet service provider to disable the access to the website.

A commercial[23] announced the updated regulation in Italy on the web and TV. In it, we initially see a boy interacting with a kind of wall or large screen in front of him. The clear reference to touchscreen technologies is mixed with a science-fiction imagery that can easily look slightly stereotypical. Due to the boy's interaction, the windows, which represent many different, inter-connected contents, increase in number, and this multiplication is visually translated into a biological, ecological metaphor: the connections are the branches of a green tree that continues to grow. A girl then enters the frame and, after looking at the boy, also starts interacting with the wall/screen, touching the windows, and the tree grows further still. The windows, i.e. content, are the fruits of the tree, and users pick them. Again, the metaphor is glaring: the Internet is like a tree, and culture is like a living organism. A voice-over comments on the images: 'We narrate emotions / We interact with people / And we invent content / Nowadays the web allows creativity to grow'. But then, something negative occurs. 'Some people are hindering this development', the impersonal speaker warns, 'by exploiting illegal content'. Staying within the ecological metaphor, illegal downloading thus becomes an act that jeopardizes the expansion of culture, considered as a living organism. In the announcement, the illegal action is ascribed to a couple formed by a man, probably a father, and a child, probably his daughter. As soon as the illegal downloading starts, the big tree becomes grey and the fruits (the content) start to fall. The message is unmistakable, albeit not ver-balized: piracy kills culture. In fact, no sooner does the daughter castigate her father, and the download is stopped, a metaphorical sap flows back into the organism, the tree becomes green again, and the web, together with culture, comes to life once again. 'Get informed, enjoy yourself and share experiences with legal digital works', concludes the narrating voice. 'You will allow culture to keep blossoming. / The regulation about copyright on the web is available on the AGCOM website / Because digital works are valuable to everybody.'

With its focus on the interaction between people and on the value of sharing experiences, the commercial seems to incorporate and sustain the features of participatory and networked culture. It also contains a clear reference to the power of creativity and how the Internet fosters it. By examining this commercial, we can clearly see how the category of *restriction* can overlap with the categories of *promotion* (it exploits 'the innovative energies' of informal practices like sharing) and of *measurement*, since it provides information about informal illegal activities in a way that apparently diverges from previous interpretations of unauthorized uses, for example as criminal and immoral actions. In fact, the commercial does not refer to downloading as stealing nor to downloaders as criminals, and in fact does not mention the word piracy. However, it simply re-proposes a typical motif of anti-piracy campaigns, namely the idea that piracy destroys culture or creativity as such. And paradoxically, despite the fact that the Regulation does not apply to users of digital works (either through down-loads or streaming), the commercial cannot avoid showing a user, the father, who is responsible for illegal downloading (and for the 'end of culture').

As mentioned, the Regulation serves a double purpose. In addition to the prevailing aim of sustaining copyright in the digital environment, it also aims to encourage the development of the 'legal offer of digital works'. Despite the Regulation's good intentions and AGCOMs explicit statements regarding the implementation of legal online content as valuable anti-piracy action, these aims imply two main problems. First, by reading the document we gain the impression that the concept of 'legal' is naturalized: in other words, it is presented as something that is simply given 'in the nature of things', or as an intrinsic feature, rather than as a specific historical condition based on a particular copyright law, which moreover has the potential for reform. Second, promoting the 'legal offer' in Italy today essentially means supporting the copyright-based window system and formal distribution broadly, while neglecting the opportunities offered by the informal areas of media distribution. It is true that the Authority claims to encourage commercially innovative offers, but the underlying association between legality and formal services tends to exclude other models from commercial exploitation, such as BitTorrent and cyberlockers, which tend to be perceived as 'inherently' illegal.

The Italian VOD market, between formality and informality

Despite the Regulation's intention to boost legal content online, the most recent improvements in this area appear related to the arrival of the true 'King Kong' (Cunningham & Silver, 2013) of the digital world on the Italian market, Netflix, approximately two years later (October, 2015). According to the most recent European Audiovisual Observatory report about SVOD revenues (EAO 2015 and 2016), the early entry of Netflix, combined with the local reaction of national players like the pay TV industry, commercial broadcasters and telecom operators, has significantly boosted consumer revenues in the last years. Moreover, it currently represents the main feature of what is labelled the 'SVOD market developed', composed of the UK (where Netflix arrived in 2012) and other Nordic countries. In 2014 the UK took EUR 393.3 million of a total consumer spending of 844 million (which amounts to EUR 2.5 billion if one considers the overall VOD market, including also TVOD [Transactional Video On Demand] and TV VOD – an additional transactional VOD service included in the subscription to a linear Pay TV). In 2014, Italy took an insignificant 1% of the overall SVOD market, equivalent to EUR 6.2 million – that rises to 117.8 million if we consider the entire VOD market (932.4 million in the UK).

Of course, this was before the entry of Netflix into the Italian market, in October 2015. Based on the most recent data provided by Statista[24], consumer revenues for SVOD services in Italy soared from 6 million in 2014 to almost 22 million in 2015, and will further rise to almost 76 million in 2020. Nevertheless, data regarding the overall Italian VOD market in 2014 provided by Statista in fact diverges from EAO data, in that Statista quantifies it as EUR 83 million (rather than 117.8). Referring to Statista, consumer spending on digital video in Italy (TVOD, EST and SVOD, without considering TV VOD) amounted to US dollars 60.7 million in 2016 and will soar to 151 million in 2021.

As already mentioned, the recent growth of the Italian market is fundamentally connected to the arrival of Netflix and the reaction of its local competitors: the main Italian pay TV operator, Sky, also launched a standalone SVOD service in Italy, Now TV (that replaced the previous model, Sky Online); and the main Italian commercial broadcaster, Mediaset, improved its pre-existing service, Infinity, which offers a hybrid model (SVOD and TVOD). One year after Netflix, its main international competitor Amazon Prime Video also entered the Italian market (December 2016), with a relatively small catalogue and a – supposedly – provisional interface in English. Other relevant players in the Italian online distribution market include: Internet pure-play and technology companies like Google (Google Play) and Apple (iTunes), or standalone websites like Chili and Wuaki TV, which all offer a TVOD service; other commercial broadcasters and the Italian public broadcaster RAI, which recently launched a re-vamped catch-up TV service called RaiPlay; ISPs such as TIM, which offers a SVOD service named TIMvision; finally, it is worth mentioning the unusual case of MYmovies.it. MYmovies.it was originally born as a website offering a mix of services that includes a film database starting from 1895, trailers, film reviews, a TV guide, information about films playing or coming soon in theatres, local showtimes and new DVD releases. In 2014 it launched a new TVOD service called Anicaondemand, which constitutes a particularly interesting experiment – despite its economic irrelevance – in view of its collaboration with ANICA, the association that represents the Italian film industry. The experiment quickly failed and was forgotten, and today MYmovies.it hosts a mix of three different services: a niche, art film catalogue based on a TVOD model; a live, multicast streaming service that can be used for free, by reserving a place in a virtual theatre where you can also chat and exchange opinions with other users participating in the live screening; and finally, an innovative service called 'Trovastreaming'/'Findthestreaming', that allows users to compare the costs for digital rental or download on iTunes, Chili, Google Play, Wuaki TV, Infinity and RaiPlay of more than 9,000 movies.

In short, the entry of Netflix into the Italian market has inevitably triggered the growth of online content (both number of platforms and richness of catalogues), and digital audiovisual distribution is currently going through an advanced phase of consolidation. This phase is mainly characterized by new aggregators that are external (or partially external) to the film and television industry, such as Amazon, Google, Apple and Netflix, and by specific business models, particularly the SVOD, which fundamentally challenges the traditional window system and emphasizes the crucial role of online catalogues, prioritizing access rather than ownership. Moreover, the online distribution landscape is characterized by a new consumption culture that implies audience engagement and, above all, the expectation for ubiquitous and personalized access (think of Netflix taste-based algorithms) to vast catalogues, where user experience and curatorship are added values. However, within this general framework of change and innovation, some critical aspects can be highlighted.

Despite the warning that 'major film and television companies must radically realign their business models around fresh modes of delivery or risk losing their audiences to a host of new rivals in the digital space' (Curtin, Holt, & Sanson, 2014: 2), traditional formal players tend to continue to promote an 'inefficient and restrictive business model' (Currah, 2006: 441), 'which poses no threat to the existing structure of the industry (Currah, 2006: 452). In Italy, for instance, ANICA has noted how 'broadcasters acquire VOD rights from the producers not as much to develop a rich, competitive legal offer, but rather to weaken it or to keep it internal, in order to defend their assets'.[25] More generally speaking, and going beyond the rhetoric of infinite access and disintermediation, it is necessary to consider carefully the persistent effort of copyright and technology companies to control access. In addition to stressing 'the continued efforts of major media conglomerates to develop better mechanisms for controlling where, when, and how content is circulated', Chuck Tryon points out that 'changes in distribution may offer viewers a wide range of viewing options, but they take place within a media industry that has developed a carefully structured business model designed to maximize profit' (Tryon, 2013: 7). It is in this frame, which entails new forms of 're-intermediation' rather than disintermediation, that Michael Gubbins has proposed the provocative idea of 'illusion of choice':

> The problem is that the new on-demand world makes it more difficult to discover films that might change, or broaden tastes, or access unfamiliar and challenging content. The paradox of greater than ever access to content and yet more difficulty in being seen might be called the Illusion Of Choice.
>
> (Cine-Regio, 2014: 79)

It is therefore in this specific frame, which often proposes to the audience non-competitive prices and poor cultural diversity, that informal distribution services and unauthorized forms of 'social distribution' continue (despite the AGCOM Regulation) to play a fundamental role in consumers' viewing habits and choices. In this respect, and despite the fact that innovative 'economic models that depend on consumers acting as distributors' (Moore, 2013: 141) are not yet fully developed in the formal industry, the idea of social distribution continues to show its potential on informal platforms such as linking and torrent sites. It is in the field of informal distribution that the 'curatorial' impulse of consumers or fans, irrespectively of any expectation of profit, emerges, and a 'collective archival activity' (Denison, 2015: 63) produces catalogues shared by communities. Even today, 'fan-made' or file sharers' catalogues are often more effective in their structure than the libraries of formal services, movies presentations are more detailed and precise, and the user experience may prove to be even more enjoyable and satisfying. Finally, models that depend on consumers acting as distributors appear to reproduce activities of commentating and discussion more intimately: within the field of informal and social distribution, cataloguing and viewing activities tend to acquire a powerful relational component, which generally remains underdeveloped on the side of formal distribution.

4 How formality depicts informality: the Italian case

In Section 1, I discussed several critiques of quantitative methodologies used previously in piracy research, which were based on the *substitution* argument and sought to demonstrate the financial harm that piracy caused to the cultural industries. In turn, the broader aim was to encourage changes in national and international copyright laws. As mentioned above, financial harm has moreover been interpreted often as a form of 'theft' and associated to strategies of criminalization and moral blame (Loughlan, 2008). More recent approaches to measurement have attempted to demonstrate a sort of indirect economic damage, and to emphasize piracy's *dispersal* rather than *substitution* effects (Incopro, 2015).

In the last few years, and in Italy since at least 2013 – when the latest AGCOM Regulation was ratified – a new phase appears to have materialized. Rather than focusing on piracy as a crime to fight, this tendency frames creativity, creative workers and cultural production as values to protect. The shift has been accompanied by a partial change in measurement strategies and objectives, too: rather than quantifying piracy, nowadays the impetus is to quantify the creative industries. These changes, of course, also concern the content and forms of institutional communication. There are still public campaigns (indeed, many resources were spent on the 2016 campaign 'Io faccio film'/'I make movies'), but forms such as contests, educational projects and reports about the impact of the creative industries have been used with increasing frequency. These seem to be characterized by a twofold strategy. On the one hand, there is an evident strategy of humanization/personalization of the creative sector, which is categorized as a large group of people who work with passion and talent, and deserve adequate remuneration. On the other hand, we can identify the promotion of creativity, as expressed through contests, educational initiatives and reports, and based on an underlying definition of creativity as 'individual expression'. Examining these strategies in light of the theoretical framework provided by Lobato and Thomas (2015) can help us to understand in greater detail precisely how they work, and to assess more accurately this historical change.

From piracy to creativity: the cases of 'I make movies' and 'respect creativity'

The campaign 'I make movies. Those who love cinema will not betray it' was launched during the 73rd Venice Film Festival (2016), and promoted by

ANICA, the FAPAV, the MPA and Univideo (the Italian association of audiovisual publishers). It consists of several short videos aimed at narrating and promoting the role of lesser-known film professionals such as dog trainers, integrated VFX supervisors, sound technicians, electricians, and so on, in order to show the faces, stories and skills of those people who are essential to filmmaking. In addition to its central website,[26] the campaign was also developed on social networks and complemented by a contest called 'Share and win', where users could upload a photo portrait, edit it with a branded frame reproducing the campaign's logo, and share it on Facebook.[27] Branded pictures could also be shared on Instagram and Twitter. Six months after the launch, organizers claimed that the campaign was a success, with over 1,800,000 users on Facebook and more than 1,700,000 views of its clips (Fabbri, 2017). As in the case of the commercial promoting the AGCOM Regulation, the incentive to share 'branded' photos on Facebook and other social networks can be easily read as a way to take advantage of the innovative energies of informal practices, or, in other words, to *promote* informality (by exploiting it) in order to sustain formality. More significantly, the campaign also provides a good example of *outsourcing*. As mentioned, *outsourcing* concerns the direct acquisition, by a formal entity, of informal labour: in this case, audience engagement and the inclination to share content online, participating in media circulation, is exploited to expand the campaign's scope and strengthen its message.

It is possible to interpret a group of educational projects in terms of *outsourcing*, too. Let us consider the example of 'Rispettiamo la creatività'/ 'Respect creativity' (two editions, 2015/16 and 2016/17). The initiative, aimed at 'raising awareness about the value of creativity and the rights of its protagonists',[28] addresses junior high school children and promoted by the EMCA (European Multimedia Copyright Alliance) in collaboration with its Italian partners in the fields of music and cinema. The educational project (consisting of a multimedia teaching kit for teachers, supplemented by online materials) appears to be particularly representative of the humanization strategy, trying to emphasize the personalities, and their rights and needs, from across the entire world of music and cinema professionals. As already happened in the past (Gates 2006), the project enables the *outsourcing* of copyright enforcement by entrusting it to teachers, who are provided with pre-designed teaching material. The project also implies another form of *outsourcing* by offering the students a competition based on designing the promotional poster of the next edition.

'Rispettiamo la creatività' also contains a questionnaire, allowing students to assess their knowledge of copyright. In the questionnaire, copyright law is defined as a system of rules meant to protect the work of creative people and guarantee their salary. In this way, the project tends to take for granted copyright as the greatest (and maybe unique) incentive to creation, and that to enforce copyright rules means to foster creation – assumptions that academic literature calls into question.[29] As a result, borrowing Lobato and

Thomas' terms, only the category of *restriction* is presented as an incentive to creation and creative industries, and there is no mention of the positive functions that informality can exert with respect to formality – like *taste-testing*, *priming* and *educating*. On the contrary, all these functions are rejected or neglected. Let us consider some examples.

Should we answer the sixth question of the same questionnaire that copying music or films and sharing them with friends is legal because no one profits that way, we are immediately warned that this is an act of copyright infringement, irrespectively of profit. Further informative materials clearly assess the difference between commercial and non-commercial piracy similarly, with the aim of asserting the illegality of the latter. Beyond the problematic nature of this distinction, as we have already discussed, it is interesting to note that there are no references to the function of *priming* and *taste-testing*, that is, to the promotional effects that sharing practices can have on sales or on the reputation of musicians and filmmakers, as well as the possibility for formal actors to understand better their audience's tastes. The issues of UGC (User Generated Content) and fair use are only superficially addressed. At question no. 4 ('Which of the following actions does not involve copyright infringement?'), these issues are approximated in the (wrong) answer: 'Sharing online a short clip made by me, where I used a song of my favourite artist'. This clearly overlooks the *taste-testing* function of piracy, but more interestingly still it also neglects the basic function of *educating*, and thus the key role of informal practices in helping young people to acquire skills in new technologies (such as video and sound editing software).

Much more could be said about how the digital media are depicted. Let us return to question no. 6, on sharing music and movies. The response that 'we do it because everybody does' (i.e., it is socially, rather than legally, acceptable) is mistaken, since 'the fact that new media allow us to copy and share music and films does not mean this is legal. A car can reach a speed of 250 km/h, but driving at this speed is forbidden!' Such an approach completely ignores both Jenkins' research about the value and economic potential of sharing practices, and Lessig's studies on how copyright laws applied to a digital environment tend to be 'overprotective'. In Lobato and Thomas' terms, this approach implies ignoring the functions of *priming*, *taste-testing* and *education*, as well as the effects of market *extension* (new markets that capitalize on unauthorised uploads) and *reconfiguration* – that is, the need to innovate business models. The relevant issue of *reconfiguration* also emerges in question 2. Answering that copyright is a set of rules determining how much a CD or DVD cost is once again incorrect, because 'the cost of CDs and DVDs is determined according to economic criteria used by producers'. As such, the questionnaire ignores users' perception of decreased marginal costs.[30] The same happens elsewhere in the website, for instance when legal online content is promoted with no references to its costs. The relevant question of the profits made by intermediary services, as well as the greater need for innovation, are completely overlooked; to employ Lobato and Thomas' terms once again, the effects of *revaluation* and *reconfiguration* that informality can have on formality are simply ignored.

Creative Italy

The last example worth citing is the report *Italia creativa* (EY, 2015a). The report contributes to a wider, international debate about the economic and, above all, social value of the cultural and creative industries. Furthermore, it stands out with respect to other similar reports (like the French report in 2015 [EY, 2015b] or the report produced by Unesco in 2013) for its particular emphasis on the impact of piracy and the role of copyright in the overall structure – as well as for the many interviews to music, film, TV and publishing professionals. Among the multiple sectors and issues addressed in the report, I will focus on online media distribution and consumption.

It is interesting to note that while the equivalent French report counts revenues for DVDs and Blu-Rays within the film industry sector, and VOD revenues are divided between film and TV sectors, In the Italian report both physical video and VOD[31] are only counted in the TV industry sector. This choice is particularly surprising considering that, elsewhere in the Italian report, much emphasis is placed on the fact that film 'secondary' markets (like home video) have not been 'secondary' (in any sense) for a long time, and that remuneration for creativity in the digital media has become a very urgent and critical point. More precisely, the report identifies a 'value gap' on digital channels, which is defined as 'the gap between the revenues obtained by some technical intermediary services (like content aggregators and search engines) by distributing content (like music, videos, news), and what is paid to copyright holders'. The expression 'technical intermediary services' refers to players like YouTube or Facebook, which are presumed not to be responsible for content management and editing (as in the case of 'passive' intermediary services, like Internet service providers). The reports states that, while players like Netflix or Spotify spend around 70% of their turnover on acquiring content, players like YouTube pay no more than 10–20%. The report concludes:

> Only an effective copyright law can promote cultural production. It should be noted that there has been a shift from ownership to access, resulting in changes in the market and the emergence of 'new values' and new business models. This phase requires adjustments in copyright law in order to guarantee remuneration in the new scenario
>
> (EY, 2015a: 42)[32]

The report also mentions a 'possible positive value of these intermediary services', related to their contribution to 'viral dissemination' of content and thus to additional, indirect revenues for traditional players. However, while concern for the effects of *substitution/dispersal* produced by informal, illegal (pirate) activities in the formal sector is at the core of the report, other ongoing changes that bear no elements of illegality but are related to informal components (new players, new business models) are not considered in relation to their potential for market *extension*. Most importantly, the need for a profound *reconfiguration* of the entire cultural and creative industries sector is not really taken into consideration: on the contrary, it is copyright law that should be partially 'reconfigured' in order to maintain the *status quo* and protect the interests of traditional intermediaries. In other words, *restriction* and *authorization* strategies are presented as the only possible responses to *dispersal* and *substitution*.

Before concluding, I would like to underline one last aspect concerning the Italian report on creative industries. Differently from other similar surveys, both editions of *Italia creativa* make no reference to the idea of the informal economy, thus leaving aside a relevant set of theoretical tools and concepts that are useful in a fast-changing market. This choice is not as obvious as it may appear, since other reports in fact do include informality in their analysis. This can lead to odd consequences, as in the *Cultural Times* report (EY, 2015c),[33] where the new category of the 'underground economy' is introduced and divided into two sub-categories: on the one hand physical and digital piracy; on the other the informal economy, or the 'supply of goods and services in exchange for payment, but which is not covered or is insufficiently covered by formal arrangements'. This strategy of separating the informal economy from piracy is irreparably far from providing effective solutions to the dramatic challenges of the contemporary creative market. Nevertheless, a far more interesting and productive account of the value of the notion of informality comes from the Unesco *Creative Economy Report* (2013). Here, a consideration of the idea of informal economy provides a truly fresh perspective on the creative sector, which includes several key attributes: attention to the social and collective dimension of creativity; the attempt to map cultural domains by going beyond the traditional arts and copyright industries (including, for instance, also creative practices related to intangible cultural heritage); and reference to models that operate predominantly in non-Western, developing countries, which present challenging combinations and interactions between formal and informal areas – such as insight into the case of Nollywood (the Nigerian movie industry), as provided by Lobato (UNESCO, 2013: 26). However, Nollywood is still far, far away from Italy.

Concluding remarks

Contemporary anti-piracy communication in Italy is predominantly aimed at validating and strengthening the preservation of a *status quo* that, within the current framework of copyright enforcement, supports an established industrial structure that maximizes intermediary profits, while denying the possibility to elaborate on crucial questions such as the duration of rights, the window system, exclusivity, or consumers' rights, not to mention the potential to develop innovative business models. More precisely, thanks to the theoretical framework provided by Lobato and Thomas (2015), we can clearly see how different anti-piracy policies all tend to reject or neglect the positive *functions* that informal elements can inspire when used within formal media market, such as *taste-testing, priming* and *educating*. At the same time, it is possible to identify the function of *outsourcing*, both in the engagement of the audience that exploits content, which strengthens messages and improves dissemination, and in the form of audience's needs, as in the case of teachers, who are provided with educational material and invited to participate in the work of copyright enforcement. As for the *effects* of informality on formality, we can clearly see how *dispersal* and *substitution* are still largely emphasized, while other effects, such as *revaluation*, market *extension* and *reconfiguration* – i.e. the need for innovative business models – are addressed approximately or totally neglected. Finally, when it comes to *controls*, the category of *restriction* is presented as an incentive for creativity and the creative industries, while *promoting* is limited to encouraging informal practices only when they are aimed at sustaining formal economy and formal players.

Through its application to specific discursive practices – such as contemporary, Italian anti-piracy communication – this chapter has aimed to show the use of Lobato and Thomas' theoretical model, as well as its more general implications. First, the categories applied to the analysis of the multiple and varied relationships between formal and informal areas/actors can provide new perspectives in digital piracy research, and new tools to examine anti-piracy strategies. Second, they allow us to relate anti-piracy communication to the development of online media distribution, and thus to demonstrate and account for the ways that formal players, in specific contexts and/or in a transnational perspective, seek to shape the digital market evolution and the social perception of informal activities.

Notes

1 For a plural definition of piracy see (among others) Johns, 2009; Crisp, 2015; Lobato, 2012a, and particularly Chapter 5, 'Six Faces of Piracy'.
2 My discussion draws in particular from Karaganis, 2011; Lobato, 2010, 2012a, and 2014; Lobato & Thomas 2012 and 2015; Crisp 2015.
3 With regard to Jenkins' and Lessig's research, it is worth specifying that in this chapter I will not discuss extensively the specific issues connected to the interactions between copyright laws, digital technologies, fair use and private copying. On this I refer to Lessig, 2008 and also Jenkins, Ford and Green (2013: 54): 'New technologies enable audiences to exert much greater impact on circulation than ever before, but they also enable companies to police once-private behavior that is taking on greater public dimension. Some people describe these shifts as a crisis in copyright and others a crisis in fair use.'
4 For analyses of the use of the term 'piracy', see (among others): Brown, 2014; Crisp, 2015; Gates, 2006; Logie, 2006; Loughlan, 2006 and 2008; Yar, 2008; Johns, 2009; Patry, 2009; Karaganis, 2011; Mirghani, 2011; Yu, 2011; Lobato, 2012a; Parkes, 2013; Re, 2014.
5 Evidently, the relationship between morality and piracy is a very complex issue. Adrian Johns, for instance, has referred to 'the moral economy of music piracy' to

explain the commercial, piratical activities of jazz and opera aficionados in the 1950s, who legitimated their action in terms of preserving an artistic heritage from major companies (Johns, 2009). Motivations for sharing in contemporary online communities are widely discussed in Crisp 2015 and Andersson Schwarz and Larsson, 2014. Brown (2014) provides a detailed overview of recent qualitative research on the motivations of file sharers. It is certainly worth reflecting on the ambivalence of the piracy metaphor, and its possible moral upside: users can interpret the metaphor by focusing on positive aspects such as freedom, social equality, and free access to culture.

6 For a wider discussion of other examples of 'ethical sharing', see Crisp, 2015.

7 '550 sites out of the 622 [examined] (88.4%) carried advertising and 142 sites offered at least one form of payment method. The overlap between the two groups gave a total of 122 sites that contained both advertising and payment methods. 52 sites did not carry either advertising or accept payment' (Incopro, 2015: 9).

8 I will come back later in the chapter also to the issues related to corporate reports and statistics.

9 See also Karaganis (2011: 41): 'Piracy has undoubtedly been a catalyst for the emergence of [...] low-cost models, insofar as it resets consumer expectations around cheaper, on-demand availability.'

10 Karaganis makes the same claim: 'What we know about media piracy usually begins, and often ends, with industry-sponsored research' (Karaganis, 2011: 1). See also the idea of the 'anti-piracy industry' proposed by Lobato and Thomas (2012), and especially what they define as the 'knowledge generation sector'.

11 My translation. Unless otherwise indicated, all translations from Italian are my own.

12 As we will see later in greater detail, in the wake of the 2011 FAPAV/IPSOS report, communication produced by industries and corporate associations has partially changed. However, a very recent report published in Italy (FAPAV/IPSOS 2017) insists nonetheless on using the substitution argument, and estimates that the economic damage to the audiovisual market in 2016 was 686 million euros.

13 For different interpretations of the closure of Megaupload, see for instance Danaher and Smith, 2013 and Peukert, Claussen and Kretschmer, 2017.

14 See, for instance, in relation to Italy, the press release by Confindustria Cultura Italia, which represents the main copyright industries associations, 14 December 2010. See also De Vany and Walls, 2007.

15 See, for instance, AGCOM, 2010b and Hargreaves, 2011.

16 See, for instance, Danaher, Dhanasobhon, Smith and Telang, 2010; Danaher and Waldfogel 2012.

17 See at least Yar, 2008, Karaganis, 2011 and Brown, 2014.

18 For an updated overview of the debate, see at least Crisp, 2015.

19 'Informality is neither good nor bad: everyday life is a combination of formal and informal activities, transactions and interactions. Seen from this perspective, media systems take up ever-shifting positions along a spectrum of formality. Piracy becomes an after-effect of changes in regulatory structure' (Lobato, 2014: 131).

20 TVOD is a pay-per-view model that incorporates purchase and/or rental. The SVOD (Subscription Video on Demand) model provides access to a catalogue for a monthly flat rate.

21 See also the metaphor of 'symbiosis' proposed in Crisp, 2015.

22 Unless otherwise indicated, all quotations in this section are taken from Lobato and Thomas 2015.

23 Available at: www.youtube.com/watch?v=DeblW6o0Eso (accessed 30 April 2017).

24 See www.statista.com (accessed 30 April 2017).

25 'Piattaforma di proposta politica Anica per una nuova cultura dell'industria audiovisiva in Italia'/'Anica Political Proposal for a New Culture of the Italian

Audiovisual Industry', available at: www.anica.it/news/news-anica/piattaforma-di- prop osta-politica-anica-per-una-nuova-cultura-dellindustria-audiovisiva-in-italia   (accessed 30 April 2017).

26 Cf. http://iofacciofilm.it (accessed 30 April 2017).

27 For other examples of contest, see also 'Il protagonista'/'The protagonist', two editions from 2014, promoted by ANICA, the FAPAV, the MPA and Univideo, in collaboration with YouTube, www.ilprotagonista.eu/# (accessed 30 April 2017), and 'Diventa pioniere'/'Become a pioneer', promoted in 2014 by the AESVI (the Italian association of videogame industries), https://vimeo.com/130447169 (teaser; accessed 30 April 2017), in the context of the public campaign 'All4Games'.

28 This is reported on the project's website: http://www.rispettiamolacreativita.it (accessed 30 April 2017).

29 For an overview of the debate see Spedicato 2013.

30 This does not mean that users all believe online content should be accessed for free, as the film producer Domenico Procacci claims in the interview included in the *Italia creativa* report (EY, 2015a: 103). Procacci seems to use the idea of *revaluation* to downplay the need for a more general *reconfiguration*.

31 Considered as 'OTT TVs', i.e. OTT platforms that are independent from broadcasters. This category is not used in other international reports, and data provided about revenues diverges from that which is provided by Statista and EAO.

32 It must be added that at the time of writing the second edition of *Italia creativa* has been published (EY 2016). In it, the film and TV industries have been combined into a single 'audiovisual sector'. However, value gap and piracy are still referred to as 'the two mains threats to the Italian creative industries' (EY 2016: 18), and piracy is defined as 'a crime against creativity' (p. 28). Further considerations would necessitate a more detailed analysis.

33 The report is promoted by the CISAC (International Confederation of Societies of Authors and Composers).

Bibliography

AGCOM. (2010a), 'Copyright issues in the electronic communications sector'. Online. Available www.agcom.it/documentazione/documento?p_p_auth=fLw7zRht&p_p_id= 101_INSTANCE_kidx9GUnIodu&p_p_lifecycle=0&p_p_col_id=column-1&p_p_col_ count=1&_101_INSTANCE_kidx9GUnIodu_struts_action=%2Fasset_publisher%2Fv iew_content&_101_INSTANCE_kidx9GUnIodu_assetEntryId=959868&_101_INSTA NCE_kidx9GUnIodu_type=document [Accessed 30 April 2017].

AGCOM. (2010b), 'Lineamenti di provvedimento concernente l'esercizio delle competenze dell'autorità nell'attività di tutela del diritto d'autore sulle reti di comunicazione elettronica'. Online. Available www.agcom.it/documentazione/documento?p_p_a uth=fLw7zRht&p_p_id=101_INSTANCE_kidx9GUnIodu&p_p_lifecycle=0&p_p_ col_id=column-1&p_p_col_count=1&_101_INSTANCE_kidxGUnIodu_struts_acti on=%2Fasset_publisher%2Fview_content&_101_INSTANCE_kidx9GUnIodu_asse tEntryId=849541&_101_INSTANCE_kidx9GUnIodu_type=document   [Accessed 30 April 2017].

AGCOM. (2011a), 'Libro bianco sui contenuti'. Online. Available: www.agcom.it/il-li bro-bianco-sui-contenuti [accessed 30 April 2017].

AGCOM. (2011b), 'Schema di regolamento in materia di tutela del diritto d'autore sulle reti di comunicazione elettronica'. Online. Available: www.agcom.it/documentazione/ documento?p_p_auth=fLw7zRht&p_p_id=101_INSTANCE_kidx9GUnIodu&p_p_ lifecycle=0&p_p_col_id=column-1&p_p_col_count=1&_101_INSTANCE_kidx9G

UnIodu_struts_action=%2Fasset_publisher%2Fview_content&_101_INSTANCE_ki
dx9GUnIodu_assetEntryId=891943&_101_INSTANCE_kidx9GUnIodu_type=doc
ument [Accessed 30 April 2017].

AGCOM. (2013a), 'Schema di regolamento in materia di tutela del diritto d'autore sulle
reti di comunicazione elettronica e procedure attuative ai sensi del decreto legislativo 9
aprile 2003, n. 70'. Online. Available: www.agcom.it/documentazione/documento?p_p_a
uth=fLw7zRht&p_p_id=101_INSTANCE_kidx9GUnIodu&p_p_lifecycle=0&p_p
_col_id=column-1&p_p_col_count=1&_101_INSTANCE_kidx9GUnIodu_struts
_action=%2Fasset_publisher%2Fview_content&_101_INSTANCE_kidx9GUnIo
du_assetEntryId=667482&_101_INSTANCE_kidx9GUnIodu_type=document
[Accessed 30 April 2017].

AGCOM. (2013b), 'Regolamento in materia di tutela del diritto d'autore sulle reti di
comunicazione elettronica e procedure attuative ai sensi del decreto legislativo 9
aprile 2003, n. 70'. Online. Available: www.agcom.it/documentazione/documento?p_p_a
uth=fLw7zRht&p_p_id=101_INSTANCE_kidx9GUnIodu&p_p_lifecycle=0&p_p_col
_id=column-1&p_p_col_count=1&_101_INSTANCE_kidx9GUnIodu_struts_action=
%2Fasset_publisher%2Fview_content&_101_INSTANCE_kidx9GUnIodu_assetEntry
Id=771920&_101_INSTANCE_kidx9GUnIodu_type=document [Accessed 30 April
2017].

Anderson, C. (2009) *Free*, London: Random House.

Andersson Schwarz, J., Larsson, S. (2014) 'The justification of piracy: differences in
conceptualization and argumentation between active uploaders and other file-
sharers', in M. Fredriksson, J. Arvanitakis (eds) *Piracy: Leakages from Modernity*,
Los Angeles, CA: Litwin Books.

Brown, S.C. (2014) 'Approaches to digital piracy research: A call for innovation',
Convergence, 2: 129–139.

Cine-Regio. (2014) *Audience in the Mind*. Online. Available: www.cine-regio.org/libra
ry/digital_revolution_2014/ [Accessed 30 April 2017].

Confindustria Cultura Italia.(2010) 'Fondamentale il provvedimento AGCOM per
tutelare i contenuti culturali', press release. Online. Available: www.confindustria
culturaitalia.it/index.php?option=com_content&view=article&id=27:confindustria-c
ultura-italia-fondamentale-il-provvedimento-agcom-per-tutelare-i-contenuti-culturali
&catid=2:comunicati-stampa&Itemid=6 [Accessed 30 April 2017].

Crisp, V. (2013) 'The piratical is political', *Soundings*, 55: 71–80.

Crisp, V. (2015) *Film Distribution in the Digital Age*, Basingtoke: Palgrave Macmillan.

Cunningham, S., Silver, J. (2013) *Screen Distribution and the New King Kongs of the
Online World*, London and New York: Palgrave.

Currah, A. (2006) 'Hollywood versus the Internet: The media and entertainment
industries in a digital and networked economy', *Journal of Economic Geography*, 6:
439–468.

Curtin, M., Holt, J., Sanson, K. (2014) 'Introduction', in Ibid. (eds), *Distribution
Revolution: Conversations about the Digital Future of Film and Television*, Oakland:
California University Press.

Danaher, B., Dhanasobhon, S., Smith, M.D., Telang R. (2010) 'Converting pirates
without cannibalizing purchasers'. Online. Available: https://ssrn.com/abstract=
1381827 [Accessed 12 August 2017].

Danaher, B., Waldfogel, J. (2012) 'Reel piracy: The effect of online film piracy on
international box office sales'. Online. Available: https://ssrn.com/abstract=1986299
[Accessed 12 August 2017].

Danaher, B., Smith, M.D. (2013) 'Gone in 60 seconds: The impact of the megaupload shutdown on movie sales'. Online. Available: http://dx.doi.org/10.2139/ssrn.2229349 [Accessed 12 August 2017].

Denison, R. (2015) 'Redistributing Japanese television drama: The shadow economies and communities around online fan distribution of Japanese media', *The Velvet Light Trap*, 75 (1): 58–72.

Digital Citizens Alliance. (2015) *Good Money Still Going Bad: Digital Thieves and the Hijacking of the Online Ad Business*. Online. Available: www.digitalcitizensalliance. org/cac/alliance/content.aspx?page=GMGB2 [Accessed 4 February 2017].

EAO (2015) *The SVOD Market in the EU. Developments 2014/2015*. Online. Available: www.obs.coe.int/en/industry/video/-/asset_publisher/H7fRZzJl0wZv/content/dgcnect-note-3-the-svod-market-in-the-eu-developments-2014-2015?_101_INSTANCE_H7fR ZzJl0wZv_redirect=http%3A%2F%2Fwww.obs.coe.int%2Fen%2Findustry%2Fvideo %3Fp_p_id%3D101_INSTANCE_H7fRZzJl0wZv%26p_p_lifecycle%3D0%26p_p_ state%3Dnormal%26p_p_mode%3Dview%26p_p_col_id%3Dcolumn-1%26p_ p_col_ count%3D1&_101_INSTANCE_H7fRZzJl0wZv_articleResourceGroupId=205595& _101_INSTANCE_H7fRZzJl0wZv_articleResourceArticleId=8412027 [Accessed 30 April 2017].

EAO. (2016) *Trends in Video-on-Demand Revenues*. Online. Available: www.obs.coe.int/ en/industry/video/-/asset_publisher/H7fRZzJl0wZv/content/obs-refit-note-b-2-vod-rev enues?_101_INSTANCE_H7fRZzJl0wZv_redirect=http%3A%2F%2Fwww.obs.coe.in t%2Fen%2Findustry%2Fvideo%3Fp_p_id%3D101_INSTANCE_H7fRZzJl0wZv%2 6p_p_lifecycle%3D0%26p_p_state%3Dnormal%26p_p_mode%3Dview%26p_p_col_i d%3Dcolumn-1%26p_p_col_count%3D1&_101_INSTANCE_H7fRZzJl0wZv_article ResourceGroupId=205595&_101_INSTANCE_H7fRZzJl0wZv_articleResourceArtic leId=8434043#p_101_INSTANCE_H7fRZzJl0wZv [Accessed 30 April 2017].

European Commission (2016) *Copyright Factsheet*. Online. Available: https://ec. europa.eu/digital-single-market/en/news/factsheet-copyright [Accessed 4 February 2017].

EY. (2015a) *Italia creativa*. Online. Available: www.italiacreativa.eu/prima-edizione/ [Accessed 30 April 2017].

EY. (2015b) *Création sous tension*. Online. Available: www.ey.com/Publication/ vwLUAssets/EY-2e-panorama-de-l-economie-de-la-culture-et-de-la-creation-en-Fran ce/%24FILE/EY-2e-panorama-de-l-economie-de-la-culture-et-de-la-creation-en-Fra nce.pdf [Accessed 30 April 2017].

EY. (2015c) *Cultural Times*. Online. Available: www.ey.com/Publication/vwLUAssets/ ey-cultural-times-2015/$FILE/ey-cultural-times-2015.pdf [Accessed 30 April 2017].

EY. (2016) *Italia creativa*. Online. Available: www.italiacreativa.eu/settore/scarica-lo-s tudio/ [Accessed 30 April 2017].

FAPAV, IPSOS. (2011) *La pirateria audiovisiva in Italia*. Online. Available: www.fapav. it/1/osservatorio/1/ [Accessed 4 February 2017].

FAPAV, IPSOS. (2017) *Indagine sulla pirateria audiovisiva in Italia*. Online. Available: www.fapav.it/1/osservatorio/1/ [Accessed 12 August 2017].

Fabbri, F. (2017) '"Io Faccio Film" alla Casa del Cinema di Roma, presentati oggi i risultati a sei mesi dal lancio', *key4biz*, 2 March. Online. Available www.key4biz.it/ io-faccio-film-alla-casa-del-cinema-di-roma-presentati-oggi-i-risultati-a-sei-mesi-dal -lancio/182961/ [Accessed 30 April 2017].

Gates, K. (2006) 'Will work for copyrights: The cultural policy of anti-piracy cam-paigns', *Social Semiotics*, 1: 57–73.

Hargreaves, I. (2011) *Digital Opportunity. A Review of Intellectual Property and Growth*. Online. Available: www.gov.uk/government/publications/digital-opportuni ty-review-of-intellectual-property-and-growth [Accessed 30 April 2017].

Howkins, J. (2007) *The Creative Economy*, London: Penguin Press (Kindle edition).

Incopro. (2015) *The Revenue Sources for Websites Making Available Copyright Content without Consent in the EU*. Online. Available: www.incopro.co.uk/resources-news-events/case-studies-reports/ [Accessed 4 February 2017].

Jenkins, H. (2006) *Convergence Culture*, New York: New York University Press.

Jenkins, H., Ford, S., and Green, J. (2013) *Spreadable Media*, New York and London: New York University Press.

Johns, A. (2009) *Piracy*, Chicago and London: The University of Chicago Press.

Karaganis, J. (2011) (ed.), *Media Piracy in Emerging Economy*, Social Science Research Council, 2011. Online. Available: http://piracy.ssrc.org [Accessed 4 February 2017].

Lessig, L. (2004) *Free Culture*, London and New York: Penguin.

Lessig, L. (2008) *Remix*, London and New York: Penguin.

Lobato, R. (2010) 'Creative industries and informal economies', *International Journal of Cultural Studies*, 4: 337–354.

Lobato, R. (2012a) *Shadow Economies of Cinema*, London: BFI-Palgrave.

Lobato, R. (2012b) 'A sideways view of the film economy in an age of digital piracy', *Necsus. European Journal of Media Studies*, 1. Online. Available: www.necsus-ejms. org/a-sideways-view-of-the-film-economy-in-an-age-of-digital-piracy-by-ramon-loba to/ [Accessed 4 February 2017].

Lobato, R. (2014) 'The paradoxes of piracy', in L. Eckstein, A. Schwarz (eds), *Postcolonial Piracy: Media Distribution and Cultural Production in the Global South*, London: Bloosmbury Academic.

Lobato, R., Thomas, J. (2012) 'The business of anti-piracy: new zones of enterprise in the copyright wars", *International Journal of Communication*, 6: 606–625.

Lobato, R., Thomas, J. (2015) *The Informal Media Economy*, Cambridge and Malden, MA: Polity Press (Kindle edition).

Logie, J. (2006) *Peers, Pirates, and Persuasion*, West Lafayette, IN: Parlor Press.

Loughlan, P.L. (2006) 'Pirates, parasites, reapers, sowers, fruits, foxes… The metaphors of intellectual property', *Sydney Law Review*, 2: 211–226.

Loughlan, P.L. (2008) '"You wouldn't steal a car": Intellectual property and the language of theft', *European Intellectual Property Review*, 10: 401–405.

Mirghani, S. (2011) 'The war on piracy: Analyzing the discursive battles of corporate and government-sponsored anti-piracy media campaigns', *Critical Studies in Media Communication*, 2: 113–134.

Moore, C. (2013) 'Distribution is queen: LGBTQ media on demand', *Cinema Journal*, 53, 1: 137–144.

Oxera and O&O. (2016) *The Impact of Cross-border Access to Audiovisual Content on EU Consumers*. Online. Available www.oxera.com/Latest-Thinking/Publications/Rep orts/2016/The-impact-of-cross-border-access-to-audiovisual-c.aspx [Accessed 4 February 2017].

Parkes, M. (2013) 'Making plans for Nigel: The industry trust and film piracy management in the United Kingdom', *Convergence: The International Journal of Research into New Media Technologies*, 1: 25–43.

Patry, W. (2009) *Moral Panics and the Copyright Wars*, Oxford and New York: Oxford University Press.

Pellicanò, F. (2014) 'AGCOM adopts a regulation on copyright protection', *Iris*, 3, 31. Online. Available: http://merlin.obs.coe.int/article.php?id=14571 [Accessed 30 April 2017].

Peukert, C., Claussen, J., Kretschmer, T. (2017) 'Piracy and box office movie revenues: evidence from Megaupload'. Online. Available: https://ssrn.com/abstract=2176246 [Accessed 12 August 2017].

Spedicato, G. (2013) *Interesse pubblico e bilanciamento nel diritto d'autore*, Milan: Giuffrè.

TNT Village. (2005) 'Statute'. Online. Available: http://forum.tntvillage.scambioetico. org [Accessed 4 February 2017].

Tryon, C. (2013) *On-demand Culture*, New Brunswick, NJ: Rutgers University Press.

Ulin, J.C. (2009) *The Business of Media Distribution*, New Yor and London: Focal Press.

UNESCO. (2013) *Creative Economy Report*. Online. Available www.unesco.org/new/ en/culture/themes/creativity/creative-economy-report-2013-special-edition/ [Accessed 30 April 2017].

United Nations (1948) 'Universal declaration of human rights'. Online. Available: www.un.org/en/universal-declaration-human-rights/ [Accessed 4 February 2017].

Van Eijk, N., Poort, J., and Rutten, P. (2010) 'Legal, economic and cultural aspects of file sharing', *Communications & Strategies*, 77: 35–54.

Yar, M. (2008) 'The rhetorics and myths of anti-piracy campaigns', *New Media Society*, 4: 605–623.

Yu, P.K. (2011) 'Digital copyright and confuzzling rhetoric', *Vanderbilt Journal of Entertainment and Technology Law*, 13: 881–939.

Section II

Approaches to understanding digital piracy

5 The social and applied psychology of engagement in music piracy

Amanda Elizabeth Krause and
Steven Caldwell Brown

Introduction

The only way to experience music in earlier centuries was to experience it live. However, the new technologies of the twenty-first century are influencing the ways in which people are able to experience and interact with music (Avdeeff, 2012; Nill & Geipel, 2010; North, Hargreaves, & Hargreaves, 2004; Sloboda, Lamont, & Greasley, 2009). The way individuals are able to access, acquire, and store music, has changed due to the popularity of digital music (Kibby, 2009). Consequently notions of 'music consumption' have shifted (Molteni & Ordanini, 2003). One of the most striking changes is of course that music is now easily accessible for free, via a mixture of legal and illegal sources.

By empowering people to listen to more music than ever before, music piracy has given people more control over what they hear, and in different environments. In general, portable devices broaden when, where, and how people engage with music (Heye & Lamont, 2010; Juslin, Liljeström, Västfjäll, Barradas, & Silva, 2008; Sloboda et al., 2009). As Avdeeff (2012: 269) stated, "digital technology is the primary means by which most people consume music and, as such, it affects the relationship between music and listener". Consuming music is not just about listening, but how it relates to both personal and social lives (O'Hara & Brown, 2006). Accordingly, an understanding of how individuals use music in the everyday context must account for technological advancements, including music piracy (Gaunt & Hallam, 2009).

Digital technological advancements have allowed for blurring between the consumption and production of music (Ebare, 2004; O'Hara & Brown, 2006; see also North, et al., 2004; Hargreaves, Miell, & MacDonald, 2002). A long held hierarchy that assigns the greatest amount of power with regard to music to the role of composer, a subordinate middle-tiered role to the performer, and the bottom position to the listeners as merely *passive recipients* of music is outdated (Cook, 1998; North & Hargreaves, 2008). With the advent of digital technology, and with its strong influences on musical activities, technology is causing the boundaries of the old hierarchy to break down. North and Hargreaves (2008) press further by wondering whether the boundaries between the roles should be re-defined, or if any hierarchy should even be arranged. Indeed, in the digital era, music listeners are considered to be quite *active* consumers (Krause, North, & Hewitt, 2015; Sloboda et al., 2009) With most songs skipped on Spotify within the first five seconds, it is clear consumers are not simply listening to anything (Guardian Music, 2014).

Why music psychology?

Music is a social phenomenon, and the ubiquity of music in everyday life means that it is important to question how and why people experience it (Chamorro-Premuzic & Furnham, 2007). People interact with music regardless of their level of proficiency with music – 'musicians' and 'non-musicians' (however defined) alike experience and enjoy music. People develop friendships because of shared interests; gather to hear and talk about music; use music as a backdrop to many situations; use music in mood regulation; and even use it in constructing their identity. Working from a social and applied psychology of music perspective, we can understand the role music occupies in everyday modern life and the factors that explain our experiences of music. Thus, music piracy is not just a legal, criminological issue.

The psychology of music, as a discipline, has a long-standing history. It began its development as an independent discipline in the middle of the nineteenth century with preliminary research in the perception of sound (Thaut, 2009). It developed in the 1970s and 1980s into two clear sub-fields: cognitive psychology of music and developmental psychology of music. While not wholly independent of each other, these two sub-fields continued to grow, establishing an informal paradigm for music psychology (North & Hargreaves, 2008).

By the 1980s, researchers, including Vladimir Konečni and Dean Simonton, began questioning the utility of laboratory-based research to fully explain real responses to music (North & Hargreaves, 2008). Konečni (1982: 500) asserted that music is enjoyed, "in the stream of daily life", prompting the argument that much of the laboratory research from the past fails to explain the modern-day reality of music listening (Juslin et al., 2008; Lamont & Greasley, 2009; North & Hargreaves, 2008; Sloboda et al., 2009). Thus, the most notable shift in the field of psychology of music since the mid-1980s has concerned a shift toward social factors, and the emergence of an identifiable social psychology of music (North & Hargreaves, 2008).

North and Hargreaves (2008) noted that within the social psychology of music there has also been a focus in applying research findings to the practical world. Importantly, North and Hargreaves open their book, *The Social and Applied Psychology of Music*, stating that "an approach based in social and applied psychology can explain the position of music in the modern world" (2008: vi). Given the strong interest in how research can be applied to "real world" problems and issues, the field has developed to emphasize research using real music and real contexts, with efforts to define the purpose of music in the modern, everyday world (North & Hargreaves, 2008). Importantly, topics of interest address people's relationship to music as it is experienced in an attempt to determine why music matters (North & Hargreaves, 2008). There is an interest in how music is embedded in everyday life, with the fact that so many people now dedicate large amounts of their waking lives listening to music.

Topics which are of central importance to research in music psychology include creativity, performance, and emotion; and these are present in the second edition of the *Oxford Handbook of Music Psychology* (Hallam, Cross & Thaut, 2016), providing a comprehensive overview of them. There is a section on the role of music in everyday life. Despite research in the field flourishing, the field employs a *topics-based* approach to research, which has the consequence of "little or no cross pollination between" closely related research topics (North & Hargreaves, 2008: 5). Consequently, related disciplines have tended to progress independently. For example, Music Information Retrieval (MIR) research occurs largely independent of the music psychology field; not to mention work concerning piracy with regard to law, copyright etc.

This chapter aims to draw together relevant theory and recent research findings in order to provide a detailed, psychological overview of why people engage in music piracy, by first taking into account research into why people listen to music. The authors of this chapter are particularly interested in the implications of how people access and select music to listen to (including the idea of unlimited access to music), given the volume of options available. It is against this backdrop that this chapter is situated, adopting a psychological approach to understanding why individuals *do* or *do not* engage in music piracy. Music is specifically singled out due to the research interests of both authors.

Thus, this chapter also considers music piracy within a broader social psychological context, contextualising its outcomes, including those that are not commercial. In doing so, this chapter exposes the shortcomings of other disciplines that have focused solely on the negative consequences of music piracy. Put simply, this chapter will identify some of the far-reaching outcomes of widespread engagement in music piracy, including the impact on the live music sector, typically absent from any critical evaluation of music piracy, focusing solely on the recorded music sector.

Why do people listen to music?

People listen to music for many different reasons. Schäfer, Sedlmeier, Städtler, and Huron (2013) reduced an aggregated list of more than 500 functions to three underlying dimensions: to achieve self-awareness; to regulate arousal and mood; and as an expression of social relatedness. It is thought that it is the impact on mood that accounts for the positive effects of listening to music (Chanda & Levitin, 2013; MacDonald, Kreutz & Mitchell, 2012) and indeed one of the most often cited reasons for listening to music is for mood management (see Swaminathan & Schellenberg, 2015 for a review). Listeners may change, release, and match emotions just as they may be listening to enjoy, comfort, or de-stress themselves (Juslin & Sloboda, 2013). Individuals can regulate and attempt to enhance their moods and emotions with music (Juslin, 2009). Indeed, DeNora (2000) explained that almost all of her participants exhibited an awareness regarding the music they 'needed' in different contexts. This includes attempts to alter moods and states of feeling, as well as activity levels (relaxing or energizing). Additionally, the music might provide a virtual realm to vent or work through aggression or violence, as it can confine the feelings to a temporal space (DeNora, 2000). Part of the criteria for the 'right' music was how well it 'fit', or was suitable for the purpose or situation they wished to achieve (DeNora, 2010).

This kind of 'use of music' by listeners involves goal achievement (Sloboda, 2010), and the growing literature on such uses (e.g., DeNora, 2000; Sloboda, et al., 2009) demonstrates how people choose music to accompany a range of daily activities (e.g., travel, exercise, physical work, intellectual work, mood management). What joins these different pairings of music and activities, Sloboda and Juslin (2010) explained, is that the listener's intentions are principal to the causal process. The listeners are using music to help achieve some sort of goal, which can be related to emotions/moods.

The respondents in DeNora's (2000) study made articulations between musical pieces and styles with desired modes of agency, using the music to inspire, elaborate, or remind them of those modes of agency and the associated emotions (DeNora, 2010). These articulations were made on the basis of the individual's perceptions – perceptions regarding what the music can afford, about previous associations between musical materials and biographical or situational occurrences, as well as their cultural and social notions of the emotional implications of different musical genres, styles, and devices (DeNora, 2010). Hargreaves and North's (2010) research that indicates that people use music as a resource to achieve certain psychological states (and that different arousal states are considered appropriate to different situations). This then relates to arousal-state goals, which in their prior work was influential to preference, also mirrors mood goals as well. As a result, this then places music as a very active resource on which individuals can employ for emotional work (goal achievement, more broadly). Listeners are able to rely upon it to satisfy particular needs.

Research into music listening typically focuses on young people, the cohort principally engaged in and benefiting from musical engagement. For instance, adolescents have been the subject of the aforementioned ability of music to enhance mood (Saarikallio & Erkkilä, 2007), and much research demonstrates how adolescents and young adults in particular use music preferences to reinforce how they view themselves, communicating to others (Saarikallio, 2012). As will be shown elsewhere, research into music piracy typically focuses on young people also and this is not a coincidence – we listen to more music during adolescence than in any other period of our lives, aiding self-definition and identity (Powell, 2016).

The cultural and commercial impact of the digital revolution on contemporary music listening practices

As mentioned at the beginning of the chapter, the so-called digital revolution has changed the ways in which we now consume, enjoy, and pay for music. MacDonald, Kreutz, and Mitchell (2012: 4) explained that:

> The technological revolution that has taken place in terms of music listening means that we can now listen to our own musical choices 24 hours a day ... We can, in effect, listen to our own music in virtually every context imaginable.

While younger generations may take this for granted, as scholars we must not. Music listening is becoming integrated into our personal and social lives (Krause & Hargreaves, 2013), and we must remain curious about such changes so we can trace them over time.

We shall not re-tell the whole story of Napster – that story has been told many times, including by David (2016) and elsewhere in this book. What we shall say is that though music piracy has existed for decades, it was not until Napster (and other peer-to-peer services in its wake), that music piracy occurred on a scale large enough to warrant intervention by the recording industry. Technology has long posed threats to the music business, as well as opportunities. To hone in solely on methods of reproduction, *radio* meant that curious teens were able to listen to music that parents might not have approved of. This brought black music to white listeners, and with it, spawned rock and roll. *Music television* shifted the focus away from the music altogether, focusing attention on visuals. This brought charismatic performers such as Michael Jackson and Madonna into the forefront of popular music, inspiring generations. The *Internet* brought threats to the very core driver of the business of music – *that consumers pay for it* – and the industry is still wrestling with this.

By some margin, the Internet has posed the biggest threat to music as an industry, leading to the upheaval alluded to above and elsewhere in this book. Scharf (2013) defined a holy trinity that triggered widespread digital piracy: the Internet; the MP3; and peer-to-peer technologies. The music industry has never looked back from these advancements, and it has no reason to. The music industry, as we now know it, is becoming increasingly more digital, or more specifically, more streaming-based. The latest industry reports emphasise that streaming now accounts for 59% of digital revenues (IFPI, 2017).

Music has now become a shared, communal resource (not always owned), something that could not have been said a generation ago. Wade and Powers (2015: 109) discussed how, "Streaming's aquatic and luminous connotations also play on the notion of music and media as a kind of 'utility'", noting that discourse about the constant free-flowing access to music speaks of ideals concerning control. With ease, you can share what you are listening to with anyone, anywhere in the world. Naturally, people now do this – because they can. Oftentimes, this will involve sharing music illegally, but not always. Anderson (2014: 77) argues that, "What makes Spotify's service exceptional is the emphasis it has placed on convenient sharing", discussing its integration with ubiquitous social media platform Facebook (also noted by Wade & Powers, 2015). Yet, empirical investigation into sharing features on Spotify finds that most subscribers share music selectively (Hagen & Lüders, 2016) suggesting that music listened to demonstrates one's identity (Levinson, 2014). Interestingly, personality accounts for not only preferred music (Greenberg et al., 2016), but wider music listening behaviours too – individuals open to experience report greater levels of browsing music by mood (Ferwerda et al., 2015). Who we are is reflected in our musical choices.

Technology has freed up the opportunity to listen to a wide variety of music (Waldfogel, 2014) and qualitative research supports the notion that people are listening to a wider range of music than before (Greasley, Lamont, & Sloboda, 2013). Yet, Ward, Goodman and Irwin (2014) found that although consumers state a preference to listen to unfamiliar music, familiarity with music positively predicts preference for songs, playlists, and radio stations. Ward et al. (2014) argued that the need for familiarity is motivated by a desire for low levels of stimulation; this is certainly plausible, given music listening via mobile devices or on computers would be expected to be an accompaniment to other activities. Alternatively, choosing to listen to known music may be due to the paradox of choice (see Dobelli, 2013), wherein the volume of options available simply leads to bewilderment and so consumers opt for the familiar (Bylin, 2014; Luck, 2016). By focusing briefly on streaming, we can already see contradictions between what appears to be the unique selling points of subscription services (ability to share and discover new music) and what research has found. The nature of streaming is not finalised; however, there exists one constant shared by all subscription services: the more media you consume, the cheaper the media.

We can, however, consider ownership relative to streaming from established psychological theory. Sinclair and Tinson (2017) argued that an enhanced feeling of psychological ownership will lead to long-term loyalty, greater word-of-mouth, customer empowerment and feelings of satisfaction. The authors cite Kirk et al. (2015) who have proposed that the use of new technologies which facilitate discovery, providing opportunities for control, are likely to experience enhanced feelings of *psychological ownership*. Pierce et al. (2003) explain that we can cultivate strong feelings of ownership both for material and immaterial possessions, and that ownership is not the same as legality. In terms of control, Sinclair and Tinson explain that streaming allows listeners to feel empowered by the ability to control music, create content, project identity and even control mood and manage daily routines.

It could be said that music streaming has or will enable consumers with the tools required to satisfy their needs, as well as perhaps creating entirely new ones; playlists are now seemingly used to creatively for courtship (Lang,

2017). To this end, the long-term ramifications of the emergence of playlists (see Fenby-Hulse, 2016) as a dominant mode of listening are worthy of scholarly investigation. As of May 2016, playlists accounted for almost one third of total listening time; this is almost 1.5 times that of album listening (Savage, 2016). Having created playlists people feel as though effort has been exerted and so feel a sense of ownership (Pierce et al., 2003, cited in Sinclair & Tinson, 2017). Playlists are therefore likely to play a central role in the continued subscription to a particular streaming service. To switch between streaming services is to surrender all of the effort put in creating playlists Hagen (2015: 642) stated that, "The playlist represents what is unique to the individual in the context of a much larger, generic platform, and it demonstrates the persistence of the collector's uniqueness despite the circumstances".

It would appear that Spotify, in fact, encourages playlists as a dominant mode of listening with their 2016 yearend ad campaign providing a rundown of popular (and obscure) playlists listened to across the year (see Roberts, 2016). It also emphasised the social side of music listening by highlighting what other people have been listening to, with one billboard in UK reading: "Dear 3,749 people who streamed 'It's The End Of The World As We Know It' the day of UK's Brexit Vote. Hang in There." The campaign also underscored the application of big data, by sharing personal listening to wider audiences, anonymously. Musicians themselves have even started referring to albums as playlists (Petridis, 2017).

To return to the focal point of this book, Mulligan (2015) forecasted that streaming leads to 'shallower engagement' – that although more music is being listened to than ever before, people are not engaging with it in the same way. This, Mulligan argued, leads to more casual fan relationships, and will hit musicians in the live music sector with the future of live music being festivals and multiple act tours, resulting in artists receiving a smaller slice of revenues. Why spend, let's say, £30 to see a band when you literally only know and like three songs you have on a playlist for driving to work in the morning? At £10 per song, that's an expensive way to spend your disposable income – and in world in which people have less of it.

The ramifications of having unlimited access to music, literally at our fingertips, has widespread ramifications for society. Some are visible, others invisible. To hone in on one of the more visible outcomes, the live music sector provides a useful case study.

The changing relationship between the recorded and live music sector

It could be said that the ultimate outcome of the digital revolution, both from a cultural and commercial perspective, is the resulting changes in the live music sector. Increased access to recorded music, including via music piracy, appears to have boosted interest in the live music sector (Brown & Knox, 2016a).

The live music sector is thriving (Cloonan & Williamson, 2016), despite ticket prices having increased beyond the rate of inflation (Brennan &

Webster, 2010; Holt, 2010). Ticket prices rose by some 39% on average between 2001 and 2010 (Houghton, 2012), indicative of a continued willingness to pay for live concerts – even beyond the retail price. The 'true' cost of a ticket has risen due to the emerging market of ticket scalping, facilitated by technological advancements (Black, Fox, & Kochanowski, 2007). An entire secondary ticketing industry (reselling concert tickets, often at exuberantly marked up prices) thrives on music fans' willingness to pay to see their favourite artists, with the industry referring to the profits made via the secondary ticketing market as an example of the so-called 'value gap' (IFPI, 2016), wherein much of the money now made from music does not make its way back to content creators. And, Page (2013) finds an increase in music piracy immediately after music festivals. Live music cannot then be said as necessarily translating into recorded music sales, as would have been the case historically. Spotify has struck a deal with Ticketmaster, replacing previous partner Songkick – this has major implications for the live music sector, with plans to email subscribers with concert recommendations, etc. (Gumble, 2016).

What is it that makes live music performances so appealing? Unlike recorded music, live performances are scarce – this creates demand. The motivation to pay exuberant sums to attend concerts and festivals contrasts with an apparent reluctance to pay anything for recorded music, at least if working from estimations of engagement in music piracy.

Research demonstrates that live music attendance is motivated by aspects concerning the 'experience' (Brown & Knox, 2016a; Packer & Ballantyne, 2011); indeed, Holt (2010) argued that live concerts remain unique experiences, measurable in their atmosphere, performance, and social interaction. There is something about *being* there, experiencing events as they unfold with likeminded others, which appeals to concertgoers. Notably, there are so many things that could interfere with having a good time, and research finds that sound quality and volume, amongst the most variable, were ranked the most important factors which determined audience satisfaction (Minor et al., 2004). With recorded music, no such speculative risk exists – you get exactly what you pay for, every time.

There is no question that it now costs more to stage events, but, importantly, the escalating cost also appears to be related to music piracy trends. For instance, Gayer and Shy (2006) found that demand for live performances is reduced when music piracy is prevented, and an awareness of smaller artists as a result of music piracy has been observed (Fer & Baarsma, 2016; Mortimer, Nosko & Sorensen, 2012). Jones (2015: 29) argued that, "As we discover more ways to consume music digitally, music consumers seem to be craving music in the live form".

David (2016) explained that, "The most profound legacy of the copyright-infringing free sharing of music online has been in reinforcing the significance of live performance as a means for musicians to get paid" (p. 63). That the lasting outcome of music piracy has been to encourage live performances (David, 2016), is echoed by Tschmuck (2016) who further explained that income streams for musicians with a sizeable fan base now predominantly come from live performances. Whilst musicians can expect to make far more from live performances than from sales or streams of recorded music, musicians may not make as much as consumers might expect (Mulligan, 2015). Though Wikström (2011) optimistically noted that artists receive approximately 85% of the profits as compared to around 10% for recorded music, business practices vary considerably and it is unlikely most musicians earn anywhere near as much. Just 1% of musicians account for 77% of all recorded music revenue (Mulligan, 2014). It is these musicians, the 1%, who are, as they say, making a killing. Broadly speaking, though, musicians' earnings have dropped. This is likely due to music piracy (Mulligan, 2014), and the secondary ticketing market exemplifies the current iteration of the longstanding trend in the music industry of unscrupulous entrepreneurs making money off the back of musicians.

The rise of the secondary ticketing market is not trivial. Seemingly always under parliamentary investigation in UK, it has been identified as a key example of the so-called 'value gap' in the music industry by the International Federation of the Phonographic Industry (IFPI, 2016). In effect, musicians and rights holders are being denied money they are entitled to. Though, there is a case to be made that the secondary ticketing market is evidence of ticketing prices not being high enough – concertgoers, and especially those who have dedicated more of their lives going to concerts, and who recognise how expensive it can now be to see live music events, are likely to disagree. However, it has been argued that some bands such as Pearl Jam have not charged as much as they could for their concerts, with many artists typically not maximising the potential revenue of seat differentiation (Courty & Pagilero, 2014).

It is important to note that the so-called music industry is, in reality, a series of inter-related industries. As far back as 2007, Williamson and Cloonan noted that the recorded music industry is in fact but one of the *music industries* that struggles to adapt with the new business environment, as a result of the digital revolution. The rhetoric of discussing the 'music industry' is misleading, and Cloonan and Williamson (2016) explained that the recorded music sector is a mere blip on the timeline of 'music' which has predominantly been live. Recorded music now sells live music – not the other way around. This is a fundamental change in how musicians make a living, with the benefits ultimately passed onto the consumer as they now have more opportunity to see their favourite artists in the flesh. Changes such as this ought not to be ignored when evaluating the impact of music piracy on culture, especially when observing how the live music sector is, "No longer enjoying the economic boom period it experienced during the 2000s" (Brennan, 2015: 220). Accordingly, if musicians are aiming to counterbalance losses from recorded music (be it from music piracy or from free and paid-for streaming) then charging more for concert tickets might prove unsuccessful.

As a final word on live music, it is interesting that so-called ticket scalpers are generally found to be repulsive – they are only to be approached under desperate circumstances, and never to be thanked. Yet when engaging in music piracy, someone, somewhere, is profiting – and the profits can be substantial. And music piracy is not an activity reserved for desperate circumstances – music has never been cheaper at any point in history.

Predictive factors of engagement in music piracy: personality and individual differences

Young males have been routinely singled out as the most likely cohort to engage in music piracy (see Watson et al., 2015). However, it is important to review any concise summary of predictive factors with regard to relevant psychological theory. In terms of gender, some possible reasons put forward by research include how females have higher *risk perceptions* and a willingness to pay for legal alternatives (Chiang & Assane, 2008), and that males and females react differently to perceptions of punishment severity (Morton & Koufteros, 2008). Males are more easily influenced by peers online (Miller & Morris, 2016). Such findings provide insight into the different *decision-making* processes of males and females, and why females may be more likely to pay for music. Elsewhere, tech savviness has been found to be predictive of engagement in piracy (Shanahan & Hyman, 2010), with young males known to engage with new technologies out of interest more than do females (Cox & Collins, 2014). Dated research finds that women viewed men as more able to understand the Internet, with females holding more negative attitudes towards computers and the Internet (Wasserman & Richmond-Abbott, 2005). There is little doubt that navigating your way around the Internet is now much easier, but it is wholly possible that a technical element remains to play a role as music piracy practices continue to change in the face of legal shifts, demanding greater technological competence. Research finds that fear of viruses is a deterrent against music piracy (Bachmann, 2011; Sheehan, Tsao & Pokrywczynski, 2012) and the whack-a-mole exercise of finding content from the myriad services providing access to music poses legitimate threats.

Findings concerning gender conform to *stereotypes* and of course criminology reminds us that gender is the strongest predictor of criminality overall (Brown et al., 2007), so perhaps it is no stereotype at all. From a psychological perspective, males would be expected to be *less moral* (see Brown, 2013, for a review of morality). Other findings show that individuals favouring music piracy are *less fair* (Brown & MacDonald, 2014). Lau and Yuen (2014) found that males are more likely to participate in immoral activities online – including piracy. It is possible however that gender trends centre on risk perceptions (as noted above) rather than proclivity towards deviance; individuals engaging in music piracy hold an *optimism bias*, believing they are at a lower risk of being of being caught than other populations (Akbulut, 2014; Nandedkar & Midha, 2012). This demonstrates further insight into the decision-making processes involved in music piracy engagement, as well as the consistent findings from criminological research into self-control.

Impulsivity is typically over-represented in criminal populations (Brown, 2015) and this applies to music piracy. A wealth of criminological research finds low self-control to be predictive of digital piracy engagement (Higgins et al., 2012; Hinduja, 2012, and elsewhere in this book) and psychological research finds individuals favouring music piracy specifically to demonstrate low levels of *conscientiousness* (Brown & MacDonald, 2014; Brown & Krause, 2017), which incorporates aspects of self-discipline and is, therefore, cognate in many respects to self-control. The *theory of planned behaviour* model has been found to account for piracy, with the theory demonstrating how attitudes towards a behaviour, subjective norms, and perceived behavioural control together shape behavioural intentions (see Fleming et al., 2017, for a meta-analysis on the theory of planned behaviour and digital piracy). Higgins and Marcum (2011: 37) explained that, "Low self-control explains all forms of crime, as crime is behaviour that pursues one's own self-interest". Indeed, Schwarz (2014) found that most people download music without uploading, suggesting a self-serving approach to engagement in music piracy. And what do pirates have to gain? Much research finds the importance of *accessing content for free* (see e.g. Cox & Collins, 2014). Related findings demonstrate other so-called utilitarian motives including *convenience* (Argan et al., 2013; Kinnally et al., 2008; Wang & McClung, 2011). Such findings appear intuitive, but it may be that it is *poor value for money* which drives piracy – not simply wanting content for free (Brown, 2016; Brown & Knox, 2016b).

In terms of age, it is often cited that younger people are time-rich and cash-poor, whereas older populations are time-poor and cash-rich. Certainly, a negative relationship has been found between household income and digital piracy engagement (Chiang & Assane, 2009; Coyle et al., 2009) and on a larger scale low gross domestic product (GDP) and other financial indexes are often found to predict higher rates of piracy (Kigerl, 2013; Mostafa, 2011). Missing in this simple dichotomy, however, is that *young people simply listen to more music* (Bonneville-Roussy et al., 2013), and so would be more inclined to seek it out. This might extend to seeking out new releases in an effort to maintain diverse collections, enhancing *musical identities* amongst likeminded peers. Notably, *peer influence* has been found to be a predictor of engagement in piracy especially amongst young people (Shanahan & Hyman, 2010). Young people listen to music for a variety of reasons, many of which are beneficial in terms of *health and wellbeing*. Williamson (2013: 75) summarises that, "Through emotional support, memory prompts, self-assurance and social facilitation the music of this period becomes an integral part of our lives". This transitory period chapter is often thought to have not really existed at all until the rise of popular music in the 50s and 60s. That is, adolescence is *socially constructed*. Being young and listening to music go hand in hand (see Miranda et al., 2015) and this may now extend to accessing music illegally. Older populations tend to seek out the same music from when they were themselves young (Bonneville-Roussy et al., 2017) and are, therefore, less motivated to seek out new music.

We would like to assert how much psychology has to offer into learning what motivates music piracy, despite the fact that such little attention has been paid to the topic in the discipline. Though we have reviewed some key findings in this section, perhaps the most transparent application of psychology in our collective understanding of music piracy can be found in Brown's (2017) review of the myths surrounding music piracy, generously highlighting the overlaps between psychology and criminology, in particular with its reliance on *criminological rationalisation theory*. The work highlights how it is possible for people with different points of view on music piracy (being for or against it, and in both instances for various reasons) to reach opposite conclusions, based on the same information. It also asserts the social element of music piracy (Brown, 2014).

The online world is not the same as the offline world, with the sense of *anonymity* afforded online can free people from the typical social norms in the real, offline world, reducing personal disinhibitions (Hinduja, 2008; Joinson, 2007; Suler, 2004). Anonymity is one of at least four factors that set the online world apart from the offline world (the other three include the reduced importance of appearance, greater control and pace of interactions, and the ease with which we can find similar others – McKenna et al., 2002). Many of these clearly apply to music piracy and accordingly, the emerging sub-discipline of *cyberpsychology* is well-positioned to expand our understanding of music piracy and indeed other cybercrimes. Returning to age, Attrill (2015) explains that the Internet is not exclusively used by young people, but that younger and older populations use the Internet to meet specific goals, needs, and motivations.

Why choose one format over another?

It has long been assumed amongst industry bodies that so-called music pirates are only interested in obtaining music illegally – that they are thieves who want music for free. Yet, a substantial volume of research suggests that those who engage in music piracy not only pay for music legally, but spend *more money* on music legally than those who do not engage in music piracy (see Huygen et al., 2009; Karaganis & Renkema, 2013; Thun, 2009; Watson et al., 2015; and Zentner, 2006). One suggestion that may account for this is that music piracy helps consumers make more informed choices about which music to seek out legally (Peitz & Waelbroeck, 2006). Certainly, participants in empirical studies make the case that this is what drives their engagement in music piracy (Brown, 2015), and with those engaging in music piracy also buying music legally, it is clear that at the very least a substitution effect is not taking place.

Those same individuals engaging in music piracy also engage in other practices to listen to or access music. In industry terms, this is known as *multi-channelling*, or simply mixing and matching between different music formats. Despite the apparent 'advantages' of digital music, both from the perspective of consumers (such as storage utility – Kinnally et al., 2008) and from industry (such as mass access to music at low cost – Curien & Moreau, 2009), most people still possess a physical music collection and actively listen to digital collections (Liikanen & Åman, 2016). Music listening now occurs across a range of delivery modes, with consumers empowered by the choice available in which to seek out and listen to music. But what is it that makes one format more appealing than other?

Uses and gratifications theory (Katz et al. 1973; Katz et al. 1974) is a framework used to study how people select and use new media (Rayburn & Palmgreen 1984; Ruggiero 2000; Stafford et al. 2004). According to the theory, people distinguish between types of media based on the *needs* they aim to satisfy as a result of media use (Katz et al. 1973), with media use considered goal-directed – that people are aware of their needs, and that people actively seek and use media. Thus, the theory views needs as, "The combined product of psychological dispositions, sociological factors, and environmental conditions" (Katz et al., 1973: 516–517) and gratifications, in turn, are the perceived fulfilment of needs as a result of a particular activity, including media use (Rayburn & Palmgreen 1984). Previously, this theory has been applied to the consideration of everyday music behaviours (e.g., reasons for listening to music – Lonsdale & North, 2011; reasons for using Facebook music listening applications – Krause, North, & Heritage, 2014). Accordingly, the theory is appropriate for researching why consumers choose one format over another, encompassing music piracy.

Sang et al. (2015) found that engagement in music piracy is predicted by utilitarian motives relating to cost and availability. Other studies considering music piracy, and digital music more broadly, identify gratifications including convenience (Argan et al., 2013; Wang & McClung, 2011) and collection utility (Sheehan et al., 2012), as well as the ability to sample new content ahead of release (Cox & Collins, 2014). Sheehan, Tsao and Yang (2010) also found that social utility (ability to increase social connections and peer inter-action) was the most important reason for engaging in music piracy, followed by collection utility and economic utility; that is, financial motives were not as important as the ability to share songs with friends, seeing what they have in their collection, and the sheer volume of music available via illegal services, corroborated by Schwarz and Larsson (2013). In what Watson et al. (2015) refer to as 'experiential utility', digital piracy (more broadly) is noted as influenced by a desire to sample new content, access niche content, or build collections. Elsewhere, Mäntymäki and Islam (2015) find that enjoyment is the main reason for continuing to use Spotify, with premium users perceiving higher levels enjoyment; discovery of new music was the strongest predictor for continuing to use premium services.

Brown and Krause (2016) recently conducted research aimed at under-standing why people might prefer and choose to listen to music using one format rather than another, electing to consider six predominant music formats: physical (i.e., CD, vinyl, cassette), digital file (i.e., MP3), free streaming, paid-for streaming, radio, and live music. As expected, differences with regard to age were found: in particular, being older was associated with preferring physical formats and the radio, whereas being younger was associated with digital formats, including free and paid-for streaming services. Importantly, however, beyond age, findings also demonstrated that music engagement was related to different format usage. Listening to more hours of music on average daily was positively associated with paid-for streaming and live music formats.

Further, Brown and Krause (2016) explored the uses and gratifications people experience in conjunction to their nominated format used most often to listen to music. An exploratory principal axis factor analysis identified eight uses and gratifications: usability and intention to use, discovery, functional utility, flexibility, connection, social norms, value for money, and playback diversity. Linking preferred format usage and music piracy attitudes, individuals using digital files and paid-for streaming services were significantly more likely to endorse positive piracy attitudes than those using physical formats. Moreover, users of free streaming services were significantly more likely to endorse more favourable piracy attitudes than users of physical formats, digital files, and the radio (Brown & Krause, 2017). Moreover, when considering how the uses and gratifications associated with music listening formats mapped onto piracy attitudes, value for money was positively associated with more favourable piracy attitudes. Value for money has been argued elsewhere as independent from simply wanting something for free (Brown & Knox, 2016b), and perceptions of value are likely to take into account a variety of utilitarian factors such as those mentioned above. Further research employing Uses and gratifications theory (Katz et al., 1973; Katz et al., 1974) may be able to unpack exactly which ones. Certainly, with those engaging in music piracy also paying for music legally, it is clear that the driver is not simply about substituting paid music with unpaid music.

Therefore, it is clear that music listening, including music piracy, is not simply about getting music for free. By utilising Uses and gratifications theory terminology (Katz et al. 1973; Katz et al. 1974), the relative pros and cons of different music formats come into focus. And the more legal services incorporate the pros of illegal services, the more likely they will appeal to music listeners. As mentioned earlier, recent research by Sinclair and Tinson (2017) found that a dominant feature of music streaming services is, in fact, an *enhanced sense of psychological ownership*, encouraged principally by the control it offers users, leading to long-term loyalty. Elsewhere, it has been proposed that those technologies which provide opportunities for control are likely to experience enhanced feelings of psychological ownership (Kirk et al., 2015). In summary, streaming appears to be here to stay – they capture feelings of ownership without the burden of ownership. As Sun (2016) explains, in her interviews with Spotify staff, Spotify provides an easy alternative to music piracy by eliminating the need for downloading altogether.

Discussion

Operating from a social psychological perspective, this chapter considered music piracy within the context of broader musical engagement. Centrally, the psychological research discussed concerning the personality and individual differences of those engaging in music piracy aides the broader understanding of consistent findings into demographics, wherein young people, and typically young males, are found to be principally engaged in music piracy. However, the contributions of other disciplines cited in this chapter provide a more in-depth overview of music piracy. Importantly, this chapter has asserted the importance of taking into consideration *why* people listen to music. While this point of view is immediately obvious to the authors as social psychologists, it appears all-but-absent in the broader scholarship concerning music piracy. By understanding why people listen to music as a foundation, more can be understood about why people do or do not choose to pay for music. Further, by contextualising music piracy practices within the larger set of music engagement practices and preferences, the chapter makes three key contributions to the scholarship into music piracy.

First, by drawing on the literature from music psychology and consumer psychology more broadly, the authors highlight one perspective that proposes that people engage in music piracy because music satisfies particular needs. Compounded with the convenience offered by digital services, both legal and illegal, it has been suggested that music is now relied upon as a sort of resource, and that access to music has become as much of a need as it is a want. Drawing predominantly from recent findings by Sinclair and Tinson (2017), it appears that legal streaming services may be able to satisfy consumer's needs and even lead to a sense of ownership over their so-called music 'collections'. Industry data such as that from IFPI (2017) indeed confirms the shift towards streaming over downloading overall, and signposts the likely future of music listening in a digital age.

Second, this chapter has highlighted the broader industry ramifications of music piracy by giving due attention to the live music sector – it has been suggested that the decline in revenues from recorded music have forced the industry to shift towards live music events, with rising costs for tickets attributable to losses from music piracy. Consumers reeling from the expense of concert tickets ought to reflect on how much money they have saved from engaging in music piracy over the years – the majority of them will be 'up', remaining there indefinitely.

Third, the most prominent contribution of this chapter is the consideration of the industry concern of so-called 'multi-channelling', including presenting initial quantitative research by the authors. Using established psychological instruments and approaches, the quantitative research confirmed the role of value for money in accounting for engagement in music piracy. This was reasoned as different from simply getting music for free. More importantly, the findings define relationships between music piracy and other, legal modes of listening – those endorsing music piracy, with positive attitudes known to be predictors of engagement, were more likely to use legal streaming services and download digital music files legally. This complicates the *common sense* notion that legal services will appease the preferences of those who engage in music piracy, converting them to legal alternatives, instead suggesting that different music formats satisfy different needs. Thus, it is not a case of choosing between one format or another; it is about mixing and matching between different preferences under different circumstances. More research is needed to better understand the dynamics at play, but one need only look to the ubiquity of *e-readers*, which have not eliminated physical book sales, to gain an initial impression of what is going on. An e-reader is perhaps convenient for all sorts of reasons: it is small; environmentally friendly; and means that people don't need to see what sort of trash you are reading when they come to your house. A hardback book is none of those things, but it does not mean you would not buy one. Again, a uses and gratifications approach (Katz et al., 1973; Katz et al., 1974) that has been highlighted in this chapter is appropriate to develop specific research questions to explore to gain a fuller understanding of how consumers now listen to, engage, and enjoy music – given the wealth of options available to them.

In terms of future directions, the implications of having unlimited and immediate access to music is an enticing research question, and one that the authors aim to explore. For instance, the omnipresence of playlist culture is worthy of scholarly investigation. Critically, playlist culture may change music listening practices in ways that no one could have anticipated. Specifically, the rise of playlists has signalled a shift in the consumption of albums, calling into question the relevance of the format from the perspective of the consumer. By mixing and matching songs, playlists allow consumers to take control over their listening. This control allows listeners to shape their listening in terms of accompanying activities and broader situational contexts. Indeed, recent research highlights that playlist preferences are influenced by situational factors (Krause & North, 2014) and even macro-level influences including the time of year (Krause & North, 2017). Further, playlists give listeners more control regarding their moods – with emotional regulation noted previously as a major driver behind music listening overall. Accordingly, a surprising legacy of music piracy then, by influencing subscription services which allow unrivalled control over what is heard, might be that it has cultivated a scenario wherein people are able to utilise music as a resource for the purposes of aiding health and wellbeing. To this end, future social psychological research is well placed to consider the full capacity of music as a public health intervention.

Returning to the focus of this chapter, the scholarly community conducting research into digital piracy overall has benefited greatly from two meta-analyses published in early 2017 (Fleming, Watson, Patouris, Bartholomew & Zizzo, 2017; Lowry, Zhang & Wu, 2017). However, the fact remains that the research to date in this area is not of the highest quality. Lowry, Zhang and

Wu explained that many studies in their meta-analysis did not contain standard correlation tables, averages, and standard deviations – and that when authors were approached for such outputs, many refused or noted it was unavailable. In the closing chapter of this book, Brown and Holt explain that with qualitative research it is typical for little detail to be provided on coding: comparable to not responding standard deviation. Such practices do little to boost the credibility to a body of work marked by scepticism, given the controversial nature of the topic itself. Future research then must adhere to higher standards, if research is to be taken seriously.

Psychology has contributed much to our collective understanding of digital piracy as a whole. In their recent scoping review, Watson, Zizzo and Fleming (2015) found that around one third of studies in their scoping review used psychological models. Looking ahead, the authors hope that the emerging sub-discipline of cyberpsychology will further understanding of music-listening practices in digital environments. In 2017, the British Psychological Society established a new Cyberpsychology section. Research that operates from a social psychological perspective while acknowledging human behaviour in online environments will enable the development of research questions which better account for the popularity of this ubiquitous cybercrime.

References

Akbulut, Y. (2014) 'Exploration of the antecedents of digital piracy through a structural equation model', *Computers & Education*, 78: 294–305.

Anderson, T.J. (2014) *Popular Music in a Digital Music Economy: Problems and Practices for an Emerging Service Industry*, New York: Routledge.

Argan, M.T., Argan, M., Ozer, A. and Kose, H. (2013) 'A study of motivational factors associated with peer-to-peer (P2P) file-sharing', *Procedia – Social and Behavioral Sciences*, 99: 180–188.

Attrill, A. (2015) 'Age verses goal-directed internet use', in: A. Attrill (ed.), *Cyberpsychology*, Oxford: Oxford University Press.

Avdeeff, M. (2012) 'Technological engagement and musical eclecticism: An examination of contemporary listening practices', *Participations: Journal of Audience & Reception Studies*, 9: 265–285.

Bachmann, M. (2011) 'Suing the genie in the bottle: The failed RIAA strategy to deter P2P network users', in: K. Jaishankar (ed.) *Cyber Criminology: Exploring Internet Crimes and Criminal Behavior*, Boca Raton, FL: CRC Press.

Black, G.C., Fox, M.A. and Kochanowski, P. (2007) 'Concert tour success in North America: An examination of the top 100 tours from 1997 to 2005', *Popular Music and Society*, 30(2): 149–172.

Bonneville-Roussy, A., Rentfrow, P.J., Xu, M.K. and Potter, J. (2013) 'Music through the ages: Trends in musical engagement and preferences from adolescence through middle adulthood', *Journal of Personality and Social Psychology*, 105(4): 703–717.

Bonneville-Roussy, A., Stillwell, D., Kosinski, M. and Rust, J. (2017) 'Age trends in musical preferences in adulthood: 1. Conceptualization and empirical investigation'. *Musicae Scientiae*, advanced online publication.

Brennan, M. (2015) 'Live music history' in: A. Bennett and S. Waksman, (eds), *The SAGE Handbook of Popular Music*, London: Sage.

Brennan, M. and Webster, E. (2010) *The UK Festival Market Report*, London: UK Festival Awards.

Brown, S.C. (2013) 'Digital piracy and the moral compass', *The Psychologist*, 26(7): 538–539.

Brown, S.C. (2014) 'Approaches to digital piracy research: A call for innovation, *Convergence*, 20(2): 129–139.

Brown, S.C. (2015) *The Psychology of Music Piracy*, PhD thesis, Glasgow Caledonian University. Available from Ethos [Accessed 27 July 2017].

Brown, S.C. (2016) 'Where do beliefs about music piracy come from and how are they shared?', *International Journal of Cyber Criminology*, 10(1): 21–39.

Brown, S.C. (2017) 'Myths about musicians and music piracy', *The Skeptic*, 26(3): 12–15.

Brown, S.C. and Knox, D. (2016a) 'Why go to pop concerts? The motivations behind live music attendance' *Musicae Scientiae*, advanced online publication.

Brown, S.C. and Knox, D. (2016b) 'Why buy an album? The motivations behind recorded music purchases', *Psychomusicology: Music, Mind, and Brain*, 26(1): 79–86.

Brown, S.C. and Krause, A.E. (2016) 'A psychological approach to understanding the varied functions that different music formats serve' paper presented at 14th International Conference on Music Perception and Cognition, San Francisco, CA, July.

Brown, S.C. and Krause, A.E. (2017). Psychological predictors of engagement in music piracy. *Creative Industries Journal*, 10(3): 226–237. DOI:10.1080/17510694.2017.1373884

Brown, S.C. and MacDonald, R.A.R. (2014) 'Predictive factors of music piracy: An exploration of personality using the HEXACO PI-R', *Musicae Scientiae*, 18(1): 53–64.

Brown, S.E., Esbensen, F.-A. and Geis, G. (2007) '*Criminology: Explaining Crime and Its Context*', 6th edition, Newark, NJ: Lexis Nexis.

Bylin, K. (2014) '*Promised Land: Youth Culture, Disruptive Startups, and the Social Music Revolution*', Leanpub (digital).

Chamorro-Premuzic, T. and Furnham, A. (2007) 'Personality and music: Can traits explain how people use music in everyday life?', *British Journal of Psychology*, 98: 175–185.

Chanda, M. and Levitin, D.J. (2013) 'The neurochemistry of music', *Trends in Cognitive Science*, 17: 179–193.

Chiang, E.P. and Assane, D. (2008) 'Music piracy among students on the university campus: Do males and females react differently?', *The Journal of Socio-Economics*, 37(4): 1371–1380.

Chiang, E.P. and Assane, D. (2009). Estimating the willingness to pay for digital music. *Contemporary Economic Policy*, 27(4): 512–522.

Cook, N. (1998) *Music: A Very Short Introduction*, Oxford: Oxford University Press.

Cloonan, M. and Williamson, J. (2016) 'Crisis what crisis? The music industries, hype, technology and research', paper presented at Marketing and Music in an Age of Digital Reproduction Symposium, Stirling, Scotland, November.

Courty, P. and Pagilero, M. (2014) 'The pricing of art and the art of pricing: Pricing styles in the concert industry', in: V.A. Ginsburgh and D. Trosby (eds), *Handbook of the Economics of Art and Culture* (Vol. 2), Oxford: North-Holland.

Cox, J. and Collins, A. (2014) 'Sailing in the same ship? Differences in factors motivating piracy of music and movie content', *Journal of Behavioral and Experimental Economics*, 50: 70–76.

Coyle, J.R., Gould, S.J., Gupta, P. and Gupta, R. (2009) '"To buy or to pirate": The matrix of music consumers' acquisition-mode decision-making', *Journal of Business Research*, 62(10): 1031–1037.

Curien, N. and Moreau, F. (2009) 'The music industry in the digital era: Toward new contracts', *Journal of Media Economics*, 22(2): 102–113.

David, M. (2016) 'The legacy of Napster', in: R. Nowak and A. Whelan (eds), *Networked Music Cultures: Contemporary Approaches, Emerging Issues*, London: Palgrave Macmillan.

DeNora, T. (2000) *Music in Everyday Life*, Cambridge: Cambridge University Press.

DeNora, T. (2010) 'Emotion as social emergence: Perspectives from music sociology', in: P.N. Juslin and J.A. Sloboda (eds) *Handbook of Music and Emotion: Theory, Research, Applications*, Oxford: Oxford University Press

Dobelli, R. (2013) *The Art of Thinking Clearly*, London: Hodder & Stoughton.

Ebare, S. (2004) *Digital Music and Subculture: Sharing Files, Sharing Styles*. Online. Available: http://firstmonday.org/ojs/index.php/fm/article/view/1122/1042 [Accessed 30 July 2017].

Fenby-Hulse, K. (2016) 'Rethinking the digital playlist: Mixtapes, nostalgia and emotionally durable design', in: R. Nowak and A. Whelan (eds), *Networked Music Cultures: Contemporary Approaches, Emerging Issues*, London: Palgrave Macmillan.

Fer, A. and Baarsma, B. (2016) 'Rockonomics revisited: The rise of music streaming services and the effect on the concert industry', *International Journal of Music Business Research*, 5(1): 6–35.

Ferwerda, B., Yang, E., Schedl, M., Tklacic, M. (2015) 'Personality Traits Predict Music Taxonomy Preferences', paper presented at 33rd Annual ACM Conference on Human Factors in Computing Systems, Seoul, Republic of Korea, April.

Fleming, P., Watson, S.J., Patouris, E., Bartholomew, K.J. and Zizzo, D.J. (2017) 'Why do people file share unlawfully? A systematic review, meta-analysis and panel study', *Computers in Human Behavior*, 72: 535–548.

Gaunt, H. and Hallam, S. (2009) 'Individuality in the learning of musical skills', in: S. Hallam, I. Cross, and M. Thaut (eds) *The Oxford Handbook of Music Psychology*, Oxford: Oxford University Press.

Gayer, A. and Shy, O. (2006) 'Publishers, artists, and copyright enforcement', *Information Economics and Policy*, 18(4): 374–384.

Greasley, A.E., Lamont, A. and Sloboda, J.A. (2013) 'Exploring musical preferences: An in-depth qualitative study of adults' liking for music in their personal collections', *Qualitative Research in Psychology*, 10: 402–427.

Greenberg, D.M., Kosinksi, M., Stillwell, D.J., Montiero, B.L., Levitin, D.J. and Rentfrow, P.J. (2016) 'The song is you: preferences for musical attribute dimensions reflect personality', *Social Psychological and Personality Science*, 7(6): 597–605.

Guardian Music. (2014) 'One-quarter of Spotify tracks are skipped in first five seconds, study reveals.' Online: www.theguardian.com/music/2014/may/07/one-quarter-of-spotify-tracks-are-skipped-in-first-five-seconds-study-reveals [Accessed 31 July 2017].

Gumble, D. (2016) 'Spotify loosens ties with Songkick to make way for Ticketmaster.' Online: www.musicweek.com/live/read/spotify-loosens-ties-with-songkick-to-make-way-for-ticketmaster/066591 [Accessed 30 July 2017].

Hagen, A.N. (2015) 'The playlist experience: Personal playlists in music streaming services', *Popular Music and Society*, 38(5): 625–645.

Hagen, A.N. and Lüders, M. (2016) 'Social streaming? Navigating music as personal and social', *Convergence*, 1–17.

Hallam, S., Cross, I. and Thaut, M. (2016) *Oxford Handbook of Music Psychology*, 2nd edition, Oxford: Oxford University Press.

Hargreaves, D.J., Miell, D. and Macdonald, R.A.R. (2002) 'What are musical identities, and why are they important?', in: R.A.R. Macdonald, D.J. Hargraves, and D. Miell (eds) *Musical identities*, Oxford: Oxford University Press.

Hargreaves, D.J. and North, A.C. (2010) 'Experimental aesthetics and liking for music', in: P.N. Juslin, and J.A. Sloboda (eds) *Handbook of Music and Emotion: Theory, Research, Applications*, Oxford: Oxford University Press.

Heye, A. and Lamont, A. (2010) 'Mobile listening situations in everyday life: The use of MP3 players while travelling', *Musicae Scientiae*, 14: 95–120.

Higgins, G.E. and Marcum, C.D. (2011) *'Digital Piracy: An Integrated Theoretical Approach'*, Durham, NC: Carolina Academic Press.

Higgins, G.E., Marcum, C.D., Freiburger, T.L. and Ricketts, M. (2012) 'Examining the role of peer influence and self-control on downloading behavior', *Deviant Behavior*, 33(5): 412–423.

Hinduja, S. (2008) 'Deindividuation and internet software piracy', *CyberPsychology and Behavior*, 11(4): 391–398.

Hinduja, S. (2012). 'General strain, self-control, and music piracy', *International Journal of Cyber Criminology*, 6(1): 951–967.

Holt, A. (2010) 'The economy of live music in the digital age', *European Journal of Cultural Studies*, 13(2): 243–261.

Houghton, B. (2012). 'Are 360 Deals A Lifeline For The Music Industry?' Online: www.hypebot.com/hypebot/2012/03/are-360-deals-a-lifeline-for-the-music-industry-infographic.html [Accessed 30 July 2017].

Huygen, A., Rutten, P., Huveneers, S., Limonard, S., Poort, J., Leenheer, J., Janssen, K., van Eijk, N. and Helberger, N. (2009) 'Ups and downs: Economic and cultural effects of files sharing on music, film and games'. Online: http://papers.ssrn.com/sol3/papers.cfm?abstract_id=1350451 accessed 27 July 2017.

International Federation of the Phonographic Industry (2016) *Global Music Report: Music Consumption Exploding Worldwide*. Online: www.ifpi.org/downloads/GMR2016.pdf [Accessed 31 July 2017].

International Federation of the Phonographic Industry (2017) *Global Music Report 2017*. Online: www.ifpi.org/recording-industry-in-numbers.php [Accessed 29 July 2017].

Joinson, A.N. (2007) 'Disinhibition and the internet', in: J. Gackenbach (ed.), *Psychology and the Internet: Intrapersonal, interpersonal and transpersonal implications*, 2nd edition, San Diego, CA: Elsevier Academic Press.

Jones, A. (2015) 'What's my scene: festival fandom and the application of the Big Day Out Stage', in: A. Jones, J. Bennett and R.J. Bennett (eds), *The Digital Evolution of Live Music*, Oxford: Chandos Publishing.

Juslin, P.N. (2009) 'Emotional responses to music', in: S. Hallam, I. Cross, and M. Thaut (eds) *The Oxford Handbook of Music Psychology*, Oxford: Oxford University Press.

Juslin, P. N., Liljeström, S., Västfjäll, D., Barradas, G. and Silva, A. (2008) 'An experience sampling study of emotional reactions to music: Listener, music, and situation', *Emotion*, 8: 668.

Juslin, P.N. and Sloboda, J. (2013) 'Music and emotion', in D. Deutsch (ed.), *The Psychology of Music*, London: Academic Press.

Karaganis, J. and Renkema, L. (2013) *Copy Culture in the US and Germany*, New York: The American Assembly.

Katz, E., Blumler, J.G., and Gurevitch, M. (1974) 'Utilization of Mass Communication by the Individual', in: J.G. Blumler and E. Katz (eds) *The Uses of Mass Communications: Current Perspectives on Gratifications Research*, Beverly Hills, CA: Sage.

Katz, E., Haas, H., and Gurevitch, M. (1973) 'On the use of the mass media for important things', *American Sociological Review*, 38(2): 164–181.

Kibby, M. (2009) 'Collect yourself: Negotiating personal archives', *Information, Communication, & Society*, 12: 428–443.

Kigerl, A.C. (2013) 'Infringing nations: Predicting software piracy rates, BitTorrent tracker hosting, and P2P file sharing client downloads between countries', *International Journal of Cyber Criminology*, 7(1): 62–80.

Kinnally, W., Lacayo, A., McClung, S. and Sapolsky, B. (2008) 'Getting up on the download: College students' motivations for acquiring music via the web', *New Media and Society*, 10(6): 893–913.

Kirk, C.P., Swain, S.D. and Gaskin, J.E. (2015) 'I'm proud of it: Consumer technology appropriation and psychological ownership', *Journal of Marketing Theory and Practice*, 23(2): 166–184.

Konečni, V. (1982) 'Social interaction and music preference', in: D. Deutsch (ed.) *The Psychology of Music*, New York: Academic Press.

Krause, A.E. and Hargreaves, D.J. (2013) 'myTunes: Digital music library users and their self images', *Psychology of Music*, 41: 531–544.

Krause, A.E. and North, A.C. (2014) 'Contextualized music listening: Playlists and the Mehrabian and Russell model', *Psychology of Well-Being: Theory Research and Practice*, 4, article 22.

Krause, A.E. and North, A.C. (2017) ''Tis the season: Music playlist preferences for the seasons', *Psychology of Aesthetics, Creativity, and the Arts*, 12(1): 89–95.

Krause, A.E., North, A.C. and Heritage, B. (2014) 'The uses and gratifications of using Facebook music listening applications', *Computers in Human Behavior*, 39: 71–77.

Krause, A.E., North, A.C. and Hewitt, L.Y. (2015) 'Music-listening in everyday life: Devices and choice', *Psychology of Music*, 43: 155–170.

Lamont, A. and Greasley, A.E. (2009) 'Musical preferences', in: S. Hallam, I. Cross, and M. Thaut (eds) *The Oxford Handbook of Music Psychology*, Oxford: Oxford University Press.

Lang, C. (2017) 'Resourceful girl broke up with a guy with a Spotify playlist.' Online: http://time.com/4732898/girl-breakup-song-playlist/ [Accessed 27 July 2017].

Lau, W.W.F. and Yuen, A.H.K. (2014) 'Internet ethics of adolescents: Understanding demographic differences', *Computers and Education*, 72: 378–385.

Levinson, J. (2014) 'Values of music', in: V.A. Ginsburgh and D. Trosby (eds), *Handbook of the Economics of Art and Culture* (Vol. 2), Oxford: North-Holland.

Liikanen, L.A. and Åman, P. (2016) 'Shuffling services: Current trends in interacting with digital music', *Interacting With Computers*, 28(3): 352–371.

Lonsdale, A.J. and North, A.C. (2011) 'Why do we listen to music? A uses and gratifications analysis', *British Journal of Psychology*, 102: 108–134.

Lowry, P.B., Zhang, J. and Wu, T. (2017) 'Nature or nurture? A meta-analysis of the factors that maximize the prediction of digital piracy by using social cognitive theory as a framework', *Computers in Human Behavior*, 68: 104–120.

Luck, G. (2016) 'The psychology of streaming: exploring music listeners' motivations to favour access over ownership', *International Journal of Music Business Research*, 5(2): 46–60.

MacDonald, R.A.R., Kreutz, G. and Mitchell, L.A. (2012) 'What is music, health, and wellbeing and why is it important?', in: R.A.R. MacDonald, G. Kreutz, and L.A. Mitchell (eds) *Music, Health, and Wellbeing*, Oxford: Oxford University Press.

Mäntymäki, M., and Islam, A.K.M.N. (2015) 'Gratifications from using freemium music streaming services: Differences between basic and premium users', paper presented at Thirty-Sixth International Conference on Information Systems, Ft Worth, Texas, December.

McKenna, K.Y.A., Green, A.S. and Gleeson, M.J. (2002) 'Relationship formation on the Internet: What's the big attraction?', *Journal of Social Issues*, 58: 9–32.

Miller, B. and Morris, R.G. (2016) 'Virtual peer effects in social learning theory', *Crime and Delinquency*, 62(12): 1543–1569.

Minor, M.S., Tillmann W., Brewerton, F.J. and Hausman, A. (2004) 'Rock on! An elementary model of customer satisfaction with musical performances', *Journal of Services Marketing*, 18: 7–18.

Miranda, D., Blais-Rochette, C., Vaugon, K.Osman, M. and Arias-Valenzuela, M. (2015) 'Towards a cultural-developmental psychology of music in adolescence', *Psychology of Music*, 43(2): 197–218.

Molteni, L. and Ordanini, A. (2003) 'Consumption patterns, digital technology and music downloading', *Long Range Planning*, 36: 389–406.

Mortimer, J., Nosko, C. and Sorensen, A. (2012) 'Supply responses to digital distribution: Recorded music and live performances', *Information Economics and Policy*, 24(1): 3–14.

Morton, N.A. and Koufteros, X. (2008) 'Intention to commit online music piracy and its antecedents: An empirical investigation', *Structural Equation Modelling: A Multi-disciplinary Journal*, 15(3): 419–512.

Mostafa, M.M. (2011) 'A neuro-computational intelligence analysis of the global software piracy rates', *Expert Systems with Applications: An International Journal*, 38(7): 8782–8803.

Mulligan, M. (2014) 'The death of the long tail.' Online: https://musicindustryblog. wordpress.com/2014/03/04/the-death-of-the-long-tail [Accessed 29 July, 2017].

Mulligan, M. (2015). 'On demand in demand.' Online. https://musicindustryblog. wordpress.com/2015/06/05/on-demand-in-demand/ [Accessed 29 July 2017].

Mulligan, M. (2015) 'Awakening: The music industry in the digital age.' CreateSpace Independent Publishing Platform.

Nandedkar, A. and Midha, V. (2012) 'It won't happen to me: An assessment of optimism bias in music piracy', *Computers in Human Behavior*, 28(1): 41–48.

Nill, A. and Geipel, A. (2010) 'Sharing and owning of musical works: Copyright protection from a societal perspective', *Journal of Macromarketing*, 30: 33–49.

North, A.C. and Hargreaves, D.J. (2008) *The Social and Applied Psychology of Music*, Oxford: Oxford University Press.

North, A.C., Hargreaves, D.J. and Hargreaves, J.J. (2004) 'Uses of music in everyday life', *Music Perception*, 22: 41–77.

O'Hara, K. and Brown, B. (2006) 'Consuming music together: Introduction and overview', in: K. O'Hara and B. Brown, (eds) *Consuming Music Together: Social and Collaborative Aspects of Music Consumption Technologies*, Dordrecht: Springer.

Packer, J. and Ballantyne, J. (2011) 'The impact of music festival attendance on young people's psychological and social well-being', *Psychology of Music*, 39: 164–181.

Page, W. (2013) 'Adventures in the Netherlands: Spotify, piracy and the new Dutch experience.' Online. https://press.spotify.com/uk/2013/07/17/adventures-in-netherlands.

Peitz, M. and Waelbroeck, P. (2006) 'Why the music industry may gain from free downloading – The role of sampling', *International Journal of Industrial Organisation*, 24(5): 907–913.

Petridis, A. (2017) 'What is Drake's More Life: A mixtape, an album or a playlist?' Online. www.theguardian.com/music/shortcuts/2017/mar/20/drake-more-life-mixtape-album-playlist-soundtrack [Accessed 30 July 2017].

Pierce, J.L., Kostova, T. and Dirks, K.Y. (2003) 'The state of psychological ownership: Integrating and extending a century of research', *Review of General Psychology*, 7(1): 84–107.

Powell, J. (2016) *Why We Love Music*, London: John Murray.

Rayburn, J.D., and Palmgreen, P. (1984) 'Merging uses and gratifications and expectancy- value theory', *Communication Research*, 11(4): 537–562.

Roberts, H. (2016) 'Spotify says: "Thanks 2016, it's been weird," in its largest ad campaign yet.' Online: http://uk.businessinsider.com/spotify-global-ad- campaign-signing-off-2016-2016-11?r=US&IR=T [Accessed 27 July 2017].

Ruggiero, T.E. (2000) 'Uses and gratifications theory in the 21st century', *Mass Communication & Society*, 3(1): 3–37.

Saarikallio, S. (2012) 'Cross-cultural approaches to music and health', in: R. MacDonald, G. Kreutz, and L. Mitchell (eds), *Music, Health, and Wellbeing*, Oxford: Oxford University Press.

Saarikallio, S. and Erkkilä, J. (2007) 'The role of music in adolescents' mood regulation', *Psychology of Music*, 35(1): 88–109.

Sang, Y., Lee, J.-K., Kim, Y. and Woo, H.-J. (2015) 'Understanding the intentions behind illegal downloading: A comparative study of American and Korean college students', *Telematics and Informatics*, 32: 333–343.

Savage, M. (2016) 'Playlists "more popular than albums".' Online. www.bbc.com/news/entertainment-arts-37444038 [Accessed 30 July 2017].

Schäfer, T., Sedlmeier, P., Städtler, C. and Huron, D. (2013) 'The psychological functions of music listening', *Frontiers in Psychology*, 4: 511.

Scharf, N.F. (2013) *Digital Copyright Law: Exploring the Changing Interface Between Copyright and Regulation in the Digital Environment*, PhD thesis, The University of East Anglia. Available from Ethos [Accessed 27 July 2017].

Schwarz, J.A. (2014) *Online File Sharing: Innovations in Media Consumption*, New York: Routledge.

Schwarz, J.A. and Larsson, S. (2014) 'Justifications of piracy: Differences in conceptualization and argumentation between active uploaders and other file-sharers', in: F. Martin and A. James (eds) *Piracy: Leakages from Modernity*, Sacramento, CA: Litwin Books.

Shanahan K.J. and Hyman, M.R. (2010) 'Motivators and enablers of SCOURing: A study of online piracy in the US and UK', *Journal of Business Research*, 63(9–10): 1095–1102.

Sheehan, B., Tsao, J. and Yang, S. (2010). Motivations for gratifications of digital music piracy among college students. *Atlantic Journal of Communication*, 18(5), 241–258.

Sheehan B., Tsao, J. and Pokrywczynski, J. (2012) 'Stop the music! How advertising can help stop college students from downloading music illegally', *Journal of Advertising Research*, 52(3): 309–321.

Sinclair, G. and Tinson, J. (2017) 'Psychological ownership and music streaming consumption', *Journal of Business Research*, 71: 1–9.

Sloboda, J.A. (2010) 'Music in everyday life: The role of emotions', in: P.N. Juslin and J.A. Sloboda (eds), *Handbook of Music and Emotion: Theory, Research, Applications*, Oxford: Oxford University Press.

Sloboda, J.A. and Juslin, P.N. (2010) 'At the interface between the inner and outer world: Psychological perspectives', in: P.N. Juslin and J.A. Sloboda, (eds) *Handbook of Music and Emotion: Theory, Research, Applications*, Oxford: Oxford University Press.

Sloboda, J.A., Lamont, A. and Greasley, A.E. (2009) 'Choosing to hear music: Motivation, process, and effect', in: S. Hallam, I. Cross, and M. Thaut (eds) *The Oxford Handbook of Music Psychology*, Oxford: Oxford University Press.

Stafford, T.F., Stafford, M.R., and Schkade, L.L. (2004) 'Determining Uses and gratifications for the Internet', *Decision Sciences*, 35(2): 259–288.

Suler, J.R. (2004) 'The online disinhibition effect', *CyberPsychology and Behavior*, 7(3): 321–326.

Sun, H. (2016) *Digital Disruption in the Recording Industry*, PhD thesis, The University of Edinburgh. Available from Ethos [Accessed 27 July 2017].

Swaminathan, S. and Schellenberg, E.G. (2015) 'Current emotion research in music psychology', *Emotion Review*, 7(2): 189–197.

Thaut, M. (2009) 'History and research', in: S. Hallam, I. Cross, and M. Thaut (eds) *The Oxford Handbook of Music Psychology*, Oxford: Oxford University Press.

Thun, C. (2009) 'Introducing Hollywood's Best Customers Vuze user vs. general internet: Comparative data.' Online. www.magid.com/sites/default/files/pdf/vuze.pdf [Accessed 27 July 2017].

Tschmuck, P. (2016) 'From record selling to cultural entrepreneurship: The music economy in the digital paradigm shift', in: P. Wikström and B. DeFillipi (eds), *Business Innovation and Disruption in the Music Industry*, Cheltenham: Edward Elgar Publishing.

Wang, X. and McClung, S.R. (2011) 'Toward a detailed understanding of illegal digital downloading intentions: An extended theory of planned behavior approach', *New Media and Society*, 13(4): 663–677.

Waldfogel, J. (2014) 'Digitazation, copyright, and the flow of new music products', in: V.A. Ginsburgh and D. Trosby (eds), *Handbook of the Economics of Art and Culture* (Vol. 2), Oxford: North-Holland.

Wasserman, I.M. and Richmond-Abbott, M. (2005) 'Gender and the Internet: Causes of variation in access, level, and scope of use', *Social Science Quarterly*, 86 (1): 252–270.

Wade, J. and Powers, D. (2015) 'Control, curation and musical experience in streaming music services', *Creative Industries Journal*, 8(2): 106–122.

Ward, M.K., Goodman, J. K. and Irwin, J. R. (2014) 'The same old song: The Power of familiarity in music choice', *Marketing Letters*, 25(1): 1–11

Watson, S.J., Zizzo, D.J. and Fleming, P. (2015) 'Determinants of unlawful file sharing: A scoping review', *PLoS ONE*, 10(6): e0127921.

Williamson, V. (2013) *You Are the Music*, London: Icon Books Ltd.

Williamson, J. and Cloonan, M. (2007) 'Rethinking the music industry', *Popular Music*, 26(2): 305–322.

Wikström, P. (2011) *The Music Industry: Music in the Cloud*, Cambridge: Polity Press.

Zentner, A. (2006) 'Measuring the effect of file sharing on music purchases', *Journal of Law and Economics*, 49(1): 63–90.

6 An examination of digital piracy behaviour through the lens of cultural and non-cultural variables

Monika Kukar-Kinney, Irena Vida and Mateja Kos Koklic

Acknowledgment

Data collection for this study was supported by the Commission of European Community, contract no. 217514 (EU – 7th Framework Programme). Authors gratefully acknowledge contributions of research partners from all countries participating in this research project.

Introduction

Today's highly competitive environment has prompted intensive efforts for sustaining competitive advantages of enterprises around the globe. One of the particularly vulnerable areas is intellectual property protection. Many industries, especially the music, film, and software industries, have been coping with the challenge of preventing piracy actions. The core topic of this chapter is digital piracy, defined as a consumer practice of illegally downloading files, such as music, movies, software, etc., from the Internet. This pervasive phenomenon in the digital era affects a number of stakeholders, including consumers, enterprises, and governments. The International Federation of the Phonographic Industry (IFPI, 2017) reports that 20 percent of Internet users worldwide regularly access unlicensed services. In response to digital piracy, companies and industry-specific associations have invested efforts into preventing consumers from pirating digital content, yet with somewhat limited success (Jeong & Khouja, 2013; Mirghani, 2011).

The phenomenon has been of particular interest to consumer researchers, with a large body of digital piracy literature illuminating its demand side (e.g., Harris & Daunt, 2011; Lowry, Zhang, & Wu, 2017). Many digital piracy consumer researchers apply ethical theoretical frameworks. This is not surprising considering that "an improved understanding of why some consumers engage in unethical behavior could be helpful in ultimately curtailing many questionable practices" (Vitell, 2003: 33). On the other hand, remarkably little attention has been devoted to applying international perspective (Ki, Chang & Khang, 2006), particularly in view of the global nature of the phenomenon and the attempts of various stakeholders to attenuate piracy-related practices at the global rather than local level.

Culture and ethics are closely intertwined concepts, as culture represents one of the broadest and most powerful influences on human behavior (Soares, Farhangmehr & Shohan, 2007) and plays an important role in affecting a person's ethical perception, ethical decision-making and attitudes (Javalgi & Russell, 2015; Vitell, King, Howie, Toti, Albert, Hidalgo, & Yacout, 2016). In discussing variations of ethical decisions across cultures, Belk, Devinney and Eckhardt contend that "culture filters our perceptions of what constitutes good or responsible consumption and what is perceived to be the consequences of violating these moral norms" (2005: 7). Yet, many single country empirical studies in digital piracy assume that factors underlying piracy behaviors are universally applicable across different national contexts.

While prior research explored a myriad of digital piracy drivers and various consumer attitudes as antecedents of illegal downloading, intentions and behaviors, there exists a lack of understanding of how individuals' perception of adverse effects of piracy shapes their behaviors (Koklic, Kukar-Kinney & Vida, 2016). Deeping the knowledge of how this perception shapes piracy behavior is important as the existing anti-piracy communication efforts, currently deemed rather ineffective, tend to exploit appeals featuring the negative effects of piracy for individuals committing the act (e.g., the risk of legal prosecution), others (e.g., struggling artists), or the society as a whole (Zamoon & Curley, 2008).

Another issue in the digital piracy literature pertains to consumers' tendency to explain away their unethical behavior by denial of injury, denial of responsibility, denial of victim and condemning the condemners – the co-called techniques of neutralization (e.g., Brown, 2016; Strutton, Vitell & Pelton, 1994; Yu, 2012). Vitell believes that "this concept has the potential to explain much as to why otherwise ethical consumers sometimes behave unethically" (2003: 45) and calls for further investigation of the concept in more depth, particularly in cross-cultural settings.

Given the shortcomings in the extant literature, this study focuses on the following two questions of significant relevance to digital piracy researchers: 1) Are perceived consequences of piracy behavior affected by cultural value orientations?, and 2) What role do the consumer perceptions of piracy consequences for individuals and for others play in shaping piracy behaviors and consumer approaches to rationalize such behaviors in cross-cultural settings? To address these questions, we examine personal cultural value orientations (uncertainty avoidance and collectivism) and non-cultural variables (personal risk and moral intensity) as antecedents to digital piracy behavior, and provide insights into rationalization as an outcome of both the perceived adverse consequences and piracy behaviors.

We make two key contributions to the digital piracy literature. First, grounded in the attitude-behavior models and the neutralization theory, we develop and test the conceptual baseline model of digital piracy to explore the links between perceived negative consequences, digital piracy behavior and rationalization. Second, we offer insights into the universality of the examined antecedents of digital piracy by demonstrating that elements of personal cultural value orientations influence not only the two sets of negative consequences of digital piracy, but also indirectly drive piracy behaviors and rationalization for such actions. A survey of adult consumer samples across three culturally distinct European Union countries provides empirical support for the conceptual model.

The structure of the chapter is as follows. First, we briefly review the existing theoretical foundations and explore the role of culture in digital piracy behavior. Next, we set out the research objective and provide a conceptual framework of the study. We then present theoretically grounded research hypotheses and discuss methodological procedures. Lastly, we report the analytical procedures and research findings along with implications and limitations.

Literature review and conceptual framework

Theoretical foundation in digital piracy literature

When exploring digital piracy issues, marketing scholars typically employ various ethical decision-making models, such as the Hunt-Vitell model (e.g., Yoon, 2012), deterrence theory (e.g., Jeong, Zhao & Khouja, 2012), or the moral intensity theory (e.g., Kini, Ramakrishna & Vijayaraman, 2003). These models rest on moral philosophies as the framework that explains the decision-making process for situations involving an ethical problem. Numerous authors have drawn on the attitude-behavior models, such as Theory of Reasoned Action and Theory of Planned Behavior (e.g., Wang & McClung, 2012; Yoon, 2011). Attitude–behavior models suggest that a single act (behavior) is derived from an attitude toward the act. Alternatively, social cognitive theory as one of the cognitive and consequential models relying on expectancy–value foundations has also been applied (e.g., Lowry et al., 2017). However, many limitations apply to these approaches. Especially problematic are a) the failure of ethical models to capture the behaviors of individuals who do not perceive digital piracy as an ethical issue, and b) the inability of attitude–behavior models to address the attitude–behavior discrepancy. As a result, some researchers utilize neutralization theory (e.g., Hinduja, 2007; Koklic et al., 2016) to explain how individuals counter feelings of guilt associated with non-normative behaviors by employing various neutralization or rationalization techniques (Grove, Vitell & Strutton, 1989). Based on the pioneering work by Sykes and Matza (1957), Strutton et al. (1994) contend that consumers use excuses to explain their negative actions and those of other consumers by appealing to issues, such as "denial of responsibility", "denial of [the] victim", "appeal to higher loyalties", "denial of injury" and "condemning the condemners."

In addition to rationalization, additional digital piracy drivers may be related to an individual's perception of possible negative consequences of engaging in digital piracy. That is, while consumers tend to be most responsive to consequences that affect them personally (e.g., perceived risk; Yoon, 2011), they are also sensitive to consequences for the society (e.g., moral intensity; Jones, 1991). These factors, along with other determinants, lead to varying rates of digital piracy that differ from one individual to another and from one country to another.

Cultural value orientation frameworks and digital piracy behavior

One conceptual framework that may help to explain the varying degree of digital piracy across individuals and countries is culture. Culture provides powerful but often overlooked behavior guidelines to consumers and its influence is well-documented (e.g., Belk et al., 2005; Shiu, Walsh, Hassan & Parry, 2015; Vitell et al., 2016). While numerous definitions exist (Soares et al., 2007), culture generally refers to a set of shared beliefs, values, attitudes and behavioral responses that form a knowledge base for navigating a person's social reality.

To map the value-based differences across countries/cultures, various value-based cultural theoretical frameworks have been put forward in the recent decades, such as those proposed by Hofstede, Schwartz, GLOBE and Trompenaars (Magnusson, Wilson, Zdravkovic, Xin Zhou & Westjohn, 2008). The validity of these frameworks has been subjected to rigorous debates in international business and marketing research (e.g., Fischer & Poortinga, 2012; Javidan, House, Dorfman, Hanges & De Luque 2006; Magnusson et al., 2008). While these frameworks share the view that each country has a shared set of core values and norms that guide their member's behaviors, they differ in the number of cultural value dimensions identified and in their position regarding which specific set of values best captures national differences. While the cross-cultural research lacks robust evidence of the frameworks that are most effective in explaining dissimilarities in consumer responses to marketing and other environmental stimuli, Hofstede framework has been the most widely applied and is believed to represent a valid approach to developing further conceptualizations (Javalgi & Russell, 2015: Sharma, 2010; Yoo, Donthu & Lenartowicz, 2011).

Hofstede conceptualized culture as a combination of six cultural dimensions: uncertainty avoidance, individualism, power distance, masculinity, long-term vs. short-term orientation, and indulgence vs. restraint, with these dimensions scored as index values for each country (Hofstede, Hofstede & Minkov, 2010). According to the authors, uncertainty avoidance captures the extent to which people feel threatened by ambiguous situations and create beliefs and institutions to avoid these. Power distance pertains to the extent to which less powerful members within a country expect and accept that power is distributed unequally. Individualism refers to preferences for loosely knit social frameworks in which individuals are expected to take care of merely themselves and their immediate families rather than look after all in-group members in exchange for unquestioning loyalty, as is the case in collectivistic societies. Masculine cultural values suggest assertiveness, achievement and acquisition of wealth as being more important in the society as opposed to feminine values that emphasize nurturing, quality of life and modesty. Long-term orientation refers to future-oriented societies that prefer to maintain time-honored traditions and norms while viewing societal change with suspicion. Indulgence refers to a society that allows a relatively free gratification of basic and natural human drives related to enjoying life and having fun. On the other hand, restraint, at the opposite side of the indulgence dimension, characterizes society that suppresses gratification of needs and regulates it by means of strict social norms. Culture has been linked to both general digital piracy behavior (Udo, Bagchi & Maity, 2016) as well as to specific types of digital piracy, such as software (e.g., Husted, 2000) and music piracy (e.g., Ki, Chang & Khang 2006). In the digital piracy domain, two cultural dimensions, i.e., individualism–collectivism and uncertainty avoidance have been identified as the strongest determinants of national differences in levels of illegal down-loading (Husted, 2000). Furthermore, these two cultural constructs have successfully explained variance in other consumer web-based behaviors (e.g., Choi & Geistfield, 2004; Lim et al., 2004; Shiu et al., 2015).

A major concern in cross-cultural research pertains to the issue of whether national culture can be measured using a global or macro measure based on existing secondary databases (such as Hofstede's framework) or whether it should be measured at the individual or micro level (Vitell et al., 2016; Yoo et al., 2011). The macro measure relies upon the indirect values inference approach (Soares et al., 2007), whereby the extrapolation of cultural values from the benchmark study to the sample being surveyed can lead to a measurement error. Specifically, such proxies cannot adequately represent the diversity in the value orientations of the actual population. Further, there tends to be more variance among individuals within a single culture or country than between different countries (Fischer & Poortinga, 2012). Existing research predominantly measures cultural influence at the national/macro level. However, several cross-cultural researchers urge the use of direct values inference approach and measure cultural value orientation at an individual level (e.g., Sharma, 2010; Yoo et al., 2011). Oyserman, Coon, and Kemmelmeier (2002) believe that employing individual level measurement may capture culture in terms of articulated mental representations that affect individual's cognitions, affect and motivation. Similarly, Shiu et al. (2015) recognize the importance of the individual-level psychological approach which assumes that cultural value orientation can be treated as an individual difference variable. Consistent with this reasoning, the present research employs the individual-level cultural value orientations.

Conceptual framework

Based on the foundations stated above, we propose a conceptual model depicted in Figure 6.1. The underlying premise of the model is that digital piracy behavior is directly influenced by two sets of negative consequences, i.e. personal risk and moral intensity, and indirectly influenced by individual-level cultural variables, i.e. uncertainty avoidance and individualism–collectivism. Furthermore, personal risk, moral intensity and piracy behavior have an influence on an individual's tendency to rationalize their piracy behavior.

In the model, *digital piracy behavior* is conceptualized as the consumers' recent engagement in digital piracy-related activities, and *rationalization* (neutralization) as the consumers' use of techniques to counter feelings of guilt associated with their piracy activities before and after the actual digital piracy behavior. *Personal risk* refers to the extent to which the consumer believes that illegally downloaded files will not perform as expected and their use might lead to damage to the consumer. *Moral intensity* is defined as the extent to which the consumer believes that pirating digital content yields a negative impact on the society at large. With respect to cultural variables, we focus on two of Hofstede's value dimensions (Hofstede et al., 2010), i.e., uncertainty avoidance and collectivism. *Uncertainty avoidance* refers to the degree to which consumers feel threatened by ambiguous situations and create beliefs and institutions that try to avoid these, and *collectivism* captures the degree to which an individual places strong emphasis on group membership, loyalty and respect for others (Hofstede & Bond, 1984). Despite the existence of six dimensions in the Hofstede framework, we limit our investigation to uncertainty avoidance and collectivism for two reasons. First, these two orientations have been found to be meaningful in explaining personal motives and behaviors in the context of digital engagement and consumer ethics when cultural value orientations are measured at the individual level (Lu, Chang & Chang, 2015; Shiu et al., 2015). Second, prior research suggests that "only the dimensions of national culture strongly tied to the constructs of interest should be included in the

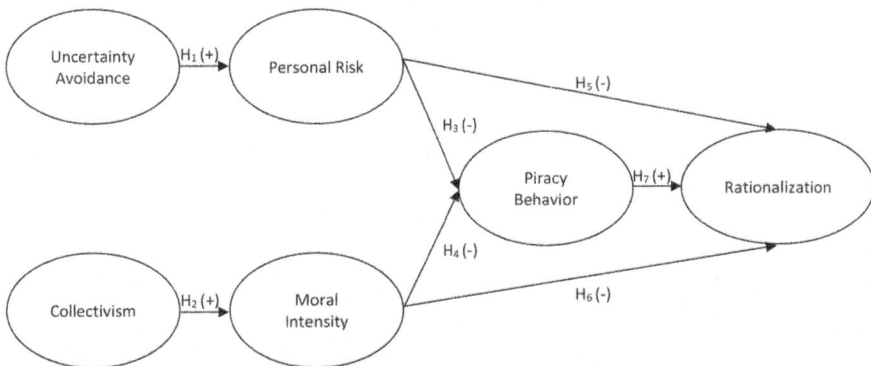

Figure 6.1 Conceptual model development

nomological network under investigation (thereby satisfying the philosophical goal of parsimony)" (Hoppner, Griffith & White, 2015: 71).

Based on this reasoning as well as the Hunt–Vitell's (1986) General Theory of Marketing Ethics, where culture is considered to be an antecedent to the process of ethical reasoning, we propose direct effects of the selected cultural value orientations. Specifically, we posit that uncertainty avoidance will directly affect an individual's perception of personal risk associated with digital activities, and that collectivistic value orientation will drive a person's moral intensity associated with digital piracy. These propositions are consistent with previous studies that examined direct effects of cultural variables on either attitudes or behaviors (e.g., Choi & Geistfelt, 2004; Lu et al., 2015; Park, Oh & Kang, 2016).

Hypotheses development

Cultural determinants of perceived consequences of piracy behaviors

The first two hypotheses address the impact of personal cultural value orientation on perceived adverse consequences of digital piracy for the individual (i.e., personal risk) and for the society (i.e., moral intensity). Among Hofstede's (1984) four major cultural dimensions, uncertainty avoidance is the most important aspect of perceived risk in a cross-cultural context (Ko et al., 2004). Perceived risk tends to increase with higher levels of uncertainty and/or a greater chance of negative consequences (Dowling & Staelin, 1994; Campbell & Goodstein, 2001). Yet, the previous literature is scarce in evaluating the relationship between uncertainty avoidance and perceived risk in the context of digital activities. For example, Al Kailani and Kumar (2011) found that individuals from high uncertainty avoidance cultures experience higher levels of perceived risk when buying over the Internet. Similarly, Choi and Geistfeld (2004) confirmed a significant positive influence of uncertainty avoidance on perceived risk in Korea, but not in the USA, in the context of e-shopping. However, Reisinger and Crotts (2009) hypothesized a positive influence of this cultural value orientation on risk perception in the travel context, but failed to provide empirical support. These contrasting findings call for further research, thus we hypothesize:

H$_1$: Uncertainty avoidance positively influences the perceived personal risk associated with digital piracy.

Numerous scholars have pointed out that culture is strongly intertwined with the process of ethical decision-making (e.g., Lu et al., 2015; Vitell et al., 2016). In particular, the individualism–collectivism dimension, more than other cultural dimensions, affects ethical decision-making by an individual (e.g., Armstrong, 1996; Husted, 2001). This cultural dimension is the extent to which the ties between individuals are loose or tight (Hofstede, 1997).

Consequently, various cultures as well as individuals are susceptible to group influences depending on their level of individualism–collectivism. Choi and Geistfeld (2004) contend that consumers with higher levels of collectivism are more concerned with others' opinions than people with higher levels of individualism. The more collectivist consumers are, the more likely they negatively perceive practices that are inconsistent with the welfare of the collective (Erez & Earley, 1993). As such, we propose that the more collectivist consumers are, the more they should be concerned about the effect of digital piracy on the society at large (i.e., moral intensity). Thus, in our conceptual model, we introduce moral intensity as one of the most prominent ethically charged constructs. Although the link between culture (or collectivism, specifically) and moral intensity has previously not been addressed, studies indicate that moral intensity varies cross-culturally (e.g., Vitell & Patwardhan, 2008). For example, Kini, Ramakrishna, and Vijayaraman (2004) demonstrate that moral intensity regarding software piracy varies in two different cultures/ environments. In sum:

H_2: Collectivism positively influences the perceived moral intensity associated with digital piracy.

Determinants of digital piracy behavior

Next, we elucidate the formation of digital piracy behavior. Consumers typically perceive each act of behavior as having either positive or negative consequences. Thus, an individual's choice of behavior rests on the expectation of consequences that follow this behavior (Limayem, Khalifa, & Chin, 2004). Given the substantial evidence of negativity bias, we expect that perceived negative consequences influence consumers more strongly than perceived positive consequences. Hence, this research examines perceived negative consequences for an individual (i.e., personal risk) and perceived negative consequences for the society (moral intensity) as determinants of digital piracy behavior.

Several scholars have examined the relationship between perceived risk and digital piracy intention as a proxy for actual piracy behavior. For example, Vida, Koklic, Kukar-Kinney, and Penz (2012) addressed the perceived risk of digital pirated products across different countries and found that it negatively affects piracy intention. Similarly, Chiou et al. (2011) confirmed a negative effect of risk perception on consumer's intention to pirate. Interestingly, Sinha and Mandel (2008) unexpectedly found that risk perception increases piracy tendencies, while Hennig-Thurau, Henning, and Sattler (2007) empirically verified the negative relationship between perceived costs (similar to perceived financial risk) and actual digital piracy behavior and discovered that search and moral costs negatively impact obtaining illegal copies, while technical costs negatively influences watching such copies. Based on these findings and the reasoning above, we hypothesize:

H₃: Perceived personal risk negatively influences piracy behavior.

The second hypothesized determinant of digital piracy behavior is moral intensity. Prior studies indicate that engaging in digital piracy behavior evokes ethical dilemmas in consumers. Chen, Pan and Pan (2009) suggest that moral intensity as an ethically charged construct is related to every stage of ethical decision-making and behavior process. Various authors propose that it is negatively related to the extent of digital piracy (Kini, Ramakrishna & Vijayaraman, 2004). In the context of music piracy, Woolley (2015) as well as Chiou, Huang and Lee (2005) have demonstrated that moral intensity predicts levels of piracy or the consumers' willingness to participate in the music piracy behavior. Similarly, evidence of a significant negative effect of moral intensity on use intention has been provided for the software piracy context (Chen, Pan & Pan, 2009). Thus, we propose:

H₄: Perceived moral intensity negatively influences piracy behavior.

Determinants of rationalization

The third set of hypotheses refers to the use of rationalization techniques and its antecedents: perceived risk, moral intensity, and piracy behavior. The literature on the relationship between perceived risk and rationalization is relatively scant. One of the exceptions is a study by Vida et al. (2012), where the authors anticipated a negative association between the two concepts in a digital piracy context, but failed to provide empirical support for their assumption. The framing effect literature suggests that consumers process negatively and positively framed information differently. Perceived risk could be interpreted as a form of negatively framed information that will lead to more intense reviewing of an individual's norms and consequently reduce the extent to which consumers use rationalization techniques (Block & Keller, 1995). Building on this theoretical reasoning, we propose:

H₅: Perceived personal risk negatively influences the consumer's rationalization of own piracy behavior.

Another antecedent hypothesized to reduce rationalization is moral intensity. Namely, we predict that the more an individual experiences the issue at hand (i.e., digital piracy) as morally intense and influential at a wider (societal) level, the less likely will he/she apply rationalization techniques as a post-hoc excuse for their behavior. For example, Zamoon and Curley (2008) find that the moral intensity of the situation reduces rationalization in the situation of software piracy. Similarly, Yu (2012) concludes that the lack of perceivable harm makes digital piracy less justifiable. As McGregor (2008) contends, being faced with a decision regarding an issue with ethical or moral imperative leads consumers to resort to rationalization techniques. The negative influence of moral intensity on rationalization has also been empirically supported by Kos Koklic et al. (2016), confirming this relationship for several countries. Hence:

H_6: Perceived moral intensity negatively influences the extent of consumer's rationalization of own piracy behavior.

The third hypothesized determinant of rationalization is digital piracy behavior. As several authors note, neutralization can either precede a misdeed or appear as after the fact rationalization, and the empirical literature offers contrasting evidence regarding the sequence of neutralization techniques. Some authors (e.g., Ingram & Hinduja, 2008) refer to neutralization techniques as those that help consumers extricate themselves from personal responsibility before the act of digital piracy is committed. Other researchers interpret neutralization as occurring after digital piracy takes place (e.g., Maruna & Copes, 2005), while several longitudinal studies indicate that timing of neutralization depends on the form of deviant behavior (Harris & Daunt, 2011; Morris & Copes, 2012). We theorize that consumers apply rationalization techniques after the act to assure themselves of appropriateness of their digital piracy behavior and to demonstrate its acceptability to others (Hinduja, 2007). Specifically, we propose that the greater the extent of individual's digital piracy behavior, the greater the feelings of guilt, and the more a person feels the need to excuse or rationalize his/her past behavior. Thus:

H_7: The extent of piracy behavior positively influences the extent of consumer's rationalization of piracy behavior.

Methodology

A survey using existing scales was utilized to collect data in three culturally diverse European Union countries: Italy, Slovenia, and United Kingdom. An initial sample of 10,000 adult consumers in each country received a self-administered mail questionnaire on various aspects of digital piracy behavior. The samples were representative of the population according to age and gender and also reflected socio-economic status in each country. The overall response rate across the three countries was 12 percent. However, for the purpose of this study, only people actually reporting past piracy behavior and their justification for the behavior were included. Based on this criterion, several responses were eliminated and the final data analysis included 1,017 usable responses (Italy n = 242, Slovenia n = 586, the U.K. n = 189).

For illustration purposes, Table 6.1 provides an overview of the cultural value orientation scores for each of the Hofstede's cultural dimensions in the countries in our sample based on the research by Hofstede, Hofstede and Minkov (2010). The dimensions are measured at the national macro level, with an index of up to 100 with a high score representing the high end of a

Table 6.1 Comparison of the selected countries based on Hofstede cultural value dimensions and software piracy rates in 2015

	Uncertainty avoidance	Individua-lism	Power distance	Mas-culi-nity	Long term orientation	Indul-gence	Software piracy rate*
Italy	**75**	**76**	50	70	61	30	45%
Slovenia	**88**	**27**	71	19	49	48	43%
U.K.	**35**	**89**	35	66	51	69	22%

Source: Business Software Alliance (2016).

specific bipolar cultural value dimension, e.g., individualistic vs. collectivistic tendencies or high vs. low uncertainty avoidance. With respect to the uncertainty avoidance dimension, with a relatively low score of 35, the U.K. residents tend to feel quite comfortable in ambiguous situations, while both Italians and Slovenes (scores of 75 and 88, respectively) exhibit a higher preference for avoiding uncertainty. In terms of the individualism dimension, based on the low score of 27, Slovenia is considered a collectivist society, valuing close relationships and long-term commitment to the member group. On the other side of the continuum are Italy and the U.K. with scores of 76 and 89, respectively, as more individualistic societies. These indices, along with those of other cultural dimensions not accounted for in our study (i.e., power distance, masculinity, long-term orientation in Table 6.1) suggest robust variation in value orientations across our three-country samples. For comparison, these countries also differ in their software piracy rates (Business Software Alliance, 2016). Specifically, Italy and Slovenia have 45 percent and 43 percent piracy rates, respectively, while the U.K. is reported to have significantly lower rate of 22 percent.

Samples and measures

The sample structure was comparable across countries. The sample of 242 Italians can be characterized as follows: 57.7 percent males with average age 39.7 years (SD =15.7 years). The majority of the sample (51.1 percent) falls into the age category 31–60 years. All except 23.4 percent of the sample obtained at least a college degree. More than half of the Italian sample (59.4 percent) works full time or part time, 12 percent are unemployed, and 14.9 percent are retired. The Slovenian sample of 586 individuals consists of 49.2 percent males. The percentage of the respondents up to 30 years old is 47.3 percent, while 45.6 percent of the sample is between 31 and 60 years. On average, the respondents are 36.1 years old (SD = 14.9). The majority of the respondents have a college degree (64 percent). Slightly more than half of the sample works full time or part time (51.4 percent). Males make up 51.9 percent of the U.K. sample, with an average age of 41.4 years (SD = 15). About one third (30.6 percent) is 30 years old or younger and 60.8 percent are 31 to 60 years old. This sample contains 67.8 percent respondents with a college degree or less. Well above half of the U.K. sample (70.4 percent) reports working full time or part time. The characteristics of the three samples are summarized in Table 6.2.

The survey items were derived from the existing literature in order to ensure that the content validity is preserved. Table 6.3 lists the specific sources, constructs, items, and their reliabilities (Cronbach's alpha) across the investigated countries. Unless noted otherwise, the respondents responded to all statements on a 5-point Likert scale anchored by "strongly disagree" and "strongly agree". All but one construct reliabilities exceed the suggested cut-off value .60 (Churchill, 1979), while the three-item uncertainty avoidance construct indicates a marginally acceptable reliability for the Italian and Slovenian samples. The uncertainty avoidance measure was composed of three statements adapted from Reardon et al. (2006), while the items measuring collectivism were based on Yoo et al. (2011). Personal risk was measured with five items adapted from Hennig-Thurau et al. (2007). We measured moral intensity with two items on a 5-point semantic differential scale consistent with Singhapakdi et al. (1996) and McMahon & Harvey (2006). Neutralization was captured with five items, each corresponding to one of the

Table 6.2 Characteristics of the sample

	Italy	*Slovenia*	*U.K.*
Variable	% / M (SD)	% / M (SD)	% / M (SD)
Gender			
Women	42.3	50.8	48.1
Men	57.7	49.2	51.9
Age (years)	39.7 (15.7)	36.1 (14.9)	41.4 (15)
– 30	36	47.3	30.6
31–60	51.1	45.6	60.8
61 +	12.9	7.1	7.6
Education			
Less than college	23.4	9.4	26.9
College	51.9	64	40.9
Graduate level	24.7	26.6	32.2
Occupational status			
Employed	59.4	51.4	70.4
Unemployed	12.8	11.4	10.6
Retired	14.9	12.5	9
Student	6.2	21.7	4.2
Other	6.7	3	5.8

Table 6.3 Constructs, construct items and reliabilities

Construct	Italy	Slovenia	U.K.
Uncertainty avoidance (adapted from **Reardon et al., 2006**)	.56	.52	.62
I am cautious about trying new and different things. I like to play games in a structured way where the rules are clear. If I am uncertain about the rules I get very anxious.			
Collectivism (adapted from **Yoo et al., 2011**)	.81	.81	.77
Group welfare is more important than individual rewards. Individuals should pursue their goals only after considering the welfare of the group. I focus on achieving societal goals more than individual accomplishments. Group rewards should take priority over individual rewards.			
Personal risk (adapted from **Hennig-Thurau et al., 2007**)	.88	.83	.92
Illegally downloading files is risky because: They might not work properly. You might have your Internet access terminated. They might infect your computer with a virus or malware. It could allow access to your data, files or passwords. They might damage your computer.			
Moral intensity (Singhapakdi et al., 1996; McMahon and Harvey 2006)	.67	.92	.93
If you illegally download files from the Internet: What would be the size of the impact on the society? (very small – very large). How likely is that this impact would be felt? (highly unlikely – highly likely).			
Neutralization (Sykes and Matza, 1957)	.69	.83	.86
I couldn't help myself; I had to illegally download the files. It's no big deal as no one was hurt. It's the industry's own fault they were taken advantage of. I was only doing what others do all the time. I wouldn't have bought the legal ones anyway.			
Piracy behavior (sum of units reported in all categories below)	NA	NA	NA
Please indicate how many units in the following categories you have illegally downloaded in the last month? (Films/TV episodes, music tracks, games software, business/application software, e-books/books/magazines/e-Zines, other).			

neutralization techniques, as suggested by Sykes and Matza (1957). Piracy behavior was measured with the number of units the respondent reported to have illegally downloaded in the previous month across various product categories. The sum of responses to all product categories was divided into five categories as equal in frequency as possible to be consistent with the five-point scaled measures of other variables in the model.

Evaluation of cross-national measurement equivalence

Equivalence in cross-cultural measurement has been raised as a serious concern in many existing cross-cultural studies (e.g., Oyserman et al., 2002; Shiu et al., 2015). To establish a meaningful comparison of the conceptual model across the three countries, we first evaluated the extent to which the measures remained cross-nationally invariant, following a procedure by Steenkamp and Baumgartner (1998). Using confirmatory factor analysis, we evaluated *configural invariance* of measures, which stipulates that the same pattern of zero and non-zero factor loadings exists in different countries (Horn, McArdle & Mason, 1983). The data showed that the model with zero loadings on non-target constructs fit the data well in all three countries (chi-square = 1,058, d.f. = 525, IFI = .93, CFI = .93, RMSEA = .03), with all salient factor loadings being substantially and significantly different from zero, and the factor inter-correlations significantly below unity. Thus, the measures achieved configural invariance.

The goal of the present research was to establish a theoretical net of the constructs of interest and test for the existence of the proposed relationships, which further requires *metric invariance* or the requirement of equal metrics or scales (Steenkamp & Baumgartner, 1998). Metric invariance allows for a meaningful comparison of the item ratings, with any differences being indicative of similar cross-national difference in the underlying construct (Steenkamp & Baumgartner, 1998). To test for metric invariance, we constrained all factor loadings to be the same across the three countries. The full metric invariance model fit the data as well as the configural model (chi-square =1,142, d.f. = 555, IFI = .93, CFI = .93, RMSEA = .03). Releasing different constraints did not lead to a substantially improvement of the model fit. Therefore, the measures exhibited full cross-national metric invariance and could be used to test the conceptual model.

Using the confirmatory factor model, we also evaluated discriminant validity of constructs. When items measuring two distinct constructs were constrained to load onto the same underlying construct, the model fit significantly worsened each time. Further, average variance extracted was greater than the squared inter-correlation for each pair of constructs within each country, providing evidence of discriminant validity and indicating that the constructs are conceptually distinct (Fornell & Larcker, 1981). We next tested the proposed conceptual model.

Analyses and results

To test the conceptual model, multi-group analysis using structural equation modeling was conducted, with all measurement weights (factor loadings) restricted to be equal across countries.

Table 6.4 Testing the conceptual model

	Italy	Slovenia	U.K.
Structural path	**Std. regr. coef. [SE] (t-value)**	**Std. regr. coef. [SE] (t-value)**	**Std. regr. coef. [SE] (t-value)**
H1+: Uncertainty avoidance → Personal risk	.24 [.11] (2.64**)	.31 [.07] (4.74**)	.20 [.10] (1.97*)
H2+: Collectivism → Moral intensity	.28 [.09] (3.31**)	.26 [.08] (5.52**)	.19 [.16] (2.19*)
H3-: Personal risk → Piracy behavior	−.11 [.10] (−3.17**)	−.08 [.10] (-3.17**)	−.14 [.10] (-3.17**)
H4-: Moral intensity → Piracy behavior	−.21 [.04] (−9.31**)	−.28 [.04] (−9.31**)	−.43 [.04] (−9.31**)
H5-: Personal risk → Rationalization	−.14 [.09] (−1.76*)	−.01 [.09] (−.32)	−.27 [.11] (−4.11**)
H6-: Moral intensity → Rationalization	−.35 [.07] (−3.70**)	−.31 [.03] (−6.77**)	−.50 [.05] (−6.66**)
H7+: Piracy behavior → Rationalization	.32 [.03] (4.18**)	.35 [.02] (7.95**)	.26 [.05] (3.70**)

Notes: ** one sided p-value < .01; * one sided p-value < .05.

Structural model fit the data well (chi-square = 1,247, d.f. = 580, IFI = .92, CFI=.91, RMSEA = .03). Table 6.4 displays individual hypotheses test statistics and results for each country. Note that only the comparison of the significance and direction of the relationships across countries is meaningful, but not the comparison of the magnitude of standardized regression coefficients.

Hypothesis 1 predicted a positive influence of uncertainty avoidance on perceived personal risk of illegally downloading Internet files. The findings support this prediction in all three countries (Italy: β = .24, *SE* = .11, *t* = 2.64, *p* < .01; Slovenia: β = .31, *SE* = .07, *t* = 4.74, *p* < .01; U.K.: β =.20, *SE* = .10, *t* = 1.97, *p* < .05). As the extent of uncertainty avoidance increases, so does the perceived risk associated with committing digital piracy. It was further expected that collectivism will positively affect the perceived moral intensity of digital piracy (hypothesis 2). The results confirm that the relationship between collectivism and perceived moral intensity was significant and positive for consumers in all three countries, offering uniform support for hypothesis 2 (Italy: β = .28, *SE* = .09, *t* = 3.31, *p* < .01; Slovenia: β = .26, *SE* = .08, *t* = 5.52, *p* < .01; U.K.: β =.19, *SE* = .16, *t* = 2.19, *p* < .05).

Hypothesis 3 predicted that the perceived personal risk will negatively influence consumers' digital piracy behavior. This hypothesis was supported in all three countries, with the extent of reported digital piracy behavior decreasing with increases in perceived risk (Italy: β = − .11, *SE* = .10, *t* = −3.17, *p* < .01; Slovenia: β = − .08, *SE* = .10, *t* = −3.17, *p* < .01; U.K.: β = −

.14, *SE* = .10, *t* = −3.17, *p* < .01). The perceived moral intensity of illegally downloading Internet files was expected to negatively influence digital piracy behavior (hypothesis 4). This hypothesis also receives consistent support across the investigated countries (Italy β = − .21, *SE* = .04, *t* = −9.31, *p* < .01; Slovenia β = − .28, *SE* = .04, *t* = −9.31, *p* < .01; U.K. β = − .43, *SE* = .04, *t* = −9.31, *p* < .01).

Perceived personal risk was also proposed to negatively affect the level of consumers' neutralization for their piracy behavior (hypothesis 5). This hypothesis receives support in Italy and U.K. (Italy: β = − .14, *SE* = .09, *t* = −1.76, *p* < .05; U.K.: β = − .27, *SE* = .11, *t* = −4.11, *p* < .01), but the proposed relationship is not significant in Slovenia (β = − .01, *SE* =.09, *t* = − .32, *p* > .10). The model also suggests that the perceived moral intensity of illegally downloading Internet files negatively influences consumers' rationalization of such behavior (hypothesis 6). This hypothesis receives consistent support across the investigated countries (Italy β = − .35, *SE* = .07, *t* = −3.70, *p* < .01; Slovenia β = − .31, *SE* = .03, *t* = −6.77, *p* < .01; U.K. β = − .50, *SE* = .05, *t* = −6.66, *p* < .01). The last hypothesis predicted that consumers' digital piracy behavior will positively influence their extent of rationalization for the behavior (hypothesis 7). As expected, this was supported in all three countries (Italy β = .32, *SE* = .03, *t* = 4.18, *p* < .01; Slovenia β = .35, *SE* = .02, *t* = 7.95, *p* < .01; U.K. β = .26, *SE* = .05, *t* = 3.70, *p* < .01), showing that the greater the extent of one's digital piracy behavior, the more the person will try to rationalize their behavior after the fact.

Discussion and implications

Theoretical implications

With the aim to contribute to the knowledge base on culture and digital piracy, the present study investigates cultural and non-cultural determinants and outcomes of consumer digital piracy behavior across three European Union countries. Overall, the vast majority of hypotheses received strong and consistent support across the three countries. The only exception was the proposed relationship between personal risk and rationalization, which was supported in Italy and the U.K, but not in Slovenia. It seems that personal risk only indirectly influences rationalization among the Slovene consumers (through behavior). It is possible that the level of risk perceived by these consumers is not sufficiently high to evoke the process of reviewing their norms.

Our findings suggest that uncertainty avoidance as one of the core cultural value orientations measured at the level of an individual significantly shapes a consumer's perception of risk with regards to digital piracy. In accordance with previous research, consumers who score highly on uncertainty avoidance perceive more personal risk of potential damage to their computer (Money & Crotts, 2003). Similarly, this study corroborates previous findings by demonstrating a significant positive relationship between collectivism and moral intensity as one of the core ethical decision-making concepts. That is, the stronger the collectivistic value orientation of a consumer, the stronger the sense of morality attached to the digital piracy issue at hand. These findings corroborate connectedness of culture and ethics, as suggested by Javalgi and Russell (2015), Lu et al. (2015), and Vitell et al. (2016).

Furthermore, we theorize and empirically confirm that digital piracy behavior is less likely to occur in situations when consumers perceive higher levels of personal risk and more negative digital piracy consequences for the society. Although the existing research offers mixed conclusions about the relationship between perceived risk and digital piracy behavior, our study findings are consistent with the majority of the studies reporting a negative association (e.g., Chiou et al., 2011; Hennig-Thurau et al., 2007; Vida et al., 2012). On the other hand, the literature offers a more uniform view of the negative relationship between moral intensity and digital piracy (Chen et al., 2009; Chiou et al., 2005; Woolley, 2015). The results of our survey in three countries are in line with these expectations. An interesting observation is that in all three samples the impact of moral intensity was substantially stronger than the impact of personal risk. This finding indicates that moral intensity with its societal focus is a more prominent deterrent of digital piracy behavior and, despite past suggestions to the contrary (e.g., Konstantakis et al. 2010), moral consideration may not be diminishing in the realm of the digitalization.

The results of this study also lend a relatively uniform support to the negative influence of perceived consequences for oneself (personal risk) and the society at large (moral intensity) and the positive influence of piracy behavior on consumer's use of rationalization techniques. While the literature provides limited evidence of the relationship between perceived risk and rationalization (e.g., Vida et al., 2012), we show that both the Italian as well as the U.K. consumers decrease their use of justification techniques as the perceived risk associated with piracy practices increases. An interesting finding is that perceived personal risk in the Slovenian sample appears to be relatively weakly related to both digital piracy behavior and rationalization. Our findings suggest that the patterns of risk perception may not be uniform across countries in determining their outcomes in the conceptual model.

Furthermore, our research reveals that moral intensity as a construct capturing societal consequences of digital piracy significantly reduces individuals' use of rationalization techniques across all three country samples. Specifically, the greater the perceived size and likelihood of the impact of digital piracy on the society, the less the consumer uses rationalization techniques to excuse their own piracy behavior. Consistent with the pattern of the effects on piracy behavior, the effect of moral intensity on consumers' use of rationalization is substantially stronger than that of the effect of personal risk across all three countries, further highlighting the importance of including moral intensity in the models of digital piracy behavior and when considering approaches to minimize it. This finding broadens the existing knowledge about the relationship between moral intensity and rationalization as two ethically charged concepts, which has previously been somewhat vaguely outlined (e.g., Yu, 2012; Zamoon & Curley, 2008).

In addition, we show dependence of rationalization upon recent digital piracy behavior in all three countries. Consistent with Maruna and Copes (2005), we demonstrate that the greater the engagement in digital piracy, the stronger the agreement with the use of various rationalization techniques after the behavior. By examining the interplay between perceived consequences, digital piracy behavior and rationalization, we add to the limited body of knowledge on temporal ordering of rationalization.

Overall, this research provides evidence of the generalizability of the conceptual model across three national samples, while applying strict psychometric criteria to ensure cross-cultural measurement equivalence.

Practical implications

This research establishes evidence regarding the universality of the examined antecedents of digital piracy across three countries and demonstrates that the examined two elements of individual cultural value orientation influence not only the two sets of negative consequences of digital piracy, but further indirectly drive piracy behaviors and rationalization for such actions. As cultural and ethical issues can markedly affect the effectiveness of the form, content and implementation of marketing communications, our results offer useful cross-cultural implications for various industries affected by digital piracy.

Specifically, the knowledge of the powerful effects of uncertainty avoidance on risk perceptions and collective values orientation on moral intensity, and subsequently on the intensity of piracy related activities and rationalization can help global marketing managers segment their international markets and develop potentially more effective communication appeals to reduce piracy activities. For instance, Reardon, Miller, Faubert, Vida and Rubyna (2006) found that individuals with high uncertainty avoidance respond more favorably to loss-framed advertisements than to benefit-framed advertisements, whereas the opposite holds for consumers with low uncertainty avoidance. On the other hand, Miller, Foubert, Reardon and Vida (2007) demonstrate that messages signaling adverse effects for other people are more effective in collectivist environments, while ads portraying the negative consequences of an action to oneself can be more effective in individualistic cultures. Hence, marketing managers are advised to investigate the extent to which their targeted market segments feel uncomfortable in the presence of ambiguity and vagueness (uncertainty avoidance) and assess consumer personal risk perceptions associated with piracy, their activities and their tendency to seek rationalizations. Similarly, measuring the relationship between the individualistic vs. the collective interests of the group to which one belongs (collectivism) can suggest consumer tendencies to activate moral intensity, and indirectly indicate the intensity of digital practices and rationalization.

Above and beyond the impact of cultural value orientations, additional areas worthy of consideration by marketers and public policy makers include perceived negative consequences for an individual (perceived risk) and the society (moral intensity), as well as the role of rationalization. This research demonstrates that both sets of adverse consequences directly drive digital piracy behavior and shape (directly and indirectly) consumer use of justification techniques. Companies aiming at discouraging digital piracy are advised to integrate information about potential negative consequences into messages targeted at end consumers, such as highlighting the potential damage to the consumer's computer as an unsolicited consequence of digital piracy, or potential harm experienced by others, such as small artists and smaller companies consumer can empathize with (Kos Koklic et al., 2016). In particular, we found that moral intensity with its societal focus is a relatively stronger deterrent of digital piracy than personal risk perceptions regardless of the country. Lastly, our finding related to the role of rationalization suggests that countering the reasons that consumers use to justify their pirating activities with solid information may discourage these activities.

Conclusions: limitations and future research

While this cross-cultural study highlights the importance of cultural as well as non-cultural variables in shaping digital piracy behavior and rationalization, several limitations that pave the way for future research should be considered. The scope of direct antecedents of digital piracy behavior was limited to negative consequences and to the two parsimoniously selected cultural value orientations. In the future, it would insightful to include positive consequences and their relationship to cultural orientations such as, for example, perceived benefits in terms of diverse content (Park et al., 2016).

While we offer evidence of the generalizability of the proposed conceptual model across three EU countries, it would be beneficial to include other cultural landscapes with varying levels of cultural orientations both nation- and individual-wise. Javalgi and Russell (2015) concluded that most ethics research in international marketing during 1960–2013 has been conducted from North-American and Western perspectives, which can limit development of new knowledge in cross-cultural ethics and marketing research. As recommended by Shiu et al. (2015), we included a sample from a recent EU member state. Future studies should further broaden the scope and the number of countries studied to increase the robustness of the model cross-culturally. For instance, would the same constellation of antecedents and relationships be revealed in a non-Western cultural setting, such as India or China?

While previous consumer research has considered mostly direct effects of cultural variables (e.g., Lu et al., 2015; Park et al., 2016; Yoo et al., 2011), researchers also examined moderating effects of cultural variables on the link between attitudes and behaviors (e.g., Udo et al., 2016; Vitell et al., 2016). Having compared both effects using the same cultural dimensions as in our study, Shiu et al. (2015) concluded that across seven EU countries, direct approach generally worked better. However, the authors also cautioned against discounting the few identified significant moderating effects, particularly in view of the fact that survey-based research is less likely to find support for theorized moderating effects relative to experimental research. Further research is needed to clarify the role of direct versus moderating cultural effects.

In conclusion, incorporating additional cultural and non-cultural antecedents of digital piracy behaviors and outcomes while adhering to rigorous methodological standards, along with the need to broaden the scope and the number of countries studied need to be addressed in the future. We hope that this chapter contributes to a better understanding of the digital piracy phenomenon in an era where globalization maintains the center stage in the business world and consumer segments are increasingly diversified (Belk et al., 2005; Douglas & Craig, 1997).

References

Al Kailani, M. and Kumar, R. (2011). Investigating uncertainty avoidance and perceived risk for impacting internet buying: a study in three national cultures. *International Journal of Business and Management*, 6(5): 76–92.

Armstrong, R.W. (1996). The relationship between culture and perception of ethical problems in international marketing. *Journal of Business Ethics*, 15: 1199–1208.

Belk, R. W., Devinney, T. and Eckhardt, G. (2005). Consumer ethics across cultures. *Consumption Markets & Culture*, 8(3): 275–289.

Block, L. G. and Keller, P. A. (1995). When to accentuate the negative: The effects of perceived efficacy and message framing on intentions to perform a health-related behavior. *Journal of Marketing Research*, 32(2): 192–203.

Brown, S.C. (2016). Where do beliefs about music piracy come from and how are they shared? *International Journal of Cyber Criminology*, 10(4): 364–378.

Business Software Alliance (2016, May). *Seizing Opportunity through License Compliance. BSA Global Software Survey.* Washington, DC: The Business Software Alliance.

Campbell, M.C. and Goodstein, R.C. (2001). The moderating effect of perceived risk on consumers' evaluations of product incongruity: Preference for the norm. *Journal of Consumer Research*, 28(3): 439–449.

Chen, M. F., Pan, C.T. and Pan, M.C. (2009). The joint moderating impact of moral intensity and moral judgment on consumer's use intention of pirated software. *Journal of Business Ethics*, 90(3): 361–373.

Chiou, J.S., Huang, C. and Lee, H. (2005). The antecedents of music piracy attitudes and intentions. *Journal of Business Ethics*, 57(2): 161–174.

Chiou, J.S., Cheng, H.I. and Huang, C.Y. (2011). The effects of artist adoration and perceived risk of getting caught on attitude and intention to pirate music in the United States and Taiwan. *Ethics & Behavior*, 21(3): 182–196.

Chiou, J. S., Wu, L.Y. and Chou, S.Y. (2012). You do the service but they take the order. *Journal of Business Research*, 65(7): 883–889.

128   *Kukar-Kinney, Vida and Koklic*

Choi, J. and Geistfeld, L.V. (2004). A cross-cultural investigation of consumer e-shopping adoption. *Journal of Economic Psychology*, 25(6): 821–838.

Churchill, G.A., Jr. (1979). A paradigm for developing better measures of marketing constructs. *Journal of Marketing Research*, 16(2): 64–73.

Douglas, S.P. and Craig, C.S. (1997). The changing dynamic of consumer behavior: implications for cross-cultural research. *International Journal of Research in Marketing*, 14(4): 379–395.

Dowling, G.R. and Staelin, R. (1994). A model of perceived risk and intended risk-handling activity. *Journal of Consumer Research*, 21(1): 119–134.

Erez, M. and Earley, P. C. (1993). *Culture, Self-identity, and Work*. New York: Oxford University Press.

Fischer, R. and Poortinga, Y.H. (2012). Are cultural values the same as the values of individuals? An examination of similarities in personal, social and cultural value structures. *International Journal of Cross Cultural Management*, 12(2): 157–170.

Fornell, C. and Larcker, D.F. (1981). Structural equation models with unobservable variables and measurement error: Algebra and statistics. *Journal of Marketing Research*, 18(3): 382–388.

Grove, S.J., Vitell, S.J. and Strutton, D. (1989). Non-normative consumer behavior and the techniques of neutralization. In R. Bagozzi and J. P. Peter (Eds), *Proceedings of the AMA Winter Educators Conference* (pp. 131–135). Chicago, IL: American Marketing Association.

Harris, L.C. and Daunt, K.L. (2011). Deviant customer behaviour: A study of techniques of neutralization. *Journal of Marketing Management*, 27(7–8): 834–853.

Hennig-Thurau, T., Henning, V. and Sattler, H. (2007). Consumer file sharing of motion pictures. *Journal of Marketing*, 71(4): 1–18.

Hinduja, S. (2007). Neutralization theory and online software piracy: An empirical analysis. *Ethics and Information Technology*, 9(3): 187–204.

Hofstede, G. and Bond, M.H. (1984). Hofstede's cultural dimensions: An independent validation using Rokeach's value survey. *Journal of Cross Cultural Psychology*, 15(4): 417–433.

Hofstede, G., Hofstede, G. J. and Minkov, M. (2010). *Cultures and Organizations: Software of the Mind* (Revised and Expanded 3rd Edition). New York: McGraw-Hill USA.

Hofstede, G. (1997). *Cultures and Organizations: Software of the Mind*. 1st edition, New York: McGraw-Hill USA.

Hoppner, J. J., Griffith, D. A.and White, R. C. (2015). Reciprocity in relationship marketing: A cross-cultural examination of the effects of equivalence and immediacy on relationship quality and satisfaction with performance. *Journal of International Marketing*, 23(4): 64–83.

Horn, J. L., McArdle, J. J.and Mason, R. (1983). When is invariance not invariant: A practical scientist's look at the ethereal concept of factor invariance. *Southern Psychologist*, 1(4): 179–188.

Husted, B. W. (2000). The impact of national culture on software piracy. *Journal of Business Ethics*, 26(3): 197–211.

Husted, B. W. (2001). *The Impact of Individualism and Collectivism on Ethical Decision Making by Individuals in Organizations*. Unpublished manuscript. Instituto Technológico y de Estudios Superiores de Monterrey and Instituto de Empresa.

IFPI (2017). Tackling music piracy. Retrieved on 18 March 2017, from www.ifpi.org/music-piracy.php.

Ingram, J.R. & Hinduja, S. (2008). Neutralizing music piracy: An empirical examination. *Deviant Behavior*, 29(4): 334–366.

Javalgi, R.G. and Russell, La Toya M. (2015) International Marketing Ethics: A Literature Review and Research Agenda. *Journal of Business Ethics*, DOI: doi:10.1007/s10551-015-2958-9.

Javidan, M., House, R. J., Dorfman, P. W., Hanges, P. J. and De Luque, M. S. (2006). Conceptualizing and measuring cultures and their consequences: A comparative review of GLOBE's and Hofstede's approaches. *Journal of International Business Studies*, 37(6): 897–914.

Jeong, B.-K. and Khouja, M. (2013) Analysis of the effectiveness of preventive and deterrent piracy control strategies: Agent-based modeling approach. *Computers in Human Behavior*, 29(6): 2744–2755.

Jeong, B.-K., Zhao, K. and Khouja, M. (2012). Consumer piracy risk: Conceptualization and measurement in music sharing. *International Journal of Electronic Commerce*, 16(3): 89e118.

Jones, T.M. (1991). Ethical decision making by individuals in organizations: An issue-contingent model. *Academy of Management Review*, 16(2): 366–395.

Ki, E.J., Chang, B H. and Khang, H. (2006). Exploring influential factors on music piracy across countries. *Journal of Communication*, 56(2): 406–426.

Kini, R.B., Ramakrishna, H.V. and Vijayaraman, B.S. (2003). An exploratory study of moral intensity regarding software piracy of students in Thailand. *Behaviour & Information Technology*, 22(1): 63–70.

Kini, R.B., Ramakrishna, H.V. and Vijayaraman, B.S. (2004). Shaping of moral intensity regarding software piracy: A comparison between Thailand and US students. *Journal of Business Ethics*, 49(1): 91–104.

Ko, H., Jung, J., Kim, J. and Shim, S.W. (2004). Cross-cultural differences in perceived risk of online shopping. *Journal of Interactive Advertising*, 4(2): 20–29.

Koklic, M.K., Kukar-Kinney, M. and Vida, I. (2016). Three-level mechanism of consumer digital piracy: Development and cross-cultural validation. *Journal of Business Ethics*, 134(1): 15–27.

Konstantakis, N.I., Palaigeorgiou, G.E., Siozos, P.D. and Tsoukalas, I.A. (2010) What do computer science students think about software piracy? *Behaviour & Information Technology*, 29(3): 277–285.

Lim, K.H., Leung, K., Sia, C.L. and Lee, M.K. (2004). Is eCommerce boundary-less? Effects of individualism–collectivism and uncertainty avoidance on Internet shopping. *Journal of International Business Studies*, 35(6): 545–559.

Limayem, M., Khalifa, M. and Chin, W.W. (2004). Factors motivating software piracy: A longitudinal study. *IEEE Transactions on Engineering Management*, 51(4), 414–425.

Lowry, P. B., Zhang, J. and Wu, T. (2017). Nature or nurture? A meta-analysis of the factors that maximize the prediction of digital piracy by using social cognitive theory as a framework. *Computers in Human Behavior*, 68: 104–120.

Lu, L. C., Chang, H. H. and Chang, A. (2015). Consumer personality and green buying intention: The mediate role of consumer ethical beliefs. *Journal of Business Ethics*, 127(1): 205–219.

Maruna, S. and Copes, H. (2005). What have we learned from fifty years of neutralization research? *Crime and Justice: A Review of Research*, 32: 221–320.

Magnusson, P., Wilson, R. T., Zdravkovic, S., Xin Zhou, J. and Westjohn, S.A. (2008). Breaking through the cultural clutter: a comparative assessment of multiple cultural and institutional frameworks. *International Marketing Review*, 25(2): 183–201.

McGregor, S. L. (2008). Conceptualizing immoral and unethical consumption using neutralization theory. *Family and Consumer Sciences Research Journal*, 36(3): 261–276.

McMahon, J. M.and Harvey, R. J. (2006). An analysis of the factor structure of Jones' moral intensity construct. *Journal of Business Ethics*, 64(4): 381–404.

Miller, C., Foubert, B., Reardon J. and Vida, I. (2007). Strategies for anti-smoking messages across cultures: An examination of directed consequences. *International Journal of Market Research*, 49(4): 515–533.

Mirghani, S. (2011). The war on piracy: Analyzing the discursive battles of corporate and government-sponsored anti-piracy media campaigns. *Critical Studies in Media communication*, 28(2): 113–134.

Money, R. and Crotts, J. (2003). The effects of uncertainty avoidance on information search, planning, and purchases of international travel vacations. *Tourism Management*, 24(2): 191–202.

Morris, R.G. and Copes, H. (2012).Exploring the temporal dynamics of the neutralization/delinquency relationship. *Criminal Justice Review*, 37(4): 442–460.

Oyserman, D., Coon, H. M. and Kemmelmeier, M. (2002). Rethinking individualism and collectivism: Evaluation of theoretical assumptions and meta-analyses. *Psychological Bulletin*, 128(1): 3–72.

Park, N., Oh, H.S. and Kang, N. (2016). Idiocentrism versus allocentrism and ethical evaluations on illegal downloading intention between the United States and South Korea. *Journal of Global Information Technology Management*: 19(4), 250–266.

Reardon, J., Miller, C., Faubert, B., Vida, I. and Rubyna, L. (2006). Antismoking messages for the international teenage segment: The effectiveness of message valence and intensity across different cultures. *Journal of International Marketing*, 14(3): 115–138.

Reisinger, Y. and Crotts, J.C. (2009). The influence of gender on travel risk perceptions, safety, and travel intentions. *Tourism Analysis*, 14(6): 793–807.

Sharma, P. (2010). Measuring personal cultural orientations: scale development and validation. *Journal of the Academy of Marketing Science*, 38(6): 787–806.

Shiu, E., Walsh, G., Hassan, L.M. and Parry, S. (2015). The direct and moderating influences of individual-level cultural values within web engagement: A multi-country analysis of a public information website. *Journal of Business Research*, 68(3): 534–541.

Singhapakdi, A., Vitell, S.J. and Kraft, K. L. (1996). Moral intensity and ethical decision-making of marketing professionals. *Journal of Business Research*, 36(3): 245–255.

Sinha, R.K. and Mandel, N. (2008). Preventing digital music piracy: the carrot or the stick? *Journal of Marketing*, 72(1): 1–15.

Soares, A.M., Farhangmehr, M. and Shohan, A. (2007). Hofstede's dimensions of culture in international marketing studies. *Journal of Business Research*, 60(3): 277–284.

Strutton, D., Vitell, S.J. and Pelton, L.E. (1994). How consumers may justify inappropriate behavior in market settings: An application on the techniques of neutralization. *Journal of Business Research*, 30: 253–260.

Steenkamp, J.-B.E.M. and Baumgartner, H. (1998). Assessing measurement invariance in cross-national consumer research. *Journal of Consumer Research*, 25(1): 78–90.

Sykes, G.M. and Matza, D. (1957). Techniques of neutralization: A theory of delinquency. *American Sociological Review*, 22(6): 664–670.

Udo, G., Bagchi, K. and Maity, M. (2016). Exploring factors affecting digital piracy using the norm activation and UTAUT models: The role of national culture. *Journal of Business Ethics*, 135(3): 517–541.

Vida, I., Kos Koklic, M., Kukar-Kinney, M. and Penz, E. (2012). Predicting consumer digital piracy behavior: The role of rationalization and perceived consequences. *Journal of Research in Interactive Marketing*, 6(4): 298–313.

Vitell, S.J. (2003). Consumer ethics research: Review, synthesis and suggestions for the future. *Journal of Business Ethics*, 43: 33–43.

Vitell, S.J. and Patwardhan, A. (2008). The role of moral intensity and moral philosophy in ethical decision making: a cross-cultural comparison of China and the European Union. *Business Ethics: A European Review*, 17(2): 196–209.

Vitell, S.J., King, R.A., Howie, K., Toti, J.F., Albert, L., Hidalgo, E.R. and Yacout, O. (2016). Spirituality, moral identity, and consumer ethics: A multi-cultural study. *Journal of Business Ethics*, 139(1): 147–160.

Wang, X. and McClung, S.R. (2012). The immorality of illegal downloading: The role of anticipated guilt and general emotions. *Computers in Human Behavior*, 28(1): 153–159.

Woolley, D.J. (2015). The association of moral development and moral intensity with music piracy. *Ethics and Information Technology*, 17(3): 211–218.

Yoo, B., Donthu, N. and Lenartowicz, T. (2011). Measuring Hofstede's five dimensions of cultural values at the individual level: Development and validation of CVSCALE. *Journal of International Consumer Marketing*, 23: 193–210.

Yoon, C. (2011). Theory of planned behavior and ethics theory in digital piracy: An integrated model. *Journal of Business Ethics*, 100(3): 405–417.

Yoon, C. (2012). Digital piracy intention: A comparison of theoretical models. *Behaviour & Information Technology*, 31(6): 565–576.

Yu, S. (2012). College students' justification for digital piracy: A mixed methods study. *Journal of Mixed Methods Research*, 6(4): 364–378.

Zamoon, S. and Curley, S.P. (2008). Ripped from the headlines: What can the popular press teach us about software piracy? *Journal of Business Ethics*, 83(3): 515–533.

7 Copyright infringement and cultural participation

Juan D. Montoro-Pons, Manuel Cuadrado-García and Miguel Puchades-Navarro

Introduction

The cultural industries offer a case study of the impact on the market of the breach of a partially enforceable legal right. The legal entitlement linked to information in the form of intellectual property has become fuzzier with the digitization of information goods, i.e. the evolution from analog to digital media, and the widespread sharing of information in the Internet. This process has had a major impact in the copyright industries, namely the cultural industries. The correlation between plummeting sales in recorded music and Internet file-sharing epitomizes the main argument used by the copyright industries, which have taken it in the past as a case in favor of stricter legislation aimed at curbing the widespread infringement of intellectual property rights. In parallel, developments in a variety of business models have taken place as an alternative way of dealing with the new environment (see Bourreau, Gensollen & Moreau, 2012).

Eventually, strategies to deal with infringement should be based on the observed effect of infringement on sales. However, as far as the empirical evidence goes, results are far from conclusive, with the impact of copyright infringement on consumption best described as ambiguous. Interestingly, most studies have approached the problem by focusing on one consumption variable, keeping other variables constant. However, this approach assumes demand in copyright industries is a homogeneous construct and does not take into account the different ways in which consumers approach cultural consumption neglecting cross-effects within a sector. To add a new perspective on this issue, this chapter jointly analyzes alternative means of cultural participation in Spain for each cultural industry (recorded music, films and books) and their interactions.

What are the salient features in these three sectors in Spain? Can we measure the impact of digitization in the three sectors, by using a consistent and widespread database on cultural consumption and habits? How does the new distribution channels of cultural contents relate to overall cultural consumption? This research aims at answering these questions and shed additional evidence to the discussion on copyright infringement. To this end we use the

Survey of Cultural Habits and Practices in Spain 2010–11, which provides individual-level information about cultural participation for a representative sample of the Spanish population over 15.

The aim of this research is twofold. On the one hand, it provides additional evidence on the impact of copyright infringement on the three sectors under scrutiny. As it will be shown, infringement is a rather generalized activity in the three sectors, with a rather strong correlation between them. However, results show that estimated effects of infringement are rather asymmetric: while the evidence shows that infringers are equally active and roughly the same individuals,[1] the measured impact across sectors is uneven. On the other hand, and based on the differential impact of infringement on the three sectors, it looks at the institutional arrangements among the three sectors and their role as potential explanation of the observed patterns. Its ultimate goal is to provide additional empirical evidence on an ongoing debate that has obvious practical implications as it may influence policy making as well as managerial strategies.

The paper is structured as follows. Next, we briefly review the findings of the economic literature on copyright infringement in recorded music, films and books. Based on this review, we put forward a set of research questions to be tested. Then we proceed with the empirical analysis. We start by analyzing the cultural consumer in Spain, and putting forward an empirical model followed by the estimation results. These will highlight cross-consumption and copyright infringement effects. Finally, we close with a discussion of the main findings and conclusions.

Review of the literature

The economic literature on information goods hypothesizes ambiguous results on the effect of copyright infringement on cultural consumption. This could be so, from a theoretical perspective, as two main offsetting effects of piracy are at play: a negative *substitution effect* and a positive *sampling effect*. The former emerges when consumers substitute the consumption of cultural goods through copyright infringement. The latter operates through more complex channels and stems from the exposure to cultural products, no matter whether these are originals or pirated. It is through consumption (any type of content consumption including piracy) that individuals become aware and discover cultural products and shape their preferences. This increased awareness and knowledge, and the discovery process that comes along with it is central to the understanding of positive exposition or sampling effects, that develop as engagement with cultural goods leads to an enlarged current legal consumption. In other words, these emerge as consumers shape their cultural preferences through piracy. When substitution and sampling effects are present, the net effect of infringement depends on their relative magnitude. To identify which one prevails, we turn to the empirical literature.

Recorded music is by far the most analyzed sector. Most studies at the aggregate level find that piracy has a net negative effect (see, for instance,

Peitz and Waelbroeck, 2004). Yet, at the individual or micro level results are ambiguous. Some papers, such as Michel (2006), Zentner (2006), Rob and Waldfogel (2006) or Waldfogel (2010), find a clear-cut negative effect. However, Andersen and Frenz (2010) find no statistically significant effect between the number of downloaded music files in file-sharing networks and CD purchases,[2] while Gopal et al. (2006) obtain an asymmetric effect as infringement reduces sampling costs that, in turn, have a positive effect on sales of less known music. In a similar vein, Bacachet-Beauvallet et al. (2015) put forward and test the hypothesis that copyright infringement has a heterogeneous impact on artists, which depends on the origin of their revenue stream, and find that the tolerance for piracy is greater in artists whose earnings are related to live performances compared to self-released acts. Using a survey on cultural participation Montoro-Pons and Cuadrado-García (2013) show that copyright infringement increases the probability of purchasing full albums (but non-significant for individual tracks) and attending live performances, showing evidence of indirect appropriation across markets. Interestingly there are significant differences in the profile of purchasers and attenders.

Looking at the effect of file-sharing and downloads on individual album sales has resulted in non-significant findings, as in Oberholzer and Strumpf (2007) or McKenzie (2013), or asymmetric ones, such as Battacharjee et al. (2007) who conclude that file-sharing increases the risk of those records at the bottom of the charts.

Several papers outline the relevance of the legal framework. Montoro-Pons and Cuadrado-García (2008) find the magnitude (and hence the potential impact) of copyright infringement to depend on the legal system that enforces intellectual property rights. Recently, Adermon and Liang (2014) isolate a natural experiment, namely the introduction of stricter copyright laws in Sweden, and its impact on Internet traffic and sales of music. The authors find a temporary increase of recorded music sales and a strong substitution effect between piracy and music sales, suggesting that most of the observed decline in sales could be the effect of copyright infringement.

Evidence for the film industry finds support for both substitution and sampling effects. De Vany and Walls (2007) estimate a time series model of change in box office revenue of a widely released movie as a function of the number of pirate copies available for download on the Internet, showing a net negative effect of downloading. Rob and Waldfogel (2007) use a sample of university under-graduate students and analyze the effect of unpaid viewing of films on several variables of film consumption – theater-going, purchase, rental or TV-viewing are used as endogenous variables – both in a cross-sectional and longitudinal analysis, finding evidence of a displacement effect of infringement. Hennig-Thurau et al. (2007) find evidence of copyright infringement displacement on movie-going and DVD rentals and purchases in a panel of German consumers. Similarly, Danaher and Smith (2014) identify a displacement effect of piracy by quantifying the effect of the shutdown of Megaupload, a file-sharing site, on the revenue increase of three major motion picture studios.

Contrary to the previous evidence, Smith and Telang (2010) use a local dataset on DVD sales for 2000–2003 and find that broadband penetration (used as a proxy for piracy) has a strong and positive effect on media sales. Although the extent of piracy is usually linked to the strength of copyright enforcement (see, for instance, Walls, 2008), Adermon and Liang (2010) do not find the implementation of stricter copyright laws in Sweden to have a significant effect on sales of theater tickets or of DVD.

The book publishing industry has only recently been affected by widespread digitization and, hence, by the drawbacks related to copyright infringement by online file-sharing. While the CD was adopted in the mid 1980s, and the DVD in the mid 1990s, book publishers have only started offering digital books with the turn of the century, although its wider acceptance has been more recent. Hence the literature on digitization and copyright infringement in book publishing is more fragmented and less focused. Nevertheless, it is worth mentioning Hu and Smith (2013), who study the impact of the availability of digital releases on print sales. By using a natural experiment (the delay of the digital release of certain books) the authors show that some digital sales are lost and hence total sales decrease. If such a strategy aims at avoiding the risks of infringement linked to digitization, it backfires: digitization does indeed increase revenue. Recently, Reimers (2014) analyzes the effect of anti-piracy effort in book publishing, and finds that piracy protection increases sales of ebooks without a statistically significant effect on print books. The determinants of the propensity to infringe copyright in books have been analyzed in Camarero, Antón and Rodriguez (2014). The authors use a survey of 227 users of ebook reader devices and find that infringement is positive related to individual's technological skills and negatively related to value consciousness.

It is noteworthy that the diversity of approaches reviewed makes results hardly comparable. In this respect, we resort to Liebowitz (2016) who, when analyzing recorded music, claims that to some extent differences in findings are to be attributed to methodological differences, namely the metrics of choice to quantify the impact of infringement. By using a similar approach across the three sectors in Spain we aim at providing comparable results, identify the traits that characterize infringers in the different sectors, and overcome some of the limitations of the previous works.

Research questions

The foregoing review allows us to put forward research questions on the impact of copyright infringement on cultural participation. These are related to four main attributes of the consumption of information goods that explain the coexistence of legal and pirate markets for cultural goods. First, consumers have heterogeneous preferences over cultural goods, which means that the willingness to pay for the same good will differ for different consumers. Second, piracy is not a costless activity: individuals face costs when infringing copyright and these differ among consumers. Third, pirated goods might not be perfect substitutes of originals if consumers perceive the former to be of lower quality applying a discount factor to them (see, for instance, Cox and Collins, 2014). Four, even with perfect substitutability and a negligible cost for piracy, the fact that fairness considerations may enter consumers' decisions rules out perfect displacement of legal markets. In this regard, it has been shown that when consumers face the choice to pay for information goods that they might as well take for free, i.e. pay-what-you-want-schemes, payments are well above the non-cooperative equilibrium (see El Harbi et al., 2014).

In short, the extent of piracy depends on individuals' preferences and the institutional framework that defines consumers' accessibility to copies of cultural products. As we have already noted, the impact of piracy is an open question. While infringement may displace or crowd-out legal consumption, in the model of rational addiction (see Stigler and Becker, 1977) consumer preferences are endogenously determined: increased actual consumption (including that of pirated contents) leads to the accumulation of consumption capital that, in turn, increases the perceived value of future consumption. This dynamic mechanism is consistent with piracy increasing cultural consumption.

The preceding discussion allows us to formulate two testable hypotheses on the direct impact of infringement on cultural participation:

H1. Infringement reduces the probability of cultural participation (substitution effect dominates).

H2. Infringement increases the probability of cultural participation (exposition effect dominates).

It should be noted that, consumer heterogeneity is an incentive for cultural organizations to provide alternative means of consuming contents. Price and product discrimination allow firms to reach out to different segments of the demand, albeit imperfectly. There are consumers who will not be enticed by the alternatives offered and might, as long as the expected costs of piracy are less than its benefits, opt for infringement. From the firm's perspective piracy is a residual market, which is endogenously defined not only by demand characteristics but also by the available supply channels. Consider that there are different market prices for the alternative channels through which consumers access cultural content; further, assume the opportunity cost individuals face when infringing copyright depends on objective factors (such as the degree of copyright enforcement) as well as on subjective ones (for instance, technological skills). Based on these, consumers face three options, namely: either access content through legal means, or infringe copyright, or stay out of the market. Substitution, that up to this point was outlined in term of lost sales, can be widely defined: substitution between channels emerges when relative costs or preferences change.

To sum up, cultural organizations' strategies can, via product differentiation (e.g. the increase of legal distribution channels and price discrimination) modify individuals' net value for the different alternatives. By providing more choices in which consumers face different subjective valuations and relative costs, marginal consumers could shift from one channel to another. In other words, legal participation could rise as infringers face a lower cost and/or better quality alternative to infringement. Hypothesis 3 follows:

H3. Increasing consumption options (variety of channels and prices) reduce the extent of a negative impact of infringement.

A final note in this respect: new channels do not only attract infringers into legal consumption. Given alternatives, some legal consumers might opt to downgrade to more affordable channels in a cannibalization process. Overall, while participation is expected to increase, net income for the industry might go down, which, on the other hand, is only reasonable given the competitive pressure piracy places on rights holders.

Descriptive analysis of cultural consumption in Spain

To identify the extent of copyright infringement and its impact on cultural participation we use data from the *Survey of Cultural Habits and Practices in Spain 2010–11* (hereafter *SCHP*), a survey that is included in the *National Statistics Plan*. The SCHP is a survey-based research undertaken by the Ministry of Education and Culture, with the collaboration of the National Institute of Statistics, which describes participation and habits in activities, related to the different cultural sectors and the arts for the Spanish population over 15.

The aim of the survey is twofold: to evaluate the development of the main indicators for cultural habits and practices of the Spanish people and, to analyze relevant aspects in the field of culture, especially with regard to cultural consumption, and to make an in-depth study into the ways of obtaining specific cultural products which are subject to intellectual property rights, such as books, recorded music, video and software. As stated in the web-portal of the survey,[3] it:

Gives continuity to the work done in 2006–2007 and again becomes a vehicle for dealing with part of the statistical information needs of the *Government's Integral Plan for the Reduction and Elimination of Activities that Violate Intellectual Property Rights*.

As for the gathering of individual information, it was done with face-to-face interviews beginning in June 2010 and:

It was done in the month following each of the quarterly periods to which most of the information refers, in order to register the activity of the quarter prior to the moment of the survey, thereby reducing the possible negative effect of a more long term memory of certain activities, and at the same time capturing the variability that plays out across a natural year. The quarterly reference periods encompass, overall, a natural year between March 2010 and February 2011, and correspond to un-natural quarters.

Regarding the sampling strategy, "[a] two-stage sampling type was used, with a stratification of first-phase units, selected census areas, with each autonomous region being considered an independent population." In this respect, "The total sample was spread out into four quarterly sub-samples, in order to appropriately estimate the differences derived from cultural behaviour patterns linked with different times of the year." Overall, the survey is directed towards a sample of 16,000 people aged 15 and older representative of the Spanish population of this age.
A quality control was in place in all the phases of the survey in order to ensure the accuracy and reliance of the collected information.

> [It] has great bearing on the content and solidity of the questionnaires and any possible difficulties encountered in the course of data collection and in the treatment of the same. The questionnaires were carefully looked at in order to detect any possible errors: the valid and invalid values were analyzed, as was the aggregated behavior of some variables and their distribution was studied according to classification variables and comparisons were made with other statistical sources. Beyond that task, the questionnaire file was subjected to a series of procedures in order to secure factors of elevation and adjustment and so constitute a file whose results could be fully exploited.

The final sample size is 14,486 individuals.

Participation and infringement

We start first by identifying participation rates across the three different industries and the means through which consumers participate, a question related to the proliferation of business models in the copyright industries. Cultural goods can be purchased on physical media (either in analog or digital format, such as with CDs or LP vinyl records for pre-recorded music, DVD or Blu-ray discs for films, and books in the publishing industry) or digitally, in which case consumers can access them in a purely digital fashion through a digital purchase (here one can consider platforms such as iTunes or Amazon for recorded music, films or ebooks).[4] Alternatively information goods can be rented, usually via streaming. Services such as Spotify, Pandora, Deezer or Apple Music for recorded music, Netflix for films and TV series, and Kindle unlimited for books rely on this business model. While the media in which cultural products are bundled does not affect its core information content, heterogeneity in consumer preferences leads to different participation means.

Tables 7.1, 7.2 and 7.3 show cultural consumers' participation in the markets for recorded music, films and books respectively. SCHP identifies consumption over different time frames: past three months, last year, more than a year, never or almost never. We present results for quarterly and annual participation. Both reflect the binary answer to whether an individual participated at least once during the last three months or year.

Starting with recorded music – Table 7.1 – we see that participation at the sample level via album purchases goes from 18.4 percent (last 12 months), down to 11.4 percent (last three months). Streaming and digital purchases represent 4.8 percent and 3.7 percent of the sample over past 12 months. However, information at the sample level hides differences in involvement that emerge once one looks at copyright infringing behavior, the most frequent participation means: 19.3 percent of the sample has engaged in copyright infringement in the last three months, a percentage that goes up to a 22.3

Table 7.1 Consumer participation: recorded music

	Purchase	Digital	Streaming	Infringement
Past 12 months				
Non-infringers	0.148	0.013	0.021	
Infringers	0.308	0.122	0.158	
Sample	0.184	0.037	0.047	0.223
Past 3 months				
Non-infringers	0.093	0.003	0.018	
Infringers	0.202	0.017	0.153	
Sample	0.114	0.006	0.048	0.193

Table 7.2 Consumer participation: movies

	Attendance	Purchase	Rental	Infringement
Past 12 months				
Non-infringers	0.396	0.137	0.135	
Infringers	0.752	0.245	0.228	
Sample	0.475	0.161	0.155	0.193
Past 3 months				
Non-infringers	0.276	0.093	0.105	
Infringers	0.556	0.154	0.157	
Sample	0.330	0.104	0.115	0.223

Table 7.3 Consumer participation: book publishing (past three months)

	Purchase	Professional	Other	Borrowing	Infringement
Non-Infringers	0.348	0.268	0.521	0.045	
Infringers	0.294	0.853	0.775	0.181	
Sample	0.347	0.276	0.525	0.046	0.014

percent when considering one year. As it becomes apparent from the data, those involved in copyright infringement are also more active at participation in general: purchases of recorded music in the past three months (12 months) go up to 20.2 percent (30.8 percent) for infringers compared to 11.4 percent (18.4 percent) for non-infringers. Similarly, 1.7 percent (12.2 percent) of infringers purchased digital music over the past three months (12 months) compared to 1.3 percent (0.3 percent) of non-infringers. Overall infringers show a greater propensity to participate.

As for films, Table 7.2 splits participation into film-going or attendance, purchase (including physical, i.e. DVD or Blu-ray, and online purchases) and rental (physical or digital via streaming through an online store or a subscription-based platform). Film-going is the most popular form of participation with 33 percent (47.5 percent) of the sample attending at least once over last three months (year), followed by purchase and rental. We also find that infringement is related to a greater participation in all three cases, but especially in movie-going. Interestingly, the percentage of infringers is similar to that found in recorded music.

Data on book consumption is shown in Table 7.3. Note that in this case there is only information about consumption over the past three months. The table includes: book purchases, sample proportion of individuals reading and motivation (profession/studies and other), proportion borrowing (library and/or friends), and infringement. Compared to recorded music and films, two facts stand out. First, infringement is marginal in the book publishing sector: just 1.4 percent of the sample, compared with roughly 20 percent in music or movies. One likely explanation has been already given, namely that book publishing is a latecomer in digitization; as copies of physical books are less convenient to store and manage than digital ones one would expect a limited extent of infringement in the sector. Second, infringement is not positively associated to book purchases, as was the case for recorded music and films. However infringement does indeed increase mean participation via reading, both for professional (85.3 percent compared with 26.8 percent) and leisure motivations (77.5 percent compared with 52.1 percent), and the borrowing of books (18.1 percent compared with 4.5 percent). Overall, we find a negative association between infringement and purchases.

Who are the pirates?

The preceding descriptive analysis raises an additional question, namely that of the similarities and differences between infringers in the three sectors. It

Table 7.4 Tetrachoric correlations: infringers in three sectors

	Music	Movies	Books
Music	1.000		
Movies	0.867	1.000	
Books	0.399	0.389	1.000

has been noted that infringement is the outcome of an individual's preferences, subjective valuations and costs of alternative distribution channels. However, how do individual traits vary across sectors? To answer this question, Table 7.4 presents the potential relationship of infringement between sectors by computing tetrachoric correlations.[5] These provide a measure of the likelihood of one individual being infringer in one sector when he is infringer in another.

We find a large correlation (equal to 0.87) between films and music meaning that infringers in one sector are, very likely, infringers in the other. This correlation is much lower, but still significant, in the case of books and films, and books and music. Therefore one could tentatively conclude that infringers in music and films are quite similar (there is a large common support between them) and share certain features with infringers in books. Again, it should be pointed out that the limited extent of infringement in books could explain the low correlation found.

To further this analysis, Table 7.5 presents the profile of infringers in all three markets and the sample average individual. As expected, there are some common features among infringers in all three sectors: infringers are younger and predominantly male. Moreover, we find single individuals and students to be over-represented among them.

Looking at educational attainment, we find that high school, vocational and university graduates are over-represented among infringers. This is especially so in the case book copyright infringers, where the share of university graduates more than doubles that found at the sample level – 36.3 percent compared with 17 percent. As for cultural participation, infringers in every sector purchase more music (both physical and digital), as well as listen more to streamed music. They also buy more albums and individual tracks, except for book copyright infringers that buy fewer albums but more individual tracks, than the sample mean.

As for films, infringers in music and movies go to the movies more (slightly so in the case of infringers in the book publishing sector), although results are fuzzier for purchases and rental (roughly the average in all cases). Finally, with respect to book purchases, the proportion for infringers in music and movies is larger than the sample one, while it is less than the average for book infringers – 29.4 percent compared with 34.7 percent. As for the number of books purchased, infringers purchase more (both for professional and other

Table 7.5 Profile of copyright infringers (by type of infringement in columns) compared to that of the whole sample

| | Infringers | | | Sample |
	Music	Movies	Books	
Age	31.78	33.08	35.75	48.22
Fem	0.45	0.45	0.45	0.52
Single	0.60	0.55	0.56	0.36
Children	0.26	0.29	0.26	0.29
Household size	3.49	3.48	3.41	3.12
Student	0.28	0.25	0.28	0.09
Vocational	0.20	0.21	0.23	0.14
High school	0.21	0.21	0.21	0.14
University	0.22	0.22	0.36	0.17
Music purchase	0.31	0.28	0.25	0.11
Music digital	0.12	0.11	0.18	0.01
Music Streaming	0.15	0.14	0.23	0.05
Albums	0.61	0.62	0.32	0.37
Tracks	1.97	1.11	14.98	0.51
Movie attendance	0.57	0.56	0.48	0.48
Movie purchase	0.15	0.15	0.16	0.16
Movie rental	0.17	0.16	0.15	0.16
Book purchase	0.51	0.52	0.29	0.35
Reads (professional motives)	0.56	0.55	0.85	0.28
Reads (other motives)	0.69	0.69	0.78	0.53
Borrows books	0.07	0.07	0.18	0.05
# Book purchases (professional)	0.79	0.79	0.68	0.41
# Book purchases (other)	31.78	33.08	35.75	48.22

reasons) than the average sample individual, a reasonable outcome in the case of music and film infringers, but somehow counterintuitive in the case of book infringers: note that the proportion of book infringers that purchase books is less than the sample proportion. The straightforward explanation is that while book infringers as a whole show a lower propensity to purchase (only 29.4 percent of book-infringers buy books compared with 34.7 percent of sample individuals), a subset of them is very active in buying. This explains the fact they also purchase more books for professional (0.68 books purchased) and non-professional motivations (1.059 books purchased) than the sample average individual (0.412 and 1.047 respectively). The stark difference in the case of professional reading suggests a functional motivation in reading which is not present in the case of the other two cultural goods analyzed. In general, all infringers read and borrow more books, especially so in the case of book infringers.

From the descriptive analysis three features stand out. First, there seems to be a reasonable similarity in the profile of infringers in the three sectors. Indeed, there is a high correlation in infringement in movies and recorded music, suggesting that infringers in both sectors are (roughly) the same individuals.[6] Second, the degree of infringement parallels the degree of digitization of the sector. Take book publishing. As a latecomer, it is less affected by copyright infringement than the other two sectors. However, digitization in the cultural industries has proven to be a highly disruptive innovation, the adoption of which has been swift. Other things equal, as all the technology that allows infringement is already there and the amount of information to be shared in books is less than that of recorded music and films, one would expect the observed gap between infringement in books and the other cultural sectors to close. Third, infringement appears to have asymmetric effects within each sector. The diversity with which cultural goods are distributed reflects the attempt of cultural industries to tailor their supply to different consumer segments and to match any latent demand. As different demand segments show a different sensitivity to infringement, we expect it to have a different impact within sectors and to depend on the distribution channel.

Empirical analysis

Estimation strategy

In this section, an empirical model to test H1–H3 is proposed. Given the nature of the data on cultural participation (responses for individual involvement with music/films/books taking two mutually exclusive values), a binary response model seems appropriate. Two elements have been taken into account in its formulation. First, the diversity of media through which information goods are consumed. Actual cultural participation is multi-dimensional, hence we define it as such: the model has as many dependent variables as channels through which individuals participate. For recorded music we consider physical and digital purchases and streaming. Film consumption includes movie-going, purchases and rental, both physical and digital. Unfortunately, SHCP does not distinguish between physical and digital book purchases; hence we only consider book purchases as a whole.[7]

Second, the fact that copyright infringement, as a way of actually consuming digital contents, is potentially determined by the same set of covariates that affects other forms of participation. Consequently, it is also included as dependent variable, although it may enter as explanatory variable for the legal consumption channels in order to test for substitution or sampling effects.

To sum up, the modeling strategy calls for a multivariate model that accounts both for the multidimensional nature of cultural consumption and the potential endogeneity of copyright infringement. We stick to the empirical strategy of the literature on cultural participation,[8] which mainly relies on survey-based qualitative-response models to identify its determinants and stresses the addictive nature of cultural consumption, a feature that explains actual preferences by prior consumption experiences, i.e. individuals shape their tastes for culture by consuming it in a process of accumulation of *cultural capital*.

Bearing all this in mind, we formulate an empirical model that assumes consumers for a cultural good participate through $k = 1...K$ alternative distribution channels. The model leads to K different participation equations for each cultural good, being y_{ik} the binary outcome individual's i participation in the k-th market.

Even though each of these equations could be individually estimated, that would neglect the potential correlation between error terms. If the unobserved heterogeneity across individuals (or preferences) drives participation, a simultaneous framework accounts for the correlation between individual participation equations. Moreover, the fact that copyright infringement, which is itself endogenous, enters as an explanatory variable for the rest of the dependent variables justifies the need for a simultaneous equations framework.

Consider joint consumption in music/films/books as a $K-$equation index function model in which a latent continuous variable y_{ik} (to be interpreted as the i individual propensity to participate in cultural market k, with $k=1,2...K$) leads to the discrete choice y_{ik} on whether or not to participate. Formally, it is formulated as follows:

$$y_{ik} = \beta \text{ j}' \ X_{ik} + \epsilon_{ik} \tag{1}$$

$$y_{ik} = 1 \text{ if } y_{ik} > 0, \ y_{ik} = 0 \text{ otherwise} \tag{2}$$

with x_{ik} a set of observed explanatory variables that influence the latent propensity to participate y_{ik}, and ϵ_{ik} being K multivariate normal errors with zero means, unit variance and $\rho_{kl} = \rho_{lk}$ correlation that account for the unobserved heterogeneity across individuals. The above equations need not include the same set of covariates. Indeed, a recursive model is proposed in which some of the dependent variables appear as explanatory variables. That does not pose a problem in the estimation of the model, as given that certain restrictions are met, the endogenous nature of the regressors does not affect the properties of the estimators.

Apart from infringement, other covariates are included as control variables in order to capture all observed determinants of cultural participation in the different markets analyzed. Firstly, socio-demographic variables are included. Here we control for being female (a binary qualitative variable), age and its square (in order to account for nonlinearities), being single (binary), having children (binary), and household size (total number of members living in the household of the survey-taker).

Second, we introduce economic related variables; specifically a set of binary qualitative variables accounts for the survey-taker's labor market situation: employer, employee, unemployed, student, homemaker or retired.

Third, education related variables are also accounted for. We include three binary variables related to an individual's educational achievement: vocational education, high school and university. While the educational attainment is frequently used as an indirect measure of the stock of cultural capital an individual holds, the fact that the survey does not offer information about income makes it also an instrument that partially captures the economic standing of survey-takers.

Fourth, geographical and habitat variables are needed in order to control for geographical differences in income and cultural supply. In this case a set of 16 binary variables for each region in Spain (17 regions overall) and four binary variables accounting for the habitat size are included. The latter split the survey-taker's habitat into: province capitals/cities with more than 100,000 inhabitants/cities with more than 50,000 inhabitants/cities with more than 10,000 inhabitants. The reference category for the latter is cities, the population of which is less than 10,000 inhabitants.

Fifth, physical capital of the household is included. We control for household equipment (which could be critical in the consumption of cultural products) by including a set of variables obtained through principal components analysis. Specifically ten principal components were obtained as the output of 21 questions related to the equipment of the household including: ebook ownership, number of physical books, number of digital books, number of computers and ownership of different peripherals such as external hard drive, number of smartphones, ownership of video player (VHS, DVD or Blu-ray), ownership of photo and/or video cameras, ownership of videogame console, access to landline and mobile broadband, ownership of HI-FI and/or portable sound equipment, and number of musical instruments.

Sixth, cultural preferences are proxied by reducing to four variables the self-reported interest in 14 different cultural activities (measured in a 0–10 scale). These activities are: reading, libraries, museums, exhibitions, art galleries, monuments, archeological sites, archives, theater, opera, operetta, dance/ballet, cinema, and music.

Finally, and in order to control for the potential seasonal pattern of cultural participation, quarterly dummies to account for the quarter in which the survey was taken are included. Note that there are demand and supply factors that lead to the seasonality of cultural participation. On the demand side, the time intensive nature of cultural consumption (at least that is the case for books and films) implies that individuals are more likely to participate during vacation periods (e.g., summer). As for the supply, cultural industries also show a seasonal pattern with releases of books, films or records being time sensitive.

The selection of the variables was driven by the literature on cultural economics, management, and the sociology of culture, and data availability. The model has been estimated by using simulated maximum likelihood – specifically the GHK simulator – as described by Cappellari and Jenkins (2003). Results proved to be robust to alternative specifications of the simulation, specifically for different seeds, when a reasonably large number of random draws was chosen. Next we present and discuss them.

Estimation results

Tables 7.6 and 7.7 display the estimation of the specification (1)–(2) for music and films respectively. In both cases we use annual data on participation and copyright infringement.

Table 7.8 presents the findings for quarterly book purchases and infringement. Sample design weights were used in the estimation of the different models, hence robust standard errors are produced.

For the sake of simplicity only results for socio-demographic, economic, and educational attainment variables, as well as cross-effects and correlations between markets are presented.[9] Additionally, all tables include a joint significance analysis (chi-square), and its p-value. Alternative specifications for the models were estimated, and results were chosen based on information criteria (both AIC and BIC were used, and consistent results were obtained in both cases).

The effect of infringement

Table 7.6 presents the main estimation results for participation in recorded music, where three alternative consumption means are included (physical and/ or digital purchases, streaming content, and copyright infringement). In it infringement enters both the purchase and streaming equations and streaming enters the purchase equation. The recursive nature of the resulting system guarantees its identifiability.

Looking at the first block of covariates we find copyright infringement to have no significant effect on the legal consumption of recorded music: the estimates in both the purchase and streaming equation have large standard errors leading to an ambiguous estimated effect. On the contrary, it is noteworthy that streaming has a negative and significant effect on purchases. While much of the debate in the sector has been about reducing the amount of infringement, and streaming has partially been considered as a legal alternative to free music, the estimates do not provide such an optimistic outcome, as there is no clear cross-effect between infringement and streaming, and there is evidence of some cannibalization of legal purchases from streaming. Nevertheless, one should be cautious about this interpretation, as this sample was drawn when streaming services such as *Spotify* were taking off. Note that in Spain the service was rolled out in October 2008, and in

Table 7.6 Multivariate probit model estimates: recorded music

	Purchase		Streaming		Infringement	
Infringement	–0.2398		0.2652			
	(.2040)		(.1952)			
Streaming	–0.4907	*				
	(.2568)					
Female	–0.1834	**	–0.0872		–0.2353	**
	(.0348)		(.0542)		(.0360)	
Age	0.0055		–0.0049		–0.0621	**
	(.0094)		(.0149)		(.0096)	
Age^2	–0.0003	**	–0.0001		0.0003	**
	(.0001)		(.0002)		(.0001)	
Single	0.04		0.1673	**	0.0832	*
	(.0411)		(.0731)		(.0460)	
Children	0.0432		–0.1184		–0.1214	**
	(.0400)		(.0720)		(.0449)	
Household size	–0.071	**	–0.0361		–0.0722	**
	(.0147)		(.0238)		(.0160)	
Employer	0.0861		0.1159		0.1307	
	(.1433)		(.2655)		(.1680)	
Employee	0.0264		0.1027		0.1386	
	(.1352)		(.2518)		(.1592)	
Unemployed	–0.0443		0.2543		0.2453	
	(.1400)		(.2545)		(.1622)	
Student	–0.1581		0.218		0.197	
	(.1490)		(.2584)		(.1694)	
Retired	0.0294		0.1092		0.2688	
	(.1515)		(.3147)		(.1877)	
Homemaker	–0.1249		–0.1529		0.0305	
	(.1474)		(.2904)		(.1776)	
Vocational	0.0953	*	0.1109		0.3368	**
	(.0489)		(.0763)		(.0493)	
High school	0.0994	**	0.0334		0.2445	**
	(.0482)		(.0748)		(.0492)	
University	0.2249	**	0.0779		0.1964	**

	Purchase	Streaming		Infringement	
	(.0455)	(.0741)		(.0515)	
Correlations					
Purchase		0.3279	**	0.2677	**
		(.1296)		(.1134)	
Streaming				0.1466	
				(.1099)	
Chi-sq	4080.9				
p-value	0				

Note: p < .05 *, p < .01**.

2011 it counted worldwide with one million paying customers (15 percent of total subscribers).[10]

To have a complete view of the intertwined impact of the endogenous variables, one needs to look at the correlation between equations, shown at the bottom of the table. From it a positive correlation between purchases and streaming, and purchases and infringement is inferred. On the other hand, no statistically significant correlation between streaming and infringement is found. This indicates that the unobserved heterogeneity that makes an individual more likely to participate through copyright infringement (or streaming), also makes him/her more likely to purchase (and the other way around). In other words, an indirect link between purchases and infringement (or streaming) via a positive correlation between both equations adds to the direct estimated link. It is important to note that the finding of significant correlation coefficients implies the inadequacy of a single equation estimation setup. Moreover, a joint test of significance for the three correlation coefficients rejects the null, hence suggesting that the multivariate model is an adequate one.

Table 7.7 presents the main estimation results for participation in films. Four markets are considered: movie-going (labeled as attendance), purchase, rental (through physical and/or digital means) and infringement. The latter is included as an explanatory variable for all legal forms of consumption, i.e. attendance, purchase and rental.

Estimates show that infringement affects rental negatively, which, as noted above, includes physical and digital rental (through cable or online platforms). That could partially explain the sluggish rolling out of major online services (such as Netflix) in Spain compared with other European markets.

As for the indirect effect between participation means, a positive correlation is found between attendance and purchase, and attendance and rental, which indicates an unobserved preference for films. A non-significant correlation is found between attendance and infringement, which suggests that cinema-goers

Table 7.7 Multivariate probit model estimates: films

	Attendance		Purchase		Rental		Infringement	
Infringement	−0.2045		−0.526		−0.5843	*		
	(.2055)		(.3206)		(.3130)			
Female	−0.1341	**	−0.2438	**	−0.16	**	−0.2696	**
	(.0339)		(.0394)		(.0420)		(.0353)	
Age	−0.0319	**	−0.0078		0.0208	*	−0.0362	**
	(.0070)		(.0099)		(.0118)		(.0096)	
Age^2	0.0001		−0.0001		−0.0005	**	0.0001	
	(.0001)		(.0001)		(.0001)		(.0001)	
Single	0.2324	**	−0.0173		0.0572		0.0432	
	(.0381)		(.0418)		(.0441)		(.0453)	
Children	−0.0726	**	0.2142	**	0.1078	**	0.0075	
	(.0360)		(.0397)		(.0416)		(.0424)	
Household size	−0.0567	**	−0.0443	**	−0.0568	**	−0.0792	**
	(.0133)		(.0160)		(.0166)		(.0153)	
Employer	0.1822		0.0688		0.2713		−0.2501	
	(.1330)		(.1692)		(.2013)		(.1530)	
Employee	0.1566		−0.0045		0.3687	*	−0.2256	
	(.1255)		(.1623)		(.1942)		(.1436)	
Unemployed	−0.085		0.0733		0.4128	**	−0.1057	
	(.1287)		(.1651)		(.1954)		(.1468)	
Student	0.1008		−0.1665		0.2759		−0.1544	
	(.1408)		(.1716)		(.2034)		(.1545)	
Retired	0.0568		0.1948		0.3987	*	−0.1001	
	(.1344)		(.1737)		(.2188)		(.1671)	
Homemaker	0.0645		−0.0162		0.2847		−0.2987	*
	(.1328)		(.1719)		(.2055)		(.1604)	
Vocational	0.2859	**	0.0581		0.0677		0.3038	**
	(.0461)		(.0557)		(.0551)		(.0474)	
High school	0.231	**	0.0434		0.0595		0.2054	**
	(.0447)		(.0503)		(.0513)		(.0483)	
University	0.3718	**	0.1698	**	0.1067	**	0.2475	**
	(.0458)		(.0498)		(.0529)		(.0504)	

	Attendance	Purchase	Rental	Infringement
Correlations				
Attendance		0.1733 **	0.1741 **	0.1662
		(.0270)	(.0310)	(.1193)
Purchase			0.153 **	0.3398 *
			(.0458)	(.1945)
Rental				0.2607
				(.1937)
Chi-sq	6785.0			
p-value	0.000			

Note: p < .05 *, p < .01**

have a specific taste for the experience of big screen cinema consumption that is not easily substituted through infringement. On the other hand, a positive correlation is found between purchase and rental, and purchase and infringement. An interpretation consistent with these correlations would be that individuals have a taste for convenient entertainment, be it legal or not. As was the case with recorded music, we cannot reject the joint significance of all the correlations, hence a simultaneous model seems appropriate.

Finally, Table 7.8 shows the estimation of a bivariate probit model in which purchases (both physical and digital) and infringement enter as dependent variables. In it, two models have been estimated. Model 1 includes the number of books purchased for professional or study motives (# professional) and other motivations (# other) as explanatory variables, while model 2 excludes them to avoid potential endogeneity problems. In both cases the effect of copyright infringement stands out: it has a negative impact on purchases, i.e. infringement decreases the probability purchasing. If we look at motivation – model 1 – it appears that infringement has functional grounds, as professionally and/or educationally driven purchases also increase the likelihood of infringement. The correlation between purchases and infringement is positive in model 1 but non-significant in model 2. In this case, each equation could be independently estimated which implies book purchasing and infringing behavior being independent. However, after so doing, the qualitative impact of infringement on purchases remains unchanged.

Socio-demographic and educational constraints

The next blocks of variables in Tables 7.6, 7.7 and 7.8 show the impact of socio-demographic characteristics, occupational status and educational attainment on the different participation variables. From these, a gender

Table 7.8 Multivariate probit model estimates: books

	Model 1				Model 2			
	Purchase		**Infringement**		**Purchase**		**Infringement**	
Infringement	−1.6446	**			−1.6607	**		
	(.3910)				(.5160)			
# professional	0.3836	**	0.7710	**				
	−0.0396		(.0894)					
# other	0.8482	**	.0558					
	(.0336)		(.1201)					
Female	0.0711	**	0.0072		0.1164	**	−0.026	
	(.0315)		(.0768)		(.0303)		(.0724)	
Age	0.0179	**	0.0279		0.018	**	0.0161	
	(.0060)		(.0234)		(.0058)		(.0232)	
Age2	−0.0002	**	−0.0003		−0.0002	**	−0.0002	
	(.0001)		(.0003)		(.0001)		(.0003)	
Single	−0.0151		0.1854	*	0.0146		0.1689	*
	(.0374)		(.1044)		(.0365)		(.1002)	
Children	0.1873	**	−0.0201		0.1655	**	−0.0208	
	(.0358)		(.1085)		(.0347)		(.1032)	
Household size	−0.0532	**	0.0094		−0.0666	**	0.0002	
	(.0133)		(.0272)		(.0131)		(.0263)	
Employer	0.3309	**	0.4819		0.3258	**	0.4614	
	(.1310)		(.3809)		(.1293)		(.3490)	
Employee	0.2321	*	0.5497		0.2259	*	0.4894	
	(.1232)		(.3625)		(.1220)		(.3304)	
Unemployed	0.2673	**	0.5994		0.2623	**	0.5172	
	(.1273)		(.3812)		(.1258)		(.3486)	
Student	0.58	**	0.7735	**	0.7408	**	0.9427	**
	(.1390)		(.3814)		(.1361)		(.3594)	
Retired	0.2672	**	1.0253	**	0.1957		0.6494	
	(.1338)		(.4403)		(.1325)		(.4109)	
Homemaker	0.2392	*	0.6944	*	0.1458		0.3864	
	(.1310)		(.4123)		(.1296)		(.3798)	
Vocational	0.066		0.3745	**	0.177	**	0.4567	**

	Model 1				Model 2			
	(.0443)		(.1054)		(.0429)		(.1041)	
High school	0.05		0.2262	**	0.178	**	0.2824	**
	(.0434)		(.1121)		(.0423)		(.1086)	
University	0.2882	**	0.2892	**	0.5472	**	0.5096	**
	(.0462)		(.1150)		(.0435)		(.1066)	
Correlations								
Purchase			0.3519	**			0.3882	
			(0.1605)				(0.2243)	
Chi-sq	3856.6				2920.7			
p-value	0.0000				0.0000			

Note: p < .05 *, p < .01**

effect, which is dependent on the sector considered, is found: being female has a negative impact on recorded music (purchases and infringement) and films (all participation variables), but a positive effect on book purchases. Age shows a rather differentiated effect on different markets: it decreases the probability of participation in purchases and infringement in recorded music and attendance and infringement in films. Interestingly, the effect is non-linear for film rental and book purchases. In the former case we find a positive effect up to 40 years of age (with a maximum positive effect is achieved at 20 years of age) and negative thereafter; while in the latter case age increases the probability of participation up to 60 years of age (maximum effect achieved at 30 years) and decreasing it thereafter.

Results on other socio-demographic variables were even more diverse. Being single increases the probability of streaming and infringement in music, attendance in films, and infringement in books. Having children decreases the likelihood of infringement in music and attendance in films. Note that both variables could proxy time availability, a key asset in explaining participation to most cultural activities, as these tend to be time intensive. On the other hand, having children increases the probability of purchase and rental in films and purchase of books. While the former stresses the existence of a market segment of entertainment for children, the latter stresses the fact that part of the book purchases are functionally motivated. The number of individuals living in the same household consistently affects negatively all participation variables except for infringement in books that could be, again, somehow linked to time availability.

Occupational status variables had no effect on music participation, while being retired or employee increased participation in film rental. For books, being a student has the major impact in both purchases and infringement. As for book purchases, being active in the labor market (employer/employee/ unemployed) increases the likelihood of participation. Except for being a student, the interpretation of which is obvious, the rest of controls are harder to interpret. An income effect might be present (being in the labor market could explain a regular income source in the case of employer and employees) but also some unobserved differences among survey-takers that has not been accounted otherwise.

Finally, educational attainment matters. Education increases the likelihood of participation in most markets, with some noteworthy differences. The more educated (university graduates) show a greater probability of purchase and infringement in music, and of participation in all markets in films and books. On the other hand vocational education and high school have a more limited impact in films (affecting attendance and infringement) and qualitatively a similar effect on participation in books is found. In short, the findings show a link between education and infringement, suggesting the need for specific technical abilities and knowledge. Here we could identify cultural capital at play, although one should not discard the estimates partially reflecting survey-takers income, a control variable that could explain cultural consumption through two channels: individuals budgetary constraints and socio-economic status. Unfortunately, the survey lacks a specific question for income, leaving us none the wiser.

Discussion

Based on a descriptive analysis of the sample, a positive association between infringement and participation is found in recorded music and films. This association turns out to be negative in the case of infringement and book purchases, although positive for infringement and borrowing. Whether these findings are related to a positive or negative effect of infringement on participation requires the formulation of a proper empirical model that includes as explanatory variables not only infringement but other potential determinants of participation. The goal is to control for potential confounding factors that might interfere in the observed association. The empirical specification and estimation of models (1)–(2) is an attempt in that direction.

Table 7.9 summarizes the main empirical results. With regards to the direct impact of infringement in each market, as given by the estimated coefficients in Tables 7.6 to 7.8 we found a variety of outcomes that we discuss next. First, there is no evidence of infringement having any impact in purchases and streaming of recorded music. The claim infringement reducing sales, framed in terms of participation, is not supported by the data, neither the existence of a net substitution effect between piracy and streaming. While the former adds more evidence to the existing empirical findings, the latter should be taken cautiously as streaming services were starting as the survey was taken. Additionally, we must note that the non-significance of the

Table 7.9 Summary of main findings

		Music	Films	Books
Descriptive	Association	(+) Infringement is positively associated to purchases (digital and physical) and streaming	(+) Infringement is positively associated to attendance, purchases and rental	(-) Infringement ios negatively associated to purchases (albeit positively to borrowing)
Model	Direct impact (coefficients)	Non-significant in all cases	Non-significant on attendance and purchases. **Negative on rental**	**Negative effect on book purchases**
	Indirect impact (correlation between equations)	Positive correlation between purchases and streaming and purchases and streaming (**taste for music**)	Positive correlation between: (i) attendance and purchases and (ii) attendance and rental (**taste for films**). Positive correlation between (i) purchase and rental and (ii) purchase and infringement (**taste for convenient film watching**)	Ambiguous: (i) positive (model 1); (i) non-significant (model 2)
	Other	Negative impact of streaming on purchases		Functional motivation of infringement: positive effect of number of books read (professional motivations) on infringement

estimates leads to an ambiguous outcome: note that predicted effects are net effects, and potentially include both substitution and sampling effects. If a negative effect is found, one could conclude with a largest substitution than sampling effect (and the other way round). When no significant effects are found, either substitution and sampling effects offset each other, or there is no impact at all. In other words, we cannot reject the hypotheses that substitution or sampling effects are zero, or that they are of (approximately) the same magnitude. Being both outcomes plausible, results provide no evidence for **H1** or **H2** in the recorded music market.

Second, only rental of movies was negatively affected by infringement. In this case there is evidence for a prevalence of substitution effects in the market. It should be noted that this result would be consistent with either (i) a substitution effect (and no sampling effect), or (ii) the existence of a sampling effect that is offset by a stronger substitution effect. The same happens with book purchases: the negative coefficient for infringement suggests similar results. Altogether, there is evidence supporting **H1** in film-rentals and in books.

What could be the source of these asymmetric results? We think it should be linked to the alternatives available to consumers. The fewer the channels through which individuals can participate, the more likely infringement becomes a relevant option, especially for those consumers who have a low net valuation of the cultural product and that do not face large transaction costs from infringing copyright. Other things equal, for a large enough group of such marginal consumers the effect of infringement would be expected to be negative. This is likely to be the case of books: as the digitization of books only recently started, individuals are still adapting to the new channels through which they participate in this market. As for movie rental, the incipiency of the deployment of online pay per view could explain the estimated effect. In short, the fact that when the survey was taken few alternatives were available is consistent with **H3**, i.e. the likelihood of infringement playing a negative role.

As a by-product of the estimation strategy, the empirical model allows us to measure the indirect link between infringement and participation via the simultaneity of the participation equations, i.e. the correlations between the underlying non-observed factors (i.e., the residuals) that affect participation across markets, including that of infringement on other distribution channels. These correlations account for the linear relation between the unobserved heterogeneity for each pair of equations, which could be interpreted as the impact of underlying preferences on any two variables. In this respect, only in the case of films was evidence of a positive correlation between the error terms of infringement and purchase of movies. The fact that the correlation between purchase and rental was also positive suggests unobserved preferences linked to the convenience and practicality of watching films at home, while the positive correlation between attendance and purchase and attendance and rental reveals a taste for films. In the recorded music market, unobserved factors that drive infringement are indirectly linked to increased participation via purchases (also correlated with streaming) in what could be a general taste for recorded music. Interestingly, for books, when model 2 is considered, there is no correlation between infringement and book purchases, suggesting these to be decisions on participation that are taken independently.

To conclude, one additional feature was identified in the recorded music participation model, namely the negative impact of streaming on purchases. This could be the counterpart to a negligible effect of infringement on legal participation means. While streaming could move marginal consumers away from infringement, it could also make actual legal participants to downgrade, hence cannibalizing more profitable distribution channels.

Conclusions

In this paper we have proposed to measure the impact of copyright infringement on participation in the cultural industries. The recorded music, film and book publishing industries share some basic features, namely they supply information goods with cultural content. The nature of cultural consumption, unlike many other goods and services, means that consumers need some basic knowledge and prior consumption experiences, which partially blurs the role of standard economic variables (such as income) in explaining consumption, and stress other such as education or time availability to mention two. This, in turn, suggests that the heterogeneity of preferences play a key role in cultural markets, which implies that a straightforward effect of infringement substituting legal consumption need not hold for every segment of the demand. To what extent this is the case in the three cultural industries considered has been the subject matter of this paper.

Interestingly, there are striking differences between these sectors, such as the different digitization stage, or the diversity of distribution channels that affect consumers' consumption possibilities. According to the hypotheses we have proposed, the better the demand is matched by supply, the less the room for substitution effects. Therefore, a second general goal has been to identify whether the different arrangements within each industry – a reflection of the different digitization stages – are related to different responses of participation to infringement.

At this point, the answer to both questions, based on the empirical evidence, goes in the same direction: the measured direct impact of infringement is negative only in some very specific instances, and the asymmetries found suggest that the different institutional arrangements within each industry are key to understand the magnitude of this impact.

One thing that has been stressed in this paper is the need to take into account the diversity of distribution arrangements within each industry in a simultaneous setup. In the proposed framework, infringement arises as one additional option that consumers face, and hence cannot be taken as exogenous to the system. When one considers the multidimensional nature of participation in the cultural industries, results are not straightforward. As already mentioned, there is an asymmetric effect of infringement both between and within industries.

On the other hand, the analysis has provided an interesting insight into unobserved individual traits. As suggested in the descriptive analysis, overall infringers show a higher propensity to participate: they listen to and buy more music, go more to the movies, and purchase and read more.[11] This propensity to participate has been captured through the correlation between equations in the different models. It shows that, in films and recorded music, infringers tend to be culturally more active: regardless of how – legally or illegally – infringers do participate, and most likely both legally and illegally. The lack of a similar evidence for books could be linked to the fact that, at this stage, infringement could be functionally motivated.

Combining all the previous evidence, it can be concluded that findings suggest that the potentially negative effect of copyright on demand is better addressed within the cultural industries. The analysis of the profile of cultural consumers shows that participants tend to access contents in diverse ways, with infringement being just another option. This implies that the more channels available, the less infringement will pose a threat to the industries. This has policy and managerial implications. While enforcement plays a role by increasing the relative price of infringement, its effectiveness is far from perfect as past experiences show. In other words, there is little that can be done just by modifying the regulatory and institutional framework, as infringement seems to be a valid option for a non-negligible share of consumers. On the contrary, strategies that aim at differentiating cultural goods and services do a better job in matching consumer's preferences widening the choice set and the range of opportunity costs individuals face, which, in turn, reduces the observed effect of infringement. The findings suggest the relevance of identifying market heterogeneity in order to better know demand segments and position alternatives ways of accessing contents to reduce the impact of infringement on legal consumption.

Notes

1 This particularly holds for films and recorded music.
2 It should be noted that Barker (2012) criticizes the findings in Andersen and Frenz (2010) mainly on methodological grounds. Specifically, the critique points to the single equation setup in the estimation process.
3 http://en.www.mcu.es/estadisticas/MC/EHC/index.html. Here one finds more information about the methodology and a summary of the main results in all areas.
4 Consumers face also hybrid models bundling physical and digital formats, such as the combination of vinyl LP+digital download, or Book+eBook.

5 Tetrachoric correlation is an appropriate measure of the correlation among latent variables that are observed as binary outcomes.
6 Yet, one must note that this does not necessarily contradict the results of Cox and Collins (2014), who found differences between heavy downloaders in music and movies. In our case we are taking into account all (and not only most intensive) infringers.
7 Nevertheless, it should be noted that ebooks, although increasingly popular, are just a marginal share of the total market. From the survey, the 95 percent interval of the proportion of the Spanish population that reads physical books is 49.4–51.3 percent, while for digital books is 2.97–3.66 percent.
8 Seaman (2006) surveys the empirical literature on cultural participation.
9 Other estimated parameters are not shown but can be provided on request.
10 See www.theguardian.com/technology/2011/mar/08/spotify-hits-1-million-paying-subscribers (accessed 24 April 2017).
11 It is true that some results are not as straightforward. Book pirates tend to participate less than the population as a whole: the proportion of infringers that buy is roughly 30 percent compared with roughly 35 percent at the sample level. However, the former also buy more books in terms of number than the latter: 1.74 books compared to 1.46. Video purchase is the other exception.

References

Adermon, A., and Liang, C. (2010). "Piracy, music and movies: A natural experiment." *IFN Working Paper* No.854. http://www.ifn.se.

Adermon, A., and Liang, C. (2014). "Piracy and music sales: The effects of an anti-piracy law." *Journal of Economic Behavior and Organization*, 105: 90–106.

Andersen, B., and Frenz, M. (2010). "Don't blame the P2P file-sharers: The impact of free music downloads on the purchase of music CDs in Canada." *Journal of Evolutionary Economics*, 20: 715–740.

Bacache-Beauvallet, M., Bourreau, M., and Moreau, F. (2015). "Piracy and creation: The case of the music industry. "*European Journal of Law and Economics*, 39(2): 245–262.

Barker, G. (2012). "Evidence of the effect of free music downloads on the purchase of music CDs in Canada." *Review of Economic Research on Copyright Issues*, 9(2): 55–78

Battacharjee, S., Gopal, R.D., Lertwachara, K., Marsden, J.R. and Telang, R. (2007) "The effect of digital sharing technologies on music markets: A survival analysis of albums on ranking charts." *Management Science*, 53: 1359–1374.

Bourreau, M., Gensollen, M., and Moreau, F. (2012). "The impact of a radical innovation on business models: Incremental adjustments or big bang?" *Industry and Innovation*, 19(5): 415–435.

Camarero, C., Antón, C., and Rodríguez, J. (2014). "Technological and ethical antecedents of e-book piracy and price acceptance: Evidence from the Spanish case." *The Electronic Library*, 32(4): 542–566.

Cappellari, L., and Jenkins, S.P. (2003). "Multivariate probit regression using simulated maximum likelihood." *The Stata Journal*, 3(3): 278–294.

Cox, J., and Collins, A. (2014). "Sailing in the same ship? Differences in factors motivating piracy of music and movie content." *Journal of Behavioral and Experimental Economics*, 50: 70–76.

Danaher, B., and Smith, M.D. (2014). "Gone in 60 seconds: The impact of the mega-upload shutdown on movie sales." *International Journal of Industrial Organization*, 33: 1–8.

De Vany, A.S. and Walls, W.D. (2007). "Estimating the effects of movie piracy on box-office revenue." *Review of Industrial Organization*, 30(4): 291–301.

Gopal, R.D., Bhattacharjee, S. and Sanders, G.L. (2006). "Do artists benefit from online music sharing?" *Journal of Business*, 79: 1503–1533.

El Harbi, S., Grolleau, G. and Bekir, I. (2014). "Substituting piracy with a pay-what-you-want option: Does it make sense." *European Journal of Law and Economics*, 37: 277–297.

Hennig-Thurau, T., Henning, V. and Sattler, H. (2007). "Consumer file sharing of motion pictures." *Journal of Marketing*, 71: 1–18.

Liebowitz, S. J. (2016). "How much of the decline in sound recording sales is due to file-sharing?" *Journal of Cultural Economics*, 40(1): 13–28.

McKenzie, J. (2013). "P2P file-sharing: How does music file-sharing affect recorded music sales in Australia?" In P. Tschmuck, P.L. Pearce and S. Pearce (Eds) *Music Business and the Experience Economy*. Berlin: Springer-Verlag.

Michel, N.J. (2006). "The impact of digital file sharing on the music industry: An empirical analysis." *Topics in Economic Analysis & Policy*, 6(1): 1–22.

Montoro-Pons, J.D. and Cuadrado-García, M. (2008). "Legal origin and intellectual property rights: an empirical study in the prerecorded music sector. "*European Journal of Law and Economics*, 26(2): 153.

Montoro-Pons, J. D., and Cuadrado-García, M. (2013). "Empirical insights into recorded music consumer behavior and copyright infringement." In *Music and Law* (pp. 245–267). Emerald Group Publishing Limited.

Oberholzer, F., and Strumpf, K. (2007). "The effect of file sharing on record sales: An empirical analysis." *Journal of Political Economy*, 115(1): 1–42.

Peitz, M., and Waelbroeck, P. (2004). "The effect of internet piracy on music sales: Cross-section evidence." *Review of Economic Research on Copyright Issues*, 1(2): 71–79.

Reimers, I. (2014). "The effect of piracy protection in book publishing." *Working Paper*, Boston, MA: Northeaster University.

Rob, R., and Waldfogel, J. (2006). "Piracy in the high C's: Music downloading, sales displacement, and social welfare in a sample of college students." *Journal of Law and Economics*, 49(1): 29–62.

Rob, R., and, Waldfogel, J. (2007). "Piracy on the silver screen." *Journal of Industrial Economics*, 55(3): 379–395.

Seaman, B.A. (2006). "Empirical studies for the demand of performing arts." In V.A. Ginsburgh, and D. Throsby (Eds) *Handbook of the Economics of Art and Culture*. Oxford: North-Holland.

Smith, M.D., and Telang, R. (2010). "Piracy or promotion? The impact of broadband internet penetration on DVD sales." *Information Economics and Policy*, 22: 289–298.

Stigler, G. J., and Becker, G. S. (1977). "De gustibus non est disputandum." *The American Economic Review*, 67(2): 76–90.

Waldfogel, J. (2010). "Music file sharing and sales displacement in the iTunes era." *Information Economics and Policy*, 22: 306–314.

Walls, W.D. (2008). "Cross-country analysis of movie piracy." *Applied Economics*, 40(5): 625–632.

Hu, Y. and Smith, M.D. (2013). "The impact of ebook distribution on print sales: Analysis of a natural experiment." http://ssrn.com/abstract=1966115.

Zentner, A. (2006). "Measuring the effect of file sharing on music purchases." *Journal of Law and Economics*, 49(1): 63–90.

8 Who cares if Taytay[1] gets pay pay? Shake it off

The apathy of the contemporary music consumer

Gary Sinclair

Introduction

> The challenge is to get everyone to respect music again, to recognise its value… Water is free. Music is $6 but no one wants to pay for music. You should drink free water from the tap – it's a beautiful thing. And if you want to hear the most beautiful song, then support the artist. Jay Z
>
> (Sisario, 2015)

During the launch campaign for the much-publicised *Tidal* music streaming subscription service, the hip-hop star Jay Z demonstrated a lack of understanding about two different types of consumption. The first is the economics of water consumption. This is unless he hydrates himself by opening his mouth and tilting his head when it rains. The second, more important for this chapter, is his belief that the modern music consumer will subscribe to Tidal because they 'want' to pay for music. The water analogy works in one instance in that music can be essentially accessed 'on tap', a legacy of peer-to-peer sharing, legal downloading and contemporary streaming practices. Consequently, the modern young music consumer has been socialised in an era of free or freemium formats where the misguided belief, similar to conceptions of tap water, that music has no cost and comes directly from thin air has potentially taken shape with some. Kusek and Leonhard (2005) have in fact made the argument that consumption of music should be similar to consumption of water in terms of its ubiquitous nature. However, they point out that payment of monthly fees is required for water 'on tap' just as it should always be for music that is always 'on'.

The values of artist compensation that Jay-Z champions here are something that should be taken seriously. This is easy to do once we look beyond the presentation of this argument in the shape of famous multi-millionaire musicians launching a corporate brand by appealing to consumers to pay them more money. The reality is that it is not the A-list musicians who suffer from music piracy but the smaller artists, the session musicians, the engineers, the custodians and a wide number of further stakeholders who are influenced both directly and indirectly from a decline in recording revenues and industry disruption. However, the question is whether the average consumer under-stands the level of this impact and if so, do they care? Following three sepa-rate qualitative studies (interviews and discussion groups) on music consumption I explore these specific questions.

The chapter is outlined as follows. Previous literature on piracy, with emphasis on music piracy, is reviewed in the context of the legal, fear, guilt and moral appeals/strategies that were employed by the industry. Reviewing this literature leads to a discussion of consumer apathy and an exploration of how this apathy can be understood in the emerging legal music streaming market. The ethical consumer literature is used as a means of focusing such discussion and to make sense of data presented that explores knowledge and perceptions about artist payment, justifications for consumer apathy, and the attitude-behaviour gap that exists between consumers' stated concerns and their actual behaviour as 'ethical' music consumers. Implications regarding these findings are discussed in the context of how the industry can address consumer apathy and issues around piracy and artist compensation from legal streaming.

Literature review

This review focuses mostly on literature concerning music piracy as the data presented later in this chapter is exclusively drawn from music consumption contexts. However, literature regarding film and television piracy is referred to intermittently as means of comparison. The focus of literature on the subject of piracy tends to draw from the music context. This is probably because of the high level of technological disruption that has come to be associated with the music industry over the last 20 years and the controversial means by which the industry has sought to address the issue. This review focuses on the industry's reaction to the threat of piracy (legal/fear appeal, guilt and moral arguments) before considering the ethical consumer literature as a lens in which the apathy of the modern music consumer can be framed. The discus-sion in this review considers if consumer apathy is still an issue in legal music streaming contexts.

Legal/fear appeals: 'you wouldn't steal a car'

The literature on music piracy has been dominated by research that is con-cerned with how to stop music piracy. Fisher (2004) and Chiou et al. (2005) argue that perceived legal and prosecution risks affect attitudes regarding music piracy. Consequently, research (see Levin et al., 2007) suggested that the industry promote the potential legal consequences of pirating music. This is despite the significant amount of research (see Balestrino, 2008; LaRose et al., 2005; Sinclair & Green, 2015) that suggests that the threat of prosecution is not likely to influence consumer behaviour. The threat of prosecution is clearly dependent on context and the perceived likelihood that one would face prosecution, something which Rojek (2005) argues is absent in a consumption practice that has grown to be socially acceptable. It can also be argued that much of this is obviously due to the difficulty in prosecuting individual pirates.

Regardless, advertising campaigns in the early 2000s ('you wouldn't steal a car!') used legal/fear approaches to try and persuade consumers of potential prosecution. Parkes (2013) writes about how this approach was used in the film industry, for example. He argues that as piracy migrated towards online downloading and file sharing, such rhetoric became almost comical. Regardless, such threats were backed up in the UK and Ireland as well as a number of other countries with graduated response systems that worked with Internet providers to clamp down on piracy with escalating warning systems that increased punishment following each transgression. The success of this was dependent on the individual laws of each country (e.g. see Hill, 2007) and the willingness of Internet providers to work with the industry to identify individual pirates. The difficulty and expense in identifying individual pirates and the bad publicity that comes with prosecuting what are often young children/ adults for such practices most likely led to a shift in the legal approach which has focused much more exclusively on prosecuting and shutting down the spaces that facilitate the illegal content. Recently (see Sinclair, 2017), the Motion Picture Association took legal action against a number of European Internet providers (e.g. UK, Ireland, Denmark) to block streaming websites (e.g. primewire.ag and onatchseries.to). Historically, blocking orders (e.g. Pirate Bay) from the recording industry only achieved temporary reprieves from piracy as new domains and proxies are created that replicate the websites that have been shut-down in an escalating game of whack-a-mole. This more widespread legal approach clearly does more to address the source of piracy but the Motion Picture Association is likely to continue to experience the same problems as the recording music industry that stem from the notion that consumers and to an extent uploaders of this content don't seem to fear prosecution.

Guilt and moral arguments

Prosecution and fear appeal strategies are of course only one-half of the recording industry's assault on music piracy. The other half of the 'master-plan' involved appealing to consumers through guilt and moral discourses. Research which considers the guilt and moral argument, like much of contemporary piracy research, starts off with the presumption that music piracy is wrong both from a legal and moral standpoint. Conveniently sidestepping the minefield that is the legal argument (that is covered with greater expertise in other parts of the book), the moral perspective is of more interest to us here when considering the perceived apathy of consumers. Ang et al., (2001) has identified low knowledge of the social implications of downloading as a key factor that is linked to the favourable attitudes towards music piracy. Cesareo and Pastore (2014) also cite a connection between moral judgment and a potential decline in piracy and argue that music companies and new legal streaming applications should place emphasis on the unethical nature of music piracy and its potential implications on a wider number of stakeholders. It must be said that the recording industry has sought to communicate the attribution of harm that music piracy causes to the wider industry using guilt appeals. However, the evidence suggests (see Levin et al., 2007; Lysonski & Durvasula, 2008) that this has failed to have an impact in reducing the levels of piracy. However, this could be a consequence of not doing enough to communicate this message effectively.

There is still not sufficient research that explores consumer's knowledge of the impact on the wider industry and whether they care if they do understand the impact. The research by Cesareo and Pastore (2004) is based on the linking of attitudes to hypothetical behaviours and perhaps does not take into account the attitude–behaviour gap (see Cotte & Trudel, 2009) that is prevalent in ethical consumer questions of this regard. Furthermore, this presumption that piracy is morally wrong is problematic in that it immediately rules out many of the consumers' justifications for pirating music, which become increasingly complex when morals come into question. For example, Rojek (2005) highlights the empowering features of piracy in that it allows for a larger number of people to access and share music in facilitating a greater sense of social inclusion. This relates to a wider argument concerning the contested ideology of commercialising art in the first place (see Adorno, 1976) and the ethics of an industry that looks to prosecute its consumers to halt a practice that's central purpose is to disseminate that very art. Garcia-Bardidia et al. (2011) suggest that the artistic ideological arguments are convenient to make but the fact that piracy is a mainstream practice makes it inevitable that there is not a singular but 'alternative stances to activism' (2011: 179) within the marketplace.

Speaking to the different perspectives that consumers inevitably have Giesler (2008) focuses on the balance that can be achieved between the *social utilitarians* (music should be free for everyone) and the *possessive individualists* (the commercial interest of music should come first). The balance that Giesler considers in his discussion of the evolution of consumer markets is essentially that of a digital alternative that allows for the same level of access and choice of content but that also speaks to commercial needs. Giesler identified iTunes at this time but it has become clear that the advent of music streaming applications such as Spotify has done more to compromise the needs of these opposing views and importantly reduces levels of piracy (see Sinclair & Green, 2015). This trend is particularly evidenced in early adopter Scandinavian countries where Norway, for example, had a drop in piracy from 80% in 2009 to 4% in 2014 (IFPI, 2015).

Does the migration towards legal streaming mean consumers now care about artist compensation?

This trend raises an interesting question. Is this as clear an indicator as we need that consumers pirate music due to utilitarian reasons (Sinha & Mandel, 2009;

Taylor et al., 2009)? Will they only consume through legal formats if they are superior in this functional sense to piracy? One could argue that the migration to legal streaming apps adheres to the utilitarian need as well as the moral and legal quandary as the consumer is now contributing money (more than zero) to the recording industry whether it is through information and consumption of adverts in freemium models or through payment in premium models.

However, it has emerged (see Marshall, 2015) that the issue of artist payment is a big problem within these subscription models with high-profile artists such as Taylor Swift and Thom Yorke speaking out about it publically. This has regenerated traditional questions about power relations between record labels and artists that much of the early research and media attention has focused on (see Resnikoff, 2011). It must be understood that the streaming apps are not completely complicit in these unfair payment practices, the individual deals between labels and distributors if anything are more revealing about the ethical practices of other stakeholders in the industry. Regardless of who is at fault, the artist is still suffering economically from digital consumption, be it from the direct loss of sales as a consequence of piracy or because of contracts with record labels and streaming platforms that unfairly compensate them for their music. Consequently, this context actually provides us with an excellent opportunity in which to explore consumer perceptions regarding the value of art and fair payment. It provides the perfect context in which we can question the consumer's knowledge of this ethical issue and whether they actually care without the moderating factor of utilitarian factors that have influenced this line of debate in previous music piracy consumption studies.

Ethical consumption

At the crux of the matter then is an ethical and socially responsible consumption question. Consumer research on ethical issues has become increasingly prevalent as consumers attain more information and hence put more pressure on corporations to produce goods/services ethically. Mohr et al. (2001: 47) define a socially responsible consumer as 'a person basing his or her acquisition, usage and disposition of products on a desire to minimize or eliminate any harmful effects and maximize the long-term beneficial impact on society'. Hence, in this case we could base one aspect of the ethical consumption of music on how artists are treated and rewarded for their music.

The advantages of positioning a product as socially responsible have many advantages. These include greater purchase intentions (Mohr & Webb, 2005), positive word of mouth (Hoeffler & Keller, 2002) and an increased likelihood of paying higher prices. This research makes sense of the strategy that Tidal have employed, for instance. If the product is positioned as socially responsible they can charge premium rates (which they have), they can generate word of mouth (yes, even if it is not necessarily positive) and this will lead to greater purchase intentions (hang on!). Clearly, it is not as simple as positioning your product/service as socially responsible. Previous research also indicates that many consumers are confused by conflicting socially responsible messages and often have a lack of awareness about socially responsible initiatives (see Du et al., 2010). Another problem is the attitude–behaviour gap (see Cotte & Trudel, 2009) where consumers state a concern for a particular issue regarding socially responsible consumption but fail to act on it, talking the talk but not walking the walk. This is further complicated by the product category. Despite research that has suggested previously (see Peloza et al., 2013; Strahilevitz & Myers, 1998) that consumers respond more effectively to hedonic products with socially responsible attributes or messages, Green et al. (2016) found that consumers were actually more likely to incorporate socially responsible considerations into their everyday utilitarian purchases than in their consumption of music. However, more research is needed to understand why this apathy exists amongst music consumers.

Methodology

The aim of this chapter is to explore this consumer apathy through the contexts of piracy and music streaming. Piracy has been framed as a fixed problem that potentially has a fixed explanation/solution. Consequently, much of the academic research has drawn from quantitative methods that seek to explore the influence of key modifiers for predicting (e.g. Higgins, 2007) or preventing (e.g. Sinha & Mandel, 2009) piracy. However, this research is more concerned with exploring the issue of consumer apathy in a much broader manner, the complexities of which are difficult to measure. As such, an exploratory qualitative approach was deemed most suitable.

Data was collected via interviews and discussion groups across three separate research projects on music consumption (music subcultures, socially responsible consumption and music streaming) that took place over the course of seven years (2009–2016). Although piracy was not the central issue of any of the projects, it emerged as a common theme of discussion in each interview and discussion group and generated a large amount of data. It was evident that respondents were motivated to openly discuss their illegal consumer behaviour even when they hadn't signed up to do so. The long period between projects also allowed for a range of data that saw a significant shift in consumer practice over time from piracy to predominantly legal streaming and incorporated key issues and contexts relating to artist payment that were topical at the time.

Appendix 1 summarises the data corpus and methods undertaken. Overall, 51 interviews were conducted (30 male). Purposive (Merriam, 2009) and snowball (Bryman, 2015) sampling strategies were used to recruit any adult who considered themselves a consumer of music. Participants were predominantly from the Republic of Ireland and Scotland and ranged in age from 18–45 with an average age of approximately 29, representing a much smaller sample of students which have tended to be disproportionally over-represented in studies of music consumption, particularly studies relating to piracy (see Weijters et al., 2014). The discussion group consisted of 19 participants (11 female) who were recruited by a specialist marketing research group. The participants were sourced from the United Kingdom and ranged in age from 18–34. The discussion group, moderated by two different researchers, took place over the course of a week and involved discussions around a variety of music consumption themes. Piracy and consumer knowledge of the recording music industry was a topic that emerged as particularly important across the week.

Participants of both discussion groups and interviews were particularly challenged on their views regarding artist payment in order to explore the gaps between knowledge and attitude and attitude and behaviour regarding the subject. Hathaway and Atkinson's (2003) wonderfully entitled 'good cop/ bad cop' interview persona was drawn on here. They suggest that the early part of an interview should be about establishing trust and accommodating respondents. This allows for the 'bad cop' persona to ask more critical and challenging questions towards the end of the interview. For example, many of the participants talked about wanting to support small artists. The trust developed between interviewer and interviewee allowed me to challenge these claims for evidence of behaviour that supports that attitude later in the interviews without offending or embarrassing the participants.

Findings

The findings are divided into two main sections. The first is about the knowledge and perceptions regarding artist payment. This is followed by an exploration concerning the relationship between increased knowledge on the subject, consumer attitudes and action/inaction.

Knowledge and perceptions about artist payment

There is a common perception amongst the respondents that it is just established mainstream artists who suffer as a consequence of music piracy. Piracy is associated with the rich becoming slightly less rich (see Brown, 2017).

> Metallica and stuff, they are not going to be put out, they are not going to be kicked out of their house because they can't pay their mortgage because someone has downloaded their album, I know again that there are huge amounts of downloads but they are still in a mansion, they are still not going bankrupt.
>
> (John, 27)

The framing of the impact of piracy in this manner is understandable considering that it is often famous artists such as Metallica and Lily Allen that are the faces of this discussion when it is debated in the public forum. This type of discourse was common amongst the participants and played a key role in justifying their own moral ambiguity regarding the act of music piracy (more on justifications later in the analysis). Furthermore, they equated increased exposure that piracy and streaming brings to higher revenues from live performances and merchandise.

> They [musicians] are going to make so much more money out of other stuff anyway that I don't think it makes a great deal of difference. These massive stadium bands are always going to make their money from tours, like their CD sales probably aren't going to account for that much, I wouldn't have thought. And it's hard to take sympathy for someone as well because they earn so much money.
>
> (Peter, 30)

There is an element of truth to this argument. Curien and Moreau (2009) argue that piracy has had a positive impact on other segments of the music industry (e.g. live performances) that make up for the lost revenues in the recording industry, although the high levels of piracy at this time were/are in no way sustainable for long-term revenues. Regardless of the validity of this argument, most of the respondents were unable to look at the impact of piracy beyond mainstream musicians without prompting. Any guilt concerning the implications of their piracy was in some way alleviated by the legitimacy afforded by the legality of streaming services such as Spotify.

J (JOHN, 27): ... anyone I wanted to listen to has been on Spotify and the fact that I am paying for it with my tenner a month takes away the little guilt I might have had...
I (INTERVIEWER): So you stopped illegally downloading?
J: Oh yeah, everything is from Spotify. It's good for not downloading stuff.

The increasing consumption of such services has if anything made consumers even more indifferent to the concerns of fair artist payment. This issue relates back to the lack of knowledge that the average consumer possesses. I have been researching music consumption (with emphasis on piracy and streaming) for about nine years and I cannot tell you with any degree of certainty how the artist royalty system works. Consequently, it is not surprising to find a high amount of confusion from the respondents regarding artist payment from streaming.

> I have no idea... how much do they get?
>
> (Becky, 19)

> I am not really sure how it works.
> (Chris, 29)Many of the respondents understandably had little knowledge of how the artists are paid and hence had very little concern or opinion concerning the issue. The lack of transparency in the music industry has been compared to that of the movie industry, for example, in terms of its

clarity regarding the reporting of salaries and box office takings (Brown, 2017).

> I don't really have an opinion owing to the fact that I don't really know enough about the area and how much they get paid and stuff like that or how the model works.
>
> (Donal, 30)

For some of the respondents there were pockets of information and mis-information that were shared.

> I don't know too much about it. I've read stuff about Spotify that they only get a fraction of a pence or something from the tracks streamed.
>
> (Peter, 30)

Such understandings typically differed in detail but participants mostly shared in the rhetoric that artists are paid poorly on the platform. The interest for some has been awakened by exposure to the debate surrounding fair payment that artists such as Taylor Swift have brought to the mainstream media.

> I do know that Spotify pay people poorly ... I [know] from online newspapers and things like that, the places that come to mind. Like Taylor Swift, she will be one of the most missed people on the platform. But I think for the billions and billions of views she might have got on her songs with the way it streams she would have got a couple, I think it would been sixty thousand or something like that. And she's getting that on the high end of the scale I would imagine the others are not getting that. But other than what I've read I haven't actively sought out anything. So, yeah, I wouldn't actively go to try to understand.
> (Niall, 28)Niall's comments indicate that there is some degree of knowledge amongst the participants of how poorly paid artists are via the streaming platforms. However, his closing comment regarding his lack of motivation to seek out further information is indicative of the apathy that most of the participants have for the issue.

> I don't know anything really about what they get paid... I suppose I don't know enough about and I don't think we ever really know enough about it. Unless you kind of are really in to following like artists and their pay and who and all that kind of stuff. You don't really you just get on with things.
> (Sabrina, 28)The lack of knowledge and confusion around the subject has clearly created a culture of apathy and a lack of motivation to become informed on the subject. This raises an important question. When the respondents are informed about artist payment do they care, does this shift their motivation for knowledge? In ethical consumption studies (see Carrigan et al., 2014) knowledge is often connected with increased concern. However, the

notion of increased action as a consequence is much debated (see Carrington et al., 2016). In the next section of analysis I will explore this.

Does knowledge lead to concern?

I think when I first started with Napster I wasn't completely sure with the whole Napster thing as I was only a kid like. Then obviously when I found out about how it impacts artists I still didn't really care about it.

(Frank, 28)

As outlined, there is a mixed level of knowledge concerning the impact of piracy on artists and the situation surrounding payments from streaming services. This can in part explain some of the consumer apathy regarding this subject. In this section of analysis we explore the attitudes of participants who either possessed a general knowledge or were prompted regarding the 'plight' of the contemporary artist. For most, informed or increased knowledge had little impact on the sense of apathy they had for this issue. This was justified in a number of ways which included the utility of consuming music this way, the hedonic purpose of music, blaming other stakeholders and denial of harm.

Utilitarian and hedonic value

The most prominent reason for consumer apathy regarding the issue of artist payment stemmed from the obvious utility (i.e. free cost, easy accessibility) that participants gained from consuming music via piracy or streaming. Sinclair and Green (2015) identified two typologies of music pirates that justify their music consumption habits on the basis of utilitarian benefit. The first group are the 'steadfast pirates' who continue to download music illegally because of the convenience of access and low (i.e. free) cost of doing so. The participants that have been interviewed since then have mostly graduated to the 'ex-downloader' typology that no longer downloads music illegally because of the increased utility that legal music streaming services supply.

I: What stopped you from doing that [piracy]?
C (CHRIS, 29): I think Spotify really was the main thing. It's so easy and it's all there so I don't really need to. It wasn't the moral point of view or anything, it was just that Spotify was much easier and all the songs were there so there was no need to download them.

The (almost) unlimited access and choice of music, relatively cheap price and surprisingly the social utility of music streaming all contributed to the consumer movement away from music piracy. However, there is still little evidence of moral concerns for artist payment. Becky was asked about paying more money for Tidal or another competing streaming service if they were more ethical to artists.

I would just say I would go for Spotify, good quality, good price, I'll get that. I wouldn't think anything about the artist. I just think about the music. I wouldn't even consider that. Whereas Tidal is so expensive and it's basically the same thing, why would I pay that?

(Becky, 19)

Furthermore, many of the participants talked about the stress of having to delete and start new playlists again and the time they would have to spend becoming familiar with a new user interface. Sinclair and Tinson (2017) describe this as psychological ownership and suggest that music consumers who develop this sense of ownership find it very difficult to switch brands or providers because of the time and effort that has gone into curating their streaming profiles, regardless of the potential superior ethical or utilitarian offering. The difficulty in getting consumers to consider ethical artist payment as a factor in their decision-making is clearly a challenge for the industry and renders the market positioning of streaming services such as Tidal perplexing and out of touch with the modern consumer.

I: Would it in any way influence your decision about what kind of streaming app you used, or service you used? In terms of what the artist is paid?

N (NIALL, 28): No. I'm aware that sounds like I am an arsehole but…To be honest it would be based on the features the application had, the value, and what I could do with it, can I have the songs downloaded on my phone? Do I need to be in WiFi to listen to the songs? With Spotify I don't. So I would be confident enough with mobile phone apps, all of that stuff, to make a decision based on a streaming app. But regarding royalties I'm fairly cut-throat, purely for royalty purposes I would say no. The indifference for some is clearly based on what they can potentially lose if they prioritise a fairer form of artist payment in their consumer decision-making. Furthermore, the hedonic experience and sense of escape that music provides is lessened somewhat if you have to examine how the proverbial sausage is made.

S (SABRINA, 28): You don't really think about it [artist payment] much because in a way for me the whole thing is escapism. So I don't really think about it.

I: What do you mean by music is escapism?

S: Music for me is an enjoyable thing and I know…

I: You don't want to know anything about the business of it do you mean or?

S: Not really. If it was an area of my work and if it was something I was dealing with I probably would be passionate about it and really annoyed about this that and the other about what artists do and don't get but for me I do enough as it is and stress enough as it is that you know I can just get on and just want to enjoy it and that's kind of my opinion on it.

This perspective was common amongst the participants and supports the Green et al. (2016) research, which argues that consumers are less likely to be concerned with the ethical issues regarding the production/consumption of hedonic products/services than more routine utilitarian purchases (e.g. grocery shopping) as it offers the consumer a sense of escape from the pressures of everyday life. Green et al. describe how one of the pressures of modern life is the growing societal expectation to be an ethical consumer. Music is seen as an escape and hence not privy to the same societal rules. The consumption of music and other hedonic goods can consequently be considered with less of an 'ethical' consideration, an escape from the mundane everyday world and pressure to be ethical.

Justifiable apathy

This sense of apathy regarding the health of the recording industry did not emerge out of thin air. The indifference to the piracy crisis and to a lesser degree the more contemporary issues regarding artist royalties are symptomatic of wider issues many consumers have with the industry and mainstream artists that have been developed over time. The reasons for this uneasy relationship are outlined below.

The tension between commerce and art is a common theme in academic studies regarding the culture industries (Adorno, 2002). Whilst most of the participants understand that musicians need to earn a living, what is perceived as hyper-commerciality can be seen as crass and distasteful. Paul's comments on the launch of Tidal echo a number of participants' feelings about the artists that were used to promote the streaming service.

> When Beyonce and Nicki Minaj and Jay-Z and all that are complaining that they don't get enough money from it [their music], I couldn't care any less, because they're already minted and on stage complaining about how they should get another five hundred grand.
>
> (Paul, 28)

There is a romanticism associated with the struggling artist for some participants and that concern for making money shouldn't be a priority.

> I feel if you're that rich you don't need to get richer because of your music. I just think you should be making your music, and if you make money, you make money. If you don't, you don't. We [with friend] were walking along, lovely day, and there was this bloke opposite Sandy Cove Beach who had a rickety old wooden piano on a slant, like sliding down, I think it was being held up by a bucket or something. And he was just there playing and I'm pretty sure he was ad-libbing what he was playing. We were just like 'oh, my god, that guy's a gent'.... He was class. I was just thinking to myself 'yep, he's the person that deserves a few coins in his bucket'. I don't really buy into U2 trying to make money out of their stuff.

And then people were complaining, rightly so, about having to pay for a lot of mainstream music now.

(Jay, 28)

There is much praise for artists who rebel against industry commercial norms and who are perceived by their fans as focusing more on 'the music' and their relationship with their fans. Frank praised the hip-hop artist Macklemore for encouraging his fans to avoid official sales channels that sold merchandise with his name on it.

He put up a link of bootleg t-shirts, they were his own t-shirts but boot-legged versions like and I thought that even though I was not a fan of his music or whatever, I just thought that it was the cool thing to do as he knows he is making enough money from people going to the gigs without spending 50 quid on a t-shirt and a ticket and all – just enjoys it, likes the music, doesn't make it for the money.

(Frank, 28)

The participants gave further examples where artists such as Radiohead and Nine Inch Nails were praised for bypassing the usual record label distribution channels and embracing the digital age. Such discussions were normally supported by arguments that communicated a sense of anger towards the recording industry for previously treating consumers with disdain through high prices, the repackaging of the same music through a variety of changing formats (e.g. tape to CD), and even the quality of the music that the big labels pushed.

You have all these huge labels that have done nothing over the years but pump out tripe. They have made music utterly disposable for people so why are people going to want to pay for it if they are going to get it for free. If the music industry is treating it like a fucking throw away thing which it has as they view the market at a particular time and they find something to market and then they move on. People are going to ultimately move on and go I am not arsed buying the CD I am just going to download the song, download the CD.

(Dean, 36)

It is not just the consumer that is angry with the industry but other stake-holders that rely on the recording industry to make a living. The participants have made reference to high-profile artist–industry disputes that often play out in the media. For example, Thom Yorke's recent description of music streaming as 'the last desperate fart of a dying corpse' is probably familiar to readers. However, it is not just the artists that suffer but a whole variety of professions within the industry (e.g. editors, technicians, and publishers). A small number of the participants that took part in the research worked within the industry in such positions and despite potentially losing money indirectly as a consequence of piracy and/or decreasing recording revenues still directed most of their ire at an industry that has always mistreated them. Elaine describes the pressure to work for very little or free at times on projects involving the music industry.

> Music videos pay editors horrendously. We're constantly being undercut and working for free. So I feel a little bit bitter about the music industry... Maybe I'm not helping it by not supporting certain things but I just feel like I'm not giving them any more money when I already have worked. I've done three music videos which I've spent a lot of hours on and I've done them all for free. And they were ten minute long music videos. So it's like thirty minutes of editing, three or four weeks' work.
>
> (Elaine, 30)

Furthermore, this uneasy relationship escalated for many of the participants when the recording industry attempted to fight piracy with what were/are viewed as stigmatising and insulting campaigns that attacked the morality of consumers. Frank comments on the famous 'You wouldn't steal a car' anti-piracy campaign.

> They are making it laughable, it is wrong but they show like some lad stealing all these bogey CDs on some market stall. They make it out that you are buying crack cocaine.
>
> (Frank, 28)

Although Frank accepts the illegality of pirating music, he has grown completely indifferent to its impact because of the hard-sell strategies of the anti-piracy movement. Wang and McClung (2011) refer to this as the boomerang effect. Although the majority of the participants accept the illegality of the practice, they take offence when their morality is questioned.

> I accept that it is illegal, I don't really accept that its immoral and I don't really get that whole argument that there is that pot of revenue that music companies are missing out on because people are downloading stuff I don't think they would have listened to or paid for and I think that is probably 90–95% of stuff that is downloaded. I think there was a lot of stuff when I downloaded that I never would have bought. I think the other stuff that you really want, you will pay for.
>
> (Don, 32)

It is the belief that the industry is somewhat exaggerating the problem that cuts to the core of the problematic industry–consumer relationship. Even if this is not the case the participants believe that the industry/musicians can make their money back in other ways. This is referred to as the denial of harm justification in the ethical consumption literature (Sykes & Matza, 1957). Clearly, there is an element of truth to this. The participants who claimed they cared mostly cited how their consumption habits could help smaller artists.

If they're on Spotify or they have songs on YouTube then definitely, I'm more likely to go and see a band if I can check them out in advance and I actually like them than I would have been a few years ago. Like when I was going to the Sonisphere festival last year obviously I knew the big bands that were playing but a lot of the smaller bands that I'd never heard of before, like checked out in advance on Spotify and then went to see them as a result, enjoyed them at Sonisphere, so now if they ever came to Dublin I'd definitely go see them. Whereas if I hadn't checked them out in advance on Spotify and they start playing at one in the afternoon and I don't know who they are I'd probably have just stayed in the campsite and had a few extra cans rather than going in to see some band from Sweden that I've never heard of.

(Chris, 28)

However, the question is whether such potential indirect benefits to the artist are actually the product of the consumer concerning themselves about fair artist payment or whether it is just incidental.

The attitude–behaviour gap

The evidence from this section indicates that for most of the participants in this study, knowledge does not translate to caring about the 'plight' of the artist. This differs from some previous research on ethical consumption which suggests there is a relationship between knowledge and caring (Du et al., 2010). Strong justifications are used to support this attitude by the participants. However, the participants who did express concern focused this on the consequences for the smaller artists or bands that they support because of some personal connection.

There are bands that I would classify as my favourite bands that I would probably buy their record to support them. I'd see myself maybe downloading it illegally and probably buying it at the same time.

(Peter, 30)

But I find during that downloading phase, if a band I really liked brought something out I would buy that.

(Declan, 29)

The key question that is often asked in the ethical consumption literature is whether attitudes regarding ethical consumption translate into behaviour. Clearly those of an apathetic attitude have translated such feelings into piracy and consumption of legal platforms that can be argued impact artists negatively. However, the question is if those with stated caring attitudes translate into consumption activities that benefit the artist. The participants that expressed a caring attitude for artists (see quotes above) were challenged on their attitudes to see if they acted on them in their consumer behaviour. Peter was questioned about his continued support for his favourite band despite having access to their music on *Spotify*.

I: Are you going to buy the band's new album that is coming out?
P: Probably not, if I'm being honest. I think even though the last few years it's changed a lot basically everything is on Spotify or another legal platform, and I really want to support the artist. I don't think they're making lots of money off this, I think they make money off their shows and stuff so I'll go to their shows. But CDs, not so much anymore.The inconsistency between attitude and behaviour is identified by the participant so he resorts to the 'denial of harm' justification that many of participants referred to throughout the research. This form of inconsistency was typical for many participants and created feelings of cognitive dissonance, a sense of discomfort at failing to act consistently with their beliefs, when they truly reflected on their consumer actions (Festinger, 1957).

I am torn, you know, for the type of person I am, I kind of go, geez, I can't believe I do download.

(Shirley, 43)

The good news for the artist is that there are at least some consumers who do care about their livelihoods, the small artists anyway, despite the gap between attitude and behaviour. The questions that remain are how this attitude is turned into behaviour, and obviously more pressing, how the general feeling of apathy towards this issue is addressed – if it in fact can be.

Conclusion

The launch of the streaming application Tidal inspired this chapter. I was fascinated that a company that has so much financial and human capital could position their offering on the principle that the contemporary consumer cares about the ethics of artist payment. This is reflected in the data discussed in this chapter but can also be seen in the media reaction at the time of the launch, which labelled it as 'tone-deaf' and out of touch with the modern consumer (see Leonard, 2015). I see this as further evidence of how little key stakeholders in the music industry truly understand about the contemporary music consumer. It is this type of social distance and lack of deep comprehension that leads to continued mishaps and errors in this time of technological disruption.

This strategy itself is most likely borne out of a recent successful trend in consumer marketing for ethical positioning. Translating such strategies into the music industry is not as impactful because of the culture of consumer apathy that surrounds the issue of artist compensation. The findings in this research indicate that this apathy is a product of many different factors, which are summarised as follows. The lack of knowledge and perception that it is only major artists who suffer from piracy and low paying legal streaming services comes from the confusion and high level of misinformation associated with the issue and the visibility of 'rich' mainstream artists as the public talking heads of the debate around fair payment. This creates little sympathy and motivation for consumers to learn more. Furthermore, for those consumers who were informed to an extent about the implications of piracy and low streaming royalties, a sense of indifference already existed with the recording industry that many participants feel has treated them with contempt for some time. The identification of alternative revenue streams that consumers contribute to (denial of harm), ideologies around the commercialisation of art and the sense of moral grandstanding and stigmatisation that consumers have been met with in the digital age have been identified as key reasons for a sense of justifiable consumer apathy. Moreover, there is a simple logic that digital alternatives provide greater utilitarian value and that for the reasons aforementioned 'ethical' value is low on the list of factors that will impact the music consumer's decision-making.

This leaves us with the question of how such apathy can be addressed. The ideal of artist value is still fundamentally an important thing and a noble challenge to take on, despite my scepticism regarding Tidal's true motivation for promoting fair artist compensation in their product launch. The short and obvious answer to this question is that I don't know and it must be acknowledged that it is difficult for any researcher or stakeholder to claim to have the answers for addressing behaviours that are so complex. However, we must have learned something from this discussion. Identifying the key factors that have contributed to the fractured relationship between key stakeholders (in particular record labels and consumers, consumers and mainstream artists, record labels and artists) and its potential long-term implications is a simple although important point from which to start. It gives us an idea of who is best placed to tackle consumer apathy.

In short, the push has to come from the producers of the music as the record labels have eroded their trust and are also a key contributor to the problem of low streaming royalties. Furthermore, consumers are not going to demand a more 'ethical' product. Artists have to do a better job of communicating information concerning artist payment in a clear and relatable fashion, whilst demonstrating the utilitarian benefit of supporting artists. Consequently, Tidal had the right idea in communicating this issue through the voice of the artist through a vehicle that is essentially sold as 'by the artist for the artist'. However, it has been a PR disaster as they have used multi-millionaire musicians complaining about their reduced income to make this point. As we have learned from previous ethical consumption studies, there has to be an element of trust and a sense that there is a legitimate victim for consumers to vote with their hard-earned money. Consequently, the face of this issue should be the small artist and the host of other voiceless stakeholders who suffer as a consequence of lower payments. In essence it would be using the money and resources of mainstream artists to promote ethical consumption through the voices of the obscure. The evidence from this research suggests that it is the small artist that the consumer empathises with and hence tackling issues of apathy with empathetic totems can possibly be worthwhile. However, the problem is that such attitudes need to be turned into actual worthwhile behaviours which favour the artist. The sense of apathy that I have developed from researching this issue leads me to believe that this is unlikely to happen anytime soon.

Note

1 Taytay is the nickname for the popstar Taylor Swift.

Appendix 1 Research methods and samples

Date	Method	Focus of project	Sample
2009–2012	In-depth interviews	Research on Dublin subcultures	• 13 interviews • Predominantly Irish music consumers • Predominantly male (9–4 split)
2013	In-depth interviews	Socially responsible consumption	• 22 interviews • 12 female • Irish and Scottish sample
2015	Discussion groups	Music streaming	• 19 participants • UK only
2015–2016	In-depth interviews	Music streaming	• 16 interviews • 5 female • Mixture of Irish and Scottish sample

References

Adorno, T. (1976). *Introduction to the sociology of music*. Chicago: Seabury Press.
Adorno, T. (2002) Music in the background. In R. Leppert (Ed.) *Adorno – Essays on music* (pp. 288–317). Berkeley, Los Angeles and London: University of California Press.

Ang, S. H., Cheng, P. S., Lim, E. A. and Tambyah, S. K. (2001). Spot the difference: Consumer responses towards counterfeits. *Journal of Consumer Marketing*, 18(3): 219–235.

Balestrino, A. (2008). It is a theft but not a crime. *European Journal of Political Economy*, 24(2): 455–469.

Brown, S.C. (2017). Myths about musicians and music piracy. *The Skeptic*, 26(3): 12–15.

Bryman, A. (2015). *Social research methods*. Oxford: Oxford University Press.

Carrigan, M., Szmigin, I. and Wright, J. (2014). Shopping for a better world? An interpretive study of the potential for ethical consumption within the older market. *Journal of Consumer Marketing*, 21(6): 401–417.

Carrington, M., Zwick, D. and Neville, B. (2016). The ideology of the ethical consumption gap. *Marketing Theory*, 16(1): 21–38.

Cesareo, L. and Pastore, A. (2014). Consumers' attitude and behaviour towards online music piracy and subscription-based services. *Journal of Consumer Marketing*, 31(6/7): 515–525.

Cotte, J. and Trudel, R. (2009). *Socially conscious consumerism: A systematic review of the body of knowledge*. London: Network for Business Sustainability.

Chiou, J. S., Huang, G.Y. and Lee, H.H. (2005). The antecedents of music piracy attitudes and intentions. *Journal of Business Ethics*, 57(2): 161–174.

Curien, N. and Moreau, F. (2009). The music industry in the digital era: Toward new contracts. *Journal of Media Economics*, 22(2): 102–113.

Du, S., Bhattacharya, C. B. and Sen, S. (2010). Maximizing business returns to corporate social responsibility: The role of CSR communication. *International Journal of Management Reviews*, 12(1): 8–19.

Festinger, L. (1957). *A theory of cognitive dissonance*. Stanford, CA: Stanford University Press.

Fisher, W. (2004). *Technology, law, and the future of entertainment*. Stanford, CA: Stanford University Press.

Garcia-Bardidia, R., Nau, J. P. and Rémy, E. (2011). Consumer resistance and anti-consumption: Insights from the deviant careers of French illegal downloaders. *European Journal of Marketing*, 45(11/12): 1789–1798.

Giesler, M. (2008). Conflict and compromise: Drama in marketplace evolution. *Journal of Consumer Research*, 34(6): 739–753.

Green, T., Sinclair, G. and Tinson, J. (2016). Do they know its CSR at all? An exploration of socially responsible music consumption. *Journal of Business Ethics*, 138(2): 231–246.

Hathaway, A. and Atkinson, M. (2003). Active interview tactics in research on public deviants: Exploring the two-cop personas. *Field Methods*, 15(2): 161–185

Higgins, G. E. (2007). An examination of low self-control and motivation using short-term longitudinal data. *CyberPsychology & Behavior*, 10(4): 523–529.

Hoeffler, S. and Keller, K. L. (2002). Building brand equity through corporate societal marketing. *Journal of Public Policy & Marketing*, 21(2): 78–89.

Hill, C.W.L. (2007). Digital piracy: Causes, consequences, and strategic responses. *Asia Pacific Journal of Management*, 24(1): 9–25.

International Federation of the Phonographic Industry (2015). *Digital music report 2015: Charting the path to sustainable growth*. Retrieved from www.ifpi.org/downloads/Digital-Music-Report-2015.pdf.

Kusek, D. and Leonhard, G. (2005). *The future of music: Manifesto for the digital music revolution*. Boston, MA: Berklee Press.

LaRose, R., Lai, Y., Lange, R., Love, B. and Wu, Y. (2005). Sharing or piracy? An exploration of downloading behaviour. *Journal of Computer-Mediated Communication*, 11(1): 1–21.

Leonard, D. (2015). That's business, man: Why Jay Z's Tidal is a complete disaster. *Bloomber Businessweek*. Retrieved from www.bloomberg.com/news/features/2015-05-28/why-jay-z-s-tidal-streaming-music-service-has-been-a- disaster May 28.

Levin, A. M., Dato-on, M. C. and Manolis, C. (2007). Deterring illegal downloading: The effects of threat appeals, past behaviour, subjective norms, and attributions of harm. *Journal of Consumer Behaviour*, 62(3): 111–122.

Lysonski, S., Durvasula, S. (2008). Digital piracy of mp3s: Consumer and ethical predispositions. *Journal of Consumer Marketing*, 25(3): 167–178.

Marshall, L. (2015). 'Let's keep music special. F – Spotify': On-demand streaming and the controversy over artist royalties. *Creative Industries Journal*, 8(2): 177–189.

Merriam, S. (2009). *Qualitative research: A guide to design and implementation (Revised and expanded from 'Qualitative research and case study applications in education')*. Hoboken, NJ: Jossey-Bass (Wiley).

Mohr, L.A., Webb, D. J. and Harris, K.E. (2001). Do customers expect companies to be socially responsible? The impact of corporate social responsibility on buying behaviour. *Journal of Consumer Affairs*, 35(1): 45–72.

Mohr, L.A. and Webb, D.J. (2005). The effects of corporate social responsibility and price on consumer responses. *Journal of Consumer Affairs*, 35(1): 45–72.

Parkes, M. (2013). Making plans for Nigel: The industry trust and film piracy management in the United Kingdom. *Convergence*, 19(1): 25–43.

Peloza, J., White, K., Shang, J. (2013). Green and guilt-free: The role of self-accountability in influencing preferences for products with ethical attributes. *Journal of Marketing*, 77(1), 104–119.

Resnikoff, P. (2011). Distributor STHoldings pulls 234 labels from Spotify Rdio, Others. *Digital Music News*. Retrieved from www.digitalmusicnews.com/2011/11/16/stholdings/. November, 16.

Rojek, C. (2005). P2P leisure exchange: Net banditry and the policing of intellectual property. *Leisure Studies*, 24(4): 357–369.

Sinclair, G. (2017, February 10). Music industry shows movie makers the way with illegal downloads. *The Irish Times*. Retrieved from www.irishtimes.com/news/ireland/irish-news/music-industry-shows-movie-makers-the-way-with-illegal-downloads-1.2971461.

Sinclair, G., Green, T. (2015). Download or stream? Steal or buy? Developing a typology of today's music consumer. *Journal of Consumer Behaviour*, 15(1), 3–14.

Sinha, R. K., Mandel, N. (2009). Preventing digital music piracy: 'The carrot or the stick'. *Journal of Marketing*, 72(1): 246–262.

Sisario, B. (2015). Jay Z reveals plans for Tidal a streaming music service. *The New York Times*. Retrieved from www.nytimes.com/2015/03/31/business/media/jay-z-reveals-plans-for-Tidal-a-streaming-music-service.html?_r=0. March, 30.

Strahilevitz, M. and Myers, J. G. (1998). Donations to charity as purchase incentives: How well they work may depend on what you are trying to sell. *Journal of Consumer Research*, 24 (4): 434–446

Taylor, S.A., Ishida, C. and Wallace, D.W. (2009). Intention to engage in digital piracy: A conceptual model and empirical test. *Journal of Service Research*, 11(3): 246–262.

Sinclair, G. and Tinson, J. (2017). Psychological ownership and music streaming consumption. *Journal of Business Research*, 71: 1–9.

Sykes, G.M. and Matza, D. (1957). Techniques of neutralization: A theory of delinquency. *American Sociological Review*, 22(6): 667–670.

Wang, X. and McClung, S. R. (2011). Toward a detailed understanding of digital downloading intentions: An extended theory of planned behaviour approach. *New Media and Society*, 13(4): 663–677.

Weijters, B., Goedertier, F. and Verstreken, S. (2014). Online music consumption in today's technological context: Putting the influence of ethics in perspective. *Journal of Business Ethics*, 124: 537–550.

Section III

Assessments of the impact of digital piracy

9 DeLiberating the information commons

A critical analysis of intellectual property and piracy

Kevin F. Steinmetz and Alexandra Pimentel

Introduction

The current chapter advances a critical perspective on digital piracy. This perspective involves an examination of the historical roots of copyright law and the economic interests which helped shape these laws. The evolution of digital piracy is then described; a phenomenon dependent on the creation and reification of intellectual property. Having established the historical-legal context, the analysis turns toward ideological and political economic dynamics that dialectically underpin both intellectual property and piracy. In contrast to representing these two social issues as polar ends of a criminological dichotomy between "offenders" and "victims," they are revealed to be mutually sustained within the logics of capital accumulation, particularly through the ideological machinations of *liberalism*, a philosophical perspective that advances values such as freedom, privacy, and autonomy. Yet, scholars also recognize that this position – endemic in Western and particularly American society – produces and reproduces dialectical contradictions (Harvey, 2014; Losurdo, 2014; Polanyi, 1944). As argued in this chapter, understanding these contradictions is vital for a rigorous academic understanding of piracy as an emergent social problem.

If lobbyists and industry officials are to be believed, digital piracy is the creeping doom of creative content industries (movies, music, software, pornography, etc.) and perhaps creativity itself. The prophets of digital danger oft-claim that digital piracy is a cause of major economic losses globally. In 2010, the Business Software Alliance (BSA) reported that pirated software caused a yearly loss of over $110 billion dollars to the economy across 42 countries. In another report, they claimed that in 2013, "43 percent of the software installed on personal computers around the world was not properly licensed" with the value of such unlicensed uses amounting to $62.7 billion (Business Software Alliance, 2014: 1). The Recording Industry Association of America (RIAA) asserted in 2015 that "music sales in the U.S. have dropped 53 percent, from $14.6 billion to $7.0 billion in 2013," and laid blame on digital piracy.[1] Twenty percent of internet users regularly accessed unauthorized music files according to the International Federation of Phonographic

Industries (2015). The Institute for Policy Innovation – a U.S.-based think tank – estimates that music piracy costs the economy $12.5 billion annually (Siwek 2007).

The release of these statistics has coincided with cries for someone – anyone – to do something about this piracy "problem." Industries have engaged in advertising designed to stymie copyright infringement (Lessig, 2004; Parkes, 2012; Yar, 2008b). For instance, in the U.K., the Industry Trust (a film industry organization) ran multiple anti-piracy campaigns. One of these campaigns was *Knock-off Nigel,* which involved television advertisements and companion websites designed to "reframe the pirate, not as an attractive criminal but as a seedy cheapskate" in an attempt to make the activity less alluring (Parkes, 2012: 29). Civil litigation has also been brought to bear against pirates, perhaps most famously by the RIAA during a multi-year lawsuit campaign in the 2000s (Bachmann, 2007). Further, industry pressure encouraged legislators to alter laws to respond to the concerns of content industries (Lessig, 2004; Perelman, 2002; Perelman, 2014). Law enforcement activity has also increasingly been directed toward upholding the intellectual property rights of copyright holders (e.g. Zetter, 2015).

Even many academics have responded to the piracy "problem." In fact, Holt and Bossler (2014) suggest that criminology has examined digital piracy more extensively than any other form of technological crime. Large swaths of this research have focused on testing a variety of criminological and socio-logical theories to explain individual piracy behaviors. Tested theories include general deterrence theory,[2] routine activities theory,[3] social network analysis,[4] actor-network theory,[5] Mertonian strain theory,[6] techniques of neutraliza-tion,[7] as well as self-control and learning theories.[8] Others have examined individual characteristics of so-called pirates, finding that individuals who illegally download music tend to indicate higher levels of proficiency in using online resources as well as a wider variety of internet use than individuals who do not pirate (Hinduja & Higgins, 2011). Additionally, these skilled internet users tend to come from more privileged backgrounds in terms of socio-economic status and education (Hargittai, 2010). Further individual level psychological variables have been associated with increased participation in piracy, including optimism bias, in which individuals perceive themselves to be less at risk than the average person to suffer consequences as a result of engaging in piracy, as well as problems related to internet addiction (Nandedkar & Midha, 2012; Navarro et al., 2014). Some analyses have explored the various subcultural features of piracy (Downing, 2010; Holt & Copes, 2010; Steinmetz & Tunnell, 2013). These studies highlight how new and developing technologies and media help frame the formation and evolu-tion of the piracy subculture (Holt & Copes, 2010). For example, Steinmetz and Tunnell (2013) qualitatively investigate the piracy scene for shared moti-vations, techniques of neutralizations, as well as contradictions in the broader community-wide belief systems. A wide assortment of research has been con-ducted internationally, with studies ranging from qualitative examinations of the perceptions of Nigerian pirates, artists, and promotors on the piracy phenomenon and the marketing of creative products (Tade & Akinleye, 2012) to the normativity of piracy behaviors among Finnish youths (Aaltonen & Salmi, 2013). Such research is vital considering the transnational character of piracy.

A surprising amount of this research adopt official narratives about piracy and its alleged harms evinced through industry statistics (Gunter, 2009; Higgins, Wolfe & Marcum, 2008; Morris & Higgins, 2010; Smallridge & Roberts, 2013; Tade & Akinleye, 2012), references to other piracy studies (Aaltonen & Salmi, 2013; Holt, Bossler & May, 2012; Malin & Fowers, 2009), government reports (Smallridge & Roberts, 2013), or simply unreferenced statements regarding the billions of dollars lost to digital piracy (Burruss, Bossler & Holt, 2012; Moon et al., 2012). Kariithi (2011), however, cautions against the unreflective use of this information as it may contain biases in the favor of content industries. Yar (2008b) similarly warns that many of the statistics and data that proliferate in these studies "may be seen at best as 'guesstimates' which can only approximately track levels of piracy; at worst, they may be seen as the product of methodologically questionable forms of statistical inference and accounting" (Yar, 2008b: 608). Further, such businesses and other organizations "may well overstate their losses for lobbying purposes" (Yar, 2008b: 608). Elsewhere he states that:

> These industry 'guesstimates' usually become reified into incontrovertible facts, and provide the basis for further discussion and action on the 'piracy problem.' From the industry's viewpoint, the inflation of the figures is the starting point for a 'virtuous circle' – high figures put pressure on legislators to criminalize, and on enforcement agencies to police more rigorously; the tightening of copyright laws *produces* more 'copyright theft' as previously legal or tolerated uses are prohibited, and the more intensive policing of 'piracy' results in more seizures; these in turn produce new estimates suggesting that the 'epidemic' continues to grow unabated; which then legitimates industry calls for even more vigorous action. What the 'true' underlying levels and trends in 'piracy' might be, however, remain inevitably obscured behind this process of socio-statistical construction.
>
> (Yar, 2005: 690)

For these reasons, the data that bolsters the assumptions of a "piracy problem" should be regarded with tremendous skepticism. Yet this research blithely capers forward, even adopting this orientation's overly simplistic dichotomy of pitting pirates ("offenders") against intellectual property holders ("victims"). Piracy – as a global, late modern phenomenon – is more complex than youthful techno-bandits marauding the wires for free stuff at the expense of content creators and producers. In particular, most research fails to consider the political, economic, and social circumstances by which piracy becomes framed as a problem as well as the reification (and subsequent protection) of intellectual property.

Rather than propagate the simplistic offender–victim dualism, research should examine piracy as a multi-faceted phenomenon that oscillates around power, technological development, and social change. A macro-structural approach is therefore needed to understand the creation, re-creation, and management of piracy and intellectual property as social constructs. This approach involves a fundamental reexamination of "common-sense" intellectual property and piracy narratives as well as a struggle to understand societal reactions to piracy. Drawing from Marxism and radical criminology, this analysis explores the process of deviance production that renders piracy a crime problem within the "circuits of accumulation in contemporary capitalism" (Yar, 2008a: 190). To unpack the production of piracy as deviance, this chapter begins with the emergence and development of copyright.

On copyright

The legitimacy of intellectual property is widely accepted in contemporary society. As Vaidhyanathan (2012) explains, "we have become so inured to the proprietary model, so dazzled and intimidated by its cultural and political power, that any common sense challenge to its assumptions and tenets seems radical, idealistic, or dangerous" (Vaidhynathan, 2012: 24). Today, legal protections are in place for multiple forms of intellectual property including copyright, patents, trademarks, and trade secrets (Halbert, 2016). Though the historical genesis and transformation each of these forms is important for understanding contemporary information capitalism and intellectual property violations, this chapter will focus primarily on the development of copyright law as this legal realm applies most directly to digital piracy.

Copyright law emerged in eighteenth-century Britain in the wake of a civil war driven in part by the Crown's practice of awarding monopoly publication rights to intellectual content (Lessig, 2004). There were intense demands to reduce such exclusivity of ownership which was upheld by government coercion. Copyright laws arose to restrict the power of book-sellers by imposing term limits on exclusive publication rights. These laws sought to bolster competition among publishers and allow works to become freely accessible and reproducible after a set period of time. The first formal copyright law, the Statute of Anne, was established in 1710 and mandated that "all published works would get a copyright term of fourteen years, renewable once if the author was alive, and that all works already published by 1710 would get a single term of twenty-one additional years" (Lessig, 2004: 86).

Enlightenment education and an emerging philosophy of liberalism were major driving forces behind the creation of copyright law. Exclusive but *temporary* rights were permitted, as such rights were believed to give authors an incentive to create. Term limits were imposed, however, to allow information to enter what is called the "public domain." The general sentiment of the time was that knowledge proliferation and accessibility were fundamentally good for society. To protect these social ideals, copyright laws provided *short term* restrictions to the reproduction of creative content to bolster creativity and enrich society *long term* (Perelman, 2002).

When the U.S. Constitution was drafted, its authors adopted a similar approach and imposed a copyright term limit of only 14 years (Perelman, 2002). Restrictions on content reproduction would be modified over time. These changes deemphasized the protection of individual creativity and, instead, shifted to the protection of business interests (Lessig, 2004). Under the Copyright Act of 1976, term limits were expanded to 50 years *after the death of the author.* An additional 20 years was added through the Copyright Extension Act of 1998, effectively extending copyright through the life of author plus 70 years (Lessig, 2004). These modifications were supposedly necessary to protect the Disney Corporation's rights to Steamboat Willie – the first cartoon to feature Mickey Mouse – which was set to expire in the 2000s (Lessig, 2004; Perelman, 2002). If Steamboat Willie had been allowed to drift into the public domain, Disney would have lost the ability to exclusively control and monetize their beloved cartoon mouse (Lessig, 2004).

The original objective of copyright was to advance culture by allowing creative content to pass into the public domain in a timely manner. These expansions to copyright have effectively dismantled this collective resource, however. Rather than copyright working to ensure the intellectual enrichment of society, such laws have become blockades that uphold practically permanent exclusive rights to content. A return to the pre-Statute of Anne treatment of intellectual property has thus been ushered forth – the primary distinction is that today content owners are often multi-national corporations with an army of lawyers.

Originally, copyright law applied only to the reproduction of certain kinds of intellectual property through certain reproduction methods. Today, nearly all forms of creative content and duplication are subsumed under copyright law with few exceptions. One particular law was responsible for drastically expanding the scope of copyright law in recent times: The Digital Millennium Copyright Act of 1998 (DMCA). Among other provisions, this law makes it illegal to bypass copy-protection mechanisms placed on intellectual property (Lunney, 2001). Under traditional copyright law, certain uses of copyrighted material are protected through the fair use doctrine (Lessig, 2004). Fair use includes, for example, copyright exemptions for certain educational uses of content in addition to parody and satire. These exceptions were deemed necessary by lawmakers to protect free speech and promote education. While the statute was originally drafted to protect industry interests against piracy and other forms of copyright infringement in an increasingly digital age, legal scholars have argued that the DMCA strangles fair use and curtails free speech by imbuing content owners with excessive control over content (e.g: Lessig, 2004; Lessig, 2008; Schaffner, 2004; Sharp, 2002). Though the Audio Home Recording Act of 1992 (AHRA) originally protected the copying of analog and digital content for private, non-commercial purposes, the DMCA makes even these forms of content reproduction illegal if they have to bypass copy-protection mechanisms.[9] Such protections apply even to superficial or token amounts of copy-protection. The DMCA thus becomes a powerful weapon for content owners interested in preventing *any* duplication of intellectual property, regardless of context of use.

As indicated here, copyright is a concept that has evolved over time. This history is fraught with tensions between individual ownership rights and collective enlightenment. In other words, intellectual property is mired in social and economic conflict between competing interests. Before delving too deeply into the implications of such conflict, however, this analysis turns toward the concurrent history of digital piracy.

Here come the (digital) pirates

Piracy as a form of illicit content duplication and dissemination has existed long before the Internet. Johns (2002), for instance, describes the trials and tribulations of sheet music piracy in the late nineteenth century. While interesting, the historical narrative offered in this chapter begins with one of the earliest documented incidents where unauthorized *digital* content duplication was labeled piracy.[10]

In the mid-1970s, the Homebrew Computer Club (HBCC) emerged, a group of computer enthusiasts or "hardware hackers" that would inspire many budding figures in computing including Steve Wozniak of Apple fame (Levy, 1984; Wozniak, 2006). The members of the HBCC were fascinated by emerging microprocessor computers like the Altair 8800. A young Bill Gates and two colleagues were developing a BASIC interpreter for the 8800 during this period and accepted pre-orders to help finance themselves and their project. The project's release was fraught with delays, which frustrated its committed consumer base. A leaked copy of the compiler eventually made its way to members of the HBCC who eagerly produced copies for each other (Levy, 1984).

When Gates heard about the unauthorized leak and subsequent duplications, he penned a strongly worded open letter published in the HBCC newsletter that condemned these copiers. He specifically invokes the words "theft" and "piracy" to create an equivalence between unsanctioned copying and the taking of finite, tangible property. The members of the HBCC did not see the situation in the same manner, instead viewing the act as simply sharing information, a perception endemic to hacker culture since its genesis at Massachusetts Institute of Technology (Levy, 1984). As will be further explored later in this analysis, this event signaled what would become a key tension between content owners who asserted liberal notions of private property and technological subcultures that described piracy as a form of free speech (Coleman & Golub, 2008; Levy, 1984; Wark, 2004).

Since the time of the HBCC, hackers and other technologists have come together to circumvent copy-protection mechanisms ("cracking") and disseminate software and other forms of digital content in what is referred to as the "warez scene" or "the scene" (Décary-Hétu, Morselli & Leman-Langlois, 2012). In the 1980s and 1990s, pirated content was shared mostly among small groups of computer enthusiasts through bulletin board systems (BBSs), Usenet/ newsgroups, FTP (file transfer protocol)/FXP (file exchange protocol), and internet relay chat (IRC) (Cooper & Harrison, 2001; Meyer, 1989; Yar, 2013). While these media were frequently used for licit purposes, they served as key methods of transmission for pirated digital goods before Internet use exploded in the mid- to late-1990s (Mueller, 2016).

Digital piracy went mainstream in 1999 with the advent Napster, a peer-to-peer (P2P) file sharing system (Yar, 2013). Napster allowed users to make their music files available for others to download and, in turn, those users could search for music files shared by all other users in the system. Combined with the creation of the MP3 file format – which allowed music files to be significantly reduced in size without major sacrifices to audio quality – Napster made digital music piracy easy and seemingly ubiquitous. In 2001, Napster was shut down by court order as a result of copyright claims made by the Recording Industry Association of America (RIAA) and others. A multitude of alternative P2P services rose from the ashes, however, including Kazaa, Limewire, eMule, and BearShare, to name a few. Like the mythical Hydra, cutting off one head only created more. These services took P2P beyond music piracy to the reproduction of almost all forms of digital content.

Amidst the grumbling and flailing of content industries, these file-sharing services too had to duck and dive shutdown attempts. A central problem these services had to overcome was centralization; if Napster's servers were shutdown, for example, then it would be impossible for its users to continue using their services. New file sharing protocols emerged that could remain in operation if one point was taken offline. Perhaps the earliest of such programs was Gnutella. In 2001, Bram Cohen created BitTorrent which became a "game changer" in piracy. It was a decentralized P2P file-sharing method that would prove extraordinarily resilient to shutdown attempts and legal challenge (Yar, 2013). A cornucopia of websites emerged dedicated to facilitating piracy through BitTorrent including Demonoid, KickassTorrents, and, most notoriously, The Pirate Bay.

Content industries grew increasingly concerned over the perceived epidemic of digital piracy; an anxiety that only increased following the advent of Bit-Torrent. Content industries went on the offensive. For instance, between 2003 and 2008, the RIAA "filed, settled, or threatened legal actions against at least 30,000 individuals" (Electronic Frontier Foundation, 2008: 1). Twenty-three universities received about 2,500 pre-litigation letters in 2007 from the RIAA that claimed students were using university servers to illegally download music (Lessig, 2008). This campaign pressured numerous college students to settle copyright infringement cases involving illegally downloaded MP3s for costs as high as $17,500 (Electronic Frontier Foundation, 2008). The Business Software Alliance (BSA) has also heavily promoted their "No Piracy" program where persons can get paid to turn over coworkers using authorized copies of software (Mitchell, 2012).[11] Multiple industry organizations crafted anti-piracy educational campaigns, providing industry propaganda for use by school teachers to instruct children about the alleged dangers of piracy (Yar, 2008b).

For many (including numerous pirates), digital piracy was seen as a point of resistance against an expanding – yet precarious – intellectual property regime; out with the old methods of production and distribution and in with the new. Reluctant to adapt in the face of technological change, the industry attempted to crush digital piracy, through efforts that continue today. Yet, this is not a story of simple resistance and domination. Dialectical contradictions are evident on both sides as they fluctuate within the confines of capital accumulation, particularly the contradiction between freedom and oppression. This chapter therefore turns toward examining these contradictions, with particular attention given to the influence of liberalism, as intellectual property and piracy simultaneously uphold and upend accumulation within information capitalism.

Contradictions of piracy, intellectual piracy, and accumulation under information capitalism

In 1944, Hungarian sociologist Karl Polanyi explored liberalism in his book *The Great Transformation.* He noticed a particular tendency of liberal logic to lead to what he termed a "double movement" where liberalism simultaneously propels marketization and protects the public against it. Copyright and intellectual property is also prone to a "double movement." Copyright law was originally envisioned as a mechanism to protect creative development and free speech. For individual autonomy to be fully realized, each person needed access to the collective library. In this capacity, copyright law embodied liberalism's penchant for free speech and the fostering of autonomy. Curiously, however, liberal logics also propagated the undermining of the original intent of copyright law. Early liberal philosophers like Locke and Jefferson upheld the virtues of private property as integral to the pursuit of happiness and individual liberty. This ardent belief in the value of private property would endure through various historical iterations of liberalism, from the *laissez faire* economic liberalism of the eighteenth century, all the way to contemporary versions of neo-liberalism. Over time, the scope of property would increase to a point where even ideas were subject to proprietization. Ayn Rand (1966), posterwoman for neoliberal economics, explains this perspective:

> Patents and copyrights are the legal implementation of the base of all property rights: a man's right to the product of his mind... The patent or copyright notice on a physical object represents a public statement of the conditions on which the inventor or author is willing to sell his product: for the purchaser's use, but *not* for commercial reproduction...

Intellectual achievement, *in fact*, cannot be transferred, just as intelligence, ability, or any other personal virtue cannot be transferred. All that can be transferred is the material results of an achievement, in the form of actually produced wealth... patents are the heart and core of property rights, and once they are destroyed, the destruction of all other rights will follow automatically, as a brief postscript.

(Rand, 1966: 125–128)

Boyle (2003) describes the expansion of intellectual property law – designed to uphold the freedoms of content industries – as a "second enclosure movement." Enclosure refers to the process through which commons are transformed into private property and control is delivered into the hands of legally sanctioned "owners." Marx (1842) described the first enclosure movement in his essay "Debates on Law on the Thefts of Wood," where wood gathering was transmogrified into wood "theft." Intellectual property has undergone reconceptualization through which content has been constructed as analogous to physical forms of private property (Halbert, 2016; Mueller, 2016). Language has adapted to suit this equivalency. "Theft" is used for copyright infringement as well as "piracy" which, for many, invokes images of maritime plunder ranging from the debonair swashbuckler to the crass sea dog. The very language of intellectual "property" invokes a connection between ideas and physical forms of property. As Yar (2008b) states, this language creates a perceived "straightforward equivalence between tangible and intangible properties" (Yar, 2008b: 612).

In the early days of the World Wide Web, for example, such equivalency was accomplished through the use of the "information superhighway" metaphor, which "suggests that information is trucked about like so much soap or canned soup" (Perelman, 2002: 175). The Motion Picture Association of America (MPAA) ran an advertisement in movie theaters and on DVDs in the late 2000s that equated the thefts of automobiles, televisions, handbags, and physical media (DVDs) with the unauthorized downloading of intellectual property (Parkes, 2013). Abrasive text emblazoned across the screen asserted that "stealing is against the law," and "piracy is a crime," thus cementing a connection between the theft of a physical commodity (where the user is deprived of their item) and the copying of copyrighted data (where the original owner is not deprived of access). The problem, as Halbert (2016) explains, is that "IP theft is substantively different from other forms of theft and the use of the word property to describe these actions conceals as much as it reveals" (Halbert, 2016: 261). With physical property, there is an intrinsic scarcity while intellectual property is inherently immune from this malady. Creating an equivalence between tangible and intangible properties obfuscates this fundamental difference.

In addition to equating intellectual properties to physical forms, the content industries also espouse rhetoric that insists creativity will dissipate and culture will erode without strict intellectual property protections. On the RIAAs website, they assert that "copyright law protects the value of creative work. When you make unauthorized copies of someone's creative work, you are taking something of value from the owner without his or her permission."[12] In addition, such content industry claims also tend to frame piracy as detrimental to artists (Parkes, 2013). The RIAA has argued that legal downloading means that "you'll be doing right by the people who created the music" – connecting the purchase of music produced through corporate labels as in the best interests of artists.[13] It seems that all of society benefits from the reduction of piracy according to industry claims (Parkes, 2013). The RIAA claims that industries are necessary because "we all benefit from a vibrant music industry committed to nurturing the next generation of talent."[14] The MPAA maintains that:

> to support copyright law is to support technological ingenuity that ultimately benefits everyone. Copyright protection is about providing the right incentives to make sure everyone has access to content across multiple platforms, and that the people who make that content are able to continue to do so.[15]

On the one hand, content industries assert that copyright law (intentionally modified to meet their interests) is fundamentally necessary to preserve the interests of creative workers. On the other, content industries have imperiled the public domain that was once thought to be necessary for creative development and community advancement. Further, fair use has been jeopardized as any creative or educational use of content can be crushed under the weight of litigation if it can remotely be construed as copyright infringement. It appears that the only creative content that industries are interested in protecting is that which is produced under their ownership. Of course, this is not to say that artists should not be paid for their creative labor, only that control of the production and distribution of said content is concentrated in the hands of vectoral capitalists and this control is framed as in the broader public's interests through liberalized rhetoric (Wark, 2004). Under this arrangement, artists are exploited (in a classical Marxian sense) while the content industries prosper.

Even academic freedom has been threatened in this intellectual "land grab." For instance, some critics argue that the DMCA not only harms fair use but also circumscribes the ability of researchers to discuss copy-protection circumvention measures for educational purposes. Cory Doctorow (2008) describes one example involving Dmitry Skylarov, a Russian programmer who gave a talk at a hacker convention on weaknesses in the copy protections mechanisms in Adobe's ebook platform:

> The FBI threw him in the slam for thirty days. He copped a plea, went home to Russia, and the Russian equivalent of the State Department issued a blanket warning to its researchers to stay away from American

conferences, since we'd apparently turned into the kind of country where certain equations are illegal.

(Doctorow, 2008: 8)

It is important to note that the Federal Trade Commission recently created an exemption to the DMCA that allows "security researchers who are acting in good faith to conduct controlled research on consumer devices so long as the researcher does not violate other laws such as the Computer Fraud and Abuse Act" (Alva, 2016). This exemption is currently acting only on a two-year trial run and is specific to persons looking for technological security vulnerabilities. It does not cover research that "facilitates copyright infringement." In other words, the DMCA has been relaxed, which may protect cases like Skylarov's. Only time will tell if such exemptions will endure.

In short, the idea that copyright law upholds the public good of information development and dissemination seems difficult to support within the current socio-legal context. Pirates are a bogeyman used to stoke fear and drive legislative changes and international enforcement efforts. Over time, through the smoke and mirrors, what copyright law has really become is a weapon designed to secure information monopolies for content industries. Like Ouroboros, the mythological Greek snake, liberalism begins to eat its own tail – freedom through private property for one person means the oppression of another through the enclosing of commons and the exclusion of ownership over the means of production (material and intellectual). Such efforts circumscribe the public domain and fair use and thereby limit the freedom of others to access the broadest intellectual palette possible (at least without going through a paywall). Copyright law has been transformed into a legal weapon to uphold the freedoms of some and limit the freedoms of others. Ayn Rand and her acolytes justify this tendency through their philosophy of objectivism which holds selfishness as a virtue. Marxists, however, recognize this phenomenon as a result of the contradictions of capital accumulation, particularly the dialectical relationship between freedom and oppression (Harvey, 2014).

The contradiction between freedom and oppression not only operates between content industries, copyright law, and creative production, but also manifests within the piracy subculture. Building from prior research and theorizing (Coleman & Golub, 2008; Warnick, 2004; Yar, 2014), there appears to be a particular strand of liberalism that seems to permeate various technological subcultures including hackers and pirates we can term "technological liberalism" (see also: Steinmetz, 2016; Steinmetz & Gerber, 2015).[16] This form of liberalism contains its own double movement which provides the seeds of resistance against corporate control of content but simultaneously allows piracy to be reabsorbed into accumulation under information capitalism.

Technological liberalism is characterized by three features. The first is an appreciation of *liberal values* including freedom, autonomy, meritocracy, and privacy, to name a few (Coleman & Golub, 2008). Also involved is a cautious acceptance of the state, rather than a wholesale rejection of government authority, as is stereotypically articulated for piracy and hacker cultures. The second feature is a *technological ontology* (Warnick, 2004). Pirates, hackers, and related technologists have a tendency to view the world and its various systems through the ontological metaphor "the world is a computer" (Warnick, 2004). In this capacity, society and its various institutions and organizations are believed to function best under the circumstances optimal for computational performance. The third feature of technological liberalism endemic to pirates, hackers, and related groups is *technological utopianism*, a belief that all problems can be solved through the judicious application of science and technology (Yar, 2014). Further, utopian thinking "gestures to other possibilities and other times" (Yar, 2014: 3). It is inherently future oriented. Thus there is a belief that problems are not only solvable through science and technology, but that the problem applications of science and technology will pull us toward a better world. Conversely, perceived *misapplications* – such as government surveillance and, as will be discussed, copy-protection mechanisms – are imagined as leading to dystopic alternatives (Yar, 2014).

The three components of technological liberalism – liberalism, technological ontology, and technological utopianism – combine together to explain many of the behaviors and perspectives of pirates and related subcultures. For instance, digital piracy subculture(s) often express views toward intellectual property that mirror the oft-cited hacker belief that information "wants to be free" (Brand & Herron, 1985; Décary-Hétu, Morselli & Leman-Langlois, 2012; Stallman, 2002). Steinmetz and Tunnell (2013) have previously termed this perspective the "sharing is caring ethos" (57). Coleman and Golub (2008) describe these kinds of sentiments among hackers and other techno-logists as "moral expressions" of liberalism. Such expressions, however, are more than articulations of liberalism. These expressions also are founded on the belief that if computer systems function best when data flows freely between hard drive, memory, processor, and other parts, then society must operate optimally under similar conditions. The particular moral expressions of liberalism found among pirates is processed through this technological ontology.

One noteworthy example of how technological liberalism manifests among pirates is through the Pirate Party, an international political organization which began in Sweden in 2006 (Erlingsson & Persson, 2011). According to the Pirate Parties International (2017), the Pirate Party advocates:

> for the promotion of the goals its members share such as protection of human rights and fundamental freedoms in the digital age, consumer and author rights-oriented reform of copyright and related rights, support for information privacy, transparency and free access to information.[17]

These organizations emerged at least partially as a reaction to shutdown attempts made against The Pirate Bay, one of the most significant online piracy websites to emerge in recent years. There are currently dozens of Pirate

Parties now scattered throughout the world dedicated to advancing a political agenda dedicated primarily to digital freedoms.

"Sharing is caring" is thus more than a moral dictum – it is a declaration of computational politics. This adherence frequently puts pirates in conflict with content industries. While pirates eschew restrictions on content as an expression of freedom and free speech, business interests seek to preserve their own freedoms as embodied by intellectual property ownership – it is "their" content and no one should be able to use it without their permission. Both sides are brought into conflict through alternative expressions of liberal values.

Pirates provide resistance against the commercialization and control of content. As previously stated, since the origins of the warez scene, pirates and hackers actively work to break copy-protection mechanisms on content. These protections obstruct sharing and the ability to transmit and consume content. For this reason, many pirates abhor copy-protections on principle. Breaking copy protection mechanisms is a prominent method of garnering status among pirates (Mueller, 2016). While content producers frantically create copy-protections protocols and devices, pirates work to undermine such approaches.[18]

In addition to the crafting copy-protections, content industries have deployed other strategies to deal with piracy. Perhaps the most notable are lawsuits and other forms of legal action. The Pirate Bay, for example, has evaded repeated shutdown attempts from industry organizations who take umbrage with their hosting of torrents file for pirated content as well as their anti-industry politics. The group has relocated to a multitude of hosting servers and web addresses. In addition, Internet service providers across the world actively block access to The Pirate Bay, which has led to the proliferation of proxies.[19] In response to each attempt to block access to pirated material, The Pirate Bay defiantly evades control from the content industries.

In the face of legal challenges, many pirates have also turn to various privacy-enhancing technological measures like VPNs or virtual private networks, measures that are thought to be on the rise among pirates (Larsson, Svensson & de Kaminski, 2012). These services route users' network traffic through their servers to hide the user's IP address which makes it more difficult to trace who is doing the piracy. Pirates have also begun returning to Usenet, a distribution system for the exchange of text-based messages, providing services similar to a set of publicly archived email lists (Turner et al., 2005). Despite the technology being decades old, it is considered by many to be the most effective way to share content while maintaining privacy. Other pirates have also turned to filelocker services. These websites allow for persons to store content on their servers and share download links with others, frequently through online discussion boards. A recent piracy crackdown involved one such site, Megaupload, whose owner (Kim Dotcom) was arrested in New Zealand through an international law enforcement sting (Zetter, 2015). For pirates, these approaches not only comprise self-protection methods, but also means to preserve privacy. Thus, at the same time pirates assert that "sharing is caring" and "information wants to be free," they also seek technological measures to protect their private information (like their identity and whereabouts). In this capacity, technology is viewed as a key mechanism for expressing liberal values like free speech, individual autonomy, and personal privacy.[20] True to Polanyi's (1944) notion of the double movement, we can see that liberalism provides the foundation for both intellectual property *and* its undermining via piracy.

Yet this tension would seem to situate pirates as diametrically opposed to the markets which represent intellectual property interests and their interpretations of liberal values. The particular rhetoric and strategies adopted by pirates, however, may also paradoxically support content industries and information capitalism more broadly. One of the key motivations espoused by pirates in previous studies, for example, is a desire to sample content (e.g. Gopal, Bhattacharjee & Sanders, 2006; Peitz & Waelbroack, 2006; Mueller, 2016). The so-called "sampling" or "exposure effect" is the idea that people may purchase content once that have sampled or otherwise been exposed to said content without purchase (Liebowitz, 1985; Peitz & Waelbroack, 2006). The idea is that content deemed to be of sufficient quality will be rewarded through legitimate purchase. Steve Wozniak echoed this sentiment during a panel discussion at the 1985 Hacker Convention:

> Some pirates copy software and they'll copy everything and put it in their collection, but if they find something that they do like and decide it's a good one, they'll go out and buy it because the producer deserves the money.
>
> (as quoted in Brand & Herron, 1985)

The idea of *paying* for content is not necessarily rejected by many pirates – only that compensation should be reserved for quality content. Interestingly, this logic is surprisingly pro-market: those who produce quality content will be rewarded while those who do not will be discarded (Brown & Knox, 2016).

Further, some pirates resort to illegal downloading out of an inability to afford content (Steinmetz & Tunnell, 2013), a motivation that conjures criminological strain theory.[21] For these pirates, there is an implication that they would be willing to pay if the costs were more commensurate with their expectations or pocketbooks. Thus the idea of *paying* for content may not be the problem for many. Rather, content may be viewed as priced too highly for the value it affords or pirates may have limited access to funds. If payment is a minimal obstruction to content, resistance is less pronounced. Viewed from Mertonian (1938) perspective, a cultural pressure exists in contemporary society consume massive quantities of creative content. Any blockage to such consumption may create a strain. As Steinmetz and Tunnell (2013) explain:

> Pirates exist in a 'consumer society' and are socialized into hyperconsumption (Baudrillard, 1970/1998). Within current political economies

and using a contemporary form of innovation, pirates across the globe replace socially approved means of acquiring digital content with illegal ones (Merton, 1938).

(Steinmetz & Tunnell, 2013: 59)

Larsson, Svensson, and de Kaminski (2012) similarly find that the adoption of anonymity services by filesharers may similarly be explained through Mertonian strain.

Such financial strain may lead to the conclusion that pirates are either cheap or outright nefarious – that they are reluctant to purchase content period. Interestingly, though pirates by definition pirate, research indicates that they also purchase significantly more content legitimately than non-pirates (Kantar Media, 2013; Karaganis & Renkema, 2013; Mueller, 2016). One study that involved phone surveys of a randomized sample of 1000 Germans and 2,303 Americans found that:

> P2P file sharers, in particular, are heavy legal media consumers. They buy as many legal DVDs, CDs, and subscription media as their non-file-sharing, Internet-using counterparts. In the US, they buy roughly 30% more digital music. They also display a marginally higher willingness to pay.

(Karaganis & Renkema, 2013: 5)

In another study conducted by Kantar Media (2013), they found that the top 20 percent of copyright infringers "accounted for 11% of the legal content consumed" and "spent significantly more across all content types on average" than other pirates and non-pirates (Kantar Media, 2013: 3). In other words, the people who engage in the most *illicit* content consumption also consume the most *legal* content as well. These findings fly in the face of most portrayals of digital pirates and contradicts the claim that pirates are largely to blame for industry losses. Most importantly, however, it suggests that some of the most prolific pirates are not diametrically opposed to paying for content and, in fact, pay into the system more than most.

Further, many pirates argue that file-sharing and related technologies offer an alternative to mainstream business models (Steinmetz & Tunnell, 2013). In this sense, making a profit from content is not necessarily condoned. Rather, pirates view content industries as antiquated behemoths that get in the way of technological progress. File sharing technologies are also said to allow artists to directly market and sell their content to consumers. In this capacity, network technologies are viewed as a utopian mechanism to allow equal participation in an open market place of intellectual property, where producers can directly connect to consumers – we can see technological liberalism at work. In this capacity, capitalist markets themselves are generally not eschewed but, rather, business models that are viewed to run counter to technological trends are rejected.

Conclusion

The ultimate point is that understanding piracy is not a simple matter. Instead, piracy is firmly enmeshed in the undulations of late modern capitalism – it is simultaneously a product of and an ulcer within it. The individual act of digital piracy is only possible in an age of high-technology and globalized content production. Piracy, as a crime, can only occur under a legal regime that protects the interests of industries dependent on control and ownership of information – a late modern form of what Spitzer (1975) describes as "deviance production." Copyright did not emerge out of some categorical imperative. Instead, it was the product of social conflict where vested interests worked toward a second enclosure movement surrounding creativity (Boyle, 2003; Halbert, 2016). Digital piracy emerged alongside the rampant production and proprietization of data. Piracy becomes a social problem during critical moments of expansion of industries that depend on the creation of artificial scarcities of ideas – a commodity that fundamentally resists scarcity (Perelman, 2002). Notions of intellectual property are reified as something fundamentally natural and worth protecting rather that something aberrant and chiefly in the interests of content owners and distributors. The bigger the content industries become and the more money to be made, the more energy is expended in the defense of intellectual property against the social banditry of pirates. These efforts have not only failed to stop piracy, but they have also harmed the social goods that copyright originally sought to protect including fair use and the public domain.

Piracy is produced under the same historical circumstances that birthed intellectual property – one cannot exist without the other. While it may be tempting to juxtapose piracy as solely a mechanism of resistance against the order imposed by proprietization, piracy itself subscribes to ideologies that also underpin the creation of intellectual property. Liberalism is isolated here though other influences are undoubtedly at work. On the one hand, the liberal value of property ownership as an expression of freedom undergirds intellectual property. The actions of content industries are Randian in their objectivism and eschew many of the social goods originally linked to liberalism:

> The world understood through these reports is not an open system where knowledge is shared for the sake of learning, poverty alleviation, or economic development, but instead one where knowledge is owned and controlled by industrial and state actors and its existence as a secret must be preserved and protected at all costs.
>
> (Halbert, 2016: 260)

On the other hand, liberalism also supports the view of pirates that expressive content is akin to speech and, as such, any limit on its circulation is fundamentally amoral. Further, piracy reimagines the enlightenment values of sharing information as a social good. Both piracy and intellectual property can thus be seen as two conflicting ends of liberalism within the context of capital accumulation (Coleman & Golub, 2008; Steinmetz, 2016). Even beyond liberalism, however, pirates still do not wholly resist the logics of accumulation as they still appear to support commercial consumption of content (albeit in forms generally not engaged in by many content corporations).

In light of this complexity – of which this chapter can only superficially cover its vastness – the idea that piracy can be simplified to individual factors like low self-control is, frankly, laughable. This is not to say that individual-level factors are not at play, but that these can only be reasonably considered within their broader contexts. Yet, most of criminology – specifically main-stream or orthodox criminology – appears satisfied to examine piracy through a pinhole. Its focus has been almost exclusively on describing and attempting to explain the behaviors and characteristics of individual pirates while implicitly or explicitly adopting the myopic assumption that piracy is a problem based simply on official narratives proffered by industry and political elites. Each facet of these narratives should instead be viewed skeptically by criminologists. Halbert (2016: 262) argues that:

> While it is arguable that the industry has lost anywhere near the amounts of money it claims, what has been successfully accomplished is the uncritical acceptance of the IP theft narrative at all levels of American government as a truth.

We would hold criminology complicity in this as well. Going forward, rather than focus exclusively on the behavioral dynamics underpinning intellectual property infringement/file-sharing, criminology should also examine the macro-structural and cultural threads that join the multifarious facets of piracy ranging from individual file sharers, law, content owners, political groups (including the Pirate Party), among others.

Notes

1 The webpage originally hosting this quote has since gone offline. A copy of the page is preserved at Archive.org through their "Wayback Machine" dated to December 4, 2015. The original URL for the page containing the quote was www. riaa.com/physicalpiracy.php?content_selector=piracy-online-scope-of-the-problem.
2 See Gunter (2009).
3 See Holsapple, Iyengar, Jin, and Rao (2008).
4 See Décary-Héntu, Morselli, and Leman-Langlois (2012).
5 See Hinduja (2012b).
6 See Larsson, Svensson, and de Kaminski (2012) and Steinmetz and Tunnell (2013).
7 Multiple studies have examined the techniques of neutralization in piracy (Higgins & Marcum, 2011; Ingram & Hinduja, 2008; Skinner & Fream, 1997; Smallridge & Roberts, 2013; Steinmetz & Tunnell, 2013).
8 Multiple studies have applied low self-control theory and social learning theories to the study of digital piracy (Burruss, Bossler, & Holt, 2012; Donner et al., 2014; Gunter, 2009; Higgins, 2004; Higgins, Marcum, Freiburger & Ricketts, 2012; Holt,

Bossler, & May, 2012; Malin & Fowers, 2009; Moon, McCluskey, & McCluskey, 2010; Moon et al., 2012).

9 The Audio Home Recording Act did provide anti-circumvention measures but they were not as strict as those imposed under the DMCA.

10 In addition, focus is given to the core subculture of piracy or the "warez scene." This group is the engine that propels contemporary piracy by providing and managing most of the piracy websites and file sharing protocols as well as cracking the file protection and uploading more digital content than "casual" or "lay" pirates. As such, this analysis focuses primarily on tensions between the subculture of piracy and capital, though many of these insights can likely be applied to casual pirates as well.

11 The BSA still accepts reports of copyright infringement at the time this chapter was written. The form can be located at the BSA's website.

12 Quote is from the RIAA's "About Piracy" page, located at www.riaa.com/resour ces-learning/about-piracy/.

13 Quote is from the RIAA's "About Piracy" page, located at www.riaa.com/resour ces-learning/about-piracy/.

14 Quote is from the RIAA's "For Students and Educators" page, located at www. riaa.com/resources-learning/for-students-educators/.

15 Quote is from the MPAA's "Why Copyright Matters" page, located at www.mpaa. org/why-copyright-matters/.

16 Other authors have taken varying perspectives on hacker/technological politics. Coleman (2017) argues, for example, that there is tremendous political diversity among hackers that range from libertarian, liberal, anarchistic, and socialistic that cannot be safely subsumed under a single umbrella. Other authors, have argued that hackers tend to subscribe to more libertarian sensibilities, which Jordan and Taylor (2004) describe as "technolibertarianism."

17 Additional technological liberties and policies are advocated by various Piracy Parties as well, some of which are enumerated on the Pirate Party Wikipedia page: https://en.wikipedia.org/wiki/Pirate_Party.

18 While most copy-protection mechanisms are broken regularly, a recent DRM (digital rights management) protocol has been giving crackers tremendous difficulty termed Denuvo. Even when cracked, creating stability in the digital content is tenuous at best. In the future, we may see an increasing arms race between content industries and crackers *or* pirates may turn toward other approaches for content acquisition.

19 A list of The Pirate Bay proxies can be found at https://thepiratebay-proxylist.org/.

20 For some, this may appear to be a contradiction. Power, however, is a key variable. Consistent with liberalism, ideal privacy protections are typically held to be inversely proportionate with the degree of power and control held by a person, organization, institution, or state. Regardless, the tension between privacy, secrecy, and information freedom is evident. Contradictions in pirate beliefs have been noted previously (Steinmetz & Tunnell, 2013).

21 Other scholars have explored the role of strain on music piracy as well. For example, Hinduja (2006; 2012a) has applied Agnew's (1992) General Strain Theory. The Mertonian strain has also been explored (Larsson, Svensson, & de Kaminski, 2012; Steinmetz & Tunnell, 2013).

References

Aaltonen, M. and Salmi, V. (2013) 'Specialized pirates? A comparison of correlates of illegal downloading and traditional juvenile crime', *Journal of Scandinavian Studies in Criminology and Crime Prevention*, 14(2): 188–195.

Agnew, R. (1992). Foundation for a general strain theory of crime and delinquency. *Criminology*, 30(1): 47–88.

Alva, A. (2016, October 28). 'DMCA security research exemption for consumer devices', *Federal Trade Commission Tech@FTC*. Retrieved January 1, 2017 from www.ftc.gov/news-events/blogs/techftc/2016/10/dmca-security-research-exemption-consumer-devices.

Andy. (2016) 'Fox "stole" a game clip, used it in Family Guy & DMCA'd the original', *TorrentFreak*. Retrieved May 23, 2016 from https://torrentfreak.com/fox-stole-a-game-clip-used-it-in-family-guy-dmcad-the-original-160520/.

Bachmann, M. (2007) 'Lesson spurned? Reactions of online music pirates to legal prosecutions by the RIAA', *International Journal of Cyber Criminology*, 1(2): 213–227.

Baudrillard, J. (1970/1998) *The consumer society*, Thousand Oaks, CA: Sage.

Boyle, J. (2003) 'The second enclosure movement and the construction of the public domain', *Law and Contemporary Problems*, 66: 33–74.

Brand, S., and Herron, M. (1985) '"Keep Designing": How the information economy is being created and shaped by the Hacker Ethic', *Whole Earth Review*, 46: 44–52.

Brown, S. C. and Knox, D. (2016) 'Why buy an album? The motivations behind recording music purchases.' *Psychomusicology: Music, Mind, and Brain*, 26(1): 79–86.

Burruss, G.W., Bossler, A.M., and Holt, T.J. (2012) 'Assessing the mediation of a fuller social learning model on low self-control's influence on software piracy', *Crime & Delinquency*, 59(8): 1157–1184.

Business Software Alliance. (2014) *The compliance gap: BSA global software survey*. Accessed July 28, 2016 at http://globalstudy.bsa.org/2013/downloads/studies/2013GlobalSurvey_Study_en.pdf.

Coleman, G.E. (2017, Online First) 'From Internet farming to weapons of the geek.' *Current Anthropology*, 58(15).

Coleman, G E., and Golub, A. (2008) 'Hacker practice: Moral genres and the cultural articulation of liberalism', *Anthropological Theory*, 8: 255–277.

Cooper, J. and Harrison, D. M. (2001) 'The social organization of audio piracy on the Internet', *Media, Culture & Society*, 23: 71–89.

Décary-Hétu, D., Morselli, C., and Leman-Langlois, S. (2012) 'Welcome to the scene: A study of social organization and recognition among warez hackers', *Journal of Research in Crime and Delinquency*, 49: 359–382.

Doctorow, C. (2008) ©*ontent: Selected essays on technology, creativity, copyright, and the future of the future*, San Francisco, CA: Tachyon Publications.

Downing, S. (2010) 'Social control in a subculture of piracy', *Journal of Criminal Justice and Popular Culture*, 14(1): 77–123.

Electronic Frontier Foundation. (2008, September 30) RIAA v. The People: Five Years Later. Retrieved May 23, 2016 from www.eff.org/files/eff-riaa-whitepaper.pdf.

Erlingsson, G. Ó. and Persson, M. (2011) 'The Swedish Pirate Party and the 2009European Parliament election: Protest or issue voting?' *Politics*, 31(3): 121–128.

Gopal, R., Bhattacharjee, S., and Sanders, G.L. (2006) 'Do artists benefit from online music sharing', *Journal of Business*, 79: 1503–1534.

Gunter, W.D. (2009) 'Internet scallywags: A comparative analysis of multiple forms and measurements of digital piracy', *Western Criminology Review*, 10(1): 15–28.

Halbert, D. (2016) 'Intellectual property theft and national security: Agendas and assumptions', *The Information Society*, 32(4): 256–268.

Hargittai, E. (2010) 'Digital na(t)ives? Variation in internet skills and uses among members of the "Net Generation"', *Sociological Inquiry*, 80(1): 92–113.

Harvey, D. (2014) *Seventeen contradictions and the end of capitalism*, New York: Oxford University Press.

Higgins, G.E. (2004) 'Can low self-control help with the understanding of the software piracy problem?', *Deviant Behavior*, 26(1): 1–24.

Higgins, G.E. and Marcum, C. D. (2011) *Digital piracy: An integrated theoretical approach*, Raleigh, NC: Carolina Academic Press.

Higgins, G.E., Marcum, C.D., Freiburger, T.L. and Ricketts, M.L. (2012) 'Examining the role of peer influence and self-control on downloading behavior', *Deviant Behavior*, 33(5): 412–423.

Higgins, G.E., Wolfe, S.E. and Marcum, C.D. (2008) 'Digital piracy: An examination of three measurements of self-control', *Deviant Behavior*, 29(5): 440–460.

Hinduja, S. (2006) *Music piracy and crime theory*, New York: LFB Scholarly Publishing.

Hinduja, S. (2012b) 'The heterogeneous engineering of music piracy: Applying actor network theory to internet-based wrongdoing', *Policy and Internet*, 4(3): 229–238.

Hinduja, S. and Higgins, G.E. (2011) 'Trends and patterns among music pirates', *Deviant Behavior*, 32(7): 563–588.

Holsapple, C.W., Iyengar, D. Jin, H. and Rao, S. (2008) 'Parameters for software piracy research', *The Information Society*, 24(4): 199–218.

Holt, T.J. and Bossler, A.M. (2014) 'An assessment of the current state of cybercrime scholarship', *Deviant Behavior*, 35(1): 20–40.

Holt, T.J., Bossler, A.M. and May, D.C. (2012) 'Low self-control, deviant peer associations, and juvenile cyberdeviance', *American Journal of Criminal Justice*, 37: 378–395.

Holt, T.J. and Copes, H. (2010) 'Transferring subcultural knowledge on-line: Practices and beliefs of persistent digital pirates', *Deviant Behavior*, 31(7): 625–654.

International Federation of Phonographic Industries. (2015) 'Digital music report 2015: Charting the path to sustainable growth', Retrieved from: www.ifpi.org/down loads/Digital-Music-Report-2015.pdf.

Johns, A. (2002) 'Pop music pirate hunters', *Daedalus*, 131(2): 67–77.

Jordan, T. and Taylor, P. (2004) *Hacktivism and cyberwars: Rebels with a cause*, New York: Routledge.

Kantar Media (2013) 'OCI tracker benchmark study "Deep Dive" analysis report.' Prepared for Ofcom. Retrieved June 9, 2016 from http://stakeholders.ofcom.org.uk/ binaries/research/telecoms-research/online-copyright/deep-dive.pdf.

Karaganis, J., and Renkema, L. (2013) *Copy culture in the US & Germany*, New York: The American Assembly, Columbia University. Retrieved June 9, 2016from http://p iracy.americanassembly.org/wp-content/uploads/2013/01/Copy-Culture.pdf.

Kariithi, N.K. (2011) 'Is the devil in the data? A literature review of piracy around the world', *The Journal of World Intellectual Property*, 14(2): 133–154.

Larsson, S., Svensson, M., and de Kaminski, M. (2012) 'Online piracy, anonymity and social change: Innovation through deviance', *Convergence: The International Journal of Research into New Media Technologies*, 19(1): 95–114.

Lessig, L. (2004) *Free culture: The nature and future of creativity*, New York: Penguin Books.

Lessig, L. (2008) *Remix: Making art and commerce thrive in the hybrid economy*, New York: Penguin Press.

Levy, S. (1984) *Hackers: Heroes of the computer revolution*, New York: Penguin Group Inc.

Liebowitz, S. J. (1985) 'Copying and indirect appropriability: Photocopying of journals', *Journal of Political Economy*, 93(5): 945–957.

Losurdo, D. (2014) *Liberalism: A counter-history*, New York: Verso.

Lunney, G. S. (2001) 'The death of copyright: Digital technology, private copying, and the Digital Millennium Copyright Act', *Virginia Law Review*, 87: 813–920.

Malin, J. & Fowers, B.J. (2009) 'Adolescent self-control and music and movie piracy', *Computers in Human Behavior*, 25: 718–722.

Marx, K. (1842, October 25) 'Debates on the law on thefts of wood', *Rheinische Zeitung*, 298. Accessed January 23, 2017. English translation retrieved from www.marxists.org/archive/marx/works/download/Marx_Rheinishe_Zeitung.pdf.

Merton, R. K. (1938) 'Social structure and anomie', *American Sociological Review*, 3: 672–682.

Meyer, G. R. (1989). *The social organization of the computer underground*. Northern Illinois: Univ De Kalb.

Mitchell, S. (2012) 'The BSA's "nauseating" anti-piracy tactics.' *Alphr*, March 14. Retrieved May 23, 2016 from www.alphr.com/news/enterprise/373567/the-bsas-nauseating-anti-piracy-tactics.

Moon, B., McCluskey, J.D., and McCluskey, C.P. (2010) 'A general theory of crime and computer crime: An empirical test', *Journal of Criminal Justice*, 38: 767–772.

Moon, B., McCluskey, J. D., McCluskey, C. P., and Lee, S. (2012) 'Gender, general theory of crime and computer crime: An empirical test', *International Journal of Offender Therapy and Comparative Criminology*, 57(4): 460–478.

Morris, R.G., and Higgins, G.E. (2010) 'Criminological theory in the digital age: The case of social learning theory and digital piracy.' *Journal of Criminal Justice*, 38: 470–480.

Mueller, G. (2016) 'Piracy as labour struggle', *Communication, Capitalism & Critique*, 14: 333–345.

Nandedkar, A. and Midha, V. (2012) 'It won't happen to me: An assessment of optimism bias in music piracy', *Computers in Human Behavior*, 28: 41–48.

Navarro, J. N., Marcum, C.D., Higgins, G. E., and Ricketts, M. L. (2014) 'Addicted to pillaging in cyberspace: Investigating the role of internet addiction in digital piracy', *Computers and Human Behavior*, 37: 101–106.

Nill, A. and Shultz, C. (2009) 'Global software piracy: Trends and strategic considerations', *Business Horizons*, 52: 289–298.

Parkes, M. (2013) 'Making plans for Nigel: The Industry Trust and film piracy management in the United Kingdom', *Convergence: The International Journal of Research into New Media Technologies*, 19(1): 25–43.

Peitz, M., and Waelbroeck, P. (2006) 'Piracy of digital products: A critical review of the theoretical literature', *Information Economics and Policy*, 18: 449–476.

Perelman, M. (2002) *Steal This Idea: Intellectual Property Rights and the Corporate Confiscation of Creativity*, New York: Palgrave Macmillan.

Perelman, M. (2014) 'The political economy of intellectual property', *Socialism and Democracy*, 28: 24–33.

Pirate Parties International (2017) 'About PPI.' Retrieved January 6, 2017 from https://pp-international.net/about-ppi/.

Polanyi, K. (1944) *The great transformation: The political and economic origins of our time*, Boston, MA: Beacon Press.

Rand, A. (1966) 'Patents and copyrights', in A. Rand (author) *Capitalism: The Unknown Ideal* (pp. 125–129), New York: New American Library.

Schaffner, D. J. (2004) 'The Digital Millennium Copyright Act: Overextension of copyright protection and the unintended chilling effects on fair use, free speech, and innovation', *Cornell Journal of Law & Public Policy*, 14: 145–169.

Sharp, J. (2002) 'Coming soon to pay-per-view: How the Digital Millennium Copyright Act enables digital content owners to circumvent educational fair use', *American Business Law Journal*, 40: 1–81.

Siwek, S. E. (2007) 'The true cost of sound recording piracy to the U.S. economy', The Institute for Policy Innovation. Retrieved from: http://ipi.org/ipi_issues/detail/the-true-cost-of-sound-recording-piracy-to-the-us-economy.

Skinner, W. F. and Fream, A. F. (1997) 'A social learning theory analysis of computer crime among college students', *Journal of Research in Crime and Delinquency*, 34: 495–518.

Smallridge, J. L. and Roberts, J. R. (2013) 'Crime specific neutralizations: An empirical examination of four types of digital piracy', *International Journal of Cyber Criminology*, 7(2): 125–140.

Spitzer, S. (1975) 'Toward a Marxian theory of deviance', *Social Problems*, 22(5): 638–651.

Stallman, R. (2002) *Free software free society: Selected essays of Richard M. Stallman*, Boston, MA: Free Software Foundation, Inc.

Steinmetz, K. F. (2016) *Hacked: A radical approach to hacker culture and crime*, New York: New York University Press.

Steinmetz, K. F. and Gerber, J. (2015) 'Hacking the state: Hackers, technological liberalism, and state crime', in G. Barak (ed.) *The Routledge Handbook of the Crimes of the Powerful* (pp. 503–514), New York: Routledge.

Steinmetz, K. F. and Tunnell, K. D. (2013) 'Under the pixelated jolly roger: A study of on-line pirates', *Deviant Behavior*, 34: 53–67.

Tade, O. and Akinleye, B. (2012) '"We are promoters not pirates": A qualitative analysis of artists and pirates on music piracy in Nigeria', *International Journal of Cyber Criminology*, 6(2): 1014–1029.

Turner, T.C., Smith, M.A., Fisher, D., and Welser, H.T. (2005) 'Picturing usenet: Mapping computer-mediated collective action', *Journal of Computer-Mediated Communication*, 10(4). doi:10.1111/j.1083–6101.2005.tb00270.

Vaidhyanathan, S. (2012) 'Open source as culture/culture as open source', in M. Mandiberg (ed.) *The social media reader* (pp. 24–31). New York: New York University Press.

Wark, M. (2004) *The hacker manifesto*, Cambridge, MA: Harvard University Press.

Warnick, B.R. (2004) 'Technological metaphors and moral education: The hacker ethic and the computational experience', *Studies in Philosophy and Education*, 23: 265–281.

Wozniak, S. (2006) *iWoz*, New York: W. W. Norton & Company.

Yar, M. (2005) 'The global "epidemic" of movie "piracy": Crime-wave or social construction?', *Media, Culture & Society*, 27(5): 677–696.

Yar, M. (2008a) 'Computer crime control as industry: Virtual insecurity and the market for private policing', in K. F. Aas, H. O. Gundhus, and H. M. Lomell (eds.) *Technologies of Insecurity: The Surveillance of Everyday Life* (pp. 189–204), New York: Routledge-Cavendish.

Yar, M. (2008b) 'The rhetorics and myths of anti-piracy campaigns: Criminalization, moral pedagogy and capitalist property relations in the classroom', *New Media & Society*, 10: 605–623.

Yar, M. (2013) *Cybercrime and society* (2nd ed.), Thousand Oaks, CA: Sage.

Yar, M. (2014) *The cultural imaginary of the internet*. New York: Palgrave Macmillan.

Zetter, K. (2015) 'Judge rules Kim Dotcom can be extradited to US to face charges', *Wired Magazine*, December 22,Retrieved May 24, 2016 from www.wired.com/2015/12/kim-dotcom-extradition-ruling/.

10 The criminality of digital piracy

Is it a pathway to more serious offending?

George Burruss and Cassandra Dodge

Introduction

The allure of free, bootleg digital content – music, movies, software, games – is hard to refuse for four chief reasons. First, most of this content is intangible: it can be downloaded without touching a physical product. This makes the act of digital piracy seem less consequential than traditional larceny theft such as shoplifting. The physical act of stealing requires the offender to consider detection by bystanders and sneaking the item or items from a location. Digital piracy does not require a detectable, tactile action. Second, the act of digital piracy can be done anonymously. Hiding behind anonymous user accounts or by using anonymized web browsing reduces the risk of detection, which is generally perceived as low. Rarely does someone learn a friend or relative has been prosecuted for illegally obtaining digital media. The prospect of deterring digital piracy is therefore negligible at best (Hinduja, 2008). Third, the victims of digital piracy are perceived as large corporations or rich artists and producers. Denying harm to these victims is easy to rationalize (Hinduja, 2007; Ingram & Hinduja, 2008). Fourth and finally, those who engage in digital piracy (for profit or use) know the act is illegal but ubiquitous: if everyone does it, it cannot be deviant. This also makes the act easy to rationalize.

Criminologists have been interested in studying the act of digital piracy because it allows for testing general theories of crime, and it may be a pathway to other more serious online behaviors. That is, digital piracy is likely done by hackers, though not all digital pirates are hackers. Gaining access to a sample of hackers in the wild has proven difficult so digital pirates provide a much easier target to study. Learning about the perceived benefits and low risks of illegal downloading can aid in studying other forms of illegal online behavior that have similar methods, such as cyberbullying and intrusion. Thus, knowing something about the motivations and methods for digital piracy may inform our understanding of other kinds of cybercrime.

There is some evidence digital piracy co-occurs with other forms of off-line property crime. Brunton-Smith and McCarthy (2016), for example, found that online piracy offenders in a representative sample of English and Welsh survey respondents were also likely to engage in traditional property offending. More specifically, they measured 'offline property offenses' as including vehicle-related theft, criminal damage, burglaries, and other thefts, aggregating these offenses into one measure. They found that mostly young offenders who also committed one offline property crime were twice as likely to commit digital piracy, and about three times as likely if they committed two or more offenses. This research suggests that underlying motivations for traditional crimes are the same as online crimes.

The opportunity that allows illegal copying of digital media is the same as other kinds of cybercrime, like hacking and spreading malware infections. In essence, opportunities are created by computing devices (desktops, laptops, tablets, and smart phones) linked through cellular networks or the Internet. We use 'cyber' in this context to simply mean the interaction between humans and technology. Cyber opportunities include anonymity, intangibility, global access to targets, asynchronous activity, lack of capable guardianship, and shifting technology. For example, anonymous browsing when using networked computing devices decreases the likelihood of detection when engaging in criminal activity; asynchronous activity means cybercrime offenders can attack networked devices without the necessity of the victim being present online. With a growth in digital content of books, music, videos, news, valuable personal data, financial data, software, games, and other content, it is not surprising that digital piracy has become a world-wide phenomenon.

For the purposes of this discussion, we define digital piracy as "the unauthorized use or illegal copying of digital media without compensation to the copyright holder" (borrowed from Hinduja's definition of software piracy (2008: 391)). This definition leaves out the motivation of the offender, which would be provided by the scholars' use of a criminological theory. In this chapter, we will focus on the harm caused by digital piracy as well as its relationship to other forms of online offending. We will also discuss how an escalation in online offending might fit into existing scholarship on pathways to criminal behavior.

We have two goals in this chapter: (1) establish that digital piracy is a serious offense that can have widespread financial impact, especially when individual acts are scaled; and (2) consider digital piracy as a gateway or co-occurrence with other forms of online deviance. Both goals are difficult given the data in hand. The difficulty with determining the financial harm felt by producers of digital content (both corporations and individual artists) is that most estimates are provided by victims who have an interest in inflating the value of lost sales. We report what has been offered to date, but note the limitations. Regarding digital piracy's value in researching other forms of cybercrime, we offer some findings with cross-sectional data from two sources, but these too suffer from methodological limitations. Regardless, we feel this information provides some evidence supporting both contentions.

The methods of digital piracy

Methods of digital piracy can be simple or complex. Some methods can be learned with a simple Google search; others require advanced technical knowledge. Regardless of the complexity, there are three elements common to all forms of digital piracy: the acting participants in the piracy transaction; the product, such as an e-book file; and the environment in which the exchange happens. Regarding the actors, there is always at least a distributor and a recipient. One of the most straightforward methodologies is the act of ripping a CD or DVD and distributing a copy to someone else. This kind of single actor-to-actor piracy is common, but it is hard to track as the process can be completed without ever distributing the files through cyberspace. Stream ripping initially involves a single actor downloading the file from a legitimate streaming service. Peer-to-peer bit torrents, on the other hand, involve a larger number of participants and the transaction takes place in an online environment. These methods will be covered in more detail below.

Central to digital piracy is the violation of a copyright in which individuals do not have the right to copy or distribute a product, but they do with or without the goal of making money. So how does someone get a hold of the original product to distribute it? One way is through copying the legitimate product. For music and film piracy, ripping the data directly from a CD or DVD would be sufficient. Similarly, software installation files can also be ripped from installation disks. Publication pirates (those who copy and distribute content from physical and digital books and other written media) could simply scan physical copies of the text for distribution as a digital version, such as a portable document format (PDF) file. However, initially copying the text could take many hours per book (Linder 2010). In some cases, a legitimate form of the product may not exist or is not accessible. Filming a movie in the theater (colloquially known as a 'cam rip') is common with new film releases. As industries add additional layers of security, the methods of making and distributing digital copies must become more complex. Ebooks, for example, are locked from access using copy protection codes. When the books are purchased, permissions to access the book are granted to the account owner. A skilled hacker, however, can get past the coding, remove the protections, and upload the e-book file to a virtual storage site (Zimerman, 2011).

Once the files are obtained, they need to be made available for distribution. As stated before, the delivery of digital content can be completed simply through a single distributor to a single recipient. Email, chat interfaces, and physical delivery are possible options for these types of transactions. If the distributor has multiple recipients, she may choose to utilize a cyberlocker. The cyberlocker user files are made accessible with proper authentication.

Wider file distribution requires a more complex system. A peer-to-peer (P2P) file transfer protocol known as BitTorrent allows users to share large files online. To utilize BitTorrent, a user must download the torrent file for the associated product. Torrent files do not contain the distribution content. They are metadata files that facilitate the process of downloading. After opening the torrent file with BitTorrent client software, users can download and upload file segments simultaneously with other peers in their assigned group, called a swarm. Often, users will be required to maintain a contribution ratio to continually download material. That is, participants in the P2P system are both recipients and distributors, allowing other peers to download file fragments directly from their computer through the client software. If the upload to download ratio becomes too small (the user does not maintain the required quota), then access to material will be restricted. They can regain access once they upload, or seed, enough data to maintain their quota.

Identified by Ipsos Connect as the most common process used to pirate audio media, stream ripping is also categorized as form of direct download (Ipsos Connect, 2016). However, unlike P2P methods, this type of piracy can be accomplished individually. The IFPI defines stream ripping as the process of "creating a downloadable file from music that is available to stream online" (IFPI, 2017: 37). Using software, such as browser extensions, users access streaming websites (legitimate or not) and download, or rip, the audio from the stream. This can be completed for personal use or the files can be uploaded to a cyberlocker, P2P system, or other websites such as YouTube-MP3.org to be shared amongst other users. In 2016, 30 percent of all internet users admitted to engaging in stream ripping in the previous six months, with 49 percent of 16 to 24-year-olds admitting their participation (Ipsos Connect, 2016).

Direct downloads are not the only way pirated material is distributed. Much like legitimate streaming services, pirated films, television programs, and music can be streamed online. The legality of these streaming sites is questionable. In the frequently asked questions section of GoMovies.to, it is claimed that "[w]atching is totally legal. We also do not host the movies, we link to them" (GoMovies, 2017: n.p.). Many of the streaming films have not been released on DVD, and some of the streams are identified as cam rips. Clearly, the majority of the films were ill-gotten, but by acting as facilitators rather than hosts, GoMovies avoids legal responsibility. Otherwise, the model for pirated streaming services is very similar to its legitimate counterpart, though they use advertising (banner ads, commercials) to generate revenue rather than charge membership fees. Much like the free streams available on Hulu, advertisements will interrupt the stream at selected intervals. The streaming website is paid for by advertisers, just like advertisements shown on television.

The scope of the digital piracy problem

Digital piracy is a phenomenon that affects multiple industries. Typically, public discussion of digital piracy centers on the music, television, and film industries. Less discussed, digital piracy also affects the software and publication industries. While there are various definitions and methodologies of digital piracy, the framework is consistent. Individuals who do not hold the copyright for a piece of digital property gain access to the data and distribute it at a reduced price or for free. This transaction occurs through multiple means, such as through peer-to-peer file sharing services (e.g., Napster, LimeWire, and BitTorrent), streaming services (e.g., GoMovies.to), or direct downloads (Price, 2013).

The prevalence of piracy is extensive. According to a report by brand protection company NetNames, an estimated three hundred and twenty-seven million users engaged in digital piracy in 2013. This estimate was derived through analyses of bandwidth consumption by known BitTorrent portals, video streaming sites, video streaming hosts, direct download cyberlocker link sites, and direct download cyberlockers (Price, 2013). While this report illustrates the extent of digital piracy, it does not specifically identify how individual industries are victimized by piracy. The methods used by digital pirates are similar across industries. However, some are impacted more, and each one estimates its losses in a variety of ways.

In a 2007 study, Siwek calculated the total global losses experienced by the sound recording industry using data from the International Federation of the Phonographic Industry (IFPI). According to the IFPI, approximately 20 billion illegal downloads occurred worldwide in 2005, assuming 66 percent of downloads were U.S. recorded music (Siwek, 2007). As of 2015, the research firm MusicWatch reported that 20 million people in the United States still download music through peer-to-peer services (Faughnder, 2015). In his 2007 report, Siwek acknowledged that not all users would purchase the recordings legally even if piracy was not an option. Accordingly, Siwek assumed that only 20 percent of downloads could be considered when calculating revenue loss. It is unclear how this final percentage was determined. The computed weighted-average legitimate price of U.S. music worldwide was $2.30 per song. This value was multiplied by the net return to the record producer (60.72 percent) and the total estimated song substitutions (2.6 billion). The revenue loss experienced by the recording industry caused by digital piracy was estimated to be approximately $3.7 billion (Siwek, 2007).

In 2005, the Motion Picture Association of America commissioned consulting firm L.E.K. to estimate lost revenue from digital and physical piracy. The full report was never released. A summary of the study was included in the appendix of another report by Stephen Siwek (2006). The study included 20,600 participants from 22 countries, who either were interviewed or participated in focus groups. Revenue loss was calculated by determining the number of legitimate purchases, including movie ticket and DVD purchases, that would have been completed if the pirated versions were unavailable. The total revenue lost to digital piracy was determined to be approximately $2.3 billion (Siwek, 2006). Without the full report, it is impossible to determine the accuracy or generalizability of these results.

Digital piracy in the publishing industry is not as prolific as in other markets, such as music or film. That said, publication piracy has long existed online, and has one of the more straightforward, if labor-intensive, methodologies of photocopying text (Linder, 2010). This time commitment has its own deterrent effect. Unfortunately, with the advent of e-readers and e-publishing formats within the last decade, piracy has been a rising concern for publishers and authors. As this consumer market is relatively new, there is little research exploring the scope of the problem. However, in 2009, the North American e-book revenue was reported to be 500 million dollars (Statista, 2016). This is particularly interesting as e-readers, Barnes and Noble's Nook and Amazon's Kindle, were first released internationally in 2009, and then Apple's eBook for the iPad in 2010. Unlike the scans of hard copy publications, e-publication files are significantly smaller in data size. Once copy protection codes are hacked, the material is available for use (Zimerman, 2011). It stands to reason that the expanding availability of e-books will only increase the number of pirated publications, as the methods for procuring these published materials become less labor intensive. According to the Association of American Publishers, U.S. publication companies are currently losing 80 million to 100 million dollars per year from piracy (MUSO, 2016a). Unfortunately, there is no information available as to how this estimate was calculated.

The leading report about software piracy is the annual BSA Global Software Survey. More than 20,000 home and enterprise PC users completed the survey online or by phone. The survey targeted thirty-two global markets, which was representative in levels of IT sophistication, geographic distribution, and cultural diversity. BSA's second survey targeted 2,200 IT managers in 22 countries. BSA calculated the total amount of unlicensed software units deployed on PCs in the consumer market at $52.2 billion worldwide (BSA 2016). Unfortunately, the BSA reports are not useful in documenting the scope of digital piracy because the BSA report is designed to assist software companies in targeting potential revenue sources. From a business perspective, the legality of how the software was originally acquired is not the report's authors' primary concern. Valid license keys can be purchased regardless of the circumstances.

The changing commercial landscape of digital media has made the analysis of the true scope of digital piracy difficult to discern. Analytic companies regularly track trends in sales, streams, and downloads of various digital content. A few of these companies also track peer-to-peer downloads, creating a rich source of information on piracy in real time. Some analytic reports would be made available publicly to gain clientele while also serving as a resource for piracy research. Occasionally, these analytic companies are bought by their clients. This gives the new owners an advantage on industry competitors because they now have exclusive access to the analytic data. Public access to these data is restricted. The 2015 acquisition of Semetric, the parent company of the Musicmetric analytics service, by Apple, Inc. is a prime example. Since then, the Musicmetric Digital Music Index – one of the largest public data sets available for peer-to-peer music downloads – has been taken offline, and no public analytics have been offered by Apple since the buyout.

While other independent analytic services exist, many charge for the service and are unlikely to publish full reports online. Third-party analytics are a for-profit enterprise. What little information is released by these organizations will support the idea that digital piracy is a real threat to media industries and creators, especially when these organizations offer products designed to curtail piracy. Overestimating the actual damage caused by digital piracy helps fuel the demand for the analytic and anti-piracy products. Muso, a digital analytics company, for example, employs such tactics. Muso released their most recent Global Film and TV Piracy Insight Report in July of 2016. The webpage advertising the report includes information on the growing piracy trend from streaming services and mobile device use. New clients can purchase the full report for a minimum of $7,500 (MUSO, 2016c).

Industry reports that include estimates of monetary loss are often criticized because the authors typically do not explain how property loss values were calculated. Court documents, however, may explain the value calculations. In the 2008 case against Tanner Hills, an expert from the Motion Picture Association of America (MPAA) valued bootleg DVDs at approximately $19 a disc (Kravets 2008). Alternatively, cases against large-scale operations that included the seizure of pirating equipment incorporated the value of DVDs not yet produced into their estimations of piracy costs. For example, a case in Hong Kong led to the arrest of four people, the seizure of 6,200 DVDs, and the bootlegging equipment. This case was estimated to be worth a potential 20 million dollars. By itself, the DVDs in this case would appear to be valued at an astronomical $3,225.80 per DVD. This discrepancy is the result of the MPAA's inclusion of DVDs that could have been created within a year using the equipment seized, an additional seven million units (Kravets 2008).

Generally, industry report authors often fail to provide the methodology for their estimates. For example, the previously mentioned report by the consulting company L.E.K. for the MPAA was an internal document and was not released publically. Any knowledge of the study resulted from its inclusion in Siwek's 2006 report. Without including detailed methodologies, it is exceedingly difficult, if not impossible, to compare industry loss estimates. Additionally, as noted, many organizations collecting and analyzing piracy data benefit from casting piracy as a grave threat. These organizations provide the problem and its solution. While digital piracy is widespread, its financial impact may be overestimated by stakeholders who benefit from selling protective solutions.

When computing monetary losses, it is not unusual for industry estimates to categorize each download as a single unit loss in revenue. However, this is based on the assumption that the users would have purchased the product if the pirated copy had not been available. This assumption may be wrong. Users may download illegal copies simply because there is no cost in trying out the illegal copy. Had there been a choice to buy the product, they would have passed. Also, users may decide to illegally download products because what they want is not available on the open market. For example, a user in the United States may choose to torrent a film that has only been released in the United Kingdom. If a legal option were available, this pirated download would have been unnecessary. An illegal download does not always translate to financial loss. As a result, many of these market reports overestimate the true financial burden of digital piracy.

In sum, there is no single accepted method for estimating the true monetary cost of digital piracy within industries. Many of these estimates are biased and reported without a transparent methodology making it impossible to evaluate their accuracy. To have a valid and accurate accounting of the losses for digital piracy, the research and estimations should be conducted by a neutral third party. The monetary losses should be calculated through the product of the total number of unit losses to digital piracy and the average retail value of one unit of the product (DVD, music track, book, etc.). The total number of unit losses must be actual loss, not hypothetical. A crime does not occur hypothetically. More difficult to determine is whether every single instance of piracy equates to monetary loss. On one hand, the act of piracy is a form of theft, much like shoplifting. The stolen product has value that should be considered. On the other hand, stolen data is much more abstract. Physical items are finite, making their loss more substantial. You cannot make a profit from product that is not there. Digital piracy does not remove access to the item, so a profit is still possible. Rather than choose a side in this argument, it may be in the best interest of the research to include estimations of both the absolute monetary loss and the estimated retail loss. Industry estimates are limited in that they consider the monetary harm felt by the industry itself. Beyond monetary costs to these industries, we should consider the harm inflicted on authors and artists, consumers, and the overall economy.

What's the harm?

As noted above, the monetary harm caused by piracy typically focuses on the direct harm it presents to the related industries. Less common are discussions about harm to the global economy. In his interlocking economy argument, Swiek described the potential detrimental effect piracy has on the supply and demand chain. Piracy decreases industry revenues, leading to fewer investments in production (2006; 2007). The decrease in demand for retail music, for example, is an approximate $890 million loss in retail revenue in 2006 (Siwek, 2007). The reduction of revenue is also connected to the loss of employment on both the production and retail aspects of the economy. According to estimates, the music industry lost over 70,000 jobs and over 140,000 in film (Siwek, 2006 and 2007).

Beyond harm to industries and producers, piracy also presents hidden harm to consumers as a malware vector. BSAs Global Software Study from 2016 suggested there is a strong positive correlation between the use of unlicensed software and the presence of malware. Some software packages may have included the malware in the original download. Additionally, some software will not check for or access security updates unless it has a valid license. This leaves the computer system vulnerable to security breaches. Every illegal download potentially opens a computer and its associated systems to vulnerabilities that can be exploited by hackers.

Concerns about malware and viruses have been shown to deter digital piracy in general. In their study of university students, Wolfe, Higgins, and Marcum (2008) found that individuals who feel they are likely to download a virus are more likely to refrain from participating in piracy. Additionally, Holt and Copes (2010) interviewed established pirates who indicated their wariness to use particular torrent programs that were prone to hosting malware. The research participants also indicated that they would avoid downloading torrent files that contained red flags, such as the types of files in the torrent, comments indicating the quality of the download, and unusual seeds to comment ratios (Holt & Copes, 2010).

The personal harm done to digital content creators, especially within the creative arts, is often overlooked. In 2000, the heavy metal band Metallica made headline news when members went after the notorious peer-to-peer company, Napster. In compliance with the lawsuit, more than 300,000 user accounts identified as trading in Metallica material were terminated by Napster. As a result, Metallica's members were perceived by the public as sell-outs who cared more about money than their fans. Fans justified their participation in piracy citing purchases of concert tickets, t-shirts, and other merchandise as sufficient payment for the downloaded files. Criticism even came from fellow rock band Mötley Crüe. Their bassist, Nikki Sixx, said, "They make enough off t-shirts and concert events and other forms of corporation. I think that it's not acceptable behavior for an artist to do that to their fans" (Simon, 2000: n.p.).

More than a decade has passed since the Metallica lawsuit; digital piracy has only grown. Metallica's members have come to terms with the presence of digital piracy. In fact, several members have participated in piracy (Pasbani 2014). Regardless, there are still strong feelings regarding the issue. Lars Ulrich recently cited the lack of control over their music as a major sticking point. "The whole thing was about one thing and one thing only – control… If I wanna give my shit away for free, I'll give it away for free. That choice was taken away from me" (Pasbani, 2014: n.p.).

Alternatively, fellow bandmate, Kirk Hammett, believes that digital piracy ultimately had a detrimental effect on the quality of music being produced by upcoming acts:

> [I]t ended up changing music and the way it even sounds. Now, it just seems like there's less of a drive to be the best musician you can be or the best band that you can …It used to be that you had to really work hard to earn the respect selling albums, competing with all the other great bands making great albums – that just doesn't exist anymore
>
> (Abellera, 2014: n.p.)

Similar sentiments are found in the publishing industry. Self-published, best-selling author S.E. Smith has had extensive experience with the piracy of her own books. Said Smith, "I don't think most people realize they are pirating a book, or if they do, the impact it has on the artist. This is our livelihood" (MUSO, 2016b: n.p.). Most information regarding digital piracy has been focused on the bottom-line for major industries. These faceless monoliths are easy to criticize and disregard. However, it is not just the executives of these industries that are affected. For less established artists, writers, and creators, the income from product sales are a necessity for their quality of life. Without that income, they may end their artistic careers in pursuit of more mundane but financially reliable jobs. The creative and cultural loss is immeasurable.

While most acknowledge digital piracy's harm, some industries are more resigned to its presence and accept its consequences. For example, the Recording Industry Association of America (RIAA) stopped actively pursuing litigation against consumers of pirated music in 2008, despite the clear financial costs (Kravets, 2010; U.S. Copyright Office, 2014). In a round-table session with the United States Copyright Office, representatives from the (RIAA), Spotify, and the Digital Media Association (DiMA) indicated piracy does damage to their bottom line, as it is hard to compete with "free." The fight against piracy is perceived as a losing battle due to its pervasiveness. It is in the best interest for some industries to accept its presence and focus their efforts elsewhere (U.S. Copyright Office, 2014).

Does digital piracy correlate with other forms on online deviance?

Clearly digital piracy causes much financial harm, even if a precise value is difficult to calculate. The value of digital piracy as an indicator of cybercrime or online deviance is often questioned because of its ubiquity and relative simplicity. That is, if everyone does it and it is easy to do, is it the same kind of harmful online behavior as hacking or distributing malware? As demonstrated above, the means to commit digital piracy varies from using ripping apps to the more technically demanding use of bit torrents. While this argument skeptical of digital piracy's research potential has face validity, it is an empirical question that should be evaluated.

People adept at technology tend to embrace its use in many different facets of their lives (e.g., work, play, communication). This is certainly true of hackers who value technology as part of their subculture (Holt, 2007). It is reasonable to assume that digital piracy co-occurs with other deviant online acts. Digital piracy might also be a 'gateway' behavior that leads to more harmful ones once an offender experiences the benefits of digital theft with scant chance of detection. That is, because deterrence is unlikely and the rewards easy, digital piracy is a rational choice when one is motivated to get free content. While we did not have the data to test this proposition here, we did make some inferences using baseline data.

Using two student datasets (one a high school sample and the other a college sample), we looked at the correlations among various online behaviors to determine whether digital piracy (copying or trading either media or software) were correlated with other online acts. This kind of analysis cannot tell us whether digital piracy causes the other kinds of online behaviors, but a negative or zero correlation would certainly falsify the causal hypothesis. Furthermore, if a correlation exists between a simple and more complex act, we can infer the simple act precedes the complex one. It seems unlikely that someone more skilled at hacking for profit would not have the knowhow or motivation to engage in digital piracy.

The first dataset we analyzed was a sample of Kentucky high school and middle school students, who were surveyed in 2008 (reported in Bossler, Holt, and May 2011). The students were mostly from the suburbs in a large city. The survey was administered online to all eighth graders and the freshman class of high school students for a total sample size of 518. The respondents were asked a battery of questions about various online activity, some risky to the respondent and some harmful to others. There were eight online behaviors addressed: (1) post a picture of yourself in a public place on-line; (2) send a picture of yourself to someone that you met on-line; (3) post personal information in a public place on-line; (4) knowingly use, make, or give to another person a "pirated" copy of commercially sold computer software; (5) knowingly use, make, or give to another person "pirated" media (music, television show, or movie); (6) post mean or threatening messages about another person for others to see; (7) post to websites to view sexual materials on purpose; and (8) access another's computer account or files without his/her knowledge or permission to look at information or files. We included measures for two other offline deviant behaviors (Purposely damaged or destroyed property not belonging to you and skipping classes without an excuse), which are discussed later.

The prevalence of all items was measured on an ordinal scale that ranged from never (0), once or twice a year (1), once every 2–3 months (2), once a month (3), once every 2–3 weeks (4), once a week (5), 2–3 times a week (6), once a day (7), or 2–3 times per day (8). These measures were therefore ordinal in scale, which provides a crude but ordered escalation in the incidents of these behaviors.

To correlate the eight online behaviors given the ordinal nature of the measures, we used polychoric correlation, which adjusts for the scale of the variables given they are ordered and not continuous. If, for example, the data were measured on a continuous scale as the number of times one engaged in a behavior, we would have used Pearson correlation. A polychoric correlation has the same properties as a Pearson correlation (e.g., a scale from -1.00 to $+1.00$, where zero means no co-relationship and one means a perfect co-relationship). It is important to use the appropriate form of correlation given how the data were measured. For example, a Pearson correlation between media and software piracy is 0.590 while the polychoric correlation is 0.762.

Both report a positive correlation, but the polychoric shows a stronger relationship. In addition to the correlations, measures of central tendency, percentage ever participating, and variation are included in Table 10.1.

What is evident in the descriptive statistics in Table 10.1 is that most students in this sample did not engage in the behaviors except for posting a picture; all the categories have a mode of zero. In the two measures of digital piracy, 19 percent of the sample did not engage in software piracy and 43 percent did not engage in media piracy. The fact that media piracy is more prevalent may be due the difficulties in breaking and copying software. While most students did not engage in these online behaviors, a non-trivial number of students engaged in at least some online deviant or risky acts. This low level of prevalence is common in measures of delinquency. To determine the concurrence of the activities, we looked at the correlations.

The pattern evident in the correlation matrix is that most behaviors have a moderate to strong relationship. In the case of software piracy, it has a correlation above 0.400 across other behaviors except for post picture ($r = 0.365$). Not surprisingly, media and software piracy are strongly correlated ($r = 0.763$). Those who pirate software also tend to pirate other digital media. Software piracy is also moderately related to accessing an account without permission ($r = 0.541$), which can be thought of as a general measure of hacking behavior.

The high school sample data also included statements about definitions favorable toward digital piracy (the results not included in Table 10.1). On a four point Likert agreement scale from 1 (strongly disagree) to 4 (strongly agree), respondents were asked about pirating software, music, and media. For the statement "it is okay for me to pirate commercial software because it costs too much" about 67 percent disagreed (that is, strongly disagree and disagree combined). For pirating music, the statement read, "It is okay for me to pirate music because I only want one or two songs from most CDs." Forty-eight percent disagreed with this sentiment. Finally, for media: "It is okay for me to pirate media because the creators are really not going to lose any money." Sixty-four percent disagreed with this statement. Despite a common perception that piracy is easy to justify, the modal response to media and software piracy was disagreement with the statements justifying the behavior. Music piracy was just below 50 percent.

Turning to a sample of college students surveyed in 2006, we looked at similar online behaviors and the correlations among predictors (this sample was the same one in Burruss, Bossler & Holt, 2012). For this sample, there were seven online behaviors: (1) Knowingly use, make, or give to another person a 'pirated' copy of commercially-sold computer software; (2) Knowingly use, make, or give to another person 'pirated' media (music, television show, or movie); (3) Look at pornographic or obscene materials; (4) Guess another's password to get into his/her computer account or files; (5) Access another's computer account or files without his/her knowledge or permission to look at information or files; (6) Add, delete, change, or print any information in

Table 10.1 Polychoric correlations among online behaviors for Kentucky high school sample (n = 489)

	1.000	2.000	3.000	4.000	5.000	6.000	7.000	8.000	9.000	10.000
1. Pirate software	1.491									
2. Pirate media	0.762	2.077								
3. Post picture	0.366	0.423	2.018							
4. Send picture	0.483	0.378	0.664	1.339						
5. Post information	0.446	0.405	0.653	0.622	2.057					
6. Post message	0.431	0.485	0.500	0.624	0.494	1.148				
7. View sexual material	0.451	0.360	0.274	0.415	0.310	0.364	2.055			
8. Access account	0.540	0.445	0.376	0.556	0.402	0.607	0.454	1.346		
9. Damage property	0.515	0.413	0.317	0.514	0.385	0.593	0.480	0.556	1.335	
10. Skip class	0.437	0.367	0.202	0.316	0.218	0.420	0.372	0.304	0.526	1.236
Mean	0.538	1.280	1.855	0.417	1.305	0.415	0.963	0.517	0.493	0.552
Mode	0.000	0.000	0.000	0.000	0.000	0.000	0.000	0.000	0.000	0.000
Median	0.000	0.000	1.000	0.000	0.000	0.000	0.000	0.000	0.000	0.000
% ever	18.81	42.74	64.01	15.34	45.40	19.43	25.15	22.49	21.65	27.81

Note: All correlations are polychoric and statistically significant. Standard deviations are in the matrix diagonals. The range of the variables is from 0 (never) to 9 (2–3 times per day).

another's computer files without the owner's knowledge or permission; and, (7) Use someone else's wireless Internet connection without their authorization to surf the Web or otherwise access on-line content? The prevalence of all the online behaviors were measured on a scale from (1) never to (5) ten or more times.

As with the high school data, correlations among online behaviors for the college students were calculated as polychoric correlations reported in Table 10.2. The overall pattern is the same as the high-school sample: pirating media and software are moderately correlated with other behaviors. In the case of pirating software, only about 20 percent ever engaged in the activity in the 12 months prior to the survey. For media piracy, the percentage who ever did so in the past 12 months increased to about 48 percent. These rates were about the same as the high school students. For cyber-intrusion behaviors (gaining access, guessing passwords, altering accounts), the correlations among the piracy variables suggest that if one engages in one of the various online behaviors, they will have also tended to engage in digital piracy (r's > 0.400).

Like the high school sample, the college students were given the same statements about definitions favorable toward digital piracy on the same four-point Likert scale, which are summarized in Table 10.3. For the statement "it

Table 10.2 Polychoric correlations among online behaviors for North Carolina college sample (n = 766)

	1	2	3	4	5	6	7
1. Pirate software	0.844						
2. *Table 2. Polychor*	0.654	1.456					
3. View pornography	0.446	0.456	1.231				
Guess password	0.538	0.444	0.308	0.664			
Access account	0.441	0.453	0.353	0.891	0.662		
Alter files	0.540	0.461	0.377	0.877	0.881	0.493	
Access wireless	0.419	0.428	0.266	0.475	0.419	0.556	1.063
Mean	1.346	2.123	1.607	1.228	1.225	1.102	1.473
Mode	1.000	1.000	1.000	1.000	1.000	1.000	1.000
Median	1.000	1.000	1.000	1.000	1.000	1.000	1.000
% ever	19.97	47.78	25.07	14.10	13.84	5.48	21.93

Note: All correlations are polychoric and statistically significant. Standard deviations are in the matrix diagonals. The range of the variables is from 1 (never) to 5 (10 or more times).

Table 10.3 Comparison of disagreement with definitional statements in favor of piracy

	High and middle school sample	College sample
Pirate commercial software	67 %	69 %
Pirate music	43 %	48 %
Pirate media	64 %	65 %

is okay for me to pirate commercial software because it costs too much" a similar 69 percent disagreed. For pirating music, the statement read, "It is okay for me to pirate music because I only want one or two songs from most cds." Forty-three percent disagreed with this sentiment (compared with 48 percent of high-school students). For media: "It is okay for me to pirate media because the creators are really not going to lose any money." Sixty-five percent disagreed with this statement. The results were therefore virtually the same between samples: most respondents did not support piracy of media and software, a small majority supported pirating music.

The analysis presented here is only speculative because we used correlations from two samples to suggest that the various online behaviors are related. While the results presented here do not prove that engaging in one causes the other, it does suggest a relationship between piracy and risky online behaviors, including cyber intrusion. We conclude this correlation analysis does not falsify the pathway hypothesis. To truly understand if there are pathways into cybercrime, we would need longitudinal data on a variety of cybercrime activities, including digital piracy. We would also need to include theoretical variables and controls to determine an overall effect. Nevertheless, we next discuss what a cyberpathways model might look like, informed by this exploratory analysis.

Toward a cyberpathways model for criminal behavior

In delinquency research, scholars have established a developmental pathways model describing how some young juveniles start with minor deviant and defiant behavior and then escalate to serious forms of delinquent offending (Loeber et al., 1993). This delinquency pathways model as a way to think about the escalation in cyber offending would be useful given the correlational findings above. The development pathways model has four key features that could apply to cybercrime. First, those who engage in the most serious forms of offending also displayed less serious forms of problematic behaviors earlier in their lives. Black-hat hackers, for example, may have engaged in piracy early in their online criminal careers. Second, the early forms of problematic behavior continue to be displayed by the more serious and chronic offenders. Those same hackers would likely continue to engage in digital piracy. Third, most people who start out displaying early and minor forms of offending do not progress to the most serious forms of behavior; only a small subset of offender become chronic and persistent. Fourth, not everyone progresses in a sequential, predictable trajectory, but many do.

The delinquency developmental pathways model has three pathways: the overt pathway, the covert pathway, and the authority conflict pathway (Loeber et al., 1993). The overt pathway includes an escalation in aggressive behaviors from bullying (minor aggression) to physical fighting (assaults) to violence (rape, strong-arm robbery). The covert pathway starts with minor covert behavior (shoplifting) and escalates through property damage, moderate delinquency, and then serious delinquency. Finally, the authority conflict pathway begins with stubborn behavior, then escalates to defiance and disobedience, and finally to authority avoidance (like truancy and running away from home).

Applied to cybercrime, including digital piracy, a developmental pathways model would suggest minor forms of problematic online behavior begins with testing the limits of deviance online, such as posting provocative messages, viewing pornography, and searching for ways to benefit socially or financially such as digital piracy. Potential serious offenders might then progress along a continuum of behaviors from trolling, penetration testing, or becoming a script kiddie that leads to serious criminal acts, like spreading ransomware, hacking, or launching DDoS attacks. Similar to the delinquency pathways, cybercrime might include overt and covert paths. A covert path in cybercrime might include aggressive behaviors, like trolling and then cyberbullying. A covert pathway might include digital piracy and then DDoS attacks. It is not clear that there is a straight forward analog to authority avoidance, but it could simply be the same as in delinquency: young online offenders continue to push the limits of what they can to online as a form of disobedience to authority.

Without empirical data, this proposed pathway model is only speculative, though some research has begun to address this issue (see Goldsmith & Brewer, 2015; and National Crime Agency, 2017). While online offending does have some distinct methods from traditional offending, however, it stands to reason that what motivates juveniles in an escalation toward serious offending would have a digital analog. Whether there are pathways and what the specific pathways entail would need to be explored empirically. The delinquency pathways model was developed from large longitudinal datasets; the same would need to be collected for online offending. Several recent studies have used panel data on student online behaviors from South Korea (e.g., Yang et al., 2013).

Another issue is whether cybercrime requires its own pathway model. It could be that online behaviors can simply be folded into existing pathways to serious criminal behavior. For example, we are still debating whether cyberbullying is something different from regular bullying; whether hacking is different from trespass and burglary; or whether trading in child pornography digitally is different from trading in photographs physically. The delinquency pathways model, for example, has bullying as part of the overt pathway, minor aggression. Cyberbullying might simply fit into the delinquency schema without the need for a separate cyberpathways model. However, even if the behaviors are not necessarily distinct from traditional crimes, the opportunity structure surely is different and thus a different pathway model may be useful. As social learning theory tells us, criminal behavior is learned like any other behavior and learning develops as it builds upon prior knowledge. Learning the methods of minor online offending helps to learn methods for more serious online offending; that is, from digital piracy to hacking.

As for the question of whether forms of online deviance are related to off-line forms, we had two measures of traditional deviance (destroying property and skipping school) for the middle- and high-school samples. As with the findings from Brunton-Smith and McCarthy (2016), both offline and online behaviors were moderately correlated (see last two rows in the correlation matrix in Table 10.1). For damaging property and pirating software, the correlation was moderate (r = 0.515), as was skipping school and damaging property (r = 0.413). For pirating media, damaging property, and skipping school, the relationship was less pronounced but still moderately correlated (the correlations with pirating media were r = 0.437 and 0.637 respectively). Again, this suggests, though does not prove, that online deviance is related to offline deviance. And this relationship may be, and probably is, caused by a third causal factor such as low self-control or deviant peers.

If digital piracy is a pathway to serious online offending, then we should see an escalation in online deviant behavior as offenders map the opportunity structure of online communications and then learn more sophisticated forms of cybercrime. To establish such a pathways model for cybercrime, scholars would need longitudinal data to understand what pathways and trajectories might exist. The academic literature review by Edwards and Bossler (see Chapter 11 in this book) suggests that digital piracy can be explained by existing criminological theory, including social learning and routine activities (see also two meta analyses: Lowry, Zhang, and Wu (2017), and Taylor, Ishida, and Melton (2014)). Pathways to serious cybercrime, perhaps starting with digital piracy, seems likely.

We attempted to address academic concerns whether digital piracy is a useful topic for the study of cybercrime. Digital piracy is ubiquitous and often considered a minor form of offending despite the impact it has on the various industries that create and distribute digital media. We documented the financial harm offered from various sources, noting the estimates are problematic at best. To shed some empirical light on the interrelated nature of digital piracy and other forms of online offending, we looked at the correlations among various forms of offending and found that digital piracy does share a respectable amount of variation with other forms of online and offline deviant and risky behaviors.

Conclusions

Overall, our discussion points to the value of digital piracy as an important area of study in the wider scholarship of cybercrime. Digital piracy does present low hanging fruit for researchers given that college student samples include technically savvy users with access to numerous online portals. Students also tend to consume much digital content as they are comfortable with various technical devices, apps, and websites, and they have much free time. Complaints that these kinds of samples are hardly generalizable ring true (Popham, 2011; Krawczyk, Tyrowicz & Kukla-Gryz, 2015); however, empirical samples that include young children and elderly adults would be unrepresentative of likely victims and offenders. But as people across the age distribution become comfortable with using the Internet in all aspect of their lives, finding representative samples becomes more important.

We believe that future research should continue to use digital piracy as a key dependent variable given its relationship to other online deviant and criminal behaviors. Furthermore, the relationship in digital piracy as a link in a pathway to more serious offending should be evaluated. Researchers should attempt to find the causal link between offline offending, minor online offending, and serious online offending, whether collecting cross-sectional or longitudinal data. Certainly, qualitative researchers could explore the timing and impact of various online behaviors from samples of hackers or malware writers, which could inform further quantitative research.

Factors that predict software piracy and other forms of offending should continue to come from criminological theories, such as social learning, a general theory of crime, strain theory, and routine activities. Given the relationship between various forms of on- and offline offending shown here, the predictive factors should be relevant for explaining digital piracy. But it will also be important to track how the legitimate distribution of digital content changes as this will impact the opportunity structure. More streaming content at a reduced price, for example, would likely reduce the prevalence of piracy. It could also be that as more artists, writers, and musicians openly complain or withdraw from making content, the stigma of piracy as stealing would also reduce piracy as it becomes defined as deviant.

As indicated in our discussion of financial harm, much empirical fine-tuning needs to be done here as well. Despite reports documenting astronomical losses in billions of dollars, industry leaders should make the methodology of their estimates clear and transparent to improve credibility. The losses are likely going to be quite high anyway, but if their veracity is in question, the reports provide little value to understand the problem in terms of scope, trends, and scale. Industry should employ academic economists to develop reasonable estimates of the costs of digital piracy. Thomas Carlyle (1849) called economics "the dismal science" because the fiscal realities of slavery offset his reasons for supporting it. Even if economists estimate losses considered dismal from industry's perspective, we would have a more valid picture of the problem. For example, we might be able to estimate the actual dollar value saved from piracy for each legitimate digital item that is streamed. Digital piracy may in fact be on the decline as more content is offered through streaming services.

From our discussion, we believe that the value of digital piracy in studying and understanding cybercrime has been supported. It is clear that we need more discussion, better data, and further analysis of the problem to really understand how digital piracy informs our understanding of crime and deviance in the age of the Internet.

References

Abellera, J. (2014) We blacked out at Kirk Hammett's horror festival. *Noisy.* February 20. Retrieved from https://noisey.vice.com/en_us/article/we-blacked-out-at-kirk-hammetts-first-annual-fear-festevil.

Bossler, A. M., Holt, T. J., and May, D. C. (2011) Predicting online harassment victimization among a juvenile population. *Youth and Society,* 44(4): 500–523.

Brunton-Smith, I., and McCarthy, D.J. (2016) Explaining young people's involvement in online piracy: An empirical assessment using the offending crime and justice survey in England and Wales. *Victims and Offenders,* 11(4): 509–533.

BSA. (2016) *Seizing Opportunity Through License Compliance. BSA Global Software Survey. May 2016.* Washington, DC: Business Software Alliance.

Burruss, G. W., Bossler, A., and Holt, T. J. (2012) Assessing the mediation of a fuller social learning model on low self-control's influence on software piracy. *Crime and Delinquency* 59(8): 1157–1184.

Carlyle, T. (1849) Occasional Discourse on the Negro Question. *Fraser's Magazine* 40 (December): 670–9. Reprinted in *Collected Works of Thomas Carlyle.* Volume 11, 171–210.

Faughnder, R. (2015, June 28) Music piracy is down but still very much in play. *Los Angeles Times.* Retrieved from www.latimes.com/business/la-et-ct-state-of-stealing-music-20150620-story.html.

Goldsmith, A. and Brewer, R. (2015) Digital drift and the criminal interaction order. *Theoretical Criminology.* 19(1): 112–130.

GoMovies.to (2017) Frequently asked questions. Retrieved from https://gomovies.to/site/faq#faq1.

Hinduja, S. (2007) Neutralization theory and online software piracy: An empirical analysis. *Ethics and Information Technology,* 9: 187–204. doi:10.1007/s10676–10007–9143–9145.

Hinduja, S. (2008) Deindividuation and Internet software piracy. *Cyber Psychology and Behavior,* 11: 391–398.

Holt, T. J. (2007) Subcultural evolution? Examining the influence of on- and off-line experiences on deviant subcultures. *Deviant Behavior,* 28(2): 171–198.

Holt, T. J., and Copes, H. (2010) Transferring subcultural knowledge on-line: Practices and beliefs of persistent digital pirates. *Deviant Behavior,* 31(7): 625–654.

Ingram, J. R., and Hinduja, S. (2008). Neutralizing music piracy: An empirical examination. *Deviant Behavior,* 29(4): 334–366.

International Federation of the Phonographic Industry. (2017) *Global music report 2017: Annual state of the industry.* Retrieved from www.ifpi.org/downloads/GMR2017.pdf.

Ipsos Connect. (2016) *Music consumer insight report 2016.* Retrieved from www.ifpi.org/downloads/Music-Consumer-Insight-Report-2016.pdf.

Kravets, D. (2007 November 21) MPAA talks turkey; pirating costs based on futuristic fantasy. *Wired*. Retrieved from www.wired.com/2007/11/mpaa-talks-turk/.

Kravets, D. (2008) MPAA waffling on piracy costs; RIAA says illicit CDs worth $13.74 each. *Wired*. Retrieved from www.wired.com/2008/08/mpaa-waffling-o/.

Kravets, D. (2010) Indie filmmakers sue thousands of BitTorrent users. *Wired*. Retrieved from www.wired.com/2010/03/bittorrent-legal-attack/.

Krawczyk, M., Tyrowicz, J. and Kukla-Gryz, A. (2015) "Piracy is not theft!" Is it just students who think so? *Journal of Behavioral and Experimental Economics*, 54: 32–39.

Linder, B. (2010) Is eBook piracy the next big thing?, weblog, available at: www.lexisnexis.com (accessed 13 December 2016).

Loeber, R., Wung, P., Keenan, K., Giroux, B., Stouthamer-Loeber, M., Van Kammen, W.B. and Maughan, B. (1993) Developmental pathways in disruptive child behavior. *Developmental Psychopathology*, 5: 101–132.

Lowry, P. B., Zhang, J., and Wu, T. (2017) Nature or nurture? A meta-analysis of the factors that maximize the prediction of digital piracy by using social cognitive theory as a framework. *Computers in Human Behavior*, 68: 104–120. Retrieved from http://doi.org/10.1016/j.chb.2016.11.015.

MUSO. (2016a) Authors, it's time to "Check your books" for World IP Day. Retrieved from: www.muso.com/magazine/publishing/authors-its-time-to-check-your-books-for-world-ip-day/.

MUSO. (2016b) Being your own boss: S. E. Smith talks online piracy. Retrieved from: www.muso.com/magazine/publishing/s-e-smith-self-publishing-interview/.

MUSO. (2016c) Main page. Retrieved from: www.muso.com.

National Crime Agency (2017). Pathways into cybercrime. Retrieved from www.nationalcrimeagency.gov.uk/publications/791-pathways-into-cyber-crime/file.

Pasbani, R. (2014January 31) Lars on his favorite Megadeth song, Napster, favorite new metal bands and cutting his hair; highlights of his Reddit AMA. *Metal Injection*. Retrieved from www.metalinjection.net/latest-news/lars-on-his-favorite-megadeth-song-napster-favorite-new-metal-bands-highlights-of-his-reddit-ama.

Popham, J. (2011) Factors influencing music piracy. *Criminal Justice Studies*, 24(2): 199–209.

Price, D. (2013) Sizing the piracy universe. *Netnames*. Retrieved from http://illusionofmore.com/wp-content/uploads/2013/09/NetNames-Sizing_Piracy_Universe-Report-2.5.pdf.

Simon, R.B. (2000) Metallica's anti-Napster crusade inspires backlash. *MTV*. May 31. Retrieved from: www.mtv.com/news/971500/metallicas-anti-napster-crusade-inspires-backlash/.

Siwek, S. E. (2006) *The true cost of motion picture piracy to the US economy*. Lewisville, TX: Institute for Policy Innovation.

Siwek, S. E. (2007) *The true cost of sound recording piracy to the US economy*. Lewisville, TX: Institute for Policy Innovation.

Statista. (2016) *Global e-book revenue from 2009 to 2016*, by region (in million U.S. dollars)*. Retrieved from www.statista.com/statistics/280249/global-e-book-revenue-by-region/.

Taylor, S.A., Ishida, C. and Melton, H. (2014) A meta-analytic investigation of the antecedents of digital piracy. In R.T. Rust, M.-H. Huang (Eds.), *Handbook of service marketing research*, Cheltenham: Edward Elgar, 437–464.

United States Copyright Office. (2014) *Music licensing public roundtable.* Washington, D.C.: Neal R. Gross.

Wolfe, S. E., Higgins, G. E., and Marcum, C. D. (2008) Deterrence and digital piracy: A preliminary examination of the role of viruses. *Social Science Computer Review,* 26(3): 317–333.

Yang, S. J., Stewart, R., Kim, J. M., Kim, S. W., Shin, I. S., Dewey, M. E., Maskey, S., and Yoon, J. S. (2013) Differences in predictors of traditional and cyber-bullying: A 2-year longitudinal study in Korean school children. *European Journal of Adolescent Psychiatry,* 22: 309–318.

Zimerman, M. (2011) E-books and piracy: Implications/issues for academic libraries. *New Library World, 112*(1/2): 67–75.

11 Criminology's contribution to the study of digital piracy

Tyler Edwards and Adam Bossler

Introduction

One of the most common forms of cybercrime is the downloading of digital media, such as music, movies, and software, over the Internet, which is known as digital piracy. Digital piracy may be the most commonly committed form of cybercrime, with estimates suggesting that up to 86 percent of college students commit piracy at some point in their lives (Gunter, 2009; Higgins, 2006; Higgins et al., 2009; Hinduja, 2003; Skinner & Fream, 1997; Vandiver et al., 2012). Although popular, digital piracy is still a form of cybercrime that leads to significant financial harm for copyright holders. Its popularity and significant financial impact are two of several reasons why criminologists have focused heavily on this form of cybercrime in comparison to others.

Criminologists have greatly contributed to our knowledge of digital piracy by examining the ability of traditional criminological theories to explain this technology-enabled offense. Scholars have consistently found that core criminological concepts from deterrence theory, social learning, the general theory of crime, and techniques of neutralization can help explain why pirates download copyrighted materials without the authorization of copyright holders. Criminologists have found that pirates weigh the costs and benefits of piracy, can be deterred, have lower levels of self-control, associate with peers who pirate, hold beliefs supportive of digital piracy, are socially reinforced by others for their piracy, and hold justifications and rationalizations that attempt to justify this behavior in order to view themselves as not being criminal and to be able to continue this behavior into the future. Current research on digital piracy in the social sciences has several limitations, including the use of convenience college and youth samples and cross-sectional data. The chapter concludes with suggestions on how to move the field forward, including collecting samples of non-college aged adults, studying piracy through a life-course perspective, modifying criminological theories, and evaluating policies and legislation that can decrease digital piracy.

What is digital piracy?

Digital piracy can be defined as "a form of cybercrime encompassing the illegal copying of digital media such as computer software, digital sound recordings, and digital video recordings without the explicit permission of the copyright holder" (Holt, Bossler, & Seigfried-Speallar, 2015: 114). As the definition indicates, digital piracy includes more than just the illegal downloading of music and movies, but also the violation of copyright laws that affect other form of media as well, such as the unauthorized use of software and video games. Digital piracy derived its name from the physical act of piracy, where pirates would raid ships and ports and sail away to sell the stolen goods at lower prices to make easy money. Unlike the original pirates, however, there are few life-threatening dangers that come from committing digital piracy (Higgins & Marcum, 2011).

In order for piracy to be committed, the creative work in question must be from another entity that did not express consent to the product being reproduced (Yar, 2013). Copyright laws protect these creative works from being reproduced without the consent of the owner; these laws offer legal recourse for the owner and the State in order for them to pursue criminal and civil penalties against the offender. As will be shown throughout this chapter, even with the presence of these laws, pirates easily justify the morality of their behavior and find ever changing ways to obtain these products.

Digital piracy has evolved from the 1970s and 1980s when individuals used multiple audio and videocassette recorders to make copies of music tapes and movies to the 1990s and 2000s when the use of the Internet allowed for the instantaneous downloading of any music and movie file one desires, with great variation in download speed in the early years depending on Internet speed. Over the last several years, the increased use of torrents – software that allows for concurrent uploading and downloading of files from multiple sources – has increased the efficiency of downloading files while also making it harder for law enforcement to respond (Holt et al., 2015). Although the evolution of technology has made it easier to access a wider variety of files for a larger group of people, thus greatly increasing the opportunity structure for this type of offense to be committed, the basics of digital piracy, such as what it is and why people commit it, have not significantly changed. Thus, the explanations of why the average person pirated 20 years ago is similar to that of today and 20 years from now.

As piracy became easier to commit, one would hypothesize that the rate of its commission would rise as well. Software piracy, however, has seen a modest global decrease, dropping from 43 percent in 2013 to 39 percent (BSA, 2016). Global trends show that the most frequent perpetrators of software piracy were the countries in the Asia-Pacific region, with 61 percent of the software on an average computer not being properly licensed. The Asia-Pacific region also took in the most revenue via unlicensed software ($19.1 billion), which is almost double the second highest amount ($10.5 billion) coming from the Western Europe region (BSA, 2016).

Some argue that the perceived "decrease" in pirating could simply be because of changes in how individuals gain access to desired files. File-sharing experienced a growth of 44 percent from 2008 to 2014 (Price, 2013; Steele, 2015). Offenders could simply be appreciating the advantages of file-sharing websites, such as BitTorrent, to achieve their ends instead of using illicit sites that promote piracy (Steele, 2015). The availability of streaming websites, like Pandora or Netflix, could also have a role in reducing the occurrence of music or movie piracy (Graham, 2012; Luckerson, 2013). The overall ease and affordability of streaming services allow individuals to obtain media legally and without worry of viruses, making it sensible to pay for the files (Kresten, 2012; Luckerson, 2013).

Who are the individuals responsible for pirating? Popham's (2011) examination of a representative Canadian sample found that piracy occurs throughout the life course, but certain age groups were more likely to pirate. Sixteen to thirty-four-year-olds comprised 56.5 percent of all music pirates surveyed, although they only made up 27 percent of Canada's population. Older groups, however, such as those between the ages of 35–54 and 55+, were also active in music piracy (Popham, 2011). MusicWatch (2014) also found that the main age group that pirates music is the 26–35-year-old category [30 percent P2P (peer-to-peer) and 31 percent downloaders/streamrippers (streamripper records Internet radio streams in the MP3 or Vorbis formats and allows for entire batches of files to be recorded rather than specific songs previously chosen)], followed closely by 18–25-year-olds (23 percent and 26 percent). These groups were, for the most part, present during the 2001 rise of the file-sharing behemoth, Napster, with the older demographics falling into the university student range during that period and the 16–34 demographic just becoming familiar with computers (MusicWatch, 2014; Popham, 2011). The rise of Napster possibly introduced many of those to the option of piracy as a source for music files.

Studies have also generally found that men are more likely to engage in digital piracy than women (Cox & Collins, 2014; Donner, 2016; Higgins, 2007a; Hollinger, 1993; Malin & Fowers, 2009; Morris & Higgins, 2009; Udris, 2016). MusicWatch (2014) found that males made up 58 percent of the peer-to-peer (P2P) file sharing downloads and 57 percent of the illegal downloaders or streamrippers. Hinduja and Higgins (2011) also found that males were more likely than females to be habitual pirates, with 7.8 percent of the women pirating over 2,000 MP3s in their lifetime, compared with 22.8 percent of the male population. Gender differences may be explained by various reasons, including that the perceived severity of the punishment associated with digital piracy significantly affected women more than men (Morton & Koufteros, 2008) and that females had less favorable attitudes towards pirating (Tjiptono et al., 2016). Other studies, however, did not find a correlation between piracy and demographic variables, and recommended that scholars examine existing theories of criminal behavior to better understand digital piracy rather than focusing on demographics (Al-Rafee & Cronan, 2006; Borja et al., 2015; Donner, 2016; Morris et al., 2009; Yu, 2012).

Applying criminological theory to digital piracy

The greatest contribution that criminologists have made and will continue to make to the study of digital piracy is the application of its theories and understanding of how humans interact with their environment. Since piracy came to the attention of social scientists, scholars have been studying the piracy subculture to understand its norms and organizational structure. As technology advanced, scholars moved from studying piracy that involved physical copies (e.g., tapes, DVDs, etc.) to digital piracy (e.g., Cooper & Harrison, 2001). Much of the rich history of criminological research on digital piracy has focused on its subculture, including its values and roles (see Cooper and Harrison, 2001). Scholars found that the piracy subculture promotes and perpetuates the amount of pirated material on the Internet by providing information on how to pirate, justifications for pirating, the pirated media itself, and social reinforcements for participating and continuing the behavior (e.g., Steinmetz & Tunnell, 2013). A fuller discussion of the piracy subculture, and how criminologists contributed to our knowledge of it is beyond the scope of this chapter. Rather, the focus of the following sections will be discussing criminological theories meant to explain individual-level behavior, including deterrence, the general theory of crime, social learning theory, and techniques of neutralization.

Deterrence theory

One of the more popular theories that can be used to explain why offenders pirate is the Classical School's deterrence theory (Paternoster, 1987). The Classical School argued that individuals were rational actors who weighed the pleasure of the act versus the costs of the consequences. In order to deter offenders from committing forbidden acts, effective punishment must therefore be certain (the offender perceives that a punishment will follow the deviant act), swift (the punishment must occur soon after the deviant act), and appropriate (the pain of the punishment must be equal to that of the pleasure of the act). This school of thought would therefore argue that digital pirates commit piracy because they view the pleasures of digital piracy, such as immediate gratification of getting access to free materials, as being greater than the risks of punishment (Higgins, 2007b; Lowry et al., 2017; Vida et al., 2012).

To date, scholars have demonstrated that the application of deterrence theory has merit in both explaining the behaviors of pirates and policies that may be derived from these arguments. Digital pirates find the physical stealing of media to be less desirable than illegally downloading it, thus choosing digital piracy over theft (Lysonski & Durvasula, 2008; Wingrove et al., 2011). Congruent with research examining deterrence theory in the physical world (Pratt et al., 2006), scholars have found that certainty of punishment is more important in deterring pirates than increasing the severity of the punishment (Higgins et al., 2005; Kos Koklic et al., 2014; Yoon, 2011). For example,

Jackman and Lorde (2014) found that when the respondents weighed the price of the music in comparison to the costs of being caught, they decided that purchasing the product legally was more beneficial to their well-being in the long run. In addition, studies have found that specific campaigns have decreased piracy (Bachmann, 2007; Chiou et al., 2005). For instance, Bachmann (2007) found that piracy levels decreased after the RIAA started their anti-piracy campaign. Similar to other deterrent crackdowns in the traditional literature, rates slowly rose again over time. Bhattacharjee et al. (2006) found that many habitual pirates decreased their activity substantially because of the RIAA's legal recourse strategy. These studies overall indicate that a perception of increased risk in being punished decreases digital piracy.

The certainty of being caught for digital piracy, however, is quite low. The anonymity of the Internet and the challenges of tracking down individuals who engage in piracy make it highly problematic for law enforcement (Higgins et al., 2006; Wall, 2005). In addition, offenders have improved their efforts to avoid detection. Digital pirates, for example, may pirate less media at one time or use more anonymous services or tactics to increase the disconnect from the offender's physical person (Larsson et al., 2013). Law enforcement, however, does not have the resources to go after the high number of individuals who pirate a multitude of different forms of media (Borja et al., 2015; Nandedkar & Midha, 2012). Many people therefore engage in piracy because of the little concern for the consequences from the law and music industries, which can promote the initiation or continuation of engaging in digital piracy (Morton & Kouteros, 2008). Without this fear of being caught, those that are committing the act will continue to do so, which will invite others to join.

Deterrence scholars studying digital piracy have also found a similar result to that of scholars studying traditional offenses – informal sanctions matter more than legal sanctions (Casidy et al., 2017; Kos Koklic et al., 2014; Wolfe et al., 2008). The social bonds an individual maintains and the possibility of informal sanctions can persuade offenders not to engage in piracy (Higgins et al., 2007; Udris, 2016). The research on the role of guilt, however, has been mixed. Research has found that self-imposed guilt over facing informal sanctions from families or peer groups has an impact on their decision to commit piracy (Wang & McClung, 2012; Wolfe et al., 2008) and can be even a stronger effect than the fear of possibly downloading malware onto the pirate's computer (Wolfe et al., 2008; Kos Koklic et al., 2014). Other scholars (e.g., Al-Rafee & Cronan, 2006), however, did not find that committing digital piracy caused distress, usually a sign of fear of repercussions for their actions, because their social ties generally supported the offender's commission of digital piracy. Thus, future scholars will need to further examine how pirates balance feelings of guilt and shame derived from parents, families, and some friends with that of positive reinforcement they receive from possibly a majority of their friends.

General theory of crime

One of the most empirically tested theories examining the causes of traditional offenses (Pratt & Cullen, 2000) and digital piracy is Gottfredson and Hirschi's (1990) general theory of crime. This theory of crime asserts that individuals commit crime and deviant acts because they do not have adequate levels of self-control to prevent themselves from committing impulsive acts that often have long-term consequences greater than the short-term benefits. In the case of digital piracy, the act allows the offender to fulfill his or her immediate gratification (i.e. wanting a song, movie, etc.) easily and for free (Higgins, 2007a; Higgins & Marcum, 2011; Hinduja, 2012). Digital piracy in many cases requires little skill, is associated with little risk, and demonstrates a lack of empathy for copyright holders.

Scholars have consistently found that low self-control, whether measured attitudinally or behaviorally, is related to all forms of piracy in youth and college samples (e.g., Higgins et al., 2008b, 2012; Hinduja, 2012; Lowry et al., 2017; Malin & Fowers, 2009; Marcum et al., 2011). For example, Higgins et al. (2008b) used hypothetical vignettes to place the respondent in certain situations while Hinduja (2012) asked about the actual commission of digital piracy; both, however, found low self-control to be related with digital piracy. Aaltonen and Salmi (2013) found that youth who commit digital piracy also engage in other delinquent acts, which supports the argument that the cause of digital piracy (i.e. low self-control) is also the cause of other forms of deviance. With the computer being a major hub in the lives of those interviewed for the study, the presence of self-control became a major factor in regards to whether or not the youth acted in a deviant manner (Moon et al., 2010). Although most studies conducted used cross-sectional data, Higgins (2007a) found a link between low self-control and changes in digital piracy behavior over a four week period of time while controlling for demographics and motivation factors. While the above studies focused mostly on music and movie piracy, Higgins (2005) found that there was a significant relationship between low self-control and software piracy as well. Individuals with low self-control were more likely to illegally download a copy onto a disc in order to take the pirated software home to download on their personal computer.

Scholars have also demonstrated how low self-control can affect deviant associations, which can give the individual the opportunity to learn skills needed to commit crimes like digital piracy (Higgins & Makin, 2004b; Hinduja & Ingram, 2008). In fact, Burruss et al. (2013) found that the indirect effect of low self-control through the social learning process was greater than its direct effect. In other words, low self-control's effect on digital piracy was mostly explained by its effect regarding with whom the respondents associated. In addition, when the social learning process was controlled for, increases in low self-control actually decreased the odds of committing software piracy. Thus, individuals with low self-control did not have adequate patience and skill to successfully pirate software unless they were showed how to complete the task by peers.

Social learning theory

Ron Akers' (1998) social learning theory is the most empirically supported criminological theory and can explain a wide variety of criminal and deviant offenses (Pratt et al., 2009). It is not surprising then that it has also been the most widely used criminological theory to understand the commission of various forms of cybercrime, including digital piracy (e.g., Burruss et al., 2013). Social learning argues that the learning of any behavior occurs through a dynamic process that comprises at least four components (differential associations, imitation, definitions, and differential reinforcement). The process begins by associating with deviants who act as models for the deviant behavior and provide attitudes and norms supporting that behavior. Imitation is important in the earlier stages of the social learning process as the individual is first becoming accustomed to the deviant behavior. The key to the continuation of the behavior, however, is whether the individual receives either social or financial reinforcement or is punished.

While one can quickly learn how to steal a physical item and be able to abscond with the prize without repercussions, the practice of digital piracy requires some form of experience in the use of technology in order to achieve the most basic forms of piracy. However, digital piracy and physical theft are both similar in that one must continue to learn in order to complete more difficult forms of theft or pirating. In this regard, social learning theory can help explain how pirates learn the tricks of the trade and who teaches them (Holt & Copes, 2010; Morris & Higgins, 2010).

Social learning theory would argue that individuals interested in committing piracy would first have to come into association with individuals who pirate and have definitions supportive of that behavior (Gunter, 2008; Hinduja, 2007; Hinduja & Ingram, 2009; Holt et al., 2010). Scholars have consistently found that higher levels of association with peers who pirate is related to higher odds of committing piracy (e.g., Higgins & Makin, 2004b; Higgins et al., 2012; Hinduja & Ingram, 2009; Holt, Bossler, & May, 2012; Lowry et al., 2017; Marcum et al., 2011). These peers, however, do not have to be in-person, as both physical and virtual peers influence digital piracy (Miller & Morris, 2016). Peers provide information on both the methods of how to commit various forms of digital piracy and the location of the coveted material. After observing or learning from peers how to pirate, individuals can now imitate the behavior and attempt it themselves (e.g., Hinduja, 2003; Holt et al., 2010; Ingram & Hinduja, 2008; Skinner & Fream, 1997). While they learn these techniques in order to navigate their way through the process, the pirates also find that their peers acknowledge their feats of piracy when they share their stolen goods with each other (Holt & Copes, 2010; Casidy et al., 2017; Morris & Higgins, 2010). Pirates will continue their behavior as long as it is being financially (i.e. getting media they want for free) or socially reinforced (Hinduja, 2003; Holt et al., 2010; Holt & Copes, 2010; Van Rooij et al., 2017).

Scholars have also consistently found a strong correlation between digital piracy and having definitions supportive of that behavior (Higgins & Marcum, 2011; Marcum et al., 2011; Skinner & Fream, 1997; Yoon, 2012). Associating with digital pirates is related to the instilling of these definitions that favor digital piracy and support the notion that laws and regulations are more of guidelines that only "squares" follow (Higgins & Makin, 2004b; Hinduja and Ingram, 2008). For example, overall moral beliefs, such as duty to uphold the law, has been found to have a negative effect on commission of software piracy (Higgins & Wilson, 2006; Van Rooij et al., 2017). Yu (2010) also found that digital piracy was viewed as less of a crime than physical stealing because the product being "stolen" was not removed. The definitions that these offenders find themselves holding often become justifications to distance themselves from "actual criminals" (Phau et al., 2014; see next section).

Techniques of neutralization

Sykes and Matza's (1957) techniques of neutralization further addresses the "definitions" aspect of social learning previously discussed. They argue that most individuals hold conforming beliefs but that individuals commit various deviant acts occasionally because of rationalizations or neutralizations they hold before the commission of the offense that justifies why the behavior was acceptable and is not in conflict with their overall belief system. These techniques of neutralization then allow an individual to drift between deviance and conformity. Although scholars have identified additional techniques of neutralization, Sykes and Matza originally identified five techniques: (1) denial of responsibility: someone or something else is to be blamed; (2) denial of injury: no one or nothing was hurt; (3) denial of victim: there is no clear victim or the "victim" deserved it; (4) condemnation of the condemners: the condemners are hypocrites; and (5) appeal to higher loyalties: the offense was committed for someone else.

Sykes and Matza's (1957) techniques of neutralization have been commonly used to explain the justifications used for deviant and criminal behavior, including digital piracy. This theory holds that individuals that commit digital piracy have certain justifications that excuse their digital piracy as an acceptable act considering the circumstances and therefore do not view themselves as criminals. The theory has been successful in providing a framework for many of the justifications used by digital pirates to separate their conforming identities from this deviant act (Marcum et al., 2011; Yu, 2012). Moore and McMullan (2009) found that all of their participants in the study used at least one of the techniques of neutralization, citing denial of injury, denial of victim, and "everyone else is doing it" as the most popular used. It becomes difficult for individuals to believe that what they are doing is really that wrong when everyone they see is committing that behavior. In fact, if an individual is paying for media files while their friends are getting the files for free via piracy, he or she may even feel that they are being penalized for conforming. In the end, several in the group used more than one justification, which is common in order to deny any wrongdoing by the wrongdoer.

Some digital pirates deny their responsibility for their acts by arguing that they did not know what they were doing was illegal. In many cases, they were often not aware of the illegality of their actions and did not see any wrong in their theft of intellectual property (Ingram & Hinduja, 2008; Morris & Higgins, 2009). In other cases, digital pirates have argued that the Internet's mere existence and the ease of pirating made it an easy viable option that they could not resist (Ulsperger et al., 2010), thus blaming the Internet and the ease of pirating for their behavior. Ulsperger et al. (2010) also found that digital pirates denied their responsibility by arguing that they were underage, which restricted them from buying certain music legally, didn't have enough money, and they did not have enough time to purchase legal copies of the media from a store.

Similar to "victimless" deviance in the physical realm, those that engage in digital piracy usually claim that no one is truly hurt, since there are few ways to accurately discern the damage done by piracy and the inflated numbers that are claimed to be used (Kahriithi, 2011; Ma et al., 2016; McCourt & Burkart, 2003; Yar, 2005). When the offender downloads illegally copied media or software, the offender justifies their actions by claiming that no one was really harmed in the process of downloading a copied or altered version of the material (Ulsperger et al., 2010). With no physical damage done, the pirates do not feel that what they were doing is a crime (Yu, 2012).

Some pirates also discuss the contributions their digital piracy brings to the performer, particularly performers who are not well known. In Tade and Akinleye's (2012) study of pirates in an internationally famed hub for pirated goods, the pirates argued that their bootlegging of music from new and veteran artists is a way to promote them into superstardom without the expensive nature of the record companies being involved. While many of the more successful artists that were interviewed saw these "promoters'" actions as being criminal, they enjoyed the vast network of music industry connections that these pirates had built up over time and even credited them with their success in many ways. Thus, there lies a grey area in ethical stances in which the artists view the piracy as criminal behavior but also see its positives, especially those artists that are struggling or have found success through the illicit trade (Tade & Akinleye, 2012).

Digital pirates also frequently blame the victim – the copyright holders – for their victimization by arguing that the "victims" deserved it because of their actions and provocations (Ingram & Hinduja, 2008; Morris & Higgins, 2009; Ulsperger et al., 2010). Many who hold this view argue that the victim in these cases set the prices too high in order to gouge more of a profit out of the consumer (Chiou et al., 2005; McCourt & Burkart, 2003). Thus, they see the intellectual rights holders as "greedy" and that they deserved to have the media stolen from them because of the outrageous prices that are set on the items (Lysonski & Durvasula, 2008; Ulsperger et al., 2010). Interestingly, nearly half of the respondents in one study reported that the primary reason that they ceased or decreased their piracy behaviors over a one-year period was because of the availability of low-cost or free music streaming services (Graham, 2012).

Condemning the condemners is the rationalization that those criticizing the offender for their transgressions are hypocritical because they are offenders in their own way. This justification often tries to dilute the seriousness of the situation by claiming that everyone has done said act and may have gotten away with it. Considering that the majority of college students admit to some form of digital piracy (Higgins & Marcum, 2011; Holt et al., 2015, Holt & Bossler, 2016), it is safe to conclude that many students are guilty of the same transgressions in their past and have gotten away with it. Ulsperger et al. (2010) found that condemning the condemners was actually the second most common technique as students argued that everyone does it and the government does not really care about it.

Appealing to higher loyalties is a common form of rationalization for many subcultures; the piracy subculture is not an exception (Smallridge & Roberts, 2013; Holt & Bossler, 2016). Similar to the differential reinforcement component found in social learning theory (Akers, 1998), appealing to peers is seen as a vital part of social interaction, regardless of the potential repercussions that may be involved if the offender is caught. The digital piracy subculture places a strong emphasis on possessing large quantities of files and being able to share these materials with others (e.g., Cooper & Harrison, 2001). In fact, digital pirates gain reputation in the subculture by being able to share high-quality copies of files, particularly harder to find songs, movies, programs, and games (Cooper & Harrison, 2001; Holt & Copes, 2010). Ulsperger et al. (2010) found that digital pirates placed higher emphasis on their friendships than laws. Thus, a core tenet of the subculture provides justifications and reinforcements for the commission of digital piracy.

Recently, Goldsmith & Brewer (2015) used the basic concepts of drift theory (see discussion above regarding drift theory and techniques of neutralization) to help explain how the characteristics of the Internet allow individuals to engage and disengage from online communities, including criminal or deviant groups. Accessing the Internet allows social connections with individuals in environments that are disconnected from their actual identities. The anonymity afforded by the Internet releases individuals from responsibility and allows them to act in ways they would normally not (Goldsmith & Brewer, 2015). Although Goldsmith and Brewer (2015) use their adaptation to explain online terrorism and child pornography, the theory applies to digital piracy as well. Individuals are able to create usernames that are not associated with their identities and they can disconnect themselves from their "virtual identity" by simply going offline. The impersonality of the activity gives the offender room to justify their actions to themselves whereas physical acts of deviance require some form of personal interaction between the offender/assailant and the victim or his/her property.

Limitations in data collection

While there are several well-known datasets that allow for insight on the prevalence of crimes and deviant behavior (e.g., NCVS, UCR), official data on cybercrime in the U.S., including digital piracy, is scant or non-existent (Holt & Bossler, 2016; Holt et al., 2015). One of the many reasons for the lack of official data on digital piracy, in addition to apathy by the public, law enforcement, and government officials, is that digital piracy is not an "individual victimization crime," meaning that the NCVS cannot collect information from victims, and that very few individuals are arrested and prosecuted for digital piracy, making police arrest reports (e.g., UCR) not possible. In order to fill this gap, corporations with intellectual property in the music, movie, and software fields collect data and create estimates on the prevalence and costs of digital piracy.

One of the major problems with these corporations' reports is that it has behooved them historically to inflate the losses in order to gain the attention of policy makers to pass additional legislation and increase penalties to attempt to deal with copyright infringement. Kigerl (2013) argues that studies examining the damage done by pirating behavior are not objective due to the inability to have a set figure on how much piracy truly occurs. While several of the entities, like the Business Software Alliance (BSA), are independent watchdogs for these companies, many of the other reporters have some form of stake in the claim when it comes to intellectual profits. The higher the number of losses, whether monetary or by the unit, the more pressure it puts on legislative entities to corral the outlaws that engage in this deviant behavior in order to protect the companies that are being victimized (Yar, 2005). There is also an argument as to how the companies record their losses, with companies often arguing that the losses from a pirated copy leads to a loss of one unit of legitimate product or movie ticket sales (Yar, 2005). The error in this logic is that it is difficult to verify if the offender was ever going to legitimately purchase a copy of the media if they were not able to pirate it (Yar, 2005). Studies have shown, however, that piracy does impact sales. Ma et al. (2016), for example, found that there would be a 14 percent increase in annual box-office revenue if pre-release movie piracy could be eliminated, and that piracy, no matter the timing of the occurrence, leads to a negative impact on the industry. As the Internet expands at an exponential pace, so does the creation of technology that can help better track digital piracy in order to create better estimates (Tcherni et al., 2016). Until such technology can be created, researchers and policy makers will have to make do with industry provided statistics.

Another limitation of a majority of digital piracy research in the social sciences is that studies have heavily focused on college students (e.g., Higgins

& Marcum, 2011; Morris & Higgins, 2009, 2010). Scholars have gravitated towards college samples for various reasons, including: having significant interaction with computers in their daily activities (Higgins et al., 2007; Hinduja, 2003; Thatcher & Matthews, 2012); falling within a high deviant group with malleable ethics (Higgins et al., 2007; Higgins et al., 2008b; Hinduja, 2003); typically having low incomes which increases their inclination to commit digital piracy instead of legally purchasing the product (Bhattarcharje et al., 2003); and convenience (Payne & Chappell, 2008). Results based on college samples may not be so easily generalizable to non-college based populations (Higgins et al., 2007, Higgins et al., 2008a; Marcum et al., 2011; Morris et al., 2009). College students' choices of media to pirate is arguably biased towards simpler forms of digital media and files that interest them, such as music. In addition, the availability of online streaming services provides a wide variety of movies and shows at low monthly subscription rates (Graham, 2012; Luckerson, 2013). College students may also be able to ascertain needed or wanted software for free or at discounted prices, decreasing the need or desire to pirate software.

There has been a positive shift in the literature towards sampling minors, including both middle and high school students (Aaltonen & Salmi, 2013; Gunter et al., 2010; Holt et al., 2012; Malin & Fowers, 2009; Moon et al., 2010; Van Belle et al., 2007), rather than convenience college samples, to better understand digital piracy. These studies help inform us of the link between computer skill and digital piracy, whether the commission of digital piracy comes earlier as technology becomes more integrated into life at younger ages (Gunter et al., 2010), and if pirating behavior is learned around the same time as other deviant behavior (Malin & Fowers, 2009).

Another common limitation of most digital piracy studies is the cross-sectional nature of the data (see Lowry et al., 2017 for further discussion of limitations of piracy data). With cross-sectional analysis, there is no time-order established which does not allow for causal arguments to be made, especially when testing criminological theories such as social learning theory and techniques of neutralization. Rare exceptions exist. For example, analyses of longitudinal data within college samples have observed that piracy behavior fluctuates (Higgins et al., 2008b; Vandiver et al., 2012). These rare longitudinal studies, however, are often limited to one student body and use relatively short periods of time (e.g., Higgins et al., 2008b). Regardless, their success using short-term longitudinal data provides support for other scholars to collect longitudinal data to better understand piracy fluctuations and to establish time order. Even over short timespans, longitudinal studies will generally offer more insights than what can be obtained simply from cross-sectional data.

In addition, almost all piracy studies use self-report survey data (Lowry et al., 2017). As with any self-report data, respondents may not provide accurate responses for various reasons, including social desirability, memory, etc. Considering the frequency with which certain groups pirate media, and how piracy rates fluctuate (Vandiver et al., 2012), it may be challenging for most respondents to validly complete closed-ended questions regarding their digital piracy. To address time order, memory bias, and to create quasi-experiments, many scholars have chosen to use vignettes in which respondents are placed in hypothetical situations to examine whether the respondent would choose to commit digital piracy in a specific scenario (e.g., Altschuller & Benbunan-Fich, 2009; Higgins et al., 2008b; Wingrove et al., 2011). Taylor (2012), in fact, demonstrated that self-reported intentions to commit digital piracy are correlated with actual digital piracy as measured by a monitoring program capturing data on students' downloading of suspect files. This demonstrates that the collection of actual digital piracy data is beneficial but does not invalidate the findings based on self-reported intentions or behavior.

Much of our knowledge regarding the causes of digital piracy derives from quantitative studies in which respondents were provided closed-ended questions to measure criminological concepts. Closed-ended questions, however, limit the ability of the respondents to explain their actions in their own words. Thus, the collection of qualitative data through either interviews or ethnographic studies increases the validity of findings. Brown (2016) noted that the participants were eager to discuss their piracy in his ethnographic study. Qualitative analyses, of course, have their own limitations, including but not limited to smaller samples, issues with generalizability, access to respondents, and resources. There can also be the problem of maintaining the confidentiality of the participants without jeopardizing the validity of the responses, such as issues that Brown (2016) reported when studying Tweets. Mixed-method approaches allow for the collection of both quantitative and qualitative data in order to maintain the strengths of both while addressing the limitations of each. Such approaches have been successfully used to study digital piracy (e.g., Yu, 2012) and provide a good avenue for future research.

Possible steps forward

As illustrated in this chapter, scholars have successfully used traditional criminological theories to better understand why people commit digital piracy and possible steps to reduce the behavior. The further use of these theories will continue to help understand the thought process of digital pirates, the influence of the social learning process, how personal traits impact decision-making, and the justifications and rationalizations used by digital pirates to commit illegal behavior without affecting their self-identities as conformists. In addition, it will be important to continue to examine the theoretical integration of these theories to better understand the fuller process of digital piracy (e.g., Higgins & Marcum, 2011; Higgins et al., 2006; Marcum et al., 2011; Morris et al., 2009). With the commonality of traits within theories, the combination of theoretical perspectives to create a more widespread framework of the phenomena can greatly further the study of this field of criminal activity (Higgins & Makin, 2004a,b). For example, studies generally find that low self-control can help explain the selection into piracy networks (e.g., Higgins & Marcum, 2011). Integrating theories can also help us consider the impact of a concept on digital piracy differently than what the theorists originally hypothesized and what would have been discovered if each theory was examined separately. For example, Burruss et al. (2013) found that low self-control decreased digital piracy for those individuals who were not part of digital piracy networks because they did not have the ability to learn the techniques on their own.

Goldsmith and Brewer (2015) have also demonstrated with their digital drift theory how modifications to existing theories can help better explain technology-enabled offenses by incorporating aspects and characteristics of the Internet and the influence of those characteristics on individual behavior. Further examination of digital drift theory and modifications of other theories may help move the field forward, particularly if the field stalls with its theoretical exploration of digital piracy.

One of the largest limitations of the study of digital piracy in the social sciences has been the heavy analyses of data from convenience college and youth samples. As insightful as the current studies have been in explaining the occurrences of digital piracy, more studies need to be conducted on different populations of society, such as individuals who go from high school to the work force, to better understand the generalizability of our current knowledge. At this point, it is unclear whether our understanding of digital piracy is only limited to youth and college students.

Similarly, it will be important for scholars to examine digital piracy from a life-course perspective to better understand how digital piracy usage fluctuates over periods of time, especially during transitioning times in schooling (high school or college to work force) and social bonds (getting married and/or having children). During these transitioning periods, changes in peer networks, disposable income, and attachment all may occur, influencing individuals' motivations to pirate and social control levels to constrain them. In addition, collecting data on other life points may provide a different portrait of what this deviant behavior actually looks like, including trends, causes, effects of peers, and risks (e.g., more malicious software infection) (e.g., Popham, 2011; Lorde et al., 2010). Utilizing a life-course perspective will allow for several important questions to be answered, such as whether digital piracy follows the age-crime curve similar to other offenses, how access to technology at different ages affects digital piracy, the link between learning basic computer skills and piracy, whether individuals change piracy types (music, movies, software, etc.) over time, and so on. Answers to these questions will not only help us better understand digital piracy but it will provide useful information regarding possible policies and strategies that can be implemented to decrease piracy.

The examination of digital piracy through a life-course perspective, however, requires the collection and analysis of longitudinal data (Lowry et al., 2017). As discussed earlier, the existence of studies using longitudinal data is scant and they have experienced their own issues, particularly attrition. For example, Higgins' (2007a) examination of motivation and low self-control on digital piracy using longitudinal data began with 292 subjects and ended with 185, a decrease of 36 percent over a four-week period. Considering that the sample consisted of college students, more of a "captive" audience than the general public, it shows the challenges that researchers will have in collecting longitudinal data. Although challenging, it will be imperative that the field moves in this direction.

Finally, it will be important for criminologists to take a greater role in evaluating policies and legislation that affect piracy (e.g., Bachmann, 2007). The deterrence literature indicates that deterring piracy is challenging because of the strong desire by youth of the content and of the nature of the Internet (Wall, 2005). However, the literature also supports that pirates' behaviors may be curtailed by legal recourse strategies (e.g., Bhattacharjee et al., 2006). A greater strategy in reducing piracy behavior, however, is the continual afford-ability of media streaming services, which have already had a hand in reducing digital piracy (Hampton-Sosa, 2017; Wang & McClung, 2011) and will pre-sumably continue to do so in the future. These streaming services also offer the customization of the listening/viewing experience for the user (Hampton-Sosa, 2017; Wang & McClung, 2011). Although artists may not make as much through these services in comparison to if customers purchased the media, these streaming services pay for the right to legally play these songs and movies/shows, allowing artists to profit more than if the media was simply pirated and decreasing piracy in the process (Hampton-Sosa, 2017). These attempts may be more effective in decreasing piracy and increasing profits for copyright holders than other efforts, especially more controversially strategies such as torrent poisoning which involves anti-piracy groups implementing contaminated files on P2P sharing networks in order to deter pirates (Kresten, 2012).

Criminologists have made great strides in contributing to our knowledge of digital piracy. Over the next decade, technological innovations that will no doubt alter how digital piracy is committed may also improve researchers' abilities to collect data. Basic reasons why individuals commit crime, however, will probably remain relatively constant. Individuals who commit digital piracy in the future will have peers who pirate as well. Pirates will also be socially reinforced for this behavior, have lower levels of self-control, and hold beliefs supportive of digital piracy. Scholars will hopefully follow the example set by Goldsmith and Brewer (2015) to make modifications to classic criminological theories to better update them to the reality of the virtual world.

References

Aaltonen, M. and Salmi, V. (2013) 'Versatile delinquents or specialized pirates? A comparison of illegal downloading and traditional juvenile crime', *Journal of Scandinavian Studies in Criminology & Crime Prevention*, 14: 188–195.

Akers, R.L. (1998) *Social Learning and Social Structure: a general theory of crime and deviance*, Boston, MA: Northeastern University Press.

Al-Rafee, S. and Cronan, T.P. (2006) 'Digital piracy: factors that influence attitude toward Behavior', *Journal of Business Ethics*, 63: 237–259.

Altschuller, S. and Benbunan-Fich, R. (2009) 'Is music downloading the new prohibition? What students reveal through an ethical dilemma', *Ethics and Information Technology*, 11: 49–56.

Bachmann, M. (2007) 'Lesson spurned? Reactions of online music pirates to legal prosecutions by the RIAA', *International Journal of Cyber Criminology*, 2: 213–227.

Bhattarcharjee, S., Gopal, R.D., Lertwachara, K. and Marsden, J.R. (2006) 'Impact of legal threats on online music sharing activity: an analysis of music industry legal actions', *The Journal of Law and Economics*, 49: 91–114.

Bhattacharjee, S., Gopal, R.D. and Sanders, G.L. (2003) 'Digital music and online sharing: software piracy 2.0?', *Communications of the ACM*, 46: 47–76.

Borja, K., Dieringer, S. and Daw, J. (2015) 'The effect of music streaming services on music piracy among college students', *Computers in Human Behavior*, 45: 69–76.

Brown, S.C. (2016). 'Where do beliefs about music piracy come from and how are they shared? An ethnographic study', *International Journal of Cyber Criminology*, 10: 21–39.

Burruss, G.W., Bossler, A.M. and Holt, T.J. (2013). 'Assessing the mediation of a fuller social learning model on low self-control's influence on software piracy', *Crime & Delinquency*, 59: 1157–1184.

Business Software Alliance. (2016) 'Seizing opportunity through license compliance', Available at: http://globalstudy.bsa.org/2016/downloads/studies/BSA_GSS_US.pdf.

Casidy, R., Lwin, M. and Phau, I. (2017) 'Investigating the role of religiosity as a deterrent against digital piracy', *Marketing Intelligence & Planning*, 35: 62–80.

Chiou, J.S., Huang, C. and Lee, J. (2005) 'The antecedents of music piracy attitudes and Intentions', *Journal of Business Ethics*, 57: 161–174.

Cooper, J. and Harrison, D.M. (2001) 'The social organization of audio piracy on the Internet', *Media, Culture, and Society*, 23: 71–89.

Cox, J. and Collins, A. (2014) 'Sailing in the same ship? Differences in factors, motivating piracy of music and movie content', *Journal of Behavioral and Experimental Economics*, 50: 70–76.

Donner, C.M. (2016) 'The gender gap and cybercrime: An examination of college students' online offending', *Victims & Offenders*, 11: 556–577.

Goldsmith, A. and Brewer, R. (2015) 'Digital drift and the criminal interaction order', *Theoretical Criminology*, 19: 112–130.

Gottfredson, M.R. and Hirschi, T. (1990) *A General Theory of Crime*, Stanford, CA: Stanford University Press.

Graham, L. (2012) 'Increased use of free music streaming services take a bite out of illegal peer-to-peer music file sharing activity', February 26. Retrieved from: www.npd.com/wps/portal/npd/us/news/press-releases/the-npd-group-music-file-sharing-declined-significantly-in-2012/.

Gunter, W.D. (2008) 'Piracy on the high speeds: a test of social learning theory on digital piracy among college students', *International Journal of Criminal Justice Sciences*, 3: 54–68.

Gunter, W.D. (2009) 'Internet scallywags: A comparative analysis of multiple forms and measurements of digital piracy', *Western Criminology Review*, 10: 15–28.

Gunter, W.D., Higgins, G.E. and Gealt, R.E. (2010) 'Pirating youth: Examining the correlates of digital music piracy among adolescents', *International Journal of Cyber Criminology*, 4: 657–671.

Hampton-Sosa, W. (2017) 'The impact of creativity and community facilitation on music streaming adoption and digital piracy', *Computers in Human Behavior*, 69: 444–453.

Higgins, G.E. (2005) 'Can low self-control help with the understanding of the software piracy problem?', *Deviant Behavior*, 26: 1–24.

Higgins, G.E. (2006) 'Gender differences in software piracy: The mediating roles of self-control theory and social learning theory', *Journal of Economic Crime Management*, 4: 1–30.

Higgins, G.E. (2007a) 'Digital piracy: An examination of low self-control and motivation using short-term longitudinal data', *CyberPsychology & Behavior*, 10: 523–529.

Higgins, G.E. (2007b) 'Digital piracy, self-control theory, and rational choice: an examination of the role of value', *International Journal of Cyber Criminology*, 1: 33–55.

Higgins, G.E., Fell, B.D. and Wilson, A. (2006) 'Digital piracy: Assessing the contributions of an integrated self-control theory and social learning theory using structural equation modeling', *Criminal Justice Studies*, 19: 3–22.

Higgins, G.E., Fell, B.D. and Wilson, A.L. (2007) 'Low self-control and social learning in understanding students' intentions to pirate movies in the United States', *Social Science Computer Review*, 25: 339–357.

Higgins, G.E. and Makin, D.A. (2004a) 'Does social learning condition the effects of low-self control on college students' software piracy?', *Journal of Economic Crime Management*, 2: 1–22.

Higgins, G.E. and Makin, D.A. (2004b) 'Self-control, deviant peers, and software piracy', *Psychological Reports*, 95: 921–931.

Higgins, G.E. and Marcum, C.D. (2011) *Digital Piracy: an integrated theoretical approach*, Durham, NC: Carolina Academic Press.

Higgins, G.E., Marcum, C.D., Freiburger, T.L. and Ricketts, M.L. (2012) 'Examining the role of peer influence and self-control on downloading behavior', *Deviant Behavior*, 33: 412–423.

Higgins, G.E. and Wilson, A.L. (2006) 'Low self-control, moral beliefs, and social learning theory in university students' intentions to pirate software', *Security Journal*, 19: 75–92.

Higgins, G.E., Wilson, A.L. and Fell, B.D. (2005) 'An application of deterrence theory to software piracy', *Journal of Criminal Justice and Popular Culture*, 12: 166–184.

Higgins, G.E., Wolfe, S.E. and Marcum, C.D. (2008a) 'Digital piracy: An examination of three measurements of self-control', *Deviant Behavior*, 29: 440–460.

Higgins, G.E., Wolfe, S.E. and Marcum, C.D. (2008b) 'Music piracy and neutralization: a preliminary trajectory analysis from short-term longitudinal data', *International Journal of Cyber Criminology*, 2: 324–336.

Higgins, G.E., Wolfe, S.E. and Ricketts, M.L. (2009) 'Digital piracy: A latent class analysis', *Social Science Computer Review*, 27: 24–40.

Hinduja, S. (2003) 'Trends and patterns among online software pirates', *Ethics and Information Technology*, 5: 49–61.

Hinduja, S. (2007) 'Neutralization theory and online software piracy: An empirical analysis', *Ethics and Information Technology*, 9: 187–204.

Hinduja, S. (2012) 'General strain, self-control, and music piracy', *International Journal of Cyber Criminology*, 6: 951–967.

Hinduja, S. and Higgins, G.E. (2011) 'Trends and patterns among music pirates', *Deviant Behavior*, 32: 563–588.

Hinduja, S. and Ingram, J.R. (2008) 'Self-control and ethical beliefs on the social learning of intellectual property theft', *Western Criminology Review*, 9: 52–72.

Hinduja, S. and Ingram, J.R. (2009) 'Social learning theory and music piracy: the differential role of online and offline peer influences', *Criminal Justice Studies*, 22: 405–420.

Hollinger, R.C. (1993) 'Crime by computer, correlates of software piracy and unauthorized account access', *Security Journal*, 4: 2–12.

Holt, T.J. and Bossler, A.M. (2016) *Cybercrime in Progress: theory and prevention of technology-enabled offenses*, London: Routledge.

Holt, T.J., Bossler, A.M. and May, D.C. (2012) 'Low self-control, deviant peer associations, and juvenile cyberdeviance', *American Journal of Criminal Justice*, 37: 378–395.

Holt, T.J., Bossler, A.M. and Seigfried-Spellar, K.C. (2015) *Cybercrime and Digital Forensics*, 1st edn, London: Routledge.

Holt, T.J., Burruss, G.W. and Bossler, A.M. (2010) 'Social learning and cyber deviance: examining the importance of a full social learning model in the virtual world', *Journal of Crime & Justice*, 33: 31–62.

Holt, T.J. and Copes, H. (2010) 'Transferring subcultural knowledge online: Practices and beliefs of persistent digital pirates', *Deviant Behavior*, 31: 625–654.

Ingram, J.R. and Hinduja, S. (2008) 'Neutralizing music piracy: An empirical examination', *Deviant Behavior*, 29: 334–365.

Jackman, M. and Lorde, T. (2014) 'Why buy when we can pirate? The role of intentions and willingness to pay in predicting piracy behavior', *International Journal of Social Economics*, 41: 801–819.

Kariithi, N.K. (2011) 'Is the devil in the data? A literature review of piracy around the World', *The Journal of World Intellectual Property*, 14: 133–154.

Kigerl, A.C. (2013). 'Infringing nations: predicting software piracy rates, BitTorrent tracker hosting, and P2P file sharing client downloads between countries', *International Journal of Cyber Criminology*, 7: 62–80.

Kos Koklic, M.K., Vida, I., Bajde, D. and Culiberg, B. (2014) 'The study of perceived adverse effects of digital piracy and involvement: Insights from adult computer users', *Behaviour & Information Technology*, 33: 225–236.

Kresten, P.V. (2012) *Torrent Poisoning*, New York: VolutPress.

Larsson, S., Svensson, M. and De Kaminski, M. (2013) 'Online piracy, anonymity and social change: innovation through deviance', *Convergence: The International Journal of Research into New Media Technologies*, 19: 95–114.

Lorde, T., Devonish, D. and Beckles, A. (2010) 'Real pirates of the Caribbean: Socio-psychological traits, the environment, personal ethics and the propensity for digital piracy in Barbados', *Journal of Eastern Caribbean Studies*, 35: 1–35.

Lowry, P.B., Zhang, J. and Wu, T. (2017) 'Nature of nurture? A meta-analysis of the factors that maximize the prediction of digital piracy by using social cognitive theory as a framework', *Computers in Human Behavior*, 68: 104–120.

Luckerson, V. (2013) 'Revenue up, piracy down: Has the music industry finally turned a corner?', February 28. Retrieved from: http://business.time.com/2013/02/28/revenue-up-piracy-down-has-the-music-industry-finally-turned-a-corner/.

Lysonski, S. and Durvasula, S. (2008) 'Digital piracy of MP3s: Consumer and ethical predispositions', *Journal of Consumer Marketing*, 25: 167–178.

Ma, L., Montgomery, A. and Smith, M.D. (2016) 'The dual impact of movie piracy on box-office revenue: cannibalization and promotion', Available at https://ssrn.com/abstract=2736946.

Malin, J. and Fowers, B.J. (2009) 'Adolescent self-control and music and movie piracy', *Computers in Human Behavior*, 25: 718–722.

Marcum, C.D., Higgins, G.E., Wolfe, S.E. and Ricketts, M.L. (2011) 'Examining the intersection of self-control, peer association and neutralization in explaining digital piracy', *Western Criminology Review*, 12: 60–74.

McCourt, T. and Burkart, P. (2003) 'When creators, corporations and consumers collide: Napster and the development of on-line music distribution', *Media, Culture & Society*, 25: 333–350.

Miller, B. and Morris, R.G. (2016) 'Virtual peer effects in social learning theory', *Crime & Delinquency*, 62: 1543–1569.

Moon, B., McCluskey, J.D. and McCluskey, C.P. (2010) 'A general theory of crime and computer crime: an empirical test', *Journal of Criminal Justice*, 38: 767–772.

Moore, R. and McMullan, E.C. (2009) 'Neutralizations and rationalizations of digital piracy: A qualitative analysis of university students', *International Journal of Cyber Criminology*, 3: 441–451.

Morris, R.G. and Higgins, G.E. (2009) 'Neutralizing potential and self-reported digital piracy: A multi-theoretical exploration among college undergraduates', *Criminal Justice Review*, 34: 173–195.

Morris, R.G. and Higgins, G.E. (2010) 'Criminological theory in the digital age: The case of social learning theory and digital piracy', *Journal of Criminal Justice*, 38: 470–480.

Morris, R.G., Johnson, M.C. and Higgins, G.E. (2009) 'The role of gender in predicting the willingness to engage in digital piracy among college students', *Criminal Justice Studies*, 22: 393–404.

Morton, N.A. and Koufteros, X. (2008) 'Intention of commit online music piracy and its antecedents: an empirical investigation', *Structural Equation Modeling: A Multidisciplinary Journal*, 15: 491–512.

MusicWatch. (2014) '2014 annual music study', Retrieved from: www.riaa.com/wpcontent/uploads/2016/03/RIAA-Music-Consumer-Profile-2014.pdf.

Nandedkar, A. and Midha, V. (2012) 'It won't happen to me: an assessment of optimism bias in music piracy', *Computers in Human Behavior*, 28: 41–48.

Paternoster, R. (1987) 'The deterrent effect of the perceived certainty and severity of punishment: A review of the evidence and issues', *Justice Quarterly*, 4: 173–217.

Payne, B.K. and Chappell, A. (2008) 'Using student samples in criminological research', *Journal of Criminal Justice Education*, 19: 175–192.

Phau, I., Lim, A., Liang, J. and Lwin, M. (2014) 'Engaging in digital piracy of movies: A theory of planned behaviour approach', *Internet Research*, 24: 246–266.

Popham, J. (2011) 'Factors influencing music piracy', *Criminal Justice Studies*, 24: 199–209.

Pratt, T.C. and Cullen, F.T. (2000) 'The empirical status of Gottfredson and Hirschi's general theory of crime: A meta-analysis', *Criminology*, 38: 931–964.

Pratt, T.C., Cullen, F.T., Blevins, K.R., Daigle, L.E. and Madensen, T.D. (2006) 'The empirical status of deterrence theory: a meta-analysis', in F.T. Cullen, J.P. Wright and K.R. Blevins (eds) *Taking Stock: the status of criminological theory* (pp. 367–396), New Brunswick, NJ: Transaction.

Pratt, T.C., Cullen, F.T., Sellers, C.S., Winfree, T., Madensen, T.D., Daigle, L.E., Fearn, N.E. and Gau, J.M. (2009) 'The empirical status of social learning theory: A meta-analysis', *Justice Quarterly*, 27: 765–802.

Price, D. (2013) 'Sizing the piracy universe', NetNames envisional'. Available at: www.netnames.com/assets/shared/whitepaper/pdf/netnames-sizing-piracy-universe-FULLreport-sept2013.pdf.

Skinner, W.F. and Fream, A.M. (1997) 'A social learning theory analysis of computer crime among college students', *Journal of Research in Crime and Delinquency*, 34: 495–518.

Smallridge, J.L. and Roberts, J.R. (2013) 'Crime specific neutralizations: an empirical examination of four types of digital piracy', *International Journal of Cyber Criminology*, 7: 125–140.

Steele, R. (2015, July 16) 'If you think piracy is decreasing, you haven't looked at the data', Available at: www.digitalmusicnews.com/2015/07/16/if-you-think-piracy-is-decreasing-you-havent-looked-at-the-data-2/.

Steinmetz, K.F. and Tunnell, K.D. (2013) 'Under the pixelated Jolly Rogers: A study of on-line Pirates', *Deviant Behavior*, 34: 53–67.

Sykes, G.M. and Matza, D. (1957) 'Techniques of neutralization: A theory of delinquency', *American Sociological Review*, 22: 664–670.

Tade, O. and Akinleye, B. (2012) 'We are promoters not pirates: A qualitative analysis of artistes and pirates on music piracy in Nigeria', *International Journal of Criminology*, 6: 1014–1029.

Taylor, S.A. (2012) 'Evaluating digital piracy intentions on behaviors', *Journal of Services Marketing*, 26: 472–483.

Tcherni, M., Davies, A., Lopes, G. and Lizotte, A. (2016) 'The dark figure of online property crime: Is cyberspace hiding a crime wave?', *Justice Quarterly*, 33: 890–911.

Thatcher, A. and Matthews, M. (2012) 'Comparing software piracy in South Africa and Zambia using social cognitive theory', *African Journal of Business Ethics*, 6: 1–12.

Tjiptono, F., Arli, D. and Viviea (2016) 'Gender and digital privacy: Examining determinants of attitude toward digital piracy among youths in an emerging market', *International Journal of Consumer Studies*, 40: 168–178.

Udris, R. (2016) 'Cyber deviance among adolescents and the role of family, school, and neighborhood: A cross-national study', *International Journal of Cyber Criminology*, 10: 127–146.

Ulsperger, J.S., Hodges, S.H. and Paul, J. (2010) 'Pirates on the plank: Neutralization theory and the criminal downloading of music among Generation Y in the era of late modernity', *Journal of Criminal Justice and Popular Culture*, 17: 124–151.

Van Belle, J.P., Macdonald, B. and Wilson, D. (2007) 'Determinants of digital piracy among youth in South Africa', *Communications of the IIMA*, 7: 47–64.

Vandiver, D.M., Bowman, S. and Vega, A. (2012) 'Music piracy among college students: An examination of low self-control, techniques of neutralization, and rational choice', *Southwest Journal of Criminal Justice*, 8: 92–111.

Van Rooij, B., Fine, A., Zhang, Y. and Wu, Y. (2017) 'Comparative compliance: digital piracy, deterrence, social norms, and duty in China and the United States', *Law & Policy*, 39: 73–93.

Vida, I., Koklic, M.K., Kukar-Kinney, M. and Penz, E. (2012) 'Predicting consumer digital piracy behavior: The role of rationalization and perceived consequences', *Journal of Research in Interactive Marketing*, 6: 298–313.

Wall, D.S. (2005) 'The Internet as a conduit for criminal activity', In A. Pattavina (ed.) *Information Technology and the Criminal Justice System* (pp. A078–94), Thousand Oaks, CA: Sage.

Wang, X. and McClung, S.R. (2011) 'Toward a detailed understanding of illegal digital downloading intentions: An extended theory of planned behavior approach', *New Media & Society*, 13: 663–677.

Wang, X. and McClung, S.R. (2012) 'The immorality of illegal downloading: The role of anticipated guilt and general emotions', *Computers in Human Behavior*, 28: 153–159.

Wingrove, T., Korpas, A.L. and Weisz, V. (2011) 'Why were millions of people not obeying the law? Motivational influences on non-compliance with the law in the case of music piracy', *Psychology, Crime & Law*, 17: 261–276.

Wolfe, S.E., Higgins, G.E. and Marcum, C.D. (2008) 'Deterrence and digital piracy: A preliminary examination of the role of viruses', *Social Science Computer Review*, 26: 317–333.

Yar, M. (2005) 'The global epidemic of movie piracy: Crime-wave or social construction?', *Media, Culture & Society*, 27: 677–696.

Yar, M. (2013) *Cybercrime and Society*, 2nd edn, London:Sage Publications.

Yoon, C. (2011) 'Theory of planned behavior and ethics theory in digital piracy: An integrated model', *Journal of Business Ethics*, 100: 405–417.

Yoon, C. (2012) 'Digital piracy intention: a comparison of theoretical models', *Behaviour & Information Technology*, 31: 565–576.

Yu, S. (2010) 'Digital piracy and stealing: A comparison on criminal propensity', *International Journal of Criminal Justice Sciences*, 5: 239–250.

Yu, S. (2012) 'College students' justification for digital piracy: A mixed methods study', *Journal of Mixed Methods Research*, 6: 364–378.

12 Identifying paths forward in the study of piracy

Steven Caldwell Brown and Thomas J. Holt

The contributions of this book demonstrate that scholars from many disciplines are interested in digital piracy, and a multi-disciplinary approach greatly enhances our understanding of this phenomenon. As outlined in the introductory chapter, one of the core aims of this work is to draw from the expertise of scholars from different disciplines, and the preceding chapters incorporated criminology and economics, as well as areas of study not commonly recognized in this area, including popular music studies, film studies, marketing, and psychology.

Another core aim was to adopt as a global a perspective as possible by inviting contributors from all over the world. No fewer than three continents are represented: North America, Australasia and Europe. The scholarship presented demonstrates the inherent value in studying piracy as an international issue, with potential local drivers that influence individual behaviour. In addition, the implications of the research presented in this work have value for academics, industry, and policy makers alike, recognizing the global nature of intellectual property in the digital age.

At the same time, there are substantive issues that remain for inquiry into piracy and a need to identify a way forward for scholars in this area. These works demonstrate the breadth of research, but have several limitations that hinder its representative nature. In fact, Brown (2017) noted that it is possible to reach opposite conclusions on digital piracy when drawing from the same information. Thus, this chapter will provide a holistic overview of the broader questions and challenges that should shape the tenor of research on digital piracy in the future. It is intended to provoke questions not only about the state of research, but also the landscape of public policy regarding intellectual property as a whole.

'Turn and face the strange'

A recurring theme in the book is *change*, which is a constant in the creative and cultural industries – sometimes willingly, sometimes unwillingly. Regarding technology, the iconic iPod is now a dated artefact, with Apple recently discontinuing the once popular Nano and Shuffle devices (Gibbs, 2017). The rise of smartphones has revolutionized how we interact with media.

The changing relationship between the consumer and content producer was highlighted by the musician Trent Reznor of the band Nine Inch Nails in a recent interview, stating: "People listen to music while they're doing something else, you know?" (Marchese, 2017). This may influence the perception of recording artists, as Nine Inch Nails has recently embarked on a project to release three conceptually related EPs seemingly influenced by current listening preferences. This is in stark contrast with a two-hour long double album comprised entirely of instrumentals release in 2008.

These changes also affect the practices of digital pirates: PRS for Music (2017) reported that stream-ripping is now the most prevalent form of music piracy. Similar shifts have been observed with the transition from warez sharing in the 1980s to peer-to-peer file sharing services like Napster in the 90s, to the use of torrent services in the mid 2000s (Cooper & Harrison, 2001; Nhan, 2013). Advertising is the principal funding model associated with stream-ripping services, highlighting the 'value gap' discussed by IFPI (2016; 2017) as the money generated from ads does not find its way to the rightsholders who are legally and morally obliged to receive payment for their work. Much of the ads associated with ripping for film piracy is considered to be 'high-risk', associated with the sex industry, gambling, and other grey market services (Lee & Watters, 2016).

These conditions demonstrate that artists and musicians are now operating at the mercy of their fans, an observation that appears prescient in the case of film and TV. The most successful media titles in recent years seem designed to appeal to pre-existing fans, with hit films often being part of franchises.

Merrily, merrily, merrily, merrily, merrily...

The increasing prominence of streaming presents a double edged sword for artists and copyright holders. Streaming was born of a desire to combat digital piracy, though Mulligan (2015) expects that streaming will lead to consumers engaging with music less frequently. As a result, relationships between the artist and their fan base may shrink, which could directly decrease the perceived value of live concerts where musicians earn most of their money. As discussed in the chapter by Krause and Brown, why would you pay to go see a band live when you only like a few songs? Furthermore, Montoro-Pons, Cuadrado-García and Puchades-Navarro caution that whilst streaming may dissuade some from music piracy, it could also lead to those who tend to pay for music legally to switch their listening patterns to focus on streaming. Such a shift could downgrade those consumers' contribution to the music industry in financial terms.

The emerging trend for listening to songs, on playlists, is worthy of note. It is thought that the average person now spends about four hours a day listening to music (Luck, 2016; Peoples, 2016), and much of this time will be spent engaging with the content via playlists. As of May 2016, playlists accounted for nearly one-third of total listening time, and are now more popular than albums (Savage, 2016). As Reznor noted, playlists appear to be a dominant mode of listening when performing other tasks (Kamalzedah, Baur & Möller, 2012). As a consequence, people are not really listening to music; they are just hearing it.

As discussed by Mulligan (2015), the change from listening to hearing has fundamental impacts on fandom, with cascading affects for recording artists and the industry as a whole. Aiken, a cyberpsychologist, explains that: "The Internet is like a catalog of desire begging people to flip through it" (2016, p. 39). How then does one actually engage in any form of media consumption when online, given the inherent temptation to do something else instead? The notion of committing to listening to an album front-to-back is antiquated, as is watching a film start-to-finish. Media of all types now exist in surplus online, with minimal effort required in order to obtain it, thereby downgrading its value.

In terms of music, access models are fast substituting ownership models, leaving no physical symbol of music-listening culture similar to the influence of the iPod in the early 2000s (Tschmuck, 2016). The latest industry reports emphasize that streaming now accounts for 59% of digital revenues (IFPI, 2017). In a nod to the influence of streaming, it is now incorporated into chart rankings to provide a more accurate and immediate measure of what people are listening to relative to actual sales (Collins & O'Grady, 2016). Sun explains that dated notions of how music once generated revenue must be substituted as preferences for music-listening change. As discussed by Krause and Brown, playlists are now the dominant mode of music-listening – not albums. This is a massive change in how music is enjoyed and appraised, and it merits empirical investigation.

Hoffecker (2012) argues that: "Creativity is the recombination of informational units into novel arrangements or structures" (p. 89), and ultimately this is what the creation of music playlists involves. Accordingly, making playlists could be considered a new form of musical creativity, or music making. This is a novel outcome of music piracy, and can be thought to represent a cultural consequence of sorts – research is, of course, focused on commercial consequences. Steinmetz and Pimental explain that the focus of research has been to reduce piracy to individual factors, such as low self-control, in the process ignoring broader contexts; political, economic and social circumstances surrounding piracy are specifically singled out, and gaps in these areas are apparent. Such examples demonstrate the many ways to map the broader impact of digital piracy, and the need to not simply assume they are simply footnotes in any historical account of digital piracy.

What we think versus what we know

Taken as a whole, it is clear that more global accountings of piracy are needed. This work attempted to provide such a set of links, though it is not explicit in the writing. Instead, more recent works have achieved such reviews remarkably well. Lowry, Zhang, and Wu (2017) analysed 257 studies, with a resulting sample size of 126,622, to explore the major constructs and variables used in the literature to generate predictors of digital piracy engagement. The authors found that digital piracy engagement was predicted by the following: outcome expectancies (considerations of rewards, perceived risks, and perceived sanctions); social learning (positive and negative social influence and piracy habit); self-efficacy and self-regulation (perceived behavioural control and low self-control); and moral disengagement (morality, immorality, and neutraliza-tion). They also found that perceived behavioural control and low self-control are the strongest predictors of piracy. Such findings reassert that digital piracy is a crime, and those who engage in it are criminals. Research depicts them as lacking in control over their actions, as would be expected from other criminal activities.

Those who query 'what's the harm?' with digital piracy should take note of the conclusions from Burruss and Dodge that a relationship exists between engagement in digital piracy and other risk-taking behaviours online. Their chapter argues that online deviance is related to offline deviance, and that this is likely mediated by factors such as low self-control or deviant peer associations. Thus, a key implication of Burruss and Dodge's work is that digital piracy may be a gateway to more serious offending online, and this is troubling.

Also troublesome is that Lowry, Zhang and Wu (2017) found that the quality of the studies included in their review were questionable, with many not reporting standard statistical outputs. They note that:

> When approached for these statistics, several researchers refused to pro-vide it or said it was no longer available. Such practices are unacceptable in any scientific community. Researchers have an ethical obligation to publish these basic statistics or to make them readily available to other researchers; otherwise, scientific progress is impaired or even misled.
>
> (p. 117)

Such findings do little for instilling confidence in research produced by the scholarly community, and future research must simply be better. In this work, both Edwards and Bossler, as well as Krause and Brown, acknowledge the limitations that permeate the literature to date, arguing for theoretical developments that better take into account behaviour on online environments.

Additionally, the existing literature is rife with examinations of the beha-viours of downloaders, or those who actively seek out and access pirated content. Though this is a sensible position given the quantity of material currently available, there is a need to consider the predictors and behaviours of those who facilitate piracy: the uploaders. Few have considered why indi-viduals crack protections on media and make them available for others to download (see Cooper & Harrison, 2001 for an exception). Arguably, the high rates of piracy would not be possible without uploaders working to host content. The technical skills needed to actually break copyright protections on files or assemble torrent files may be greater than what is necessary to simply download content. As a result, a shift in research towards uploader activities would represent a sensible next step in order to better understand the supply chain dynamics of digital piracy, including hacking. More effort to better understand the broader, cultural consequences would also provide a richer understanding.

Qualitative research into digital piracy

Much has been said throughout this work about the strengths and weaknesses of research into digital piracy, but the majority of studies have focused on quantitative works. It is, of course, quantitative work that dominates the field, as noted by Watson and associates (2015) who found that qualitative outcome measures featured in just 8 per cent of published studies. This is sensible as quantitative scholarship enables analyses with statistical power and generalizability to broad populations. At the same time, qualitative scholarship has the ability to generate substantial breadth and depth of knowledge about the nature of offending and offender behaviour in ways that cannot be replicated by quantitative metrics.

As a result, future research should seek to appraise the quality of qualitative research into DP to better understand the scientific quality and reliability of these studies generally. Though some qualitative studies go into detail on the process of coding and the development of results, most do not provide sufficient information (see Cenite et al. 2009; Flores & James, 2012; Lewis, 2015; and Nutall et al., 2011 for exceptions). This is a weakness that must be taken into account when appraising findings. Leung (2015) explains that there is no agreed upon way in which to evaluate qualitative research, but certainly the use of the Critical Appraisal Skills Programme (CASP) Qualitative Checklist would be an agreeable approach.

In terms of recommendations for future research, there is a need for mixed-methods approaches that utilize both qualitative and quantitative data collection and analysis techniques (Lau, 2006; Weitjers, Goedertier & Vestreken, 2014; Yu, 2012). This is seemingly essential in the case of digital piracy, given the complexity of the phenomenon. For instance, utilizing a survey method to assess methods of piracy could be valuable to demonstrate prevalence. This could be augmented by interviews with participants to understand why they use one method over another, and the extent to which they change practices as a function of perceived risk of detection or access content that may not be available through other mediums.

There is also inherent value in increasing scholarship utilizing online data sources and methods (Beekhuyzen, von Hellens & Nielsen, 2011; Brown, 2016; Holt & Copes, 2010; Lau, 2006; Lewis, 2015; Sezneva, 2012; Sinclair & Tinson, 2017; and Steinmetz & Tunnell, 2013). It is intuitive that qualitative scholars would seek to monitor online activity given the nature of piracy, and it ought to be noted that the Internet offers qualitative researchers an insight into social construction, and how meaning and identity is negotiated (Silverman, 2016). It has been argued that the Internet makes it possible to: "Generate nuanced qualitative data from large numbers of respondents – whether through social networking sites or through other methods, such as designing new forms of questionnaires which allow researchers to generate in-depth data" (Silverman, 2016: 199).

Using the Internet as a research medium provides a wealth of pre-existing data from the individual's perspective, frequently in their own words (see Cooper & Harrison, 2001; Evans, Elford & Wiggins, 2008; Holt, 2013; Steinmetz & Tunnell, 2013 for examples). Forums, blogs, and social media platforms can all be mined for data, as could metrics from Torrent sites and piracy sources. A small body of researchers have also used computer-mediated communications, such as Skype and email to facilitate interviews with participants across great distances (e.g. Holt & Copes, 2010). There are, however, complex ethical considerations that arise when using online data, such as the anonymity and privacy of posts made in on-line platforms (Holt, 2015; Willig, 2013). As a result, researchers must carefully weigh the advantages and costs that emerge from online methods prior to engaging in any research study.

Concluding statement

As shown by Re, and by Tessler and Forbes, digital piracy is not easy to understand. This book presents a multidisciplinary attempt to examine various forms of piracy in a global context. Such examinations are necessary in order to demonstrate what is known and establish a roadmap for future research. The rapidly changing state of technology and media consumption demonstrates that this field can stagnate quickly. Thus, researchers must be diligent and constantly explore the issue of piracy through a diverse theoretical lens in order to identify the nuances of piracy as a phenomenon and understand its cascading impacts on intellectual property generation and production, as well as the economy and the state of cultural consumption as a whole.

References

Aiken, M. (2016). *The Cyber Effect*. St. Ives: John Murray.

Beekhuyzen, J., von Hellens, L. and Nielsen, S. (2011). Underground online music communities: exploring rules for membership. *Online Information Review*, 35(5): 699–715.

Brown, S.C. (2016). Where do beliefs about music piracy come from and how are they shared? *International Journal of Cyber Criminology*, 10(1): 21–39.

Brown, S.C. (2017). Myths about musicians and music piracy. *The Skeptic*, 26(3): 12–15.

Cenite, M., Wang, M.W., Peiwen, C. and Chan, G.S. (2009). More than just free content: Motivations of peer-to-peer file sharers. *Journal of Communication Inquiry*, 33(3): 206–221.

Collins, S. and O'Grady, P. (2016). Off the charts: The implications of incorporating streaming data into the charts. In R. Nowak and A. Whelan (Eds), *Networked Music Cultures: Contemporary Approaches, Emerging Issues* (pp. 151–170). London: Palgrave Macmillan.

Cooper, J., and Harrison, D. M. (2001). The social organization of audio piracy on the Internet. *Media, Culture & Society*. 23(1): 71–89.

Evans, A., Elford, J. and Wiggins, D. (2008). Using the Internet for qualitative research. In C. Willig and W. Stainton-Rogers (Eds), *The SAGE Handbook of Qualitative Research in Psychology* (pp. 315–333). London: Sage.

Flores, A. and James, C. (2012). Morality and ethics behind the screen: Young people's perspectives on digital life. *New Media Society*, 15(6): 834–852.

Gibbs, S. (2017). Apple kills off iPod Nano and Shuffle, marking the end of an era, July. Retrieved from: www.theguardian.com/technology/2017/jul/28/apple-kills-ip od-nano-shuffle-marking-end-of-an-era-smartphone.

Hoffecker, J.F. (2012). The evol ecol of creativity. *Developments in Quaternary Science*, 16: 89–102.

Holt, T. J. (2013). Examining the forces shaping cybercrime markets online. *Social Science Computer Review* 31: 165–177

Holt, T. J. (2015). Qualitative criminology in online spaces. In H. Copes, *The Routledge Handbook of Qualitative Criminology* (pp. 173–196). London: Routledge.

Holt, T.J. and Copes, H. (2010). Transferring subcultural knowledge on-line: Practices and beliefs of persistent digital pirates. *Deviant Behavior*, 31(7): 625–654.

International Federation of the Phonographic Industry (2016). *Global Music Report: Music Consumption Exploding Worldwide*. Retrieved from: www.ifpi.org/downloads/ GMR2016.pdf.

International Federation of the Phonographic Industry (2017). *Global Music Report 2017*. Retrieved from www.ifpi.org/recording-industry-in-numbers.php.

Kamalzadeh, M., Baur, D. and Möller, T. (2012). *A Survey on Music Listening and Management Behaviours*. Paper presented at the ISMIR'12, Porto, Portugal, October.

Lau, E.K. (2006). Factors motivating people toward pirated software. *Qualitative Market Research*, 9(4): 404–419.

Lee, S.J. and Watters, P.A. (2016). Gathering intelligence on high-risk advertising and film piracy: A study of the digital underground. In R. Layton and P. A. Watters (Eds), *Automating Open Source Intelligence* (pp. 89–102). London: Elsevier.

Leung, L. (2015). Validity, reliability, and generalizability in qualitative research. *Journal of Family Medicine and Primary Care*, 4(3): 324–327.

Lewis, J. (2015). The piratical ethos in streams of language. *Popular Communication: The International Journal of Media and Culture*, 13(1): 45–61.

Lowry, P.B., Zhang, J. and Wu, T. (2017). Nature or nurture? A meta-analysis of the factors that maximize the prediction of digital piracy by using social cognitive theory as a framework. *Computers in Human Behavior*, 68: 104–120.

Luck, G. (2016) The psychology of streaming: exploring music listeners' motivations to favour access over ownership. *International Journal of Music Business Research*, 5(2): 46–60.

Marchese, D. (2017, July). In Conversation: Trent Reznor. Retrieved from www.vul ture.com/2017/07/trent-reznor-nine-inch-nails.html.

Mulligan, M. (2015, June). On Demand In Demand [Web log message]. Retrieved from https://musicindustryblog.wordpress.com/2015/06/05/on-demand-in-demand.

Nhan, J. (2013). The evolution of online piracy: Challenge and response. In Holt, T.J. (Ed.). *Crime On-line: Causes, correlates, and context* (pp. 61–80). Raleigh, NC: Carolina Academic Press.

Nutall, P., Arnold, S., Carless, L.Crockford, L.Finnamore, K., Frazier, R. and Hill, A. (2011). Understanding music consumption through a tribal lens. *Journal of Retail and Consumer Services*, 18: 152–159.

Peoples, G. (2016). How, and how much, America listens have been measured for the first time. Retrieved from www.billboard.com/biz/articles/news/digital-and- mobile/6121619/how-and-how-much-america-listens-have-been-measured-for.

PRS for Music (2017, July). Stream-ripping takes over as most aggressive form of music piracy increases 141%. Retrieved from: https://prsformusic.com/press/2017/stream- ripping-takes-over-as-most-aggressive-form-of-music-piracy.

Savage, M. (2016). Playlists 'more popular than albums. Retrieved from www.bbc.com/news/entertainment-arts-37444038.

Sezneva, O. (2012). The pirates of Nevskii Prospekt: Intellectual property, piracy and institutional diffusion in Russia. *Poetics*, 40: 150–166.

Silverman, D. (2016). *Interpreting Qualitative Data*. London: Sage.

Sinclair, G. and Tinson, J. (2017) Psychological ownership and music streaming consumption. *Journal of Business Research*, 71: 1–9.

Steinmetz, K.F. and Tunnell, K.D. (2013). Under the pixelated Jolly Roger: A study of on- line pirates. *Deviant Behavior*, 34(1): 53–67.

Tschmuck, P. (2016). From record selling to cultural entrepreneurship: the music economy in the digital paradigm shift. In P. Wikstrom and R. DeFillippi (Eds) *Business Innovation and Disruption in the Music Industry* (pp. 13–32). New York: Dedward Elgar Publishing.

Watson, S.J., Zizzo, D.J. and Fleming, P. (2015). Determinants of unlawful file sharing: A scoping review. *PLoS ONE*, 10(6): e0127921.

Weitjers, B., Goedertier, F. and Verstreken, S. (2014). Online music consumption in today's technological context: Putting the influence of ethics in perspective. *Journal of Business Ethics*, 124, 537–550.

Willig, C. (2013). *Introducing Qualitative Research In Psychology* (3rd edition). Milton Keynes: Open University.

Yu, S. (2012). College students' justification for digital piracy: A mixed methods study. *Journal of Mixed Methods Research*, 6(4): 364–378.

Index

Note: Page numbers in **bold** indicate tables, while those in *italic* indicate figures.